Web Applications on Azure

Developing for Global Scale

Rob Reagan

apress®

Web Applications on Azure

Rob Reagan
Chattanooga, Tennessee, USA

ISBN-13 (pbk): 978-1-4842-2975-0   ISBN-13 (electronic): 978-1-4842-2976-7
https://doi.org/10.1007/978-1-4842-2976-7

Library of Congress Control Number: 2017962632

Managing Director: Welmoed Spahr
Editorial Director: Todd Green
Acquisitions Editor: Gwenan Spearing
Development Editor: Laura Berendson
Technical Reviewer: Fabio Ferracchiati
Coordinating Editor: Nancy Chen
Copy Editor: Teresa F. Horton
Compositor: SPi Global
Indexer: SPi Global
Artist: SPi Global

Distributed to the book trade worldwide by Springer Science+Business Media New York, 233 Spring Street, 6th Floor, New York, NY 10013. Phone 1-800-SPRINGER, fax (201) 348-4505, e-mail orders-ny@springer-sbm.com, or visit www.springeronline.com. Apress Media, LLC is a California LLC and the sole member (owner) is Springer Science + Business Media Finance Inc (SSBM Finance Inc). SSBM Finance Inc is a **Delaware** corporation.

For information on translations, please e-mail rights@apress.com, or visit http://www.apress.com/rights-permissions.

Apress titles may be purchased in bulk for academic, corporate, or promotional use. eBook versions and licenses are also available for most titles. For more information, reference our Print and eBook Bulk Sales web page at http://www.apress.com/bulk-sales.

Any source code or other supplementary material referenced by the author in this book is available to readers on GitHub via the book's product page, located at www.apress.com/9781484229750. For more detailed information, please visit http://www.apress.com/source-code.

Printed on acid-free paper

*For Brandi. Without your patience and encouragement,
this book would not be possible. I love you.*

Table of Contents

About the Author

Rob Reagan has been building web applications with Microsoft .NET since the release of Framework 1.0 and has a long-standing interest in how to architect sites for Internet scale. He has led projects developing web applications built for hundreds to thousands of concurrent users for companies such as ExxonMobil, Standard & Poor's, Fidelity, and Microsoft. He holds a BA in computer science from Duke, and is currently finishing his master's degree in computer science at Georgia Tech. Rob lives in Chattanooga, TN, and is the CTO at `textrequest.com`.

About the Technical Reviewer

Fabio Claudio Ferracchiati is a senior consultant and a senior analyst/developer using Microsoft technologies. He works at BluArancio S.p.A (`www.bluarancio.com`) as Senior Analyst/Developer and Microsoft Dynamics CRM Specialist. He is a Microsoft Certified Solution Developer for .NET, a Microsoft Certified Application Developer for .NET, a Microsoft Certified Professional, and a prolific author and technical reviewer. Over the past ten years, he's written articles for Italian and international magazines and coauthored more than ten books on a variety of computer topics.

Acknowledgments

I am forever grateful to the folks who helped bring this book from a concept to a finished work. Thanks to Gwenan Spearing for believing in this project, taking a chance on a new author, and offering guidance along the way. Thanks to Nancy Chen for her near-infinite patience and her work to keep me on schedule. Thanks to my technical editor Fabio Ferracchiati, who read through all of the drafts and offered great advice on how to improve this book. Thanks also to the entire Apress team who worked behind the scenes to make this book a reality.

Finally, thanks to my wife Brandi, who gave up so many evenings and weekends so that I could write and pursue a dream.

Introduction

Professional developers and hobbyists will likely build dozens of web apps throughout their careers. Some of those web apps—like the cooking blog you set up for your mother—will probably never experience heavy traffic. Occasionally, though, we catch lightning in a bottle and our web apps experience rapidly growing or even torrential traffic. When that occurs, it's best if your app is built to withstand the flood.

Several years ago, I found myself in just such a situation. Fortunately, our app was built on Azure, and we were able to scale to thousands of concurrent users, all of whom were sending several requests per minute. Along the way, though, we restructured the code multiple times to support our growing user base. I wrote this book to share the lessons that we learned when scaling. Hopefully it will shorten your learning curve and help you avoid some of the bumps and bruises we experienced.

Who Is This Book for?

This book introduces Azure technologies targeted toward building web applications, and discusses patterns, practices, and architectures that will help you take your apps from zero to thousands of concurrent users. It is written for programmers who are already familiar with building basic web applications using Microsoft ASP.NET MVC and Web API.

System and Subscription Requirements

With Microsoft's "Any Developer, Any App, Any Platform" initiative, you can now develop Azure applications on the Windows, Linux, and OSX platforms. Although it is possible to do so, the instructions and illustrations in this book apply to Microsoft Visual Studio 2015 Community Edition only.

The following is the full list of the software that you'll need to download and install to follow along with the samples in this book. All of the required software is completely free, and Chapter 1 contains more detailed instructions on downloading and installing each application.

- *Visual Studio 2015 Community Edition:* If you already have the Professional or Enterprise editions, you do not need to download Community Edition. You will be able to follow along. Community Edition can be downloaded from `https://www.visualstudio.com/vs/`

- *Azure Software Development Kit (SDK):* This includes libraries needed to program against Azure, further integration between Azure and Visual Studio, and development tools and emulators you'll need. You can download it from `https://azure.microsoft.com/en-us/tools/`

- *SQL Server Management Studio (SMSS), version 16.5 or greater:* This can be downloaded from `https://msdn.microsoft.com/en-us/library/mt238290.aspx`

- *Microsoft Azure Storage Explorer, version 0.8.5 or greater:* This can be downloaded from `http://storageexplorer.com/`

- *Redis Desktop Manager, version 0.8.8 or greater:* This can be downloaded from `https://redisdesktop.com/`

- *Azure Cosmos DB Emulator:* The latest version can be downloaded from `https://aka.ms/cosmosdb-emulator/`

- *Service Bus Explorer, version 1.0.0 or greater:* The Git repo is located at `https://github.com/paolosalvatori/ServiceBusExplorer.git`

Your Azure Subscription

To publish Azure applications to the cloud, you'll need to set up an Azure subscription.

Microsoft offers a free tier for most services. For example, you can provision an App Service Plan using the free tier, which will allow you to create several free web apps, mobile apps, or application programming interface (API) apps. Although processing power is very limited for these free services, they're perfect for learning how Azure works.

There are several services that do not allow a free instance, such as Azure SQL Databases. Fortunately, Microsoft is currently offering a $200 credit when you sign up for a free trial. The $200 credit expires after 30 days.

When signing up for an Azure trial account, you will have to verify via phone call or SMS message, and you will have to enter a valid credit card. Don't worry—your credit card will not be charged, even after your $200 credit is exhausted. Once your $200 Azure credit is consumed or expires, the billable services that you've provisioned will stop working. You'll have to explicitly upgrade your subscription from a trial to a pay-as-you-go before your credit card will ever be billed.

To set up an Azure free trial account and claim your $200 credit, browse to `https://azure.microsoft.com`. Instructions for creating a trial account are prominently displayed on the home page. We'll cover further details on setting up and managing an Azure subscription in Chapter 1.

Let's get started!

CHAPTER 1

Introducing Azure

What Is Azure?

What is Azure? According to Microsoft's own web site, "Microsoft Azure is a growing collection of integrated cloud services—analytics, computing, database, mobile, networking, storage, and web—for moving faster, achieving more, and saving money."

That's not a bad definition, but it's a little wordy. For web app developers, I'd say that Azure is a cloud-based, compute-on-demand platform and set of services that has everything you need to build reliable and scalable web applications. It can support anywhere from a handful to millions of users. Microsoft has been using Azure to host their own large-scale services such as Xbox One.

Let's start with the meaning of cloud-based, compute-on-demand, and how these concepts can save you money. Then we discuss the different categories of Azure services and talk about the services that are most applicable to web app developers.

Cloud-Based Compute-on-Demand Services

Back in the dark ages of computing (before 2006), hosting options were limited. If you wanted to launch a new web application, you had to estimate the max load that your servers could possibly experience, then lease or purchase servers that could handle the traffic. The issue was guessing exactly how much traffic your new web app would experience. It was a classic Goldilocks problem. Because adding additional servers could take weeks to purchase and configure, you didn't want to underestimate, have your site featured on Slashdot, receive a flood of traffic, and watch your servers collapse under the load. Conversely, you didn't want to overestimate and pay hundreds of thousands of dollars for servers that sat idle most of the time. I've seen both cases happen, and it generally ends with management screaming at the poor development team. What's a web developer to do?

1

© Rob Reagan 2018
R. Reagan, *Web Applications on Azure*, https://doi.org/10.1007/978-1-4842-2976-7_1

In 2006, Amazon launched their Amazon Web Services (AWS) platform to address this very issue. AWS changed how computing resources were purchased. Amazon's servers were all virtualized. As a developer, you purchased one or more server instances with guaranteed computing resources—you didn't know or care about the underlying hardware. Spinning up a new server instance could be automated and took only seconds. Now you could scale both the size of your instance and the number of instances up or down in near real time. This is compute-on-demand.

Amazon's second innovation was metered billing. As developers, we were no longer tied to commitments of purchasing or leasing servers for months at a time. With AWS, you simply paid for what you used on a per-hour basis.

Amazon made a killing on AWS and continued to improve and expand their product offering, and Microsoft took notice. As Microsoft is wont to do, they took Amazon's great idea and worked to make it even better. In 2010, Microsoft released its own suite of cloud-based, compute-on-demand services that was originally named Windows Azure. In the beginning, Azure had a limited number of services and minimal integration with Visual Studio. Now, Azure has grown to 67 separate services as of the time of this writing. If you're a .NET developer building web applications, Azure is the place to be.

Infrastructure-as-a-Service vs. Platform-as-a-Service

Infrastructure-as-a-Service (IaaS) is a category of cloud computing that refers to providing virtualized computing resources. When you provision infrastructure as a service, you receive nothing more than the virtualized resource. Examples in Azure include virtual machines, networking infrastructure such as virtual networks and load balancers, and storage services such as Backup and Site Recovery and Storage Account. With each of these, you can configure low-level details as to how the infrastructure functions. For example, with a provisioned virtual machine, you have complete control over the operating system (OS) and how it is configured.

With Platform-as-a-Service (PaaS), you receive a platform for developing applications. Unlike IaaS, most or all of the underlying infrastructure settings are fixed. For example, let's look at Azure Web Apps, which are one of the basic building blocks of Azure web applications. Azure Web Apps allow you to upload your ASP.NET application directly to a hosting environment that puts your app on the Web immediately. You have the ability to change a limited number of hosting settings such as server affinity, the .NET framework version, and whether or not to enable web sockets. The underlying OS settings are fixed and inaccessible.

Why would you want to build on PaaS instead of IaaS if you're limited to what you can configure with PaaS? The beauty of PaaS is that you do not need to worry about details such as setting up and properly configuring the underlying OS and Internet Information Services (IIS), configuring networking and managing network security, or hardening the underlying OS and keeping up to date with the most recent patches. Instead, you upload your code and verify that your site is answering requests properly. PaaS takes away a great deal of headaches and risk.

My personal recommendation is to always start a web application project with PaaS in mind. If and only if you are unable to accomplish everything you need to do within Azure's PaaS offering, then consider falling back to IaaS. Throughout this book, we discuss services from both IaaS and PaaS.

Setting Up Your Machine for Azure Development

Before diving into Azure development, you'll need to install some software on your local machine. This software ranges from software development kits (SDKs) to emulators to tools that you'll need to use when managing your live Azure services. These tools are all free and are listed here.

Visual Studio 2015 Community Edition

Visual Studio 2015 Community Edition is an excellent integrated development environment (IDE) for .NET in general, and its integration with Azure is excellent. You'll use Visual Studio for rapidly deploying code to Web Apps, WebJobs, browsing Web App server logs, remote debugging Web Apps, analyzing log files, and browsing Azure services within your subscription.

If you already have Visual Studio 2015 Professional or Enterprise installed, you do not need to install Community Edition.

Required: Yes.

Download link: `https://www.visualstudio.com/downloads/`

Azure SDK

After installing Visual Studio, it's time to install the Azure SDK. The Azure SDK includes both the SDK and Azure Tools, which provide deeper Azure integration with Visual Studio and local emulators for development. If you do not install the Azure SDK, you'll have to chase down tools and emulators one by one.

Required: Yes.

Download link: `https://azure.microsoft.com/en-us/tools`. Choose .NET SDK, then click the link for your version of Visual Studio.

SQL Server 2016 Express Edition

This is an instance of SQL Server that you can install to your local machine. It's very handy to use when developing web applications that make use of relational data. Although you can develop against an instance of Azure SQL that is provisioned in the cloud, it's much easier to develop locally and avoid latency between your local machine and an Azure regional data center.

Required: Only for developing applications that use a local relational database. Also, if you have already installed an instance of SQL Server 2016 Standard, Developer, or Enterprise on your local machine, you can skip this install.

Download link: `https://www.microsoft.com/en-us/sql-server/sql-server-editions-express`

Note   SQL Server 2016 Developer Edition is also free, but requires you to log in with your Microsoft account and answer a few questions before proceeding to the download. Developer Edition is a heavier weight install and includes all of the features of the Enterprise Edition. You are restricted by license to use the Developer Edition for development purposes only. There are no examples in this book that require the additional functionality found in the Developer Edition.

You can download and install the Developer Edition here: `https://www.microsoft.com/en-us/sql-server/sql-server-editions-developers`. Note that to download the Developer Edition, you'll have to register to do so.

SQL Server 2016 Express Installation Walkthrough

There are several options and settings that you must specify when installing SQL Server 2016. Here's a quick run-through of the installation process and recommended settings.

Step 1: Choose the Installation Type

After downloading the bits from `https://www.microsoft.com/en-us/sql-server/sql-server-editions-express`, run the application. This is simply a web downloader that will download the installer and SQL Server bits.

After launching the downloader, choose the Basic configuration (see Figure 1-1). The only difference between the Basic and Custom options is that the Custom option lets you specify the folder in which to place the downloaded binary before installation.

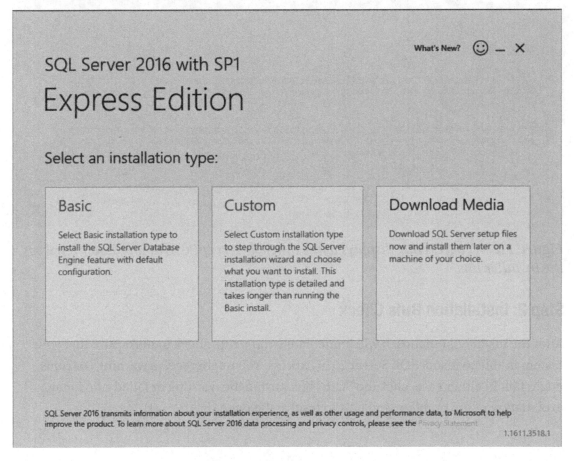

Figure 1-1. *Choose the installation type*

After you select Basic, the downloader will begin downloading the SQL Server 2016 Express bits (Figure 1-2).

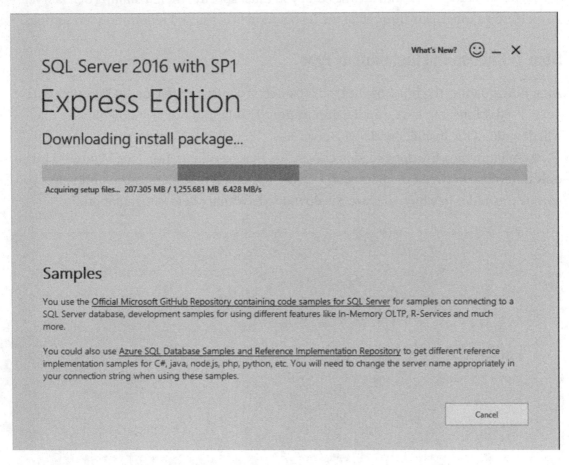

Figure 1-2. *Progress bar displays while the SQL Server 2016 downloader retrieves the installer bits*

Step 2: Installation Rule Check

After the installer launches, it will immediately run a rule check to make sure that your system is able to install SQL Server 2016 Express. You might receive warnings or rules might fail. In either case, click the Status link next to the warning or failed rule for an explanation of the problem and how to resolve the issue (Figure 1-3).

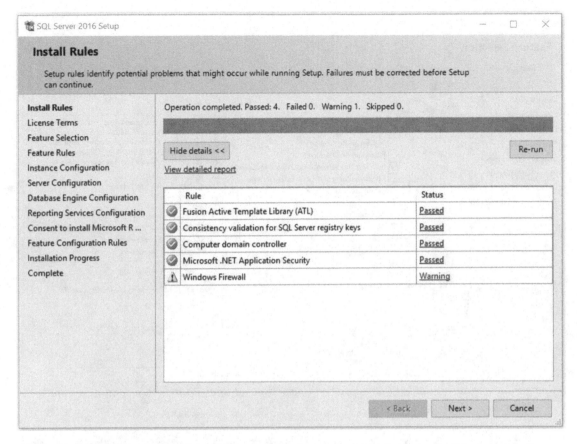

Figure 1-3. *The rule check will ensure that your system has everything needed for SQL Server. Click the hyperlink in the Status column to see a description of the problem if any rule fails or raises a warning.*

Step 3: Agree to the License Terms

The Apress legal department insists I recommend that you read the license terms in their entirety and print a copy for your own reference, but we both know that isn't going to happen. Select the I Accept the License Terms check box and click Next to continue.

Step 4: Feature Selection

The Feature Selection screen, shown in Figure 1-4, lets you choose exactly what gets installed. For the examples in this book, you do not need SQL Server Replication, R Services, or Reporting Services. You are free to install these if you choose to do so.

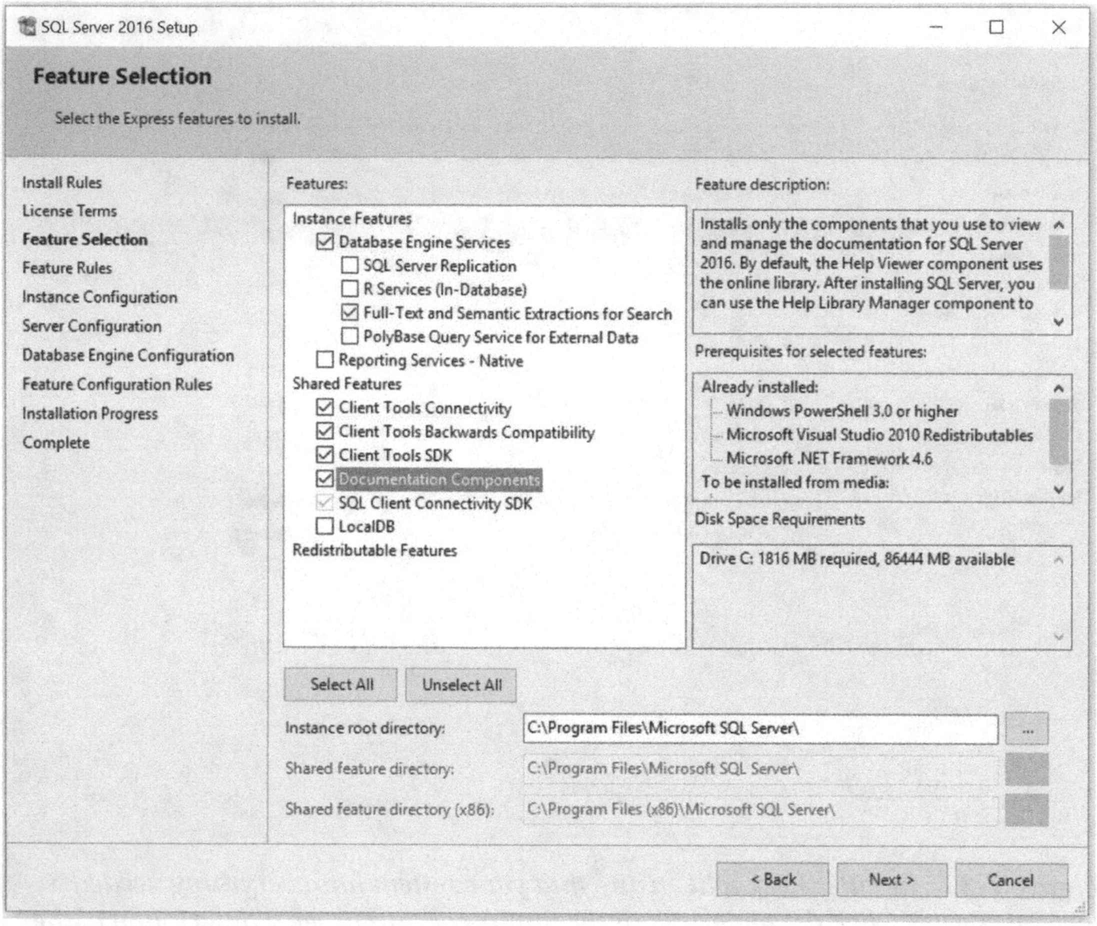

Figure 1-4. *Choose the features that you want installed with SQL Server 2016*

Click Next to continue, and the installer will run Feature Rules to ensure that your machine has the necessary prerequisites to install the features you selected. If your machine passes all Feature Rules, you will automatically be advanced to the Instance Configuration screen. If your machine fails any Feature Rules, you'll be shown a list of problems and suggestions for remediation.

Step 5: Instance Configuration

The Instance Configuration screen, displayed in Figure 1-5, allows you to choose between installing a default and named instance. On a given machine, there can be only one default instance, but as many named instances as you want. Each instance will have its own set of directories, registry entries, and services that can have unique settings apart from other instances. The only other significant difference between default and named instances is that connection strings within your code will reference a default instance by the machine name only, and named instances must be addressed in the connection string by machine name and instance name.

I recommend choosing a named instance. After making your choice, click Next to continue.

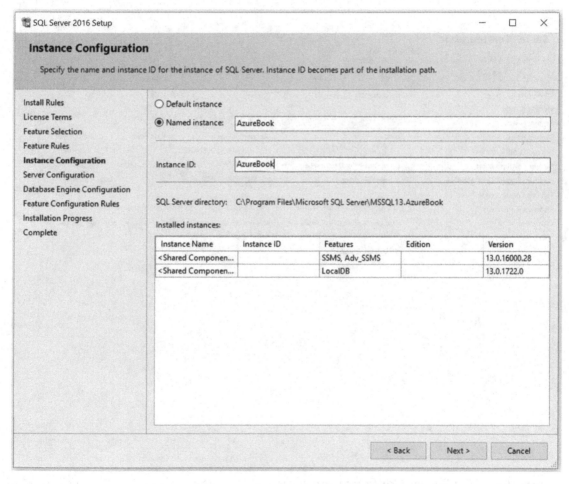

Figure 1-5. *The Instance Configuration screen*

Step 6: Server Configuration

SQL Server 2016 is composed of multiple Windows services. The Server Configuration screen, shown in Figure 1-6, allows you to specify how the SQL Server 2016 services are started. Options are Automatic (the service starts when your machine boots), Manual (you must explicitly start a service from the command line or Windows Management Console), or Disabled. Accept the defaults and click Next.

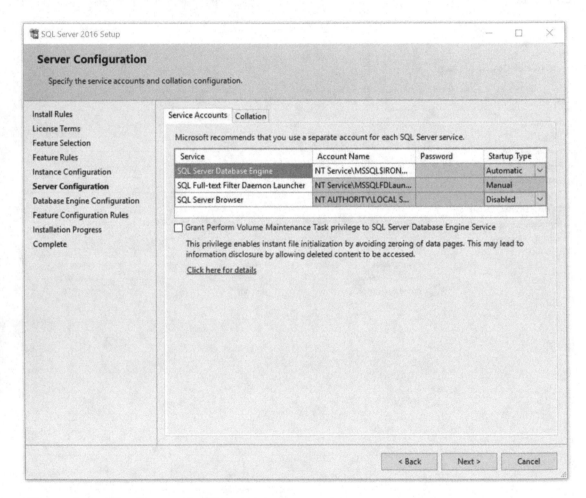

Figure 1-6. *The Server Configuration screen*

You also have the option on this screen to specify different service accounts that will be used to run the various services that make up SQL Server. By default, the installer will create separate accounts for services. I recommend using the defaults unless you have a compelling reason to do otherwise.

Step 7: Database Engine Configuration

The Database Engine Configuration screen, shown in Figure 1-7, allows you to set the authentication mode for the server, specify the default location of database and log files for each database created, nonstandard settings for the TempDB, and whether to enable FILESTREAM.

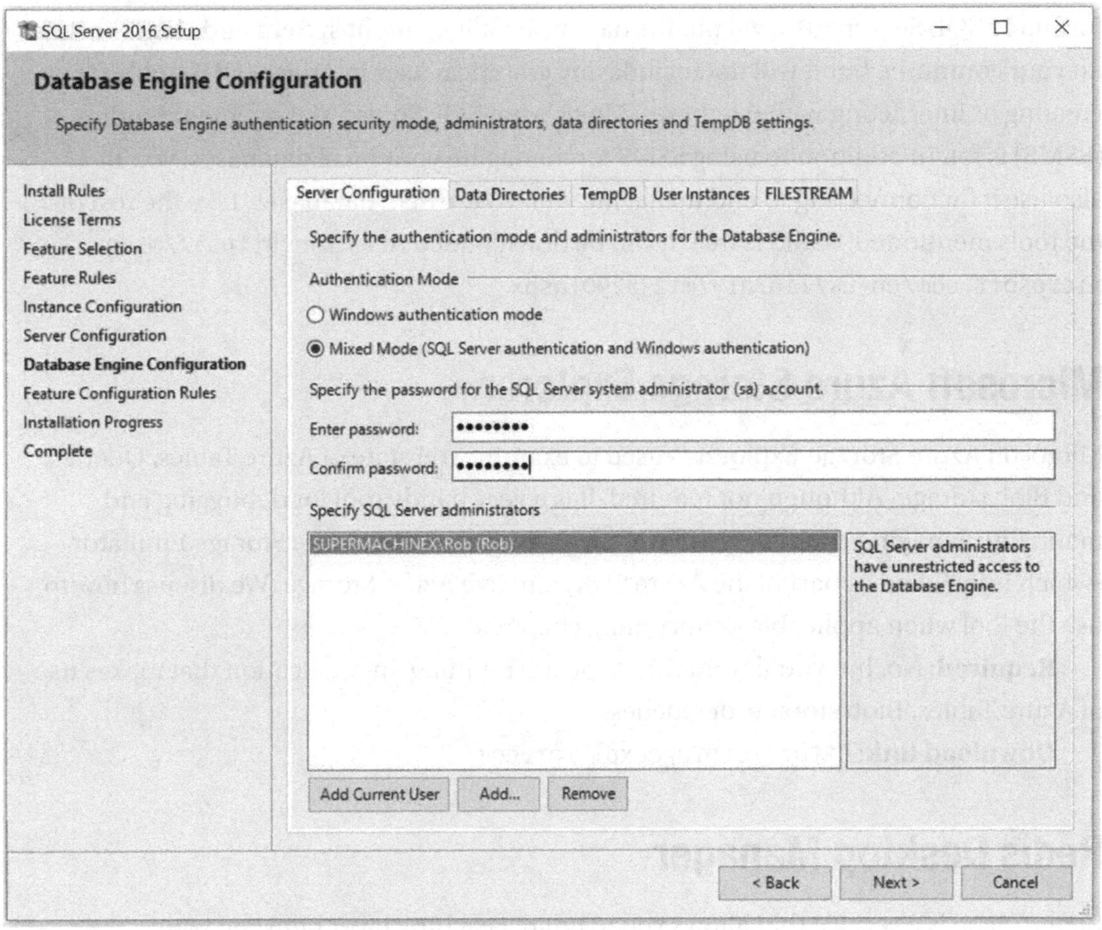

Figure 1-7. *The Database Configuration screen*

It is highly recommended that you set the Authentication Mode to Windows, which is much more secure and offers benefits such as the enforcement of password policy, handling of account lockout, and support for password expiration.

If your Windows login doesn't appear in the Specify SQL Server Administrators list, click Add Current User. Leave all other defaults on the other tabs, and click Next.

11

Complete the Installation

After the Database Configuration Screen, you'll move to the installation progress screen, where you'll sit and watch progress bars until the installation is complete.

SQL Server Management Studio

Installing SQL Server 2016 will put the database management system and client libraries on your computer, but it will not include any graphical user interface (GUI) tools for creating or interacting with databases. That's what SQL Server Management Studio (SSMS) is for. In addition to using SSMS for managing your local databases, you'll also use it for connecting to and managing your Azure SQL databases. Like the rest of the tools mentioned, SSMS is free. It can be downloaded here from `https://msdn.`
`microsoft.com/en-us/library/mt238290.aspx`

Microsoft Azure Storage Explorer

Microsoft Azure Storage Explorer is used to examine the state of Azure Tables, Queues, and Blob storage. Although not required, it is a very handy tool for debugging and manually managing content. It will work with both the local Azure Storage Emulator (which is installed as part of the Azure SDK) and live Azure Storage. We discuss how to use the tool when applicable in upcoming chapters.

Required: No, but you'll want this if you are building an application that makes use of Azure Tables, Blob storage, or Queues.

Download link: `http://storageexplorer.com`

Redis Desktop Manager

Redis Cache is a service that allows you to build a caching layer between your application and data store to speed up data access. Although the Azure SDK includes the libraries necessary to program with Redis Cache, you'll need to download the Redis Desktop Manager to view and manage the contents of your Redis Cache.

Also, note that there is no local emulator for Redis Cache. You'll need to program directly against a Redis Cache service provisioned on Azure.

Required: Only for managing applications that use Redis Cache.

Download link: `https://redisdesktop.com/`

Setting Up Your Azure Account

You can develop certain Azure solutions locally without having an Azure subscription, but you must have an Azure subscription before you can provision any services in the cloud on Azure. Microsoft offers three different types of subscriptions: free trial, pay-as-you-go, and enterprise agreements. Let's run through each.

Free Trial

At the time of this writing, Microsoft is offering a free trial membership. The trial membership consists of a $200 Azure credit that expires 30 days after creating your free trial account. Any unused portion of the $200 expires at the end of the 30-day period. You can use the $200 credit for any combination of Azure services. You cannot use the $200 credit for third-party services offered through the Azure Marketplace.

For many Azure services, Microsoft also offers a free tier. The free tier generally has limited computing power and some feature restrictions. It is intended to allow you to explore working with the service and build proof of concepts. Examples of services that include a free tier are Web Apps, Search, Notification Hubs, Application Insights, and Scheduler. Once your 30-day $200 Azure credit expires, you can still continue using the free tier of any Azure services.

After your 30-day trial period has elapsed, any paid services that you have provisioned will be decommissioned. You can continue using any paid services that you provisioned if you upgrade to a pay-as-you-go subscription before your free trial expires.

To sign up for a free trial, you'll need an e-mail address, a credit card, and a phone number. Your credit card will not be billed; it's just used as part of Microsoft's antifraud measures to weed out nefarious actors such as spam-bots and Nigerian princes. You can rest assured that even at the end of your free trial, Microsoft will not charge your credit card for any paid provisioned services unless you explicitly upgrade to a pay-as-you-go subscription. As part of the verification process when creating a free trial account, Microsoft might place a $1 verification hold on your credit card. This hold is removed in three to five days.

Now, let's sign up for your free account. The process is straightforward.

Go to `https://azure.microsoft.com`. Click Start Free or Free Account to get started.

You'll be asked to log in with your Microsoft account (Figure 1-8). If you don't have one, click the Get a New Account link. Creating a new Microsoft account requires only an e-mail address.

Figure 1-8. *To start a free trial, log in with your Microsoft account. If you don't already have a Microsoft account, click the Get a New Account link.*

After signing in, you'll need to provide your name, basic contact information, and phone and credit card identity verification. You also have to agree to the terms of the license agreement (Figure 1-9). Once these are complete, your free trial account is provisioned and you're ready to begin building applications with Azure.

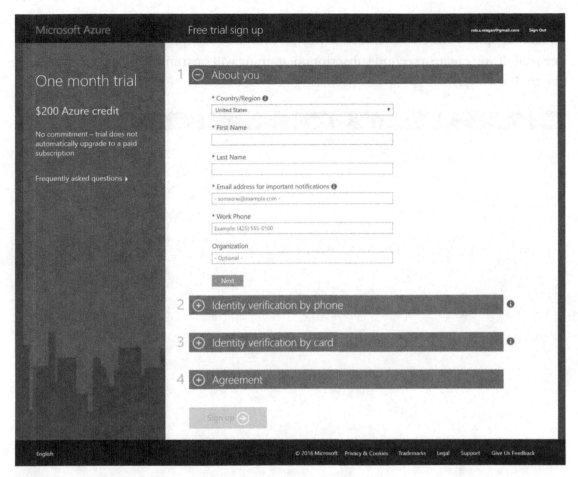

Figure 1-9. *To complete your free trial, you'll need to provide basic information and verify your identity via phone and credit card*

Purchasing an Azure Subscription

There are two ways to purchase a pay-as-you-go subscription: upgrading a free trial, and buying a subscription without setting up a free trial.

Upgrading a Free Trial

To upgrade a free trial, go to `https://account.windowsazure.com/subscriptions`. You'll see the screen shown in Figure 1-10, and can either click the Click Here to Automatically Convert to Pay-As-You-Go link or click the Add Subscription link. The difference between the two is that clicking on the former transfers all services you've provisioned as part of your free trial to a new pay-as-you-go subscription. Clicking the Add Subscription link creates a second pay-as-you-go subscription in addition to your free trial. If you create a second subscription, nothing will be transferred over from your free trial.

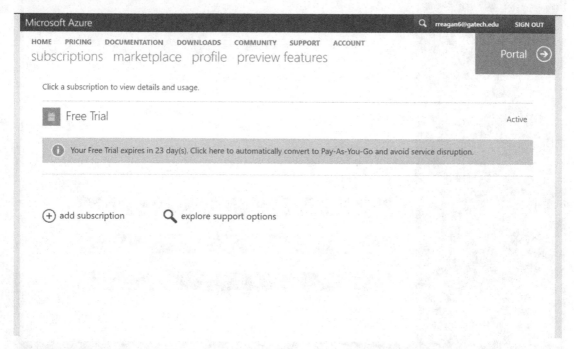

Figure 1-10. *Upgrade an existing trial subscription to a paid subscription*

Purchasing a New Subscription Without a Free Trial

If you know you want to purchase a subscription and don't want to bother with a free trial, navigate to `https://azure.microsoft.com/en-us/pricing/purchase-options`, and click Buy Now. You'll be asked to sign in to your Microsoft account, and then prompted to enter your contact information, verify via phone, and enter your payment information. Once complete, you'll be ready to provision Azure services.

Enterprise Agreements

Enterprise agreements (EAs)make sense when you or your company plan on consuming more than $1,200 of Azure services per year. The benefits of an EA are as follows:

- *Discounts on Azure services:* With an EA, you'll receive a discount on the published pay-as-you-go prices. The percentage discount varies by service and pricing tier.

- *A dedicated account executive:* If you have billing, account management, or even technical questions, your account executive will help you track down the information that you need.

- *Access to the EA Portal:* The EA Portal provides extended billing information above and beyond what you receive from a pay-as-you-go subscription. It also provides tools for managing multiple subscriptions.

So why wouldn't you elect to purchase an EA rather than a normal pay-as-you-go subscription? The main reason is that you pay for the first year of an EA up front. Afterward, you pay quarterly. You'll have to decide if the discounts on Azure services warrant yearly or quarterly prepayment.

Purchasing an EA

Microsoft does not sell EAs directly; all EA subscriptions are sold through Microsoft Partners. However, not all Microsoft Partners sell EAs. If you work at a larger company that already has a Microsoft Account Representative, the easiest thing to do is to ask your account representative to refer you to a partner who can handle selling and servicing an Azure EA. If you do not have a Microsoft Account Representative who works with your company, the real fun begins.

If you do not have a Microsoft Account Representative, your best bet for locating a partner is to call or e-mail the Azure sales team directly. You can find the country-specific sales phone number or submit an inquiry at `https://azure.microsoft.com/en-us/overview/sales-number`

Summary

In this chapter, we've discussed what Azure is and what it can do for you, how to set up your development environment to begin building Azure applications, and various options for creating an Azure subscription. Now let's get started building scalable Azure apps.

CHAPTER 2

Web Applications

Microsoft App Service Web Apps are a PaaS offering that allows developers to quickly and easily deploy web sites and applications to the Internet. Think of Web Apps as a cloud-based IIS that is already secured, configured, and just waiting for you to upload your code. In addition to hosting your application, some of the other benefits that Web Apps offer include the following:

- *Scalability*: Web Apps allow you to scale up (move to a more powerful instance) or scale out (add additional instances) almost instantaneously without having to redeploy your code. With Standard or Premium Web App instances, you can even set autoscale rules that will scale up or scale out your application based on real-time performance metrics such as CPU utilization.

- *Automatic OS updates*: Because this is a PaaS offering, you don't need to worry about upgrading or patching the underlying OS; it's handled for you.

- *Ease of deployment*: You can publish your application to Web Apps directly from within Visual Studio with just a few clicks. There are also other deployment options, such as deploying directly from Git for continuous integration. You can even script deployments using PowerShell or .NET.

- *Integration with other Azure technologies*: Your Web Apps can integrate with other services such as Azure SQL databases, Service Bus, Azure Redis Cache, and Azure Storage services such as Azure Queues and Azure Tables.

- *Simple backup and recovery*: Azure makes it very easy to back up and restore everything deployed to your Web App. You can even include an Azure SQL database as part of the backup or restore operation.

19

R. Reagan, *Web Applications on Azure*, https://doi.org/10.1007/978-1-4842-2976-7_2

- *Robust performance monitoring*: Web Apps integrate with Application Insights, which gives detailed information into requests, dependencies, exceptions, and tracing. This helps take much of the guesswork out of debugging logic errors and performance issues.

- *Multiple language support*: Web App Services support applications written in .NET, Node.js, Python, PHP, and Java. This book focuses on building Web Apps with .NET.

Of all the hosting technologies that Azure offers (Web Apps, Cloud Services, Virtual Machines [VMs], and Service Fabric), Web Apps are the simplest to use.

In this chapter, we'll start with building a very simple example web application called Verify. We'll then walk through deploying the Verify web application to Azure. Next, we'll load test our deployed application using Visual Studio Team Services performance testing tools to see how our basic deployment handles traffic. We'll then discuss various strategies for scaling Web Apps, and end this chapter with instructions on backing up and restoring your application.

Let's dive in.

Introducing the Verify App

To illustrate Web App features, we'll build a simple web application called Verify. Verify allows employers and financial institutions to enter a Social Security number (SSN) and determine if it is valid.

We'll build our Verify app using .NET Framework 4.6.1 and ASP.NET Core 1.0. We'll include an Azure SQL database for our data store, and will access it using Entity Framework Core 1.1. Don't worry about the details of Azure SQL for now; we discuss it in depth in Chapter 4.

Note   This example application is intended to demonstrate how to deploy an application to Web Apps and to provide us with something appropriate to load test and scale. It is stripped down to be as simple as possible and doesn't include functionality such as authentication, authorization, or robust client-side input validation. These features would clutter our codebase and are not important to our discussion on Web Apps.

Building the Verify Web Application

The Verify application will consist of an ASP.NET MVC web application and a SQL Server database.

In the following sections, we'll walk through building the Verify application step by step. If you are already comfortable with this tech stack, you can skip ahead and download the complete source code from the Git repo at `https://github.com/BuildingScalableWebAppsWithAzure/VerifyWebApp.git`

Creating the Database and Person Tables

Let's start by defining our data model and creating our database. Because our goal is to allow employers and financial institutions to determine if a provided SSN is valid and belongs to the appropriate person, we'll need to track the following fields:

- Social Security number
- First name
- Middle name
- Last name
- Birthdate
- If the person is deceased

Let's create a table called Person in our local SQL Server instance that has a table definition as shown in Figure 2-1.

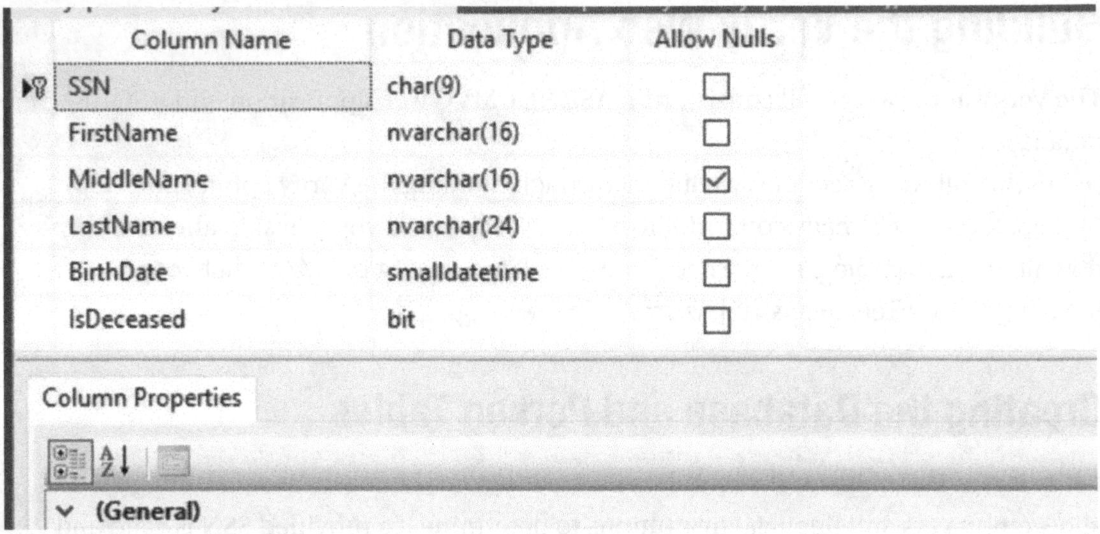

Column Name	Data Type	Allow Nulls
SSN	char(9)	☐
FirstName	nvarchar(16)	☐
MiddleName	nvarchar(16)	☑
LastName	nvarchar(24)	☐
BirthDate	smalldatetime	☐
IsDeceased	bit	☐

Column Properties

Ⅴ **(General)**

Figure 2-1. *The Person table definition in SQL Server 2016 Management Studio*

Creating the Web Application

Let's start by opening Visual Studio 2015, choosing File ➤ New ➤ Project. Under Installed ➤ Templates, choose Visual C# ➤ .NET Core and select the ASP.NET Core Web Application (.NET Core) project template. Name the project Verify.Web, select the Create Directory for Solution check box, and from the list of frameworks, choose .NET Framework 4.6.1 (see Figure 2-2). Finally, click OK. If you do not see the .NET Core project templates, you'll need to make sure that you've installed the .NET Core SDK.

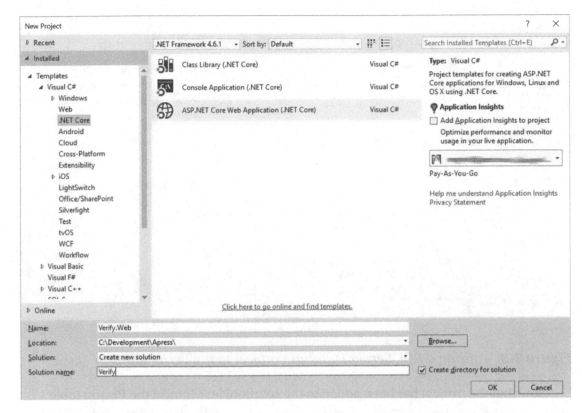

Figure 2-2. *Creating the Verify application project in Visual Studio*

Next, you'll be asked to select an ASP.NET Core Template. Choose Web Application and click OK.

Adding a SQL Server Database Project

Visual Studio SQL Server Database projects are an excellent way to handle the initial deployment of a database to a production server. They will also handle deploying changes to existing databases. Because it's a Visual Studio project, we can also keep the current state of our database under source control. We'll eventually use a SQL Server Database project to deploy our database to an Azure SQL instance.

To add a SQL Server Database project to our solution, right-click the solution within Solution Explorer, and choose Add ➤ New Project. Under Installed, select SQL Server, then select SQL Server Database Project from the list of templates. Name the project Verify.Database, and click OK (Figure 2-3).

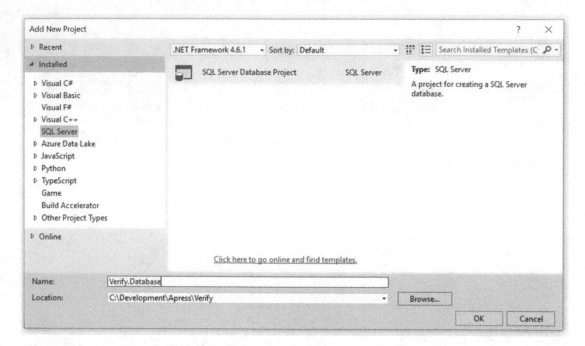

Figure 2-3. *Adding a SQL Server Database project to the Verify solution*

Now that the project has been added to the solution, let's import the Person table within our Verify database. The easiest way to do so is to right-click the Verify.Database project within the Visual Studio Solution Explorer, and select Import from the shortcut menu. This will open the Import Database dialog box. Specify your database connection by clicking Select Connection, then click Start.

After the Import Database Utility has finished running, you will see a `Person.sql` file under a new dbo ➤ Tables directory in the Verify.Database project. We're done with the Verify.Database project for the moment and will return to it when we deploy our application to Azure.

Adding Entity Framework Core to Verify.Web

Because we'll be retrieving data from a SQL Server database, we must decide how our application will communicate with our database. Entity Framework, Microsoft's object relational mapping tool, is the recommended technology for doing so.

As we'll be working with Azure SQL, there are additional connectivity issues that we have to address. Like all Azure services, Azure SQL is cloud-based. It allocates a fixed amount of memory, CPU cycles, and I/O operations to your database depending on the service tier that you choose. Once your application exceeds these limits, you will experience command timeouts, refused connections, or both. Your data access code will need to identify when these transient failures occur and automatically retry the operation. Writing this retry logic from scratch is time consuming, complicated, and difficult to get right. Fortunately, Entity Framework 6.x and Entity Framework Core 1.0+ both have retry logic automatically built in. This is one of the more compelling reasons to use Entity Framework over other data access technologies such as plain ADO.NET. We'll cover Azure SQL in further detail in Chapter 4.

We currently have two choices when using Entity Framework: using Entity Framework 6.x or Entity Framework Core. As of this writing, Entity Framework Core does not support all of the features found in Entity Framework 6.x, but it does include all of the features we'll need for this demo. Over time, Entity Framework Core will grow to feature parity with Entity Framework 6.x.

To add Entity Framework Core to our solution, right-click the Verify.Web project and select Manage NuGet Packages from the shortcut menu. Next, make sure that you've selected the Browse tab and not the Installed or Updates tabs. On the NuGet package management screen, be sure to select the Include Prerelease check box. Then search for and add the following NuGet packages:

- `Microsoft.EntityFrameworkCore`

- `Microsoft.EntityFrameworkCore.Design`

- `Microsoft.EntityFrameworkCore.SqlServer.Design`

- `Microsoft.EntityFrameworkCore.Tools`

- `Microsoft.EntityFrameworkCore.Tools.DotNet`

Generating the Entity Framework DbContext and Models Classes

When using Entity Framework, you'll need to derive a class from `Microsoft.EntityFrameworkCore.DbContext`. The `DbContext` class is responsible for querying the database, translating query results into object instances, tracking changes made to entities after they are retrieved from the database, caching, and writing changes made to entities back to the database. Think of `DbContext` as the air traffic controller that coordinates moving relational data from tables within the database to .NET object instances, and vice versa. We'll also need to create classes to hold the data retrieved from the database.

Fortunately, you don't have to write that code yourself. Because we've already created our app's database, we can use Entity Framework's `Scaffold-DbContext` command to reverse engineer our tables and generate our `DbContext` subclass and models. In Visual Studio, click Tools ➤ NuGet Package Manager ➤ Package Manager Console, then run the following command at the Package Manager prompt:

```
Scaffold-DbContext "Server=[YourSQLServerName];Database=Verify;Trusted_
Connection=True;" Microsoft.EntityFrameworkCore.SqlServer -OutputDir Models
```

After running this command, you will see a new `Models` folder in your Verify.Web project. It will contain two new classes: `Person.cs`, which is our single-model class, and `VerifyContext.cs`, which derives from `DbContext`.

Creating the Service Layer

Ultimately, we'll create a `SearchController` class that derives from `Microsoft.AspNetCore.Mvc.Controller` to process SSN search requests from users who visit our Verify application web site. It's a good idea to keep controller classes thin and not include business logic in them. We'll put our search logic within a service-tier class called `PersonService`. Because we'll be injecting a `PersonService` instance into our `SearchController`, we'll need to set up an interface called `IPersonService` that `PersonService` will implement.

1. Create a new folder in Verify.Web called `Services`.

2. Add a new interface to the `Services` folder called `IPersonService.cs`. The code for `IPersonService.cs` is as follows:

   ```
   namespace Verify.Services
   {
       public interface IPersonService
       {
           Person RetrievePersonBySSN(string ssn);
       }
   }
   ```

3.   Add a new class to the Services folder called PersonService.cs.
     The code is as follows:

```csharp
using Verify.Models;

namespace Verify.Services
{
    /// <summary>
    /// This class handles retrieving a person with a given SSN
    /// from the database.
    /// </summary>
    public class PersonService : IPersonService
    {
        private VerifyContext _verifyContext;

        /// <summary>
        /// Constructor. Our DbContext subclass is injected via
        /// the DI controller at runtime.
        /// </summary>
        /// <param name="verifyContext"></param>
        public PersonService(VerifyContext verifyContext)
        {
            _verifyContext = verifyContext;
        }

        /// <summary>
        /// Retrieves and returns a Person instance identified by
        /// their SSN. If no person with
        /// the specified SSN is found in the database, this
        /// method returns null.
        /// </summary>
        /// <param name="ssn"></param>
        /// <returns></returns>
        public Person RetrievePersonBySSN(string ssn)
        {
            ssn = RemoveNonNumericCharacters(ssn);
            Person requestedPerson = null;
```

```csharp
        if (IsSSNValid(ssn))
        {
            //we have a nine-digit SSN. Let's search to see
            //who it belongs to!
            requestedPerson = _verifyContext.Person.Find(ssn);
        }
        return requestedPerson;
    }

    /// <summary>
    /// Checks to make sure that the supplied SSN is nine
    /// characters in length.
    /// </summary>
    /// <param name="ssn">The SSN that we are validating.
    /// </param>
    /// <returns></returns>
    private bool IsSSNValid(string ssn)
    {
        bool isValid = ssn.Length == 9;
        return isValid;
    }

    /// <summary>
    /// Returns a string containing only the numeric
    /// characters found in str.
    /// </summary>
    private string RemoveNonNumericCharacters(string str)
    {
        string result = string.Empty;
        char[] charArray = str.ToCharArray();
        foreach (char currentChar in charArray)
        {
            if (char.IsDigit(currentChar))
            {
                result += currentChar;
            }
```

```
            }
            return result;
        }
    }
}
```

Specifying Our Application Settings

In previous versions of ASP.NET MVC and ASP.NET Web Form projects, application settings were stored in `web.config` files. In ASP.NET Core, we now store our application settings in the `appsettings.json` file. We need to set our connection string within our project's `appsettings.json` file so that our `VerifyContext` class will know how to connect to our database.

Open the `appsettings.json` file within the Verify.Web project. You'll need to swap out the connection string for your own. The `appsettings.json` file should look as follows:

```
{
  "ConnectionStrings": {
    "DefaultConnection": "[Your connection string]"
  },
  "Logging": {
    "IncludeScopes": false,
    "LogLevel": {
      "Default": "Debug",
      "System": "Information",
      "Microsoft": "Information"
    }
  }
}
```

Setting Up Dependency Injection

Back in the old days, developers built monolithic apps where class dependencies were hard-coded. If your front-end `SearchController` class needs a `PersonService` class to do its job, within the Search Controller you declare a variable of type `PersonService`

29

and then instantiate the PersonService class. The major downside of this approach was that it made unit testing difficult. Unit testing a front-end controller class meant that you would likely execute code all the way down to the data access layer and even hit the database itself. If a unit test failed, it was difficult to determine if the error was in the controller method under test, or in one of the dependencies that the controller method used.

Dependency injection (also called inversion of control) solved this problem. With dependency injection, we no longer hard-code class dependencies. Instead, we use a dependency injection container that is responsible for instantiating and providing dependencies at runtime. This injection of dependencies is typically done with constructor arguments. In our example, instead of declaring a variable of type PersonService within our SearchController class, the SearchController class will receive its PersonService instance via a constructor argument at runtime.

We can take this idea one step further by declaring interfaces for our dependency classes, and then specifying those interfaces for our constructor arguments in classes that rely on those dependencies. This allows us to use mocking frameworks to greatly simplify our unit tests and ensure that we are only exercising the logic within the method that we are testing and not any code from our dependencies.

Note   A full discussion of dependency injection and mocking frameworks is beyond the scope of this book. If you'd like to brush up on these concepts, Martin Fowler has written an excellent article that can be found at http://www.martinfowler.com/articles/injection.html. Although the examples are in Java, the concepts are directly applicable to .NET.

In .NET Core web applications, dependency injection is configured in the Startup class's ConfigureServices method. To make our Entity Framework's VerifyContext class and our PersonService class available for dependency injection, open the Verify. Web project's Startup.cs class and add the following code:

```
// This method gets called by the runtime. Use this method to add services
// to the container.
public void ConfigureServices(IServiceCollection services)
{
        // Add framework services.
        services.AddMvc();
```

```
//read our connection string from the appsettings.json file.
string connectionString =
        Microsoft.Extensions.Configuration.ConfigurationExtensions.
        GetConnectionString(
        this.Configuration, "DefaultConnection");

//register our VerifyContext class with the dependency injection
//container.
services.AddDbContext<VerifyContext>(options => options.UseSqlServer
(connectionString));

//add our PersonService class to the dependency injection container.
services.AddTransient<IPersonService, PersonService>();
}
```

Adding the Front-End Controllers

Our application will consist of just two pages. The first page prompts the user for an SSN. The second page shows the search results.

Because we've put our search logic in a service class, the front-end controllers become very simple. Within the Verify.Web ➤ Controllers folder, our HomeController can be slimmed down to the following code that does nothing but return the appropriate view.

```
using Microsoft.AspNetCore.Mvc;

namespace Verify.Controllers
{
    public class HomeController : Controller
    {
        public IActionResult Index()
        {
            return View();
        }
    }
}
```

Now let's add our `SearchController` to the project. Right-click the `Controllers` folder in the Verify.Web project, and select Add ➤ New Item, then select MVC Controller Class from the list of templates. Name the new Controller `SearchController.cs`. This controller will have a single method that will receive a SSN, then return the results. The code for the new controller is as follows:

```
using Microsoft.AspNetCore.Mvc;
using Verify.Models;
using Verify.Services;

namespace Verify.Controllers
{
    public class SearchController : Controller
    {
        private IPersonService _personService;

        public SearchController(IPersonService personService)
        {
            _personService = personService;
        }

        [HttpGet]
        public IActionResult Index(string ssn)
        {
            Person requestedPerson = _personService.
            RetrievePersonBySSN(ssn);
            return View(requestedPerson);
        }
    }
}
```

Finally, delete all other `Controller` classes in the Verify.Web ➤ `Controllers` folder. We won't need them.

For the sake of brevity, we'll skip the source for our Views and Cascading Style Sheets (CSS). You can find both of these in the project repo at `https://github.com/BuildingScalableWebAppsWithAzure/VerifyWebApp.git`.

Deploying to Azure

Now that we've put together a simple example app, we can deploy it to Azure. We'll first provision an Azure SQL instance and then use our SQL Server Database project to publish our database to the server. Then we'll create our App Services Web App and publish our Verify project.

To get started, log into your Azure account. If you do not yet have an Azure account set up, flip back to Chapter 1 for a discussion on creating one.

Provisioning an Azure SQL Instance

Let's create the database that will host our Person records. After logging in to the Azure portal, click the plus sign button in the upper left corner to add a new service. Next, select Databases, then select SQL Database (Figure 2-4).

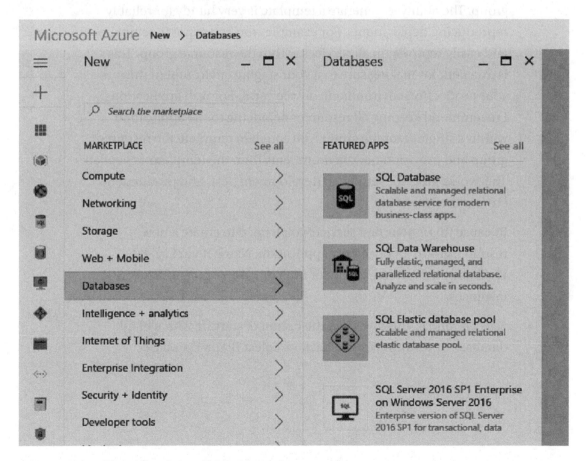

Figure 2-4. Provisioning a SQL Azure instance

Next, you'll be prompted for basic settings before the Azure SQL instance is created.

- *Database name*: This is the database name that will be created within your database server. This name must be unique within your database server only, and be descriptive so that you can identify your database resource in a list of resources. Adopting a naming convention is helpful in doing so. Let's name this `database verify-sql`.

- *Subscription*: If you have more than one subscription, you can choose which subscription you'd like to add the database to.

- *Resource group*: A resource group allows you to group one or more Azure services together for management purposes. You can specify role-based access to a resource group, lock a resource group to make sure that no resources within it can be deleted, and generate a template for automatic provisioning of resources within the resource group. The ability to generate a template is very handy for reliably reproducing deployments. For example, you can export a template and easily reprovision all services within the resource group. This is excellent for making sure that your staging environment mirrors your production environment, or vice versa. For web applications, I recommend keeping all resources belonging to the application within a single resource group. You can then template the resource group and provision new environments from the template as needed. This works great for setting up development, test, and production environments.

  Because this is your first service, you'll need to create a new resource group for our Verify application. Name it `verify-rg`. We'll use this resource group for both our Web App and Azure SQL instances.

- *Select resource*: This gives you the option of starting with a blank database or restoring from a backup. Select Blank Database.

- *Server*: Your database must live within a server. Let's provision a new one. Click the Server option, then on the Server blade, click Create a New Server. You'll be asked for a server name, server admin login, a location, and whether to use a V12 server, which is the latest version. You should create all new Azure SQL databases using V12. Choose a location and make note of it. We'll eventually place our Web App in the same region.

- *Use SQL elastic pool*: Select No. We discuss this option in detail in Chapter 4.

- *Pricing tier*: Database power is measured in database transaction units (DTUs). This measure is an amalgamation of CPU, data and transaction I/O operations, and memory. Microsoft does not publish the exact formula for calculating DTUs, but more DTUs means a more powerful server. The pricing tier basically determines how much power your database will have, measured in DTUs. We cover this in more depth in Chapter 4. For the task at hand, click the Pricing Tier option to open the Choose Your Pricing blade. Make sure that you select the View All option at the top of the blade. Select the Basic option.

- *Collation*: This option determines how SQL Server will sort and compare values. It cannot be changed after you provision the database. Accept the default, then click Create.

Now that we've created our Azure SQL database, we have a bit more configuration to do. Let's go to the management screen for our Azure SQL Server (which is different from the Azure SQL Database resource) by clicking All Resources, located directly below the Create button on the far left. This will show us every resource that we've provisioned. Find the SQL Server by name and click it to open its management blade (Figure 2-5).

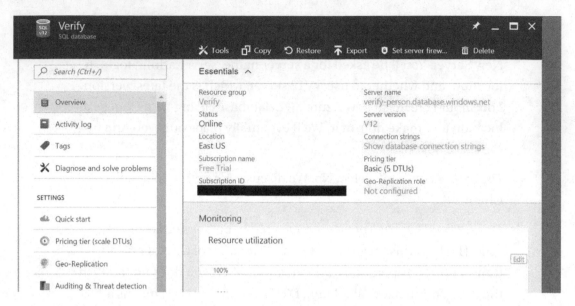

Figure 2-5. *The SQL Server management blade*

Azure SQL Servers control connectivity via an Internet Protocol (IP) whitelist at both the server and database levels. If you whitelist an IP address at the server level, the IP address can connect to all databases that live on that server. If you whitelist an IP address at the database level, the IP address can only connect to that database and no others on the server. If your IP address is *not* on the server or database whitelist, you will be unable to connect to the database at all.

It is recommended that administrators whitelist their IP addresses at the SQL Server level so that they can easily administer all databases on the server. If any other external users need access to individual databases, whitelist their IP addresses at the database level.

By default, Azure services are allowed to connect to your database. You can change this default setting if you like.

To set your firewall rules for this database, click the Show Firewall Settings link. This opens the Firewall settings blade, shown in Figure 2-6, which list all current valid firewall rules. You can define a range of IP addresses that are allowed to connect. To quickly add your current IP address, click Add Client IP. You can also toggle whether or not Azure services can connect to databases within this server.

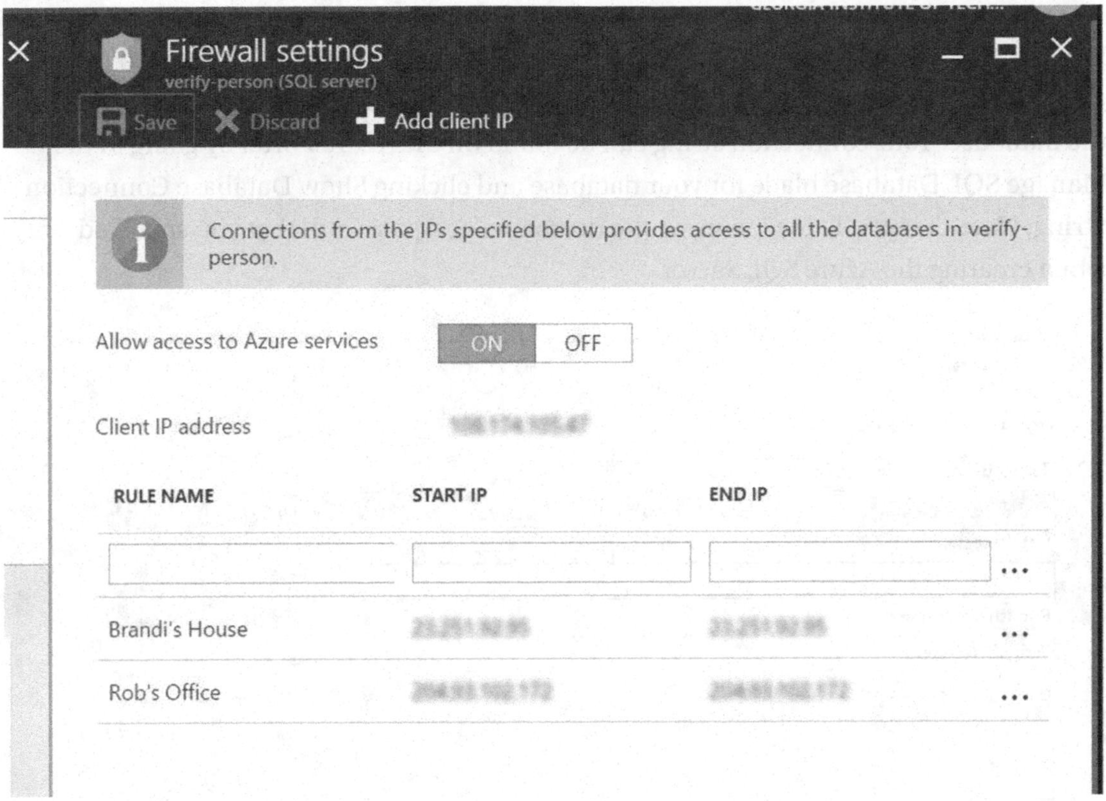

Figure 2-6. *The SQL Server Firewall settings blade*

Note that you must click Save after adding, modifying, or deleting a single rule. If you try to batch several changes together and click Save, the Firewall settings blade will refuse to cooperate.

Deploying the Verify Database

We've provisioned our Azure SQL Database, so it's time to upload our Verify database to our instance. We'll use our Verify.Database SQL Server Database project in our Visual Studio Verify solution to do so.

A SQL Server Database project can target different versions of SQL Server, and deployment will fail if you attempt to deploy to an Azure SQL Database and your project targets anything else. Let's make sure that we're targeting the correct SQL Server version. Switch back to the Verify solution in Visual Studio. Right-click the Verify.Database project, and select Properties. Once the project Properties screen appears, go to the Project Settings screen and ensure that the Target platform is set to Microsoft Azure SQL Database V12.

Now let's publish. Right-click the Verify.Database project once again, and select Publish. This will open the Publish Database dialog box (Figure 2-7). You'll need to click Edit for the Target Database Connections field to specify your connection string to the database. Your connection string can be found on the Azure Portal by going to the Manage SQL Database blade for your database and clicking Show Database Connection String. Note that you'll need to input the username and password that you specified when creating the Azure SQL Server.

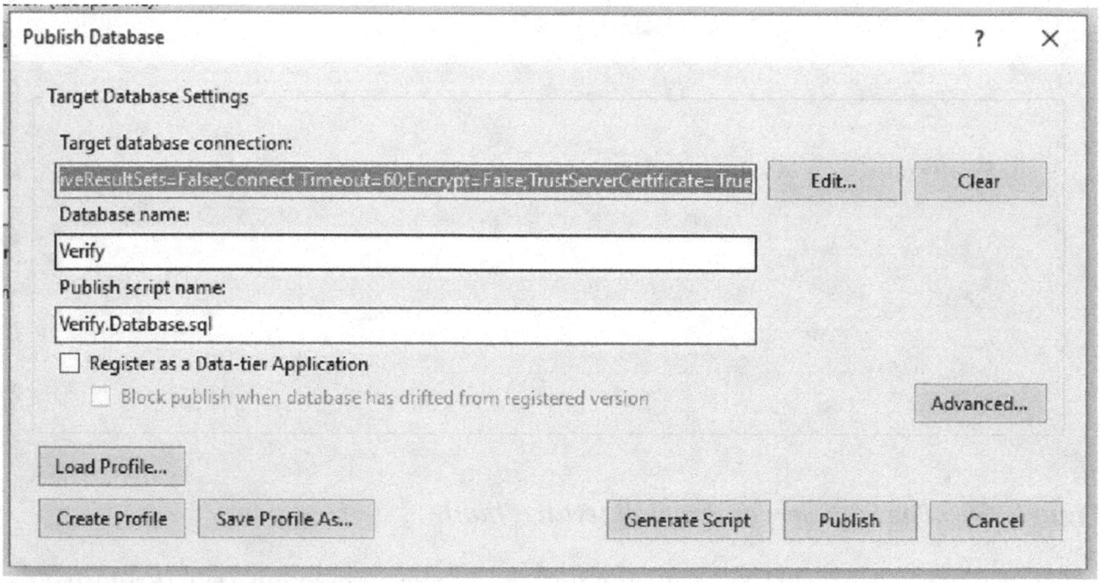

Figure 2-7. *The Publish Database dialog box*

Next, set the Database name field that you'd like to use. You can take the defaults for the Publish script name; it has no bearing on this process. Finally, you can click Save Profile to save all of these settings to disk. The next time you need to republish the database you can click Load Profile to reload your previously saved settings without having to enter them again.

Once the publishing is complete, you can use SQL Server Management Studio to connect to your database on Azure.

Creating Our App Services Web App

Now that our database is published to Azure, let's provision our Azure Web App that will host our application. We'll need to first create the Web App resource within the Azure Portal, publish our application to the Web App using Visual Studio, and then set a few configuration options for our Web App.

Log in to the Azure Portal at `https://portal.azure.com`, and click the plus sign button in the upper left corner to add a new resource. From the menu, select Web + Mobile ➤ Web App (Figure 2-8).

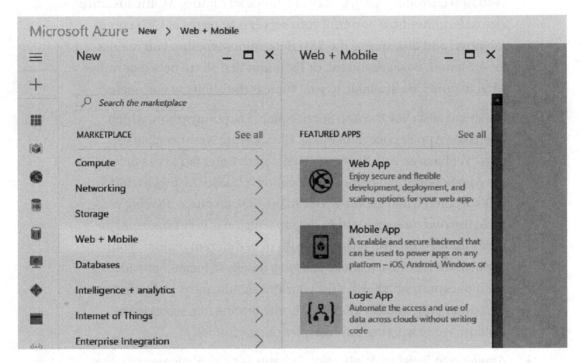

Figure 2-8. *Provisioning a new Web App*

Next, fill in the required fields to provision our new Web App resource.

- *App name*: This name must be unique across all Azure Web Apps. It will also determine the public URL for your web app, which will be `[App name].azurewebsites.net`. You can, of course, later add one or more custom domain names that will map to this Web App. In staying with my simple naming convention, I chose `verify-wa`. Because the names must be unique across all Azure Web Apps, you can't use that one. Sorry.

- *Subscription*: This is the subscription that you'd like to use for this Web App.

- *Resource Group*: Put this in the previously defined verify-rg Resource Group. We want to manage the Verify Azure SQL database and Web App together as they make up the same application.

- *App Service plan/Location*: All Web Apps belong to an App Service plan. Each App Service plan consists of a region (which is another term for an Azure datacenter), scale count (how many instances of a Web App currently exist), and the instance size and SKU. The instance size determines how powerful your server is in terms of CPU cores, memory, and disk space. The SKU determines whether you're on a Free, Shared, Basic, Standard, or Premium tier. These tiers determine what features are available to you, such as the ability to autoscale.

- Go ahead and click the App Service plan/Location option, which opens the App Service plan blade. Click Create New because you don't yet have an App Service plan defined. Enter `verify-asp` for the App Service plan name. For Location, choose the region that you specified when creating your Azure SQL resource. *Placing your Web App and database within the same region is very important for performance and cost.* If you place them in different regions, your application will have to make calls to a database located outside the datacenter, which will slow your site significantly, and will incur outbound data transfer charges. For the pricing tier, select Free because we're working through a learning exercise.

- *Application Insights*: Application Insights is an analytics service that integrates with Web Apps. It provides excellent tools for logging and analyzing requests, dependencies, exceptions, and traces. If you enable Application Insights, a free Basic Tier Application Insights resource will be provisioned. Of course, you still have to install the Application Insights library within your application to make use of the service. Because we're working through an example and minimizing complexity, turn Application Insights off. We discuss Application Insights in detail in a later chapter.

Now click Create to provision your Web App.

Publishing the Verify Application to Azure

Microsoft has done an excellent job of making the publishing process very simple. The easiest way to publish is directly from Visual Studio.

To publish, open the Verify solution in Visual Studio. Right-click the Verify.Web project, and select Publish. This opens the Publish dialog box that will step us through publishing to our Azure Web App.

Specify a Publish Profile

The first screen in the publish process is for choosing a profile (Figure 2-9). The profile specifies which Web App we're publishing to, the publishing method, and credentials for connecting to the server. The easiest ways to specify a publish profile are to choose either the Microsoft Azure App Service or Import options.

- *Microsoft Azure App Service*: Choosing this option allows Visual Studio to connect directly to your Azure account and list all available Web Apps. You can choose a Web App, and Visual Studio will download the appropriate information.

- *Import*: In the Azure Portal on the Overview screen of your Web App's management blade, you can download a publish profile (Figure 2-10). This is simply an XML text document. You can click Import on the Profile screen within the Publish dialog box, browse to the publish profile document that you downloaded, and import it.

After specifying a profile, click Next.

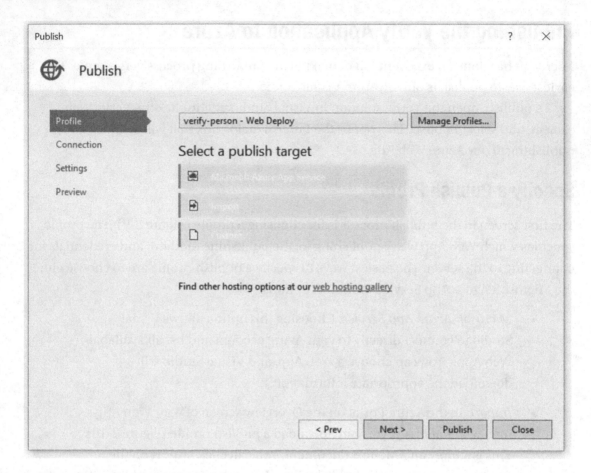

Figure 2-9. *The Publish dialog box Profile screen*

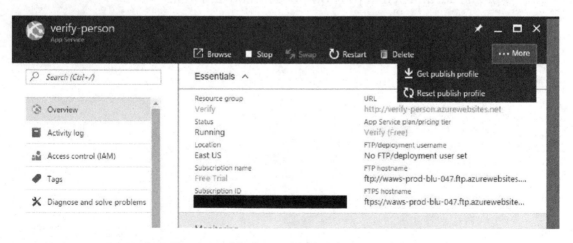

Figure 2-10. *Downloading a publish profile from the Web App management blade in the Azure Portal*

The Connection Screen

The Connection screen lets you choose a publishing method. This is simply how Visual Studio will get the bits from your computer to the Azure server. You have several options, but I recommend choosing Web Deploy because we're doing this from Visual Studio. Web Deploy performs a diff and only copies over files that have changed. It also works over a secure connection.

The other fields such as Server, Site name, User name, Password, and Destination URL will already be prefilled from your publish profile.

The Settings Screen

The Settings screen allows you to choose your Configuration, Target Platform, and override database connection strings specified in your `appsettings.json` file. We'll choose a Release Configuration and `.NETCoreApp, Version=1.0` for our Target Framework.

Expand the Databases node, and notice that the `DefaultConnection` property defined in our `appsettings.json` appears here. Replace the connection string listed here that points to your local SQL Server instance to our Azure SQL connection string. When Visual Studio performs the publish process, it will transform this connection string as it copies the `appsettings.json` file to the Azure Web App.

Click Next to continue.

Preview

The Preview screen shows the publish profile that will be used, and gives you a chance to preview what will be published. If you click Start Preview, Visual Studio will build your application, perform a diff with files on the server, and show you which files will be copied in the publishing process.

When you are ready, click Publish to publish your application to Azure. Visual Studio will churn for a bit, and you can view what is happening in the Output window. After the publish is complete, Visual Studio will launch your browser and navigate to the newly published Web App.

Scaling Web Apps

Now that we've published the Verify app to Azure, let's discuss the various ways to scale Web Apps to handle increasing amounts of traffic. There are three main ways to do so: intelligent use of threads, scaling up, and scaling out. Let's look at each.

Intelligent Use of Threads

Just like IIS, each Web App has a maximum number of threads available to service requests. When all of the threads servicing requests to a Web App are busy, new incoming requests are added to the HTTP request queue until a thread becomes available. If the HTTP request queue continues to grow faster than threads become available to service those requests, a couple of bad things can happen. First, response time grows because requests are waiting before a Web App thread becomes available and can process them. Second, if the wait time becomes too long, your users could experience HTTP request timeouts. Not only does this lead to frustrated users, it will also lead to angry bosses and will ruin your day in general.

Think of worker threads as clerks who work at the paint counter at the local hardware store. A clerk will service one customer at a time. If customers come to the paint counter faster than the clerks can help them, a line forms. Sometimes, customers just have quick questions such as "What aisle is the primer on?" Other times, customers need something more time consuming that could take five to ten minutes, such as mixing a gallon of paint.

Imagine if, when asked to mix a gallon of paint, the clerk set up the mixing machine, started the mixer, then stared at the mixer for the full ten minutes it takes to complete the job. While the clerk is staring at the mixer, customers are lining up at the counter. Customers would get pretty mad. Why couldn't the clerk start the mixer, return to the counter to help other customers, and then return his attention to the mixer after the mixing process is complete?

This, my friend, is exactly how threads servicing requests in your Web App will behave unless you make proper use of async and await. Think of those quick customer questions as simple requests such as materializing a view and returning it to the caller: It might only take the worker thread a millisecond or two to perform. Think of a long, drawn-out process like a database query as the equivalent of mixing paint. If you do not use async and await when accessing the database or performing other time-consuming processes that require waiting on an external service, your worker threads will wait until the long-running operation completes and will not service other requests in the meantime. This can very quickly lead to thread starvation and angry visitors.

Before publishing a site to production or even considering your scaling strategy, go through your code and ensure that you're making use of async and await in the following scenarios:

- Accessing external data stores (Azure SQL, Cosmos DB, and even Azure Table Storage).

- External web service calls.

- Reading and writing files on disk.

This can lead to huge improvements. It can be expensive or even impossible to scale out a Web App to handle synchronous code when your server is receiving lots of requests. In a recent consulting engagement, we identified this particular problem, properly implemented async and await, and the client was able to scale down from 13 medium Premium Web App instances to two medium Standard instances.

A thorough discussion of threading in general and async and await in particular is beyond the scope of this book. You can find an excellent treatment of this topic at `https://msdn.microsoft.com/en-us/library/mt674882.aspx`.

App Service Plans

When we created a new Web App for our Verify application, we touched briefly on what an App Service Plan is. Every Web App belongs to a single App Service Plan, and the App Service Plan determines what region the Web App runs in. It also determines the scale count, instance size, and SKU (also called the tier in various Microsoft literature).

The scale refers to how many copies of your app are running in your chosen Azure datacenter. If you set the App Service scale count to three, there will be three identical copies of your Web App servicing requests. The instance size and SKU for a Web App are also set by the App Service Plan. The instance size and SKU settings will apply to all copies of your Web App running under the App Service Plan. For example, it is impossible to run a small Standard instance and a medium Premium instance of a Web App within the same App Service Plan.

Scaling Up

If a single small Standard tier Web App is falling behind and cannot handle traffic, then fix the issue by moving to a medium Standard tier—problem solved! This is exactly what scaling up means: moving to a more powerful Web App instance size, service tier, or both.

Scaling up is done through your Web App's App Service Plan. Within the Azure Portal, you can either go directly to your App Service Plan management blade, or access it through your Web App's management blade by clicking Scale Up, or App Service Plan. If you go through the App Service Plan, you'll need to click on the App Service Plan's Scale Up link.

The Scale Up screen is straightforward (Figure 2-11). Simply choose the instance size from the list of available instances. Note that if you choose an instance that is within a different pricing tier (e.g., going from an instance in the Free to an instance in the Standard tier), the features available to you might change. Note that by default, Azure might only show you the recommended instance options. To see all available instances, make sure to click the View All link in the upper right corner of the blade.

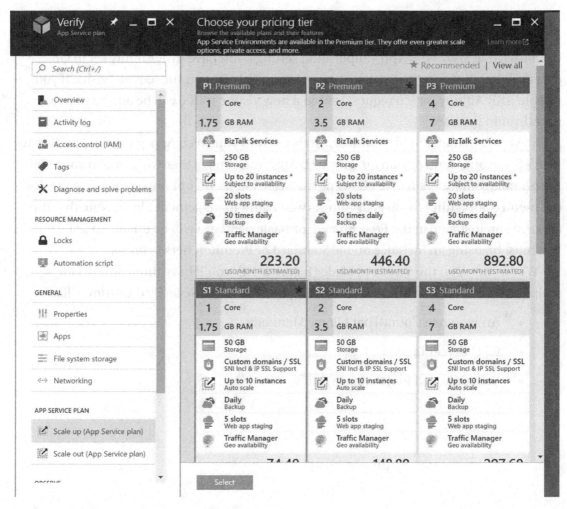

Figure 2-11. *Choosing a new instance size*

Changes will take place almost immediately. You do not need to redeploy your code.

Scaling Out

Dr. Grace Hopper once wrote "In pioneer days, they used oxen for heavy pulling, and when one ox couldn't budge a log, they didn't try to grow a bigger ox." That's why we typically scale out to handle increased load. You can scale out much further than you can scale up.

Once you add more than one instance of your Web App to your App Service Plan, Azure automatically provisions a network load balancer that will dole out traffic to your instances. If in your Web App's application settings, you have ARR Affinity set to On, users will be routed to the same instance of your Web App on subsequent visits. If you disable ARR Affinity, or if a request is from a new visitor, traffic will be allocated in a round-robin fashion.

To scale out and add (or remove) instances from your Web App, go to the App Service Plan's Scale out menu option for your Web App. You can get there by going to your Web App's management blade and choosing the Scale out menu option, or choosing the Scale out menu option directly on your App Service Plan's management blade. Note that if you are using an instance in the Free, Shared, or Basic tiers, you will be unable to scale out. You must be using an instance on the Standard or Premium tiers to do so.

When you open the Scale out blade (Figure 2-12), you'll have three options for scaling. You can choose one of the following options in the Scale By drop-down list:

- An Instance Count That I Enter Manually

- CPU Percentage

- Schedule and Performance Rules

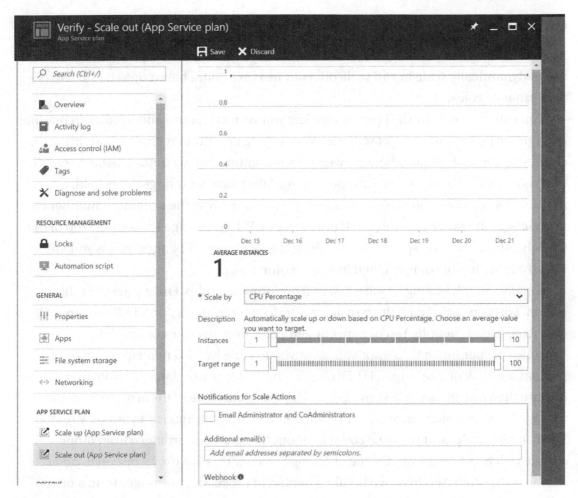

Figure 2-12. *Scale out management blade*

Selecting An Instance Count That I Enter Manually will set the instance count at the number that you specify. You will remain at that instance count until you explicitly change it. Because you pay for your Web App by the compute hour, this is usually not a very cost-effective strategy. Most web applications will experience surges and lulls in traffic. Paying for a fixed number of instances will waste dollars during traffic lulls. It is, however, a handy tool to use in a pinch if your autoscale rules are not behaving as expected and your Web App is failing due to heavy traffic.

Scaling by CPU percentage or schedule and performance rules let you scale computing resources up and down based on load. This is far more cost effective for most Web Apps, and is the topic of our next section.

Autoscale

Rather than explicitly setting your instance count, you can specify rules that Azure will use to dynamically scale in and scale out your instance count based on schedule or performance rules.

Choosing to scale by CPU percentage lets you set a minimum and maximum number of target instances and a target range for your aggregate CPU percentage. Your instance count will always be somewhere between the minimum and maximum instance count that you specify. If the average CPU percentage falls below your target threshold, Azure will scale down one instance, unless you are already at the minimum number of instances in the range that you set. If the average CPU percentage exceeds the top of the CPU threshold that you specify, Azure will add an additional instance unless you are already at the top of your specified instance count range.

Finally, there's scaling by schedule and performance rules. Once you select this option, you can click Add Rule to scale by a performance metric, or Add Profile to scale on a fixed time schedule. You can specify zero, one, or many rules or profiles.

Rules pertaining to Web Apps will allow you to scale by CPU percentage, memory percentage, disk queue length, HTTP queue length, data in, or data out. Note that if there is more than one instance in your App Service Plan, the value of these metrics will be averaged across instances. Scaling by averaged Web App metrics isn't your only option. You can also scale your instance count in or out based on performance from other services such as Service Bus Queue or Storage Queue. This is a useful option to detect that a worker Web App instance is falling behind in processing messages from a queue, and more instances are needed to drain the queue.

When a condition defined by a rule or profile is met, the scale action defined within will execute. Because you can combine multiple rules, it is possible for those rules to conflict. If two scale rules conflict, the order of precedence is as follows:

- Rules that add instances will be executed over rules that decrement the instance count.

- If more than one scale out rule is triggered, the rule that will add the largest number of instances will take precedence.

- If more than one scale in rule is triggered, the rule that will remove the least number of instances will be executed.

Limits on Scaling Out

There are fixed limits to how many instances you can add during scale out, and it's based on the service tier of your instance size. Standard instances are limited to a maximum of ten, and any instance in the Premium tier can scale up to a maximum of 20.

If you need to scale further, contact Microsoft Azure Customer Support. They are able to raise your maximum instance count to 50 for the Premium service tier.

One final caveat: Scaling out and adding additional instances is subject to instance availability within your datacenter. I have seen messages denying a request to add an additional instance due to no further instances being available at the datacenter. Generally, this is a transient condition, but it can occur. If you receive this message, try again in a few minutes.

How to Define Autoscale Rules

The obvious question from developers who are new to autoscaling is "How do I know what rules to define?" That's a great question.

Given a web application and an App Service Plan, it is nearly impossible to calculate exactly how many requests the app can handle before it nears its breaking point and requires scaling out. There are simply too many variables to account for. For different architectures and design decisions, applications will experience problems in different places as load increases. Knowing where your app will break first (CPU exhaustion, memory exhaustion, disk queue length growing, etc.) will be a clue as to what metrics you should use when defining your autoscale rules.

So how do we determine where our app will fail first as load increases? We try to break it, of course, and we can use Microsoft's load testing tools to do so.

Load Testing

Microsoft has created load testing tools that allow us to stress our applications in various ways before we unveil them to the general public. These tools allow us to specify the number of users in a pool, the URL(s) each user will hit, and the duration of the test. Azure will then spin up a botnet and dish out as much punishment to your application as you desire (and are willing to pay for). You can then examine load test metrics.

It's a good idea to understand what in your application will buckle first as traffic increases, and how much traffic it takes to break things. You can then evaluate if it's reasonable to modify your application further to handle such traffic. The answer is not always yes.

Creating a Load Test

We'll perform our load tests using Visual Studio Team Services load testing tools. You'll need a Visual Studio Team Services account before you can load test. Like most of Microsoft's developer tools, though, there's a limited free subscription that you can sign up for to get started. If you don't already have a Visual Studio Team Services account, go to `https://www.visualstudio.com/team-services/` and create one.

Note   It is possible to access Visual Studio Team Services load testing tools from directly within the Azure Portal. This option is Performance test and is found on the Web Apps blade under the Development Tools heading. However, as of the time of this writing, the integration is a bit buggy. That's why we're going directly with Visual Studio Team Services to perform our tests.

If this is the first time you've used Visual Studio Team Services, you'll be prompted to create a project. You can choose any name for your project that isn't already taken, and specify if you'll use Git or Team Foundation Version Control. Using the Visual Studio Team Services repo is not required to make use of the load testing tools.

Once you've logged into your Visual Studio Team Services account, navigate to your Account home, then select Load Test from the top menu.

You'll see that you have multiple options for creating load tests. These include the following:

- Recording a series of actions through a browser and uploading the resulting HTTP archive file to use by the testing agents.

- Hitting specified URLs to stress an application.

- Creating a Visual Studio Web Performance and Load Test project. This provides greater flexibility, takes more time to author, and requires Visual Studio Enterprise Edition.

For our purposes, we'll hit specified URLs to stress our Web App.
To create our first load test, do the following:

1. Click New on the Load Test screen. Select URL Based Test from the drop-down list.

2. Give your load test a name. I prefer uniform descriptive names so that I can identify tests when looking at a table of test results. I named my first test `FreeWABasicDB`.

3. When performing a URL-based test, you can either upload an HTTP archive file containing prerecorded actions that will be performed by the testing agents or enter one or more URLs. We'll use a single specified URL that will query an SSN from our database. For our test URL, specify `GET` for the HTTP method, `https://your-webapp-name.azurewebsites.net/search` for the URL itself, and add `ssn` for the query string parameter name, and a valid SSN attached to a `Person` record that you have already loaded into your Azure SQL database instance (Figure 2-13).

4. Now that we've specified our URL, click the Settings link to configure user load, browser mix, and the datacenter that we'll launch the test from.

   - *Run duration*: This is how long we'll run this test. I chose two minutes. Tests are billed by virtual minutes (VUMs) and are calculated as v-users × run duration. Our first test will be to blast the server with traffic and see where it fails. Future tests will be longer in duration as we set our Web App to autoscale in various ways.

   - *Load pattern*: This can be constant or step. Constant hammers your application with all of the specified v-users from the beginning of the test. Step will allow you to set an initial number of v-users, a step duration, and how many v-users to add each step. When you're not quite sure at what point your application will fail, stepping is a useful strategy. If you blast your app with a constant load pattern of 260 v-users and it fails immediately, all you know is that the app cannot handle 260 concurrent v-users × requests per v-user per second. If you step up v-users over time, you can see at what point the app failed. For this test, let's use a Step Load pattern with a max of 260 users, a start user count of 120, a step duration of 10 seconds, and a step user count of 10 users.

- Warmup duration will hit your Web App once, then wait for the duration. We will specify 15 seconds because our Web App is using the Free tier and might have been unloaded if it hasn't received any requests.

- Finally, we must choose a location to launch the test from. I prefer using the same datacenter that is hosting our Web App to reduce latency.

5. Click Save to save this test.

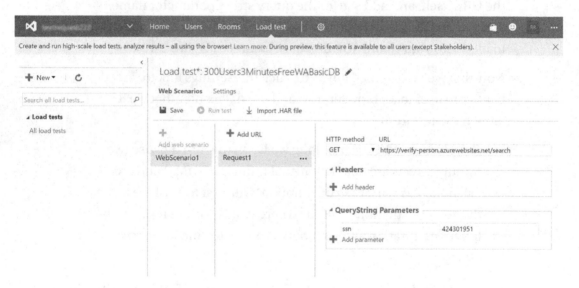

Figure 2-13. *Configuring a load test*

Now we're ready to run.

Running the Load Test

After saving a load test, it will appear in the left column under the Load Tests heading. To run a test, select it and click Run. This will queue your test as Visual Studio Team Services gathers and prepares its botnet. Once the test begins, you'll be able to view metrics in real time.

Viewing Load Test Results

On our load testing results screen, we can see the highlights (Figure 2-14).

Figure 2-14. *Results for the first load test*

We are particularly interested in the Avg. Response Time and Failed Requests results. If Avg. Response Time is reasonable and there were no failed requests, the server handled the given load quite nicely. Remember that our Verify Web App is residing on a Free tier instance, which is as small as we can go. We are also querying an Azure SQL database that is on the Basic tier, which at 5 DTUs is the smallest offered. Even with such paltry specifications, our Web App handled about 1,100 requests per second from 260 concurrent users without missing a beat. That's rather impressive. Because we weren't able to break the Web App, though, we're going to have to turn up the volume and try again.

For the next test, we'll run for a full four minutes, start with 250 users, and step up 25 users every 15 seconds. As you can see in Figure 2-15, we were able to tip over our Web App: 17,155 out of 133,044 requests failed, and the average response time was 558.3 ms.

AVG. RESPONSE TIME	USER LOAD	REQUESTS PER SEC	FAILED REQUESTS	ERRORS →	USAGE
558.3 ms	500 users	554.3 RPS	13 %	11 errors	2K VUMs
			17155 failed requests 133044 total requests	4 thresholds violated	

Learn more about metrics and criteria

Test settings

Load duration:	4 min	Requested by:	Rob Reagan	Run source:	Team Services portal
Start time:	12/20/2016 2:51:29 PM	Test:	300Users3MinutesFreeWABasicDB	Warmup duration:	15 sec
End time:	12/20/2016 2:55:32 PM	Location:	East US	Agent cores:	1

Figure 2-15. *Results for our second load test that caused errors*

The summary statistics don't tell the whole story. The average response time averages using response times from the beginning of our test where the Web App handled the given load all the way to the end of the test where our Web App was failing. Click the Charts link to see graphs for Performance and Errors (Figure 2-16). You can see from the Errors graph that errors began to occur at 1:30 into the test. Cross-referencing this with the Throughput graph, we see that errors occurred at about 1,052 requests per second. Also, note that at the 4:00 mark, our Performance chart shows that average page response time was up to 3.196 seconds.

You might wonder why this test failed at fewer requests per second than our initial test. Notice on the Charts tab that during our second run that failed, requests per second built to about 1,200 per second, then fell to about 1,052 per second around the time that errors begin to occur. This hints at some type of resource exhaustion that our initial stepped load test didn't trigger because it was shorter and didn't involve the same sustained amount of traffic over time.

From the test summary screen, we can see that requests have failed. The summary screen doesn't show us exactly what failed, though. Click the Diagnostics link to see errors that occurred in the test (Figure 2-16). We can't always tell exactly what has broken in our Web App from seeing the specific HTTP error codes, but it gives us a good place to start our investigation. We won't know for sure until we dig into various logs. The next step is to look at our logs and instrumentation within the Azure Portal to pinpoint what broke and why.

↓ Export test to Visual Studio

Summary   Charts   **Diagnostics**   Logs

Test Errors

Type	Subtype	Occurren...	Last Time	Last Text
HttpError	403 - Forbidden	630	00:01:52	403 - Forbidden
HttpError	502 - BadGateway	406	00:01:38	502 - BadGateway
HttpError	502 - BadGateway	398	00:01:38	502 - BadGateway
HttpError	502 - BadGateway	196	00:01:38	502 - BadGateway
HttpError	403 - Forbidden	187	00:01:52	403 - Forbidden
HttpError	403 - Forbidden	183	00:01:52	403 - Forbidden
ThresholdMessage	Critical	11	00:03:30	["Agent0","Processor","% Processor Time","_T
ThresholdMessage	Critical	11	00:03:30	["Agent0","Processor","% Processor Time","0'

Figure 2-16. *The Diagnostics tab from our second test run*

Note   The Visual Studio Team Services trial account includes 20,000 VUMs per month. Even if you are only using a single Web App instance from the Standard tier, you might have trouble causing errors due to load with only 20,000 VUMs available. Of course, this ultimately depends on how your application is designed. Be prepared to purchase a Visual Studio Team Services subscription, though, to be able to simulate enough load to cause a Standard tier instance to fail.

Setting Appropriate Autoscale Rules

After you've load tested your application, you can dig into performance metrics within the Azure portal to see what went wrong. Once you've found the underlying problem, you can set your scale rules accordingly. Here's a checklist to run through after you've tipped over your app by using either load testing tools or making the Reddit front page.

1. *Did the database fail to answer queries in a timely manner?* When using an Azure SQL database, the first possibility to eliminate is if database resources were exhausted, leading to application errors. To check, pull up the Azure SQL management blade, and click Edit on the chart. Set the time range to when your application experienced errors, and chart the DTU limit and DTU used. This will quickly tell you if you simply ran out of horsepower and your queries were throttled. If DTU used bumped up against the DTU limit, you need to scale your Azure SQL instance. Strategies for doing so are discussed in Chapter 4.

   To be thorough, remove the DTU limit and DTU used from the chart and add Total database size. Ensure that you haven't exceeded your database's allocated storage.

   If you've discovered a problem with either of these metrics, scaling your Web App will not help you, but you do need to scale your database. If both of these look good, let's move to your App Service's management blade.

2. *Check App Service metrics.* You'll notice that the Overview screen on the App Service management blade has a large chart. If you edit the chart, you'll see that you can graph CPU Percentage, Data In, Data Out, Disk Queue Length, HTTP Queue Length, and Memory Percentage. It just so happens that you can set autoscale rules to key from all of these metrics. Set the time period for the chart to the time period when you've experienced performance issues. Check each metric. If you find a metric indicating that a resource is stressed, you can create an autoscale rule that keys off of that metric.

Even after identifying what metric to use when setting autoscale rules, it can be useful to perform root cause analysis and see exactly what broke under load in your code, and if it is cost effective to improve that portion of your source.

Summary

In this chapter, we've created an example web application that included a SQL Server database. We've provisioned an Azure SQL database, Web App, and accompanying App Service Plan. After deploying our web application and database to Azure, we discussed scaling strategies, covered basic load testing, and saw how to set appropriate autoscale rules.

In the next chapter, we look at various Azure data storage technologies and discuss the difference between traditional relational databases and NoSQL and what Azure has to offer for each.

CHAPTER 3

Azure Data Storage Overview

Most web applications need to persist user data. Examples of data that your web application might need to persist include usernames and passwords, order history, shopping cart contents, or player high scores.

In this chapter, we discuss data storage scenarios that you might encounter when building web applications. Next, we introduce the pertinent Azure data storage services available and offer a broad overview of each. We also discuss the pros and cons of each data service, and rules of thumb for choosing between them when designing your web application.

This chapter is intended as an introduction to Azure's data storage technologies. Think of this chapter as the movie trailer for each Azure data service. This can help you orient yourself and decide which data services might be a good fit for your application. Each data service mentioned is covered in depth in upcoming chapters. If you are already familiar with Redis Cache, Azure SQL, Cosmos DB, and Azure Table Storage, you can safely skip this chapter.

Data Storage Scenarios

There are three different data storage scenarios that you might encounter when building a web application.

© Rob Reagan 2018
R. Reagan, *Web Applications on Azure*, https://doi.org/10.1007/978-1-4842-2976-7_3

Session Data

Session data involves keeping track of information that only needs to be persisted while a user is interacting with your web application. In e-commerce, items in a shopping cart or recently viewed items are good examples. After the user makes a purchase or abandons the cart, you no longer need to keep track of the data.

Back in the old days of smaller web applications built with ASP.NET web forms, many developers would simply store session data with the `System.Web.SessionState` class. The `SessionState` class was very simple to use and offered developers the option of storing data in-process, within SQL Server, or a separate session state process.

All three choices were terrible ideas for building scalable applications, and it's not hard to see why. Data stored in-process has two shortcomings: Session state can be lost in a multi-instance front-end application if a user whose session is started on Server A is then routed to Server B during his or her next request. Even in a single-server scenario, session data stored in-process is lost if the web application is recycled or crashes. Storing session data in an external store such as SQL Server or an external session state process was an improvement because multiple web front-end servers could access session state, allowing web applications to scale out by adding additional instances.

In Azure, Redis Cache is the preferred data service for storing session data.

Persisted Data

Some data needs to be stored indefinitely. In e-commerce, examples include items on a wish list, a user's purchase history, and payment information. Historically, this type of data is stored in a relational database such as SQL Server. However, relational databases run into scalability problems when building web applications at Internet scale.

The biggest problem with relational databases is that to be performant, databases usually run on a single server. It's difficult to scale a single relational database across multiple servers, and scale out is a requirement for building Internet-scale web applications. The second problem is that sometimes the relational model isn't the easiest to work with or the most efficient for certain scenarios.

Various NoSQL options have emerged such as Cosmos DB and Azure Tables to address these shortcomings.

Data Analytics

More and more companies are making use of machine learning to gain insight from massive amounts of customer or operational data that they have collected over time. Machine learning algorithms can sift through terabytes or even petabytes of data to identify relationships. Those insights are then packaged into models that make predictions or classifications. An example of a prediction might be how likely a customer is to cancel a service based on his or her interaction history. Amazon and Netflix customers are very familiar with machine learning classification models, although they might be unaware that machine learning is responsible. Amazon suggests products that you might be interested in, and Netflix suggests movies that you might like based on your past viewing history.

As mentioned, the data sets that machine learning algorithms operate on are often massive; multiterabyte data sets are not uncommon. The data is almost always heterogeneous and does not conform to a single schema. Therefore, using a relational database to store data used in machine learning is not a good idea.

Azure Data Lake is the Microsoft answer to storing massive amounts of data for consumption by analytics packages such as HDInsight. Analytics and machine learning are broad subjects and are well beyond the scope of this book. Data analytics and Azure Data Lake are only mentioned for completeness.

Relational Databases

Most developers are familiar with relational databases. Examples include SQL Server, MySQL, and Oracle. Relational databases store data in tables. Tables are made up of one or more columns, and each column has a specified data type. Each record within a table is a row.

A schema describes the columns in each table and is a set of rules specifying the name and data type for each column. Because each row within a table must specify a value for each column within the table, we say that a relational database has a fixed schema. For example, if you have a table called Employees that contains columns for each employee's Name, City, State, Birthdate, and Social Security Number, and you later want to add a Phone Number column, you must modify the table's schema and add a column for the Phone Number. Schemas are handy for two reasons.

Schemas provide error checking for a table. Once a schema is defined, data that is inserted or updated must conform to the schema. For example, if I try to insert a string value of "They're sure going to notice that, Peter!" into the employee's Birthdate field that is defined as a Date data type, the database engine will not allow the insert and will return an error.

We know exactly what type of data exists for each table and can code accordingly. We don't have to worry if the record that we're retrieving from the Employees database table actually contains department information; we know exactly what fields we'll get when we query the Employees table. This is not a true statement for NoSQL databases, which we discuss in an upcoming section.

To interact with a relational database, we use structured query language (SQL). With SQL, we can read, insert, update, or delete data within the database. We can also use SQL to define stored procedures or functions, which are packaged sets of SQL statements that we can call to interact with the database.

We've already mentioned that data in a relational database is stored in tables. How do we quickly locate a record within a table if there are many records? The simplest way to locate a record would be to search a table from the first row until we find the row that we're looking for, or until we hit the end of the table. This type of search is called a full table scan, and it's very inefficient. For a table with 1 million rows, you'd have to search all 1 million rows if the record that you're looking for is the last in the table.

Instead, we can define one or more indexes for a table. An index is a set of lookup data that "indexes into" a table. These indexes are typically stored internally within the database as B-trees, which allow log(n) search time where n is the number of records in a table. This allows us to find records that we're looking for very fast. The trick is to make sure that all queries to a database have covering indexes, which means that each query can make use of one or more indexes to quickly locate the records you're looking for.

Each table within a database should have a special index called a primary key. A primary key can be a single column or a combination of columns that uniquely identify a record within a table. Querying by a table's primary key will yield the best performance. Tables can also define columns as foreign keys. A foreign key points to another table's primary key. Primary keys and foreign keys are how we define relationships between tables in a database.

When designing a database, our goal is to translate the details that we care about from the real world that our application is concerned with into a set of tables. When creating tables, we have to decide how many tables we need, and how the data within the tables is related.

One of our goals is to be sure that data is not repeated within the database. Consider a database that contains all employees in a company and the project that each employee is currently assigned to. A simple database design would be to create an Employees table, and store the project name for each employee's currently assigned project within the Employees table. What if a project name changes? You can imagine what a pain it would be to have to update a project name stored within the database in several hundred different employee records. If you missed updating a single employee record, the database is now inconsistent: Some records use the new project name, and other records that were missed in the update still contain the old project name.

A better design would be to create a Projects table that holds all of the company's projects. Each employee record could define a foreign key that points to the appropriate Projects record's primary key. Now project names are not repeated in the database.

Making sure that we don't duplicate data within the database, and that tables relate to each other in appropriate ways, is called normalization. There are a progressively stricter set of rules called normal forms that database designers design toward. The details of database normalization could take several chapters and are beyond the scope of this book, but if you are interested in relational database design, I encourage you to investigate them in detail. The important takeaway is that normalization and correct design of relational databases is very different from the design of NoSQL databases, which we discuss shortly. In fact, attempting to design a NoSQL database as you would a relational database will generally lead to terrible performance and will fail to take advantage of the power of NoSQL technologies.

Azure SQL

Azure SQL is Microsoft's cloud-based relational database service. It very closely resembles the server-based SQL Server product. You can use almost all of the same SQL syntax between the server-based SQL Server products and Azure SQL. In fact, when developing web applications with a relational database data store, it's easiest to install a SQL Server 2016 Express or Developer Edition to your local machine and develop against a local instance. When you publish the application to Azure and use Azure SQL, the same queries for data manipulation and retrieval just work.

There are several important differences between the traditional server-based SQL Server and Azure SQL. They are covered in the sections that follow.

Billing

With a server-based SQL Server instance, you must purchase a SQL Server license for the edition of your choice. With Azure SQL, you provision a database instance on a service tier and pay by the number of hours that your database is provisioned.

Performance

A server-based SQL Server instance is limited by the machine resources available, and any restrictions you've placed on how much of the system resources SQL Server is allowed to utilize. Azure SQL is hosted in a virtualized environment in the cloud, and performance is limited by DTUs, a combination of CPU, memory, data I/O, and transaction log I/O. We're not given the exact formula for calculating DTUs, but you can think of more DTUs translating into more performance power. The number of DTUs available to your database is determined by the pricing tier that you select when provisioning an Azure SQL instance. DTUs range from 5 for a Basic instance to 4,000 for the largest Premium tier instance.

Throttling and Retry

Each Azure SQL database instance has service limits. For example, a Basic instance can only have 5 DTUs and a maximum of 30 concurrent workers. If these limits are exceeded, one or more of your queries will fail until the database engine has returned to within the service limits. This is called throttling.

The bad news is that your application must be able to handle failure in case a query is throttled. If you're using standard ADO.NET with no custom retry code, you're going to have a difficult time when your queries are throttled and your users see an error page.

The good news is that Microsoft Entity Framework 6.x and Entity Framework Core have automatic retry logic built in. It is highly recommended that you use Entity Framework to interact with Azure SQL for just this reason.

Scaling Azure SQL

There are two options for scaling Azure SQL: scaling up and sharding.

Scaling Up

Scaling up is simple: You log in to the Azure Portal and change your Azure SQL's pricing tier to a larger, more powerful instance. When you do so, there is no need to redeploy or explicitly move your database; Azure does this for you. This is by far the easiest solution to scaling. However, if your app continues to grow, you can eventually end up at the largest Premium instance with nowhere else to go. Your next option is sharding.

Sharding

Sharding involves horizontally partitioning your data so that data is split across multiple Azure SQL instances. This is typically for multitenant applications, in which one or more of your clients' accounts live in each database instance. Each Azure SQL instance will have a complete set of tables. For example, assume that your database consisted of two tables: Employees and Timesheets. Now assume that your application had four clients: clients A, B, C, and D. A traditional approach would have a single database with tables Employees and Timesheets, and all data for clients A, B, C, and D would reside in the same database. A sharded approach works a little differently. In a sharded solution, you split your clients' data across two or more databases. A sharded solution for this application might have two separate Azure SQL databases. Each database would have tables Employees and Timesheets. However, Database 1 will contain only data from clients A and B, and Database 2 will contain all data from clients C and D.

Sharding is not a new idea, and it historically causes some difficult problems, including these:

- Maintaining schema changes across all shards.

- Querying across all shards for reporting purposes.

- Mapping each request from a client to the appropriate shard.

Azure SQL has several features that take the sting out of the aforementioned problems. These tools are contained in the Elastic Database Client Library, and will assist you in mapping client requests to the appropriate shard, splitting shards, combining shards, and querying across all shards.

When to Use Azure SQL

Relational databases are familiar to most developers, and the relational model has been used with great success for more than 40 years. Its main downside is that it can only scale so far before we have to resort to tricks such as sharding. Sharding solves lots of problems for multitenant applications, but is still more difficult to maintain and can get very expensive compared to other NoSQL options.

I recommend using Azure SQL as your data store under the following scenarios.

You are migrating an application that already uses a relational database to Azure.

Your data is highly relational and your application allows your data to be sharded. Like all good craftsmen, we should choose the best tool for the job. If your data will not accommodate a NoSQL solution such as Cosmos DB or Azure Tables and can be sharded, you should use Azure SQL. When deciding if your application's data will fit into a NoSQL solution, please make sure that you consider reporting requirements.

You can use Azure SQL as part of a hybrid data store of two or more Azure data services. There's nothing wrong with storing parts of your data in different Azure data stores based on your application's needs. For example, if you're building a social media site for pets (and I'm convinced that this thought briefly crosses every developer's mind at least once), you might store user and profile information in Azure SQL, and news feed data in Cosmos DB.

Other Azure Relational Database Offerings

Azure also offers MySQL and PostgreSQL as fully managed services. These are mentioned for completeness and are not covered in this book.

NoSQL Data Stores

NoSQL simply means that a data storage technology is not a relational database. Asking if a data storage technology is NoSQL might be a useful bit of information if you're playing a geeky version of 20 Questions, but it doesn't convey much useful information.

NoSQL databases were invented to allow for horizontal scaling across multiple machines. As we've already mentioned, scaling a relational database across multiple machines is difficult. Other benefits of NoSQL databases include simplicity for certain problem domains, speed, and the replication of data across machines so that a single machine failure doesn't bring down the entire database.

Azure offers three NoSQL solutions that are of interest to web app developers: Redis Cache, Azure Tables, and Cosmos DB. Let's look at each, starting with Redis Cache.

Redis Cache

Azure Redis Cache is a caching service based on the open source Redis Cache. It is a NoSQL service that allows you to query, insert, update, and delete data based on key/value pairs. The key is always a string, and the value can be another string, a hash, a list, a set, or a sorted set. In practice, you can store any type of .NET object that can be serialized to a JSON string; you'll just be responsible for deserializing the JSON string and casting it to the appropriate type on retrieval from the cache. Think of Azure Redis Cache as a service that provides a giant dictionary in the cloud.

Azure Redis Cache is an in-memory caching service that runs on VMs outside of your Web Apps. This offers two benefits for building scalable web applications.

Because Azure Redis Cache is implemented as a service outside of your web application, you can scale out your Web Apps to multiple instances and have all instances reading from a common cache. Therefore, if the network load balancer routes users to different instances of your Web App, all data stored in the cache will be consistent.

Because Azure Redis Cache holds your data in memory, access is very, very fast, provided that your cache is provisioned in the same datacenter as your other Azure services.

When you provision an Azure Redis Cache instance, you can choose from multiple instance sizes in a Basic, Standard, or Premium tier. The Basic tier has no service-level agreement (SLA) and no replication failover. Therefore, if you try to use an instance from the Basic tier in production, be aware that if the VM hosting your cache is recycled, you will lose all data within the cache. Basic instances are cheap and perfect for development or playing around to become more familiar with the service.

The Standard and Premium tiers are recommended for production jobs. The Standard tier is replicated, has automatic failover for recovery in case the primary node fails, and offers an SLA of 99.9% availability. The Premium tier offers the same benefits as the Standard tier, along with the ability to scale out via Redis Cluster, taking and restoring snapshots of the cache for disaster recovery, and higher throughput.

Now that you know that Azure Redis Cache is an ultrafast key/value data store, the next question on your mind is probably "OK, so how do I interact with it?" That's a very good question. Because Redis is a mature open source project, there are already lots of libraries out there for interacting with and managing your Redis Cache. Microsoft recommends using StackExchange.Redis, an open source library built by, maintained by, and used by the good folks at StackExchange. Yep, that's the same company who brought us StackOverflow.com, where we all go to get answers. The StackExchange.Redis library is available via NuGet, or you can download and compile it directly from GitHub.

Now for the sort-of bad news: There's no local emulator for Azure Redis Cache. This leaves you with two options when developing solutions on your local computer.

You can install your own copy of Redis locally. For Windows users, the best bet will be to download and install the MSOpenTech Redis port. You can download the installer from `https://github.com/MSOpenTech/redis/releases`. You can still use the StackExchange.Redis library with this local installation. I personally hate this option because as developers, we are perpetually sweating aggressive deadlines, and the last thing we need is to have to set up and babysit additional infrastructure. That's why I prefer the second option.

You can provision a C0 Basic Azure Redis Cache instance, and use it for local development. This means that even though you're developing your web application and debugging on localhost, all Redis cache calls will go out over the Internet, hit the Azure Redis Cache service at the datacenter where you provisioned your cache instance, and return. It's not exactly a recipe for high performance, but it works just fine. The benefit is that you don't have to install and configure yet another local service. The bad news is that you will incur a charge of $0.055 per hour as of the time of this writing. Don't forget to shut down your Azure Redis Cache instance before you go home for the day.

Finally, here is the $64,000 question: What is Azure Redis Cache best used for in building scalable web applications? There are two scenarios in which it excels.

- *Maintaining session state in a multiweb front-end scenario*: If you need to maintain session state, Azure Redis Cache is the place to do it. All Web App instances can access the cache and see the same data.

- *Building a cache atop another persistent data store*: Imagine that you have data within your app that is accessed very frequently and is relatively expensive to read from a persistent data store. An example of such data might be user security settings such as an access control list. Rather than rereading this information every time a user accesses your web application, you can cache it in an Azure Redis Cache instance for very fast retrieval. This comes with considerations. You will need to consider how long information should live in the cache, if you're implementing a lazy loading strategy to populate the cache, and make sure that if the cached data is updated within the application, you either update or remove the stale data within the cache.

Azure Table Storage

Azure Tables are a very simple, highly scalable, and extremely cheap NoSQL service. Azure Tables store entity records, which are sometimes referred to as rows. An entity record is simply a subclass of the `Microsoft.WindowsAzure.Storage.Table.TableEntity` class that you create. Your subclass can have any properties that you wish. You can even mix different subclasses in the same Azure Table.

Azure Tables store data in tables. However, these tables are not relational, and there's no support for joining tables. I've always thought this service was poorly named; you should think of Azure Table storage as a dictionary and not a relational table. Conceptually, it is a key/value store. You provide Azure with a key, and it hands you back the associated entity record identified by the key.

Although Azure Tables is a key/value store, there's a little more complexity to delve into. Each Azure Table is made up of one or more partitions. Each partition contains one or more rows. Each record within an Azure Table is uniquely identified by the combination of a partition key and a row key. The partition key and row key together make up the "key" that was mentioned earlier.

Why did Microsoft introduce the concept of a partition into Azure Tables? Doesn't it just overcomplicate things? Those were my thoughts when I first read about this service, but partitions are part of the magic that allows Azure Tables to scale to up to 500 terabytes of data.

Each partition within your table lives on a partition server. Under the covers, Azure might move partitions around from server to server for load balancing purposes. Splitting your table data across multiple servers by partition is what allows Azure Table Storage to scale. Imagine if you had a table called ZipCodes. You defined your partitions by state so that all zip codes within a given state live in the same partition. Your row key is the five-digit zip code. This leaves you with 50 partitions that collectively contain roughly 43,000 zip code records.

If I query my ZipCodes table and pass in a partition key of Tennessee and a zip code of 37405, Azure will first figure out which partition server contains the data for the Tennessee partition. It will then jump to the unique zip code record of 37405 and return it to the caller. This type of query in which both a partition key and row key are provided is called a point query. It's blindingly fast and will return a single record. There are other types of queries such as a row range scan within a partition, a partition range scan that scans across multiple partitions, and a full table scan across all partitions and all rows.

There is support for transactions, but only within the same partition. If we're updating information on zip codes in our previous example, we can only frame a transaction for zip code records within the same state because they are all part of the same partition.

Working with Azure Table Storage is pretty easy. To interact with Table Storage, use the Azure Storage Client Library. This can be downloaded separately, but it's included with the Azure SDK. There is also an emulator that you can use during development on your local machine. Finally, there's an indispensable tool called Azure Storage Explorer that you can use to view the contents of Queues, Tables, or Blobs in Azure Storage. The Azure Storage Explorer works on both your local emulator and on Azure.

Azure Table Storage is billed by the number of gigabytes stored per month. When allocating Table Storage, you can choose between service tiers of Locally Redundant Storage (LRS), Globally Redundant Storage (GRS), and Read-Access Globally Redundant Storage (RA-GRS). LRS is the least expensive per GB per month, and RA-GRS is the most expensive per GB per month. There is also a small charge per 100,000 read and write operations. At the time of this writing, it's a paltry $0.0036.

When to Use Azure Table Storage

Azure Table Storage is by far the cheapest data storage solution available. It's also blazingly fast and nearly infinitely scalable. Its main downside is that its only index is the partition and row keys. There is no way to construct a secondary index without writing the code to do so yourself.

Use Azure Table Storage if you only need one index for retrieval (because that's all that's available) and you plan on having many gigabytes of data and a great deal of reads and writes. If you do not think that your data will grow over several gigabytes or are not sure if you will need to query on something other than one key, consider Azure SQL or Cosmos DB.

As mentioned previously, don't be afraid to mix storage services and use Azure Table Storage to store part of your application's data if Table Storage makes the most sense.

Note   Troy Hunt, the creator of haveIBeenPwned.com, wrote an entertaining and informative blog post on how he created a site using Azure Table Storage that manages more than 150 million records. You can read it at `https://www.troyhunt.com/working-with-154-million-records-on/`

Cosmos DB

Cosmos DB is a NoSQL Azure service that stores documents. Here, document doesn't refer to Excel or Word docs; it refers to a JavaScript Object Notation (JSON) document, which is nothing more than a valid JSON object. Because this can be a mind-bending concept for developers who have only worked with the relational model, here's an example of a JSON document for a musical album that could be stored in Cosmos DB:

```
{
        "album": "Abbey Road",
            "artist": "The Beatles",
            "release_date": "26 September 1969",
            "tracks": {
                    { "title": "Come Together", "written_by": "John Lennon" },
                    { "title": "Something", "written_by": "George Harrison" },
                        { "title": "Maxwell's Silver Hammer", "written_by:
                        "Paul McCartney" }
        }
}
```

Relational database designers might freak out when seeing this. After all, if we were going to represent this data in the relational database paradigm, we'd have separate tables for Artists, Albums, Tracks, and Composers. These four tables would be associated by primary/foreign key relationships.

The lack of normalization and having documents containing all information necessary to satisfy a query is part of the beauty of NoSQL in general and Cosmos DB in particular. Imagine if we are building a web application that serves up album information. To retrieve an album's information from a normalized relational database would require several joins to return its full information. In Cosmos DB, returning an album's information requires a single read.

This raises several further questions for folks coming from a relational database background. How exactly do we query for this album information? How fast is retrieval time? How are indexes created? What happens if denormalized data that is repeated throughout the database needs to change?

Querying for information is actually easy. You can query Cosmos DB using a modified SQL syntax. The syntax is surprisingly similar to the SQL used in relational databases. Developers coming from a relational background who are fluent in SQL will be able to get up to speed fairly quickly.

Retrieval times are on average very, very fast. Cosmos DB's goal is extremely low latency reads and writes. Cosmos DB ensures that the read time for at least 99% of read operations is less than 10 ms. The target latency for writes is 15 ms for at least 99% of write operations.

In relational databases, indexes are required for fast reads and writes, and database designers are responsible for defining indexes. This is typically done by examining how an application needs to access data, then creating covering indexes to ensure that database engine doesn't have to resort to table scans on large tables to locate data. Indexing in Cosmos DB is much simpler: It's automatically done for you. Yes, you did read that correctly. Every property on every document within Cosmos DB is automatically indexed. To save index space, you can explicitly exclude properties from indexing if you so choose.

In many instances, denormalized data turns out to not be such a horror as long as it's done intelligently. When deciding what type of data each document that you store in Cosmos DB will have, think in terms of exactly how an app will query and update data. Ideally, you will structure your data in such a way that interactions with an application can be completed with a single query. Also, think of what data needs to be denormalized to satisfy queries, and how likely the data is to change. In our previous album example, it is extremely unlikely that any of the information listed will change after an album is published. The risk in denormalizing with our example document is effectively zero. In the event that denormalized data does change, there are provisions for executing a transaction that updates all data via JavaScript.

Working with Cosmos DB

Cosmos DB has its own SDK. You can query a Cosmos DB database using LINQ SQL statements via an API. Microsoft also has a Cosmos DB emulator that you can install locally to work with when developing your apps.

Scaling Cosmos DB

Just like index creation, scaling is something that you don't have to consider. By default, Cosmos DB is elastic and can grow to whatever size you need. Throughput (how many queries Cosmos DB can satisfy in a given period of time) is defined by the developer. You can even instruct Cosmos DB to be globally available across two or more regions around the world. Cosmos DB instances in differing regions automatically replicate and synchronize with one another. You will need to specify a consistency policy that tells Cosmos DB exactly when other users who are potentially reading from an instance in another regions see changes made. This is a trade-off between consistency and performance.

Cosmos DB is truly global scale. If you build atop Cosmos DB, you will never lay in bed at night staring at the ceiling trying to figure out how to scale your app's data storage.

Pricing

Cosmos DB is priced by GB per month stored, and reserved request units per second (RU/s).

A request unit is a measure that Microsoft created. The Cosmos DB pricing page gives the definition of an RU as a "measure of throughput in Cosmos DB. 1 RU corresponds to the throughput of the GET of a 1KB document." In other words, we don't need to worry about CPU, I/O, memory, or drive space. If you want faster performance, simply dial up the reserved number of RUs for your Cosmos DB instance.

When to Use Cosmos DB

If you're creating a new web application, I highly recommend considering Cosmos DB. Take a look at how your application will access data and what your reporting needs will be. If it is possible to fit your data into documents, strongly consider Cosmos DB over a relational database. I can speak from personal experience: As you scale up Azure SQL databases, it gets expensive. Once you reach the top 4,000 DTU Azure SQL instance and there's not another option for scaling up, you're left with difficult decisions to further scale your application.

Summary

In this chapter, we discussed the differences between SQL and NoSQL data storage solutions, and looked broadly at what Azure offers for each. Now let's dive into the specifics of each data storage service.

CHAPTER 4

Azure SQL Databases

For nearly 30 years, SQL Server has been Microsoft's premier relational database management system (RDBMS) offering. There have been various versions released that target different scenarios. SQL Server is capable of handling the data storage needs from lightly trafficked blogs all the way to airline reservation systems. It's also been a favorite for developers writing web apps using a Microsoft stack.

Back in the old days (meaning before 2010), setting up SQL Server as the data store for a highly available and scalable web site was no small undertaking. You had to do fun things such as these:

- Set up and harden a physical or virtual machine to host SQL Server.

- Make hardware decisions regarding where the data and log files would reside.

- Create and implement a disaster recovery plan.

- Plan for and implement high availability.

- Make sure that your SQL Server deployment was secure.

- Monitor usage and tune for performance as needed.

- Keep current with patches and updates.

Getting these steps right required a highly skilled database administrator (DBA). This isn't something that developers could reasonably hope to accomplish in their spare time by skimming through a few TechNet articles. This, coupled with SQL Server licensing costs, made standing up such a database an expensive proposition.

© Rob Reagan 2018
R. Reagan, *Web Applications on Azure*, https://doi.org/10.1007/978-1-4842-2976-7_4

Introducing Azure SQL Database

Azure SQL Database is Microsoft's cloud-based relational database solution. For all practical purposes, Azure SQL Database is a fully managed version of SQL Server running within Azure. Because Azure SQL is a PaaS offering, you don't have to worry about most of the aforementioned headaches associated with setting up a stand-alone SQL Server instance.

From a developer's perspective, there's almost no difference between a stand-alone SQL Server instance and an Azure SQL Database instance. It's extremely common to develop web applications locally against a stand-alone SQL Server Express or Developer Edition, then deploy to an Azure SQL Database. We discuss strategies for doing so later in this chapter. Most of the differences between stand-alone and Azure SQL Database involve administrative TSQL commands that don't make sense in a PaaS environment, or differences in how ancillary services are provided.

Some of the benefits of Azure SQL Databases include the following:

- *Create an instance in seconds*: You can provision an instance and be ready to program against your new Azure SQL Database in less time than it takes to brew a pot of coffee.

- *Automatic performance tuning*: SQL Database will monitor your app's interaction with the database and automatically suggest indexes to improve your app's performance. You can choose to review all suggestions and choose whether to apply, or you can tell Azure to automatically add suggested indexes.

- *Automatic backups*: SQL DB will automatically perform full, differential, and transaction log backups. Storage for backups is included with your SQL Database instance at no extra charge. The backup retention period varies based on your chosen service tier. Databases in the Basic tier will retain backups for the last seven days, whereas databases in the Premium tier retain backups for 35 days. These backups enable point-in-time restores.

- *Point-in-time restore*: Using backups, you can restore to a database to a point in time. This is very handy if a database becomes corrupted, is accidentally deleted, or if a developer accidentally omits the "where" clause in a delete statement.

- *Transparent data encryption*: Transparent data encryption (TDE) automatically encrypts each database, transaction log, and backup when at rest.

- *Zero downtime for scale up and scale down operations*: You can scale up or scale down your instance size with zero downtime. This allows you to start with a smaller instance and scale up as your web application grows.

- *Manage using SQL Server Management Studio*: Connect to and manage your databases using SQL Server Management Studio, just as you would your on-premises SQL Server databases.

- *Geo-replication*: With a few clicks and keystrokes, you can replicate your database to up to four (or to the same) datacenters. Replicas are read-only and are kept in sync with the primary in near real time. The delay in data synchronization is mainly due to network latency.

  This has several benefits. You can offload read-intensive tasks to a replicated read-only instance. You can also failover and promote a read-only secondary to a primary in the event of a datacenter outage.

- *Failover groups for high availability*: Failover with geo-replication has one downside: After promoting a replicated secondary database as the new primary, the new primary will have a different connection string. This is because all secondaries in other datacenters live on other servers. Therefore, you'll need to change the connection string in your web application to point to the new primary. It's one more step that you'll have to perform as part of the disaster recovery process.

  If you add geo-replicated databases to a failover group, you can use a single connection string to address the primary database in your failover group. Azure can automatically detect that the primary is down, and will promote one of your secondaries as the new primary. Because the primary is addressed with the same connection string, though, your app doesn't have to make any changes. I'm a big fan of automating disaster recovery tasks so that I'm not interrupted at home with "The Call" from the operations team.

- *Cash flow*: Running an Azure SQL Database instance can help your company's cash flow. Although most developers don't really care, your accounting department sure does. Instead of paying for a SQL Server license up front, Azure SQL Databases are billed by the hour. It's analogous to renting a Zipcar instead of purchasing a vehicle: You only pay for the time that you use. It's a lot easier to ask your boss for $30 per month for an Azure SQL Database instance rather than several thousand dollars to purchase a SQL Server license.

Licensing

Azure SQL Database instances are billed by the hour that the instance is allocated. The hourly rate billed depends on the service tier and instance size that you select.

There are four service tiers: Basic, Standard, Premium, and Premium-RS. Each service tier has multiple instance sizes available. Here's a quick rundown of the different tiers.

- *Basic*: Instances in the Basic tier are great for hosting development databases or lightly trafficked sites. This is the cheapest tier, and instances start at around $5 per month.

- *Standard*: Consider a Standard tier instance for web applications with concurrent workloads and moderate amounts of traffic.

- *Premium*: If your web application is mission critical, has high traffic volumes, and has heavy I/O needs, go with a Premium instance.

- *Premium-RS*: The Premium-RS tier has the same high I/O performance as the Premium tier, but has a reduced SLA. Databases in this tier are great for heavy I/O tasks that aren't mission critical.

Each instance size within a service tier specifies the maximum database size and maximum DTUs.

Single Database vs. Elastic Pool

Imagine that your company has three databases that power its day-to-day operations. Each of these databases is generally quiet and only consumes a dozen or so DTUs on average. Occasionally, though, each database will burst to around 50 DTUs for a few minutes, then quiet back down to its normal level. If you had to choose an instance size for each database, you'd likely go with an S3 instance from the Standard tier, which allows up to 100 DTUs. At the time of this writing, a single S3 instance costs about $150 per month per database, for a total outlay of $450 per month.

This seems like an awful waste because most of the time, each database has almost 90 DTUs of excess capacity. This is a scenario that's perfect for elastic pools.

An elastic pool can contain multiple databases that draw on a shared pool of DTUs, which are called eDTUs. Although the sum of DTU usage of each database cannot exceed the pool's maximum DTU limit, each database within the pool can dynamically use as many DTUs as necessary.

In our previous example, we would likely place our three databases in a Standard tier 100 eDTU pool. This costs roughly $225 per month, giving us a substantial savings over provisioning each database under the single database model.

Exceeding a DTU Limit

What happens when a database experiences heavy load and hits its DTU limit? When a database instance (or databases with an elastic pool) hits the DTU limit, queries will be throttled. Response times will increase, possibly to the point that timeouts occur and exceptions occur.

The good news is that we can configure alerts within Azure to let us know when we start bumping against a DTU limit, and scaling up a database is simple to do and doesn't cause any downtime. The bad news is that there isn't currently an autoscale feature to automatically scale up and down a SQL DB instance as there is for Web Apps.

We'll talk about ways to handle errors due to throttling when walking through our sample application.

TaskZilla: Our Example Application

Imagine that we work at AwesomeTech, a software development firm. Our company has decided to develop TaskZilla, an internal-use web application to help developers track tasks that they need to perform. Taskzilla is a simple app; it will allow developers to create, read, update, and delete (CRUD) tasks. Serendipitously, this corresponds to the database CRUD operations.

Because our goal in this chapter is to explore and illustrate how to use Azure SQL databases in web applications, we won't spend much time focusing on parts of the code base that don't pertain to SQL Database.

The code is fully commented and available for download at `https://github.com/BuildingScalableWebAppsWithAzure/TaskZilla.git`.

The remainder of this chapter assumes that you are familiar with basic relational database concepts such as queries, tables, columns, and rows. You'll also need to be somewhat familiar with Entity Framework. Both of these topics are broad (and deep) and are beyond the scope of this book.

Creating the TaskZilla Project

To keep our workload to a minimum, we'll create TaskZilla as an ASP.NET Web Application that uses the MVC template. To create the project, follow these steps:

1. Open Visual Studio 2015 and choose File ➤ New ➤ Project.

2. In the New Project dialog box, select the ASP.NET Web Application (.NET Framework) template located under the Installed ➤ Templates ➤ Visual C# ➤ Web heading. Enter `TaskZilla` for the Name and Solution Name, then click OK (Figure 4-1).

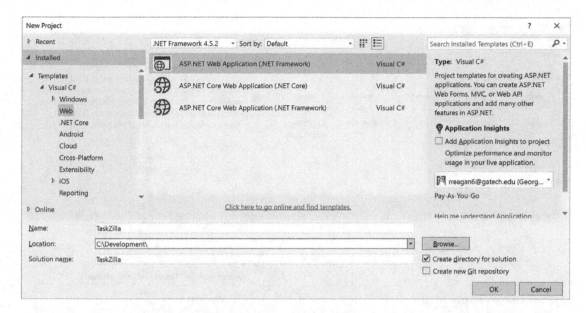

Figure 4-1. *Creating a project using the ASP.NET Web Application template*

3. On the next screen, you'll be asked to select a template. Select
    MVC and click OK (Figure 4-2).

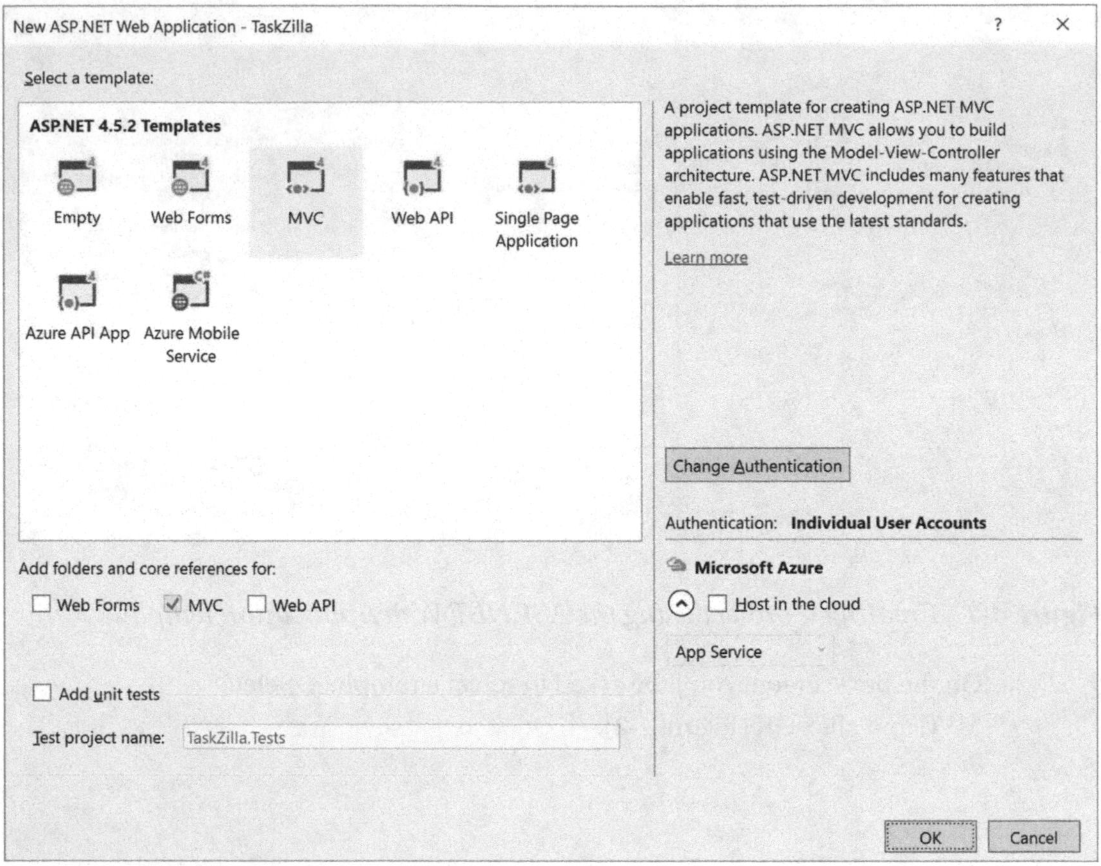

Figure 4-2. *We'll use the MVC template when creating our project*

We're now ready to move on to creating our data model.

The TaskZilla Data Model

Our requirements are simple:

- Users need to be able to list all tasks in the system.

- They should also be able to add new tasks and edit and delete existing tasks.

- Users should be able to securely log in and log out of the application.

- Tasks consist of a name, an extended description, a priority, who the task is assigned to, and the estimated time it will take to complete the task in hours.

To satisfy our secure login and logout requirements, we'll make use of ASP.NET Identity, which is already incorporated in our project template. Identity already has its own set of tables defined, which will be created in the database when the application is first run.

Creating the ASP.NET Identity Tables

Let's start by actually setting up those ASP.NET Identity tables. To do so, follow these steps.

1. First, we need to create a TaskZilla database in your local SQL Server instance. Open SQL Server Management Studio, connect to your local SQL Server instance, right-click the Databases folder on your local instance, and select New Database. In the New Database dialog box, enter `TaskZilla` as the database name, then click OK.

2. Now that our local database is created, we need to direct our TaskZilla web application to use it. Open the project's `web.config` file and find the DefaultConnection node located in the `<connectionStrings></connectionStrings>` section. Change this connection string to point to your local SQL Server instance and the new TaskZilla database that you just created.

3. Run the application. You'll see the default ASP.NET MVC welcome page, shown in Figure 4-3. Behind the scenes, though, our application used Entity Framework Code First Migrations to create the tables necessary to support ASP.NET Identity in our TaskZilla database. If you jump back over to SQL Server Management Studio and view all tables in the TaskZilla database, you'll see the Identity tables that have just been created (Figure 4-4).

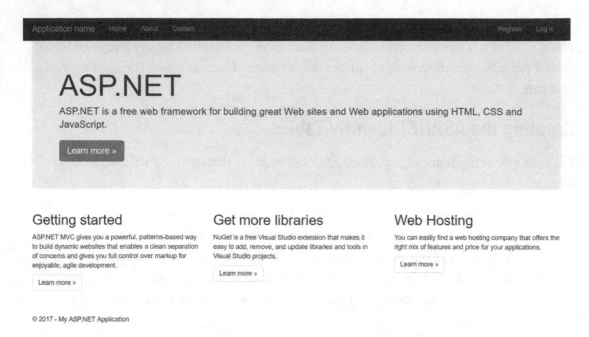

Figure 4-3. *The default ASP.NET Web Application MVC template welcome page*

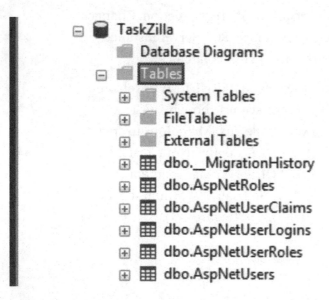

Figure 4-4. *After browsing to our TaskZilla database in SQL Server Management Studio, we can see the ASP.NET Identity tables created by our TaskZilla web application.*

Creating Our Tasks and Priorities Tables

Now we're ready to create our Tasks and Priorities tables that will store task information in our application.

To create the TaskZilla database, open SQL Server Management Studio, connect to your local SQL Server instance, and execute the TSQL shown in Listing 4-1.

Listing 4-1. The TSQL to Create Our Tasks and Priorities Tables

```
USE [TaskZilla]
GO
SET ANSI_NULLS ON
GO
SET QUOTED_IDENTIFIER ON
GO

/* Create the Priorities table. This is a lookup table that will contain
our priorities
    of Low, Medium, and High */
CREATE TABLE [dbo].[Priorities](
        [Id] [int] NOT NULL,
        [Priority] [nvarchar](24) NOT NULL,
 CONSTRAINT [PK_Priorities] PRIMARY KEY CLUSTERED
(
        [Id] ASC
)WITH (PAD_INDEX = OFF, STATISTICS_NORECOMPUTE = OFF, IGNORE_DUP_KEY = OFF,
ALLOW_ROW_LOCKS = ON, ALLOW_PAGE_LOCKS = ON) ON [PRIMARY]
) ON [PRIMARY]
GO
SET ANSI_NULLS ON
GO
SET QUOTED_IDENTIFIER ON
GO
```

```
/* The Tasks table holds our actual tasks definition. The code below
creates it. */
CREATE TABLE [dbo].[Tasks](
        [Id] [int] IDENTITY(1,1) NOT NULL,
        [Name] [nvarchar](64) NOT NULL,
        [Description] [nvarchar](2000) NULL,
        [AssignedToUserId] [nvarchar](128) NOT NULL,
        [PriorityId] [int] NOT NULL,
        [EstDurationInHours] [decimal](18, 2) NULL,
 CONSTRAINT [PK_Tasks] PRIMARY KEY CLUSTERED
(
        [Id] ASC
)WITH (PAD_INDEX = OFF, STATISTICS_NORECOMPUTE = OFF, IGNORE_DUP_KEY = OFF,
ALLOW_ROW_LOCKS = ON, ALLOW_PAGE_LOCKS = ON) ON [PRIMARY]
) ON [PRIMARY]
GO

/* We'll create a foreign key that defines a relationship between the
AspNetUsers
    table (which holds all of our users) and the Tasks table.
    This relationship will
    ensure that each task is assigned to a user */
ALTER TABLE [dbo].[Tasks]  WITH CHECK ADD  CONSTRAINT [FK_AspNetUsers_Tasks]
FOREIGN KEY([AssignedToUserId])
REFERENCES [dbo].[AspNetUsers] ([Id])
GO
ALTER TABLE [dbo].[Tasks] CHECK CONSTRAINT [FK_AspNetUsers_Tasks]
GO

/* We'll add another foreign key that defines a relationship between tasks and
priorities. Each task will have a priority. */
ALTER TABLE [dbo].[Tasks]  WITH CHECK ADD  CONSTRAINT [FK_Priorities_Tasks]
FOREIGN KEY([PriorityId])
REFERENCES [dbo].[Priorities] ([Id])
GO
ALTER TABLE [dbo].[Tasks] CHECK CONSTRAINT [FK_Priorities_Tasks]
GO
```

Note that we've made sure to define foreign key relationships between our tables. This will be very important when we set up Entity Framework in the next section.

The Data Access Tier

We've defined our model, so now let's create our data access tier. There are multiple technologies that we could use to access our database. Some of the more popular choices include ADO.NET, Dapper, and Entity Framework.

Handling Transient Faults

Before choosing a data access technology for our app, let's talk about one of the primary differences between a stand-alone SQL Server installation and Azure SQL Database: transient faults.

When working with Azure SQL Database, we occasionally encounter transient faults. A transient fault is an ephemeral error that's usually very short-lived and self-corrects. These errors can be due to an internal Azure issue. In my experience, though, transient faults are almost always the result of bumping up against a database DTU limit and having queries throttled.

If you're building an app that accesses a stand-alone SQL Server instance that sits on a local area network (LAN), you don't have to deal with throttling or spend as much time worrying about transient faults. Therefore, using ADO.NET is sufficient. If you're using an Azure SQL Database and rely on a data access technology with no automatic retry when transient faults are encountered, however, you're going to have a bad time. Occasionally, queries will fail and your users will be frustrated.

There are a couple of ways that we can deal with transient faults. Our first option is to combine ADO.NET or Dapper with Microsoft's Transient Fault Handling Application Block. The Transient Fault Handling Application Block will detect when errors occur and reissue requests.

The second option is to use Entity Framework. Starting in Entity Framework 6, Microsoft included a feature called connection resiliency and retry logic. This allows us to configure Entity Framework to retry requests that fail due to known transient issues with SQL Azure Database.

Entity Framework has other benefits such as Code First Migrations, which we will use to deploy our database to Azure SQL Database and issue future schema updates. We'll use Entity Framework in TaskZilla.

Setting Up Entity Framework

1. To keep things tidy and organized within the project, let's create a
   Persistence folder to hold our Entity Framework Context class and
   generated models. Right-click the TaskZilla project, then select
   Add ➤ New Folder. Name this new folder Persistence.

2. Right-click the new Persistence folder and choose Add ➤ New
   Item. In the Add New Item dialog box, select the Visual C# ➤
   Data menu item, and select the ADO.NET Entity Data Model
   from the list of available items (Figure 4-5). Name the new item
   TaskZillaContext and click Add.

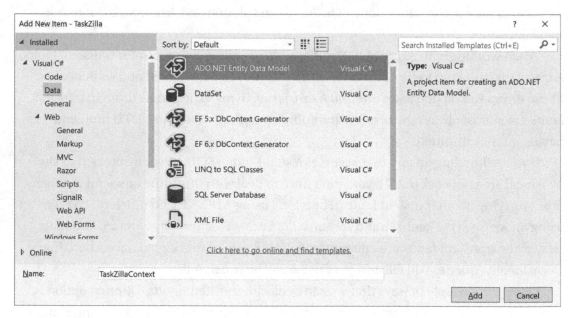

Figure 4-5. *Adding the ADO.NET Entity Data Model to our project*

3. Next, the Entity Data Model Wizard will ask how you want to set up
   Entity Framework. Select Code First from Database (Figure 4-6).
   This will instruct Entity Framework to examine our existing database
   and generate a DbContext subclass and associated model objects
   based on our existing database schema. Note that this is why it is
   very important to make sure that your database has foreign keys

that define relationships between tables. If you neglect to set up the foreign key relationships, Entity Framework has no idea how tables are related and will not create relationships within generated model classes.

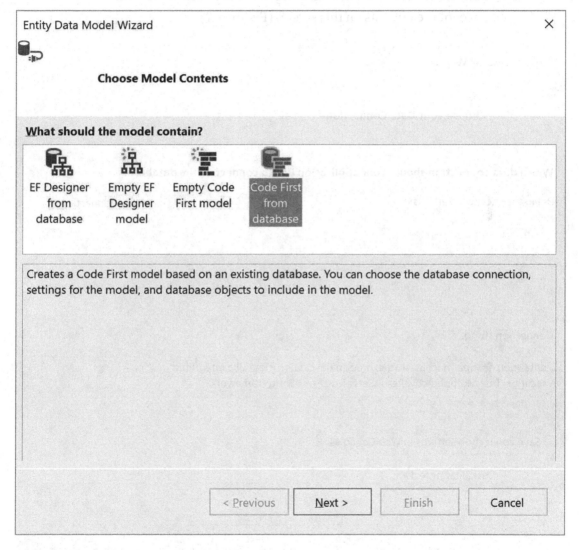

Figure 4-6. *We'll use Code First from Database to initialize our* DbContext *subclass and associated model classes*

4. The Entity Data Model Wizard now needs to know which database
    it should examine to generate our DbContext subclass and
    associated model classes. We'll need to supply a connection string
    to the database we'd like to use. Because we've already set up our
    DefaultConnection connection string in the web.config file, you
    can accept the defaults on this screen (Figure 4-7).

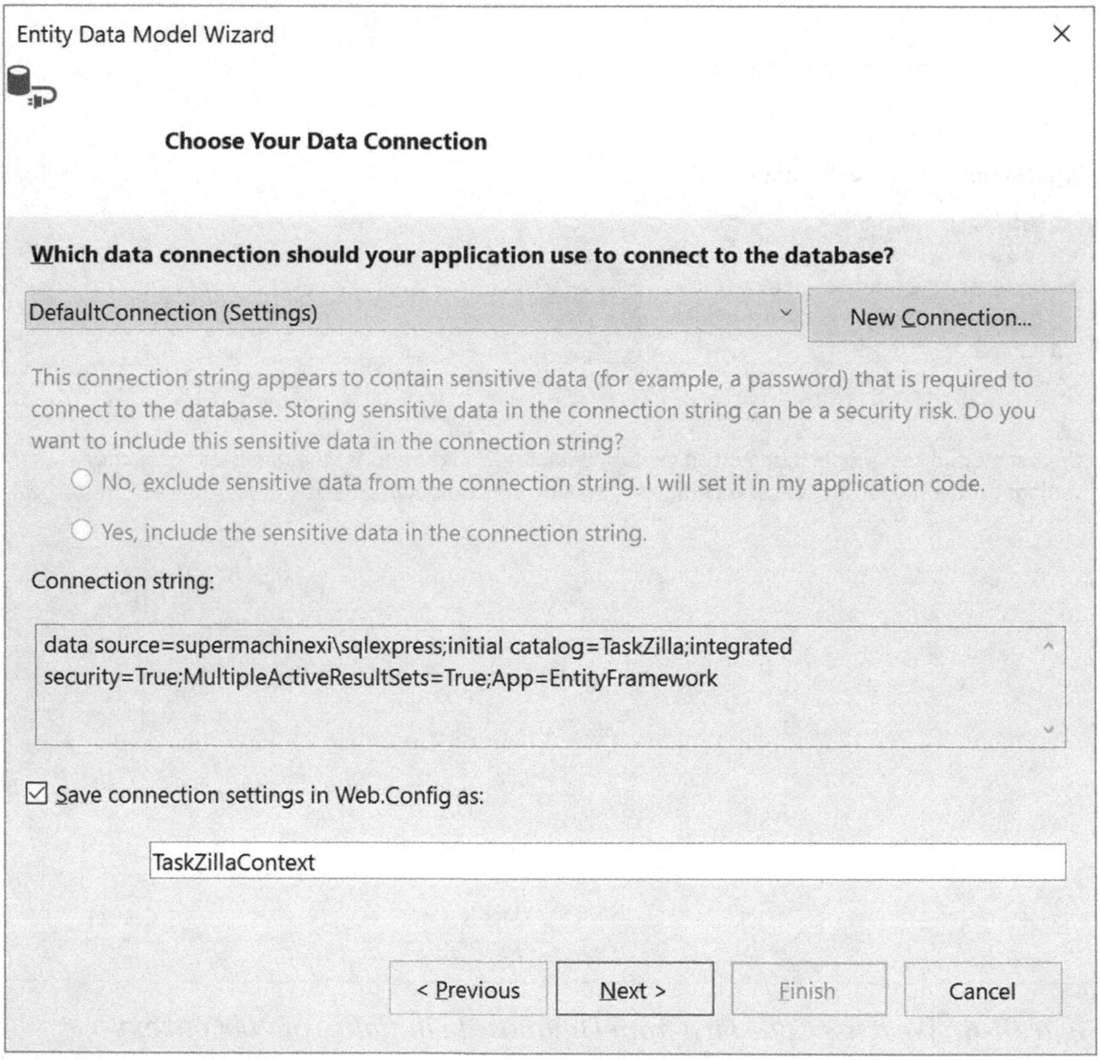

Entity Data Model Wizard   ✕

Choose Your Data Connection

<u>W</u>hich data connection should your application use to connect to the database?

DefaultConnection (Settings)   ⌄   New <u>C</u>onnection...

This connection string appears to contain sensitive data (for example, a password) that is required to connect to the database. Storing sensitive data in the connection string can be a security risk. Do you want to include this sensitive data in the connection string?

   ○ No, exclude sensitive data from the connection string. I will set it in my application code.

   ○ Yes, include the sensitive data in the connection string.

Connection string:

```
data source=supermachinexi\sqlexpress;initial catalog=TaskZilla;integrated
security=True;MultipleActiveResultSets=True;App=EntityFramework
```

☑ <u>S</u>ave connection settings in Web.Config as:

TaskZillaContext

         < <u>P</u>revious   <u>N</u>ext >   <u>F</u>inish   Cancel

Figure 4-7. *We'll need to specify a connection string to the database that we want the Entity Data Model Wizard to use when generating our DbContext subclass and associated model classes*

5. Finally, we need to tell the Entity Data Model Wizard which tables
    and views should be included in our application. Note that we
    do not want to include every table, as there are several tables
    generated to support ASP.NET Identity that we do not need. Expand
    the Tables node and select AspNetUsers, Priorities, and Tasks
    (Figure 4-8). We're including AspNetUsers because we will need to
    allow our users to assign tasks to specific users within the system.

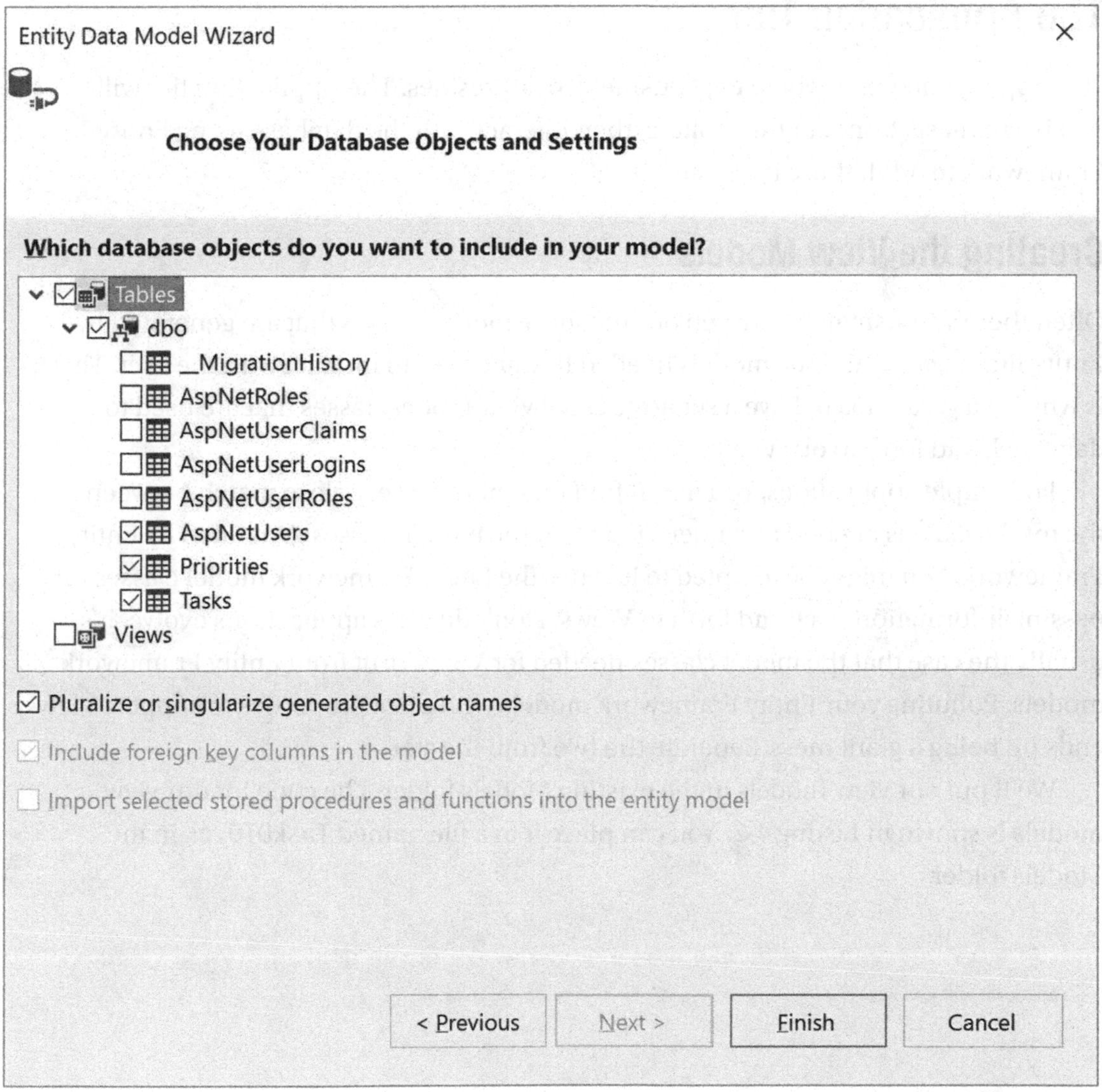

Figure 4-8. *Choosing the tables we want to include in our Entity Framework*
DbContext subclass and models

6.   Click Finish to generate our Entity Framework code.

After the wizard finishes, you'll see several new classes in our Persistence folder. The `AspNetUser.cs`, `Priority.cs`, and `Task.cs` are generated model classes. Their properties are created based on our database tables that we included. The `TaskZillaContext.cs` derives from `DbContext` and is responsible for moving our objects back and forth to our relational database.

The Application Tier

Our Application tier is where the "business logic" resides. The Application tier will receive requests from our Controllers, then interact with the database using Entity Framework to fulfill those requests.

Creating the View Models

Often there's a mismatch between our database model classes that are generated by Entity Framework, and the models needed by our Views to interact with the user. This is why it's a great idea to have a separate set of view model classes that are used to move data back and forth to our Views.

For simple applications, you might find that there's a very close match between the model classes needed to render Views and the model classes generated by Entity Framework. You might be tempted to just use the Entity Framework model classes for passing information back and forth to Views. Don't do it! As applications evolve, it's usually the case that the model classes needed for Views drift from Entity Framework models. Polluting your Entity Framework models with extra properties to support Views ends up being a giant mess. Separate the two from the start.

We'll put our view models in the existing Models folder. The code for our view models is shown in Listing 4-2. You can place it in a file named `TaskDTO.cs` in the Models folder.

Listing 4-2. Our View Model Code

```
namespace TaskZilla.Models
{
    public enum OpResult
    {
        NoOp, Success, Exception
    }

    /// <summary>
    /// Parent class for our data transport objects.
    /// </summary>
    public class BaseDTO
    {
        public OpResult Result = OpResult.NoOp;
        public string ErrorMessage;
    }

    /// <summary>
    /// Transports information about a task, the options for priorities,
    /// and the options
    /// for users who we can assign the task to back and forth from our
    /// service layer to
    /// our Controller.
    /// </summary>
    public class TaskDTO : BaseDTO
    {
        public int Id { get; set; }

        [Required]
        [StringLength(64)]
        public string Name { get; set; }

        [StringLength(2000)]
        public string Description { get; set; }

        [Display(Name = "Assigned to")]
        public string AssignedToUserId { get; set; }
```

```csharp
    [Display(Name = "Assigned to")]
    public string AssignedToLabel { get; set; }

    [Display(Name = "Priority")]
    public int PriorityId { get; set; }

    [Display(Name = "Priority")]
    public string PriorityLabel { get; set; }

    [Display(Name = "Est. Duration")]
    public decimal? EstDurationInHours { get; set; }

    public List<PriorityDTO> Priorities { get; set; }
    public List<UserDTO> Users { get; set; }
}

/// <summary>
/// Used to transport all priority types to our Views. This is mainly used
/// in binding to drop-downs where the user will pick a priority
/// </summary>
public class PriorityDTO
{
    public PriorityDTO() { }
    public PriorityDTO(int id, string priority)
    {
        this.Id = id;
        this.Priority = priority;
    }

    public int Id { get; set; }
    public string Priority { get; set; }
}

/// <summary>
/// Used to transport a list of users who are valid assignees for a
/// task. This
/// is used by our Views and is mainly bound to drop-downs where a user
/// needs to
```

```
/// be selected.
/// </summary>
public class UserDTO
{
    public UserDTO() { }
    public UserDTO(string id, string userName)
    {
        this.Id = id;
        this.UserName = userName;
    }

    public string Id { get; set; }
    public string UserName { get; set; }
}
}
```

Creating the TaskService Class

The TaskService class holds the entirety of our Application tier logic. First, create a folder called Services. Within the Services folder, create a file called TaskService.cs and enter the code shown in Listing 4-3.

Listing 4-3. The TaskService.cs Class

```
using System.Collections.Generic;
using System.Linq;
using System.Web;
using TaskZilla.Persistence;
using TaskZilla.Models;
using System.Data.Entity;

namespace TaskZilla.Services
{
    /// <summary>
    /// This is our "business logic" layer. It is responsible for working
    /// with Entity Framework
```

```csharp
/// to handle CRUD operations and translate results into view models
/// for consumption
/// by our controllers.
/// </summary>
public class TaskService
{
    private TaskZillaContext _context;

    /// <summary>
    /// Constructor. Note that in a production app, we'd inject
    /// dependencies such as
    /// the TaskZillaContext into this constructor using a dependency
    /// injection
    /// framework like Autofac
    /// </summary>
    public TaskService()
    {
        _context = new TaskZillaContext();
    }

    /// <summary>
    /// Retrieves all priorities defined in the database.
    /// </summary>
    /// <returns></returns>
    public async System.Threading.Tasks.Task<List<PriorityDTO>>
    GetPriorities()
    {
        List<Priority> prioritiesList = await _context.Priorities.
        ToListAsync();
        List<PriorityDTO> priorityDTOs = DTOHelpers.CopyPriorities
        (prioritiesList);
        return priorityDTOs;
    }

    /// <summary>
    /// Returns the task identified by taskId.
    /// </summary>
```

```
/// <param name="taskId">Primary key for the requested task</param>
/// <returns>A populated task instance, if the requested task
/// is found. Otherwise returns null.</returns>
public async System.Threading.Tasks.Task<TaskDTO> GetTaskById
(int taskId)
{
    Task t = await _context.Tasks.FindAsync(taskId);
    var taskDto = new TaskDTO
    {
        Id = t.Id,
        Name = t.Name,
        Description = t.Description,
        EstDurationInHours = t.EstDurationInHours,
        AssignedToUserId = t.AssignedToUserId,
        PriorityId = t.PriorityId,
        PriorityLabel = t.Priority.Priority1,
        AssignedToLabel = t.AspNetUser.UserName
    };
    return taskDto;
}

/// <summary>
/// returns all users defined in the system.
/// </summary>
/// <returns></returns>
public async System.Threading.Tasks.Task<List<UserDTO>> GetUsers()
{
    //we'll use a projection since we don't need to retrieve fields
    //such as password...
    var users = await _context.AspNetUsers.Select(p => new
        { Id = p.Id, UserName = p.UserName }).ToListAsync();
    List<UserDTO> userDTOs = new List<UserDTO>();
    foreach (var u in users)
    {
        userDTOs.Add(new UserDTO(u.Id, u.UserName));
    }
```

```csharp
        return userDTOs;
    }

    /// <summary>
    /// Updates a task in the database.
    /// </summary>
    public async System.Threading.Tasks.Task UpdateTask(TaskDTO task)
    {
        var taskToUpdate = await _context.Tasks.FindAsync(task.Id);
        taskToUpdate.Name = task.Name;
        taskToUpdate.Description = task.Description;
        taskToUpdate.PriorityId = task.PriorityId;
        taskToUpdate.AssignedToUserId = task.AssignedToUserId;
        taskToUpdate.EstDurationInHours = task.EstDurationInHours;
        await _context.SaveChangesAsync();
    }

    /// <summary>
    /// returns all tasks in the system. This demonstrates an inner
    /// join between
    /// Tasks, Priorities, and AspNetUsers.
    /// </summary>
    /// <returns></returns>
    public async System.Threading.Tasks.Task<List<TaskDTO>>
    GetAllTasksAsync()
    {
        var tasks = await (from t in _context.Tasks
            join p in _context.Priorities on t.PriorityId equals p.Id
            join u in _context.AspNetUsers on t.AssignedToUserId equals u.Id
            select new { Priority = p, Task = t, User = u }).ToListAsync();
        List<TaskDTO> taskDTOs = new List<TaskDTO>();
        foreach (var t in tasks)
        {
```

```csharp
        taskDTOs.Add(new TaskDTO {
            Id = t.Task.Id,
            Name = t.Task.Name,
            Description = t.Task.Description,
            PriorityId = t.Task.PriorityId,
            PriorityLabel = t.Priority.Priority1,
            AssignedToUserId = t.Task.AssignedToUserId,
            EstDurationInHours = t.Task.EstDurationInHours,
            AssignedToLabel = t.User.UserName
        });
    }

    return taskDTOs;
}

/// <summary>
/// Adds a new task to the database.
/// </summary>
/// <param name="newTask">The task to add</param>
public async System.Threading.Tasks.Task CreateTask(TaskDTO newTaskDTO)
{
    Task newTask = new Task
    {
        Name = newTaskDTO.Name,
        Description = newTaskDTO.Description,
        AssignedToUserId = newTaskDTO.AssignedToUserId,
        PriorityId = newTaskDTO.PriorityId,
        EstDurationInHours = newTaskDTO.EstDurationInHours
    };
    _context.Tasks.Add(newTask);
    await _context.SaveChangesAsync();
}

/// <summary>
/// Removes a task from the database.
/// </summary>
```

```
    public async System.Threading.Tasks.Task DeleteTask(int id)
    {
        Task taskToDelete = await _context.Tasks.FindAsync(id);
        _context.Tasks.Remove(taskToDelete);
        await _context.SaveChangesAsync();
    }
}

/// <summary>
/// Contains helper methods to copy Entity Framework Models into
/// ViewModels.
/// </summary>
public class DTOHelpers
{
    public static List<PriorityDTO> CopyPriorities(List<Priority>
    priorities)
    {
        List<PriorityDTO> dtos = new List<PriorityDTO>();
        foreach (Priority p in priorities)
        {
            dtos.Add(new PriorityDTO(p.Id, p.Priority1));
        }
        return dtos;
    }
}
}
```

Controllers and Views

Next, let's add methods to our HomeController class located in the Controllers folder. The code for our HomeController is shown in Listing 4-4.

Listing 4-4. The HomeController Class

```
using System;
using System.Collections.Generic;
using System.Web.Mvc;
```

```csharp
using TaskZilla.Services;
using TaskZilla.Models;
using System.Threading.Tasks;

namespace TaskZilla.Controllers
{
    /// <summary>
    /// Contains methods to handle views for all task-related activities.
    /// Users must be logged in to access any methods in this controller.
    /// </summary>
    [Authorize]
    public class HomeController : Controller
    {
        private TaskService _taskService;

        /// <summary>
        /// Constructor. In a production app, we'd inject all
        /// dependencies like TaskService
        /// into this constructor using a DI framework like Autofac.
        /// </summary>
        public HomeController()
        {
            _taskService = new TaskService();
        }

        /// <summary>
        /// Shows the user all tasks in the system.
        /// </summary>
        /// <returns></returns>
        public async Task<ActionResult> Index()
        {
            List<TaskDTO> tasks = await _taskService.GetAllTasksAsync();
            return View(tasks);
        }
```

```csharp
/// <summary>
/// Shows the create task screen.
/// </summary>
/// <returns></returns>
[HttpGet]
public async Task<ActionResult> Create()
{
    List<PriorityDTO> allPriorities = await _taskService.
    GetPriorities();
    List<UserDTO> allUsers = await _taskService.GetUsers();
    TaskDTO task = new TaskDTO();
    task.Priorities = allPriorities;
    task.Users = allUsers;
    return View(task);
}

/// <summary>
/// Handles the validation and creation of a new task.
/// </summary>
/// <param name="taskToCreate">The task that the user wants to
/// create</param>
/// <returns>A viewModel indicating whether the create operation
/// was successful</returns>
/// <summary>
/// Called when the user submits a new task.
/// </summary>
[HttpPost]
public async Task<ActionResult> Create(TaskDTO taskToCreate)
{
    try
    {
        await _taskService.CreateTask(taskToCreate);
        taskToCreate.Result = OpResult.Success;
    }
```

```csharp
        catch (Exception ex)
        {
            taskToCreate.Result = OpResult.Exception;
            taskToCreate.ErrorMessage = ex.Message;
        }
        return View(taskToCreate);
    }

    /// <summary>
    /// Renders a view that shows a task's details.
    /// </summary>
    /// <param name="id">The primary key of the task to view</param>
    /// <returns>A view containing the requested task's details</returns>
    [HttpGet]
    public async Task<ActionResult> Details(int id)
    {
        TaskDTO task = await _taskService.GetTaskById(id);
        return View(task);
    }

    /// <summary>
    /// Renders a view that will allow the user to edit a specific task.
    /// </summary>
    /// <param name="id">The ID of the task that we want to edit</param>
    /// <returns>A view populated with the requested task's details.
    </returns>
    [HttpGet]
    public async Task<ActionResult> Edit(int id)
    {
        TaskDTO task = await _taskService.GetTaskById(id);
        List<UserDTO> allUsers = await _taskService.GetUsers();
        List<PriorityDTO> allPriorities = await _taskService.
        GetPriorities();
```

```
            task.Priorities = allPriorities;
            task.Users = allUsers;
            return View(task);
        }

        /// <summary>
        /// Writes the edits to a task back to the database, and tells the user
        /// if the update was successful.
        /// </summary>
        /// <param name="task">The task with edits to be saved</param>
        /// <returns>A view informing the user if the update was
        /// successful</returns>
        [HttpPost]
        public async Task<ActionResult> Edit(TaskDTO task)
        {
            try
            {
                await _taskService.UpdateTask(task);
                task.Result = OpResult.Success;
            }
            catch (Exception ex)
            {
                task.Result = OpResult.Exception;
                task.ErrorMessage = ex.Message;
            }
            return View(task);
        }

        /// <summary>
        /// Deletes the specified task and tells the user if the
        /// deletion was successful.
        /// </summary>
        /// <param name="id">The ID of the task to delete</param>
```

```
        /// <returns>A view telling the user if the deletion was
        /// successful</returns>
        public async Task<ActionResult> Delete(int id)
        {
            await _taskService.DeleteTask(id);
            return View();
        }
    }
}
```

The Views for TaskZilla are both trivial and verbose, so we'll omit them here.
If you'd like to view or download them, check out the GitHub repo for this project at
https://github.com/BuildingScalableWebAppsWithAzure/TaskZilla.git.

Finishing Touches

Note that the entire HomeController class is marked with the [Authorize] attribute,
meaning that a user must be logged in to execute any of the HomeController methods.
We'll need to add a node to the <appSettings></appSettings> section of our web.config
file to let ASP.NET know where to direct users who are unauthenticated. To do so, add
"<add key="loginUrl" value="~/Account/Login" />" between thetags in the web.config.

Running the Application

After running the application, you'll be redirected to the /Account/Login screen because
you're not yet authenticated (Figure 4-9).

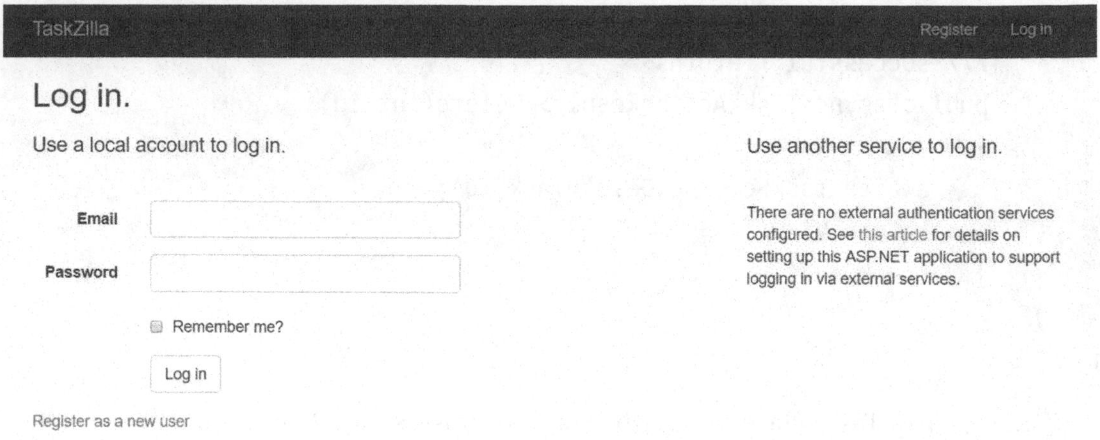

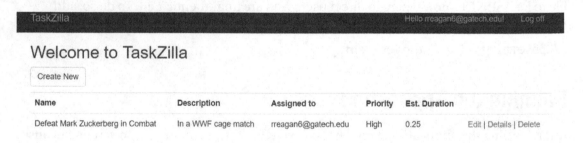

Figure 4-9. *The TaskZilla login screen*

Because this is the first time that the application has run, you'll need to click on the Register As a New User link below the login fields to create an account. After creating an account, you can log in to the site.

Once logged in, you'll see the main screen that lists all tasks in the system (Figure 4-10). From this screen, you can add, edit, view, or delete tasks.

Figure 4-10. *The /home/index page lists all tasks defined in the system*

Deployment to Azure

At this point, we're running TaskZilla against a database on our local SQL Server. It's now time to publish our database to Azure. We'll first need to create an Azure SQL Database instance.

Creating an Azure SQL Database Instance

To create an Azure SQL Database instance, perform the following steps:

1. Log into the Azure Portal. Click the Add Resource button (the plus
    sign at the top of the left toolbar), select Databases, and click the
    SQL Database menu item (Figure 4-11).

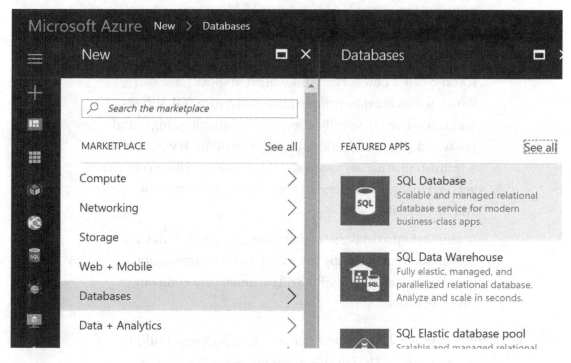

Figure 4-11.   *Creating a new Azure SQL Database instance*

2. Next, we need to enter the particulars for our new instance
    (Figure 4-12). Here's a rundown of the fields that we must specify:

    -   *Database Name*: This is the name of our new database. It must be
        unique within the server. For this exercise, enter TaskZilla.

    -   *Subscription*: This is the subscription that you'd like to bill for all
        charges for this new database.

    -   *Resource Group*: Resource groups allow you to manage resources
        that share a similar purpose as a group. We'll place our TaskZilla
        database and Web App in the same resource group. Select Create
        New, then enter rg-taskzilla as the resource group name.

- *Select Source*: When creating a new Azure SQL Database, we can start with a blank database, restore a backup of another database, or begin with an example AdventureWorks database. Select Blank database.

- *Server*: Each database must live on a server instance. You can choose one of your existing servers or create a new server. Please note that this server is not an Azure VM instance that you have to pay for separately; it's included with the pricing tier that you select for your database.

  If you create a new server, you'll need to specify a server name, which must be unique across all Azure SQL servers. You'll also need to specify a server administrative login and password. These SQL authentication credentials will provide administrative access to any database that you place on this server. Finally, you'll need to specify a region where the server will be located.

  It's important to make sure that your Azure SQL Database server and your Web App are located in the same region. Otherwise, your application will be much slower due to network latency.

- *Want to Use SQL Elastic Pool?* A SQL elastic pool lets multiple databases share DTUs. For this example, select Not Now.

- *Pricing Tier*: The pricing tier and instance size that you select will determine your database's maximum available DTUs, maximum database size, and cost. For this example, choose the Basic tier. The Basic tier will cost roughly $5 per month, but you'll only pay depending on for how many hours your database instance exists. Given how easy it is to scale up or scale down an Azure SQL Database instance, I don't agonize over choosing an instance size.

- *Collation*: Accept the default value.

Click Create to create your new database instance. Your database instance might take a minute or two to allocate.

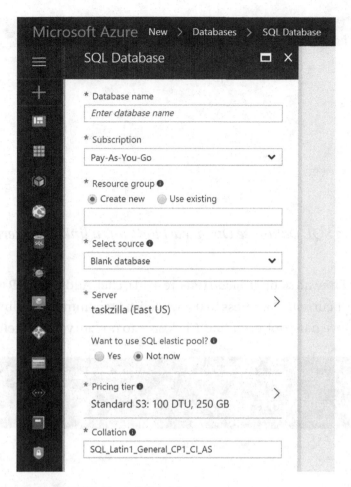

Figure 4-12. *The Create SQL Database blade*

Setting Firewall Rules

SQL Database maintains an IP address whitelist to determine who can connect to a database. By default, that whitelist is empty. Before connecting to your new database, you must add your current IP address to your server's whitelist by following these steps:

1. Log into the Azure Portal and navigate to your newly created database instance. You can do so by clicking the All Resources icon in the left menu bar, or by clicking the SQL Databases icon on the left menu bar.

2. On your new database's Overview blade, click Set Server Firewall, located in the header (Figure 4-13).

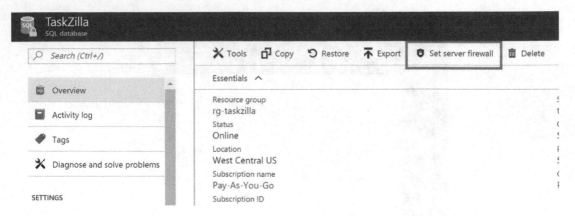

Figure 4-13. *The SQL Database Overview blade has a link to set server firewall rules*

3. On the Firewall settings blade (Figure 4-14), click Add Client IP to add your current IP address to the whitelist. I recommend adding a descriptive name for each rule. Click Save to update your whitelist.

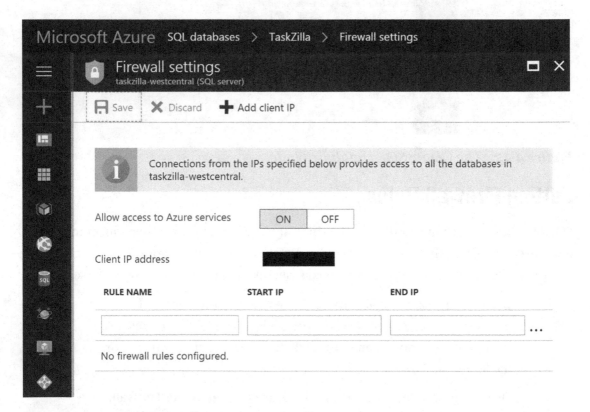

Figure 4-14. *The Firewall settings blade allows you to add IP addresses to the SQL Database IP whitelist*

Connecting to the New Instance

Let's make sure that we can connect to our new instance. Let's open SQL Server Management Studio, and do the following:

1. In SQL Server Management Studio, select File ➤ Connect Object Explorer. This will open the Connect to Server dialog box (Figure 4-15).

2. Use the following settings to connect:

   - *Server Type*: This should be Database Engine.

   - *Server Name*: This is the server name that you defined. It will be in the format of [server name].database.windows.net. I used TaskZilla as my server name, so I would enter taskzilla. database.windows.net.

   - *Authentication*: This should be SQL Server Authentication, because we are going to connect with the server administrator credentials.

   - *Login*: This is the server admin username that you specified when creating your server. It will be in the format of [username] @[server name]. If I set my server admin username as adminZilla, the login would be adminZilla @TaskZilla.

   - *Password*: This is the server admin password that you specified when creating your server.

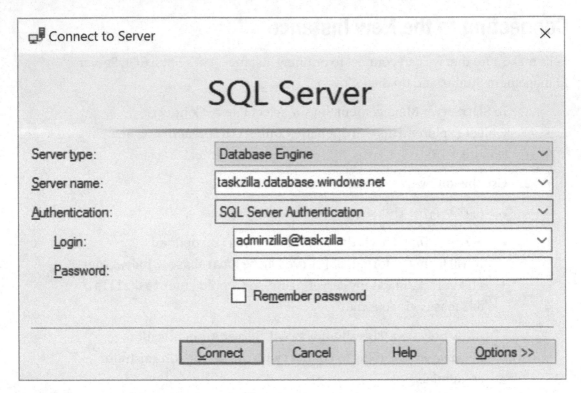

Figure 4-15. *Connecting to our new database using SQL Server Management Studio*

After entering your specific information, click Connect to create a connection.

Deploying to Azure

After connecting with our new database via SQL Server Management Studio, it's time to publish our database schema to our Azure SQL Database. We'll use Entity Framework Code First Migrations to do so.

Entity Framework Code First Migrations is a very handy tool for scripting database changes with Entity Framework. When you run the Entity Framework Code First Migrations tool, it will do the following:

1. Examine your DbContext subclass to determine your current data model.

2. Look back at your previous data model from the last time that you executed the Entity Framework Code First Migrations tool. It will then calculate what has changed.

3. Generate the database transformation code needed to bring your database schema, data, or both up to date from the last time that the Entity Framework Code First Migrations tool was run. It will also generate code to downgrade to the previous database state. You can use this downgrade code in case things go horribly wrong during your next deployment.

Let's use our TaskZilla project to walk through an example. Our goals are to enable Code First Migrations for our local database that currently contains our schema, and to initialize our Azure SQL Database instance with the necessary tables and reference data to run the TaskZilla application.

We'll start by publishing our existing database schema to our Azure SQL Database.

1. *Enable Entity Framework Code First Migrations*: Before the fun begins, we'll first need to set our project up to include Entity Framework Code First Migrations. This is done by entering a command in the Visual Studio Package Manager Console.

    a. With the TaskZilla project open in Visual Studio, go to the Tools menu option and select NuGetPackage Manager, and then Package Manager Console. This opens the Package Manager Console command prompt.

    b. Type `Enable-Migrations -ContextTypeName TaskZilla.Persistence.TaskZillaContext` at the `PM>` prompt, then press Enter. This will create a new Migrations folder in your project, along with a `Configuration.cs` file to support the use of Code First Migrations.

    The reason that we specified the `-ContextTypeName` argument is that there are actually *two* `DbContext` subclasses in this project: one for our TaskZilla database tables, and the other for the ASP.NET Identity provider. We must specify the `ContextTypeName` whenever there's more than one `DbContext` subclass in the project.

2. *Script our existing database schema*: We now need to let Code First Migrations examine our `TaskZillaContext` to understand our current data model. Code First Migrations will compare this with the previously scripted model, then calculate and script the difference between the two. Because there is no previously scripted model, Code First Migrations will script the entire database schema.

At the Package Manager Console prompt, type `Add-Migration InitialCreate`. The `InitialCreate` argument is the name applied to this new migration.

After this command finishes executing, you'll note that a new file with a name in the format of `[timestamp]_InitialCreate.cs` has been added to your project. If you open the file, you'll see that there are two methods defined, `Up()` and `Down()`. These methods contain code to modify the target database.

3. *Manually modify the generated code (if needed)*: Before executing a Code First Migration, we might need to manually tweak the generated code. You won't always need to perform this step, but it's exactly what we need to do in this case. Open the `[timetamp]_initialCreate.cs` file, and comment out the statement to create the dbo.AspNetUsers table.

This `create` statement was generated because the AspNetUsers table is part of our `TaskZillaContext`. However, we'll let the ASP. NET Identity framework handle the creation of this table, and Code First Migrations will complain if a database object already exists. You can see the complete `[timestamp]_initialCreate.cs` file with the AspNetUsers creation statement commented out in Listing 4-5.

Listing 4-5. The Generated Code First Up() and Down()Migrations

```
namespace TaskZilla.Migrations
{
    using System.Data.Entity.Migrations;

    public partial class InitialCreate : DbMigration
    {
        ///the code within the Up() method runs when we run the update-database
        ///command at the Package Manager Console prompt.
        public override void Up()
        {
            ///NOTE: We don't want our Entity Framework Code First
            ///Migration to try to create
            ///this table because it will be created when ASP.NET Identity runs
            ///for the first time.
            //CreateTable(
            //    "dbo.AspNetUsers",
            //    c => new
            //        {
            //            Id = c.String(nullable: false, maxLength: 128),
            //            Email = c.String(maxLength: 256),
            //            EmailConfirmed = c.Boolean(nullable: false),
            //            PasswordHash = c.String(),
            //            SecurityStamp = c.String(),
            //            PhoneNumber = c.String(),
            //            PhoneNumberConfirmed = c.Boolean(nullable: false),
            //            TwoFactorEnabled = c.Boolean(nullable: false),
            //            LockoutEndDateUtc = c.DateTime(),
            //            LockoutEnabled = c.Boolean(nullable: false),
            //            AccessFailedCount = c.Int(nullable: false),
            //            UserName = c.String(nullable: false, maxLength: 256),
            //        })
            //    .PrimaryKey(t => t.Id);
```

```
            CreateTable(
                "dbo.Tasks",
                c => new
                    {
                        Id = c.Int(nullable: false, identity: true),
                        Name = c.String(nullable: false, maxLength: 64),
                        Description = c.String(maxLength: 2000),
                        AssignedToUserId = c.String(nullable: false,
                        maxLength: 128),
                        PriorityId = c.Int(nullable: false),
                        EstDurationInHours = c.Decimal(precision: 18, scale: 2),
                    })
                .PrimaryKey(t => t.Id)
                .ForeignKey("dbo.Priorities", t => t.PriorityId)
                .ForeignKey("dbo.AspNetUsers", t => t.AssignedToUserId)
                .Index(t => t.AssignedToUserId)
                .Index(t => t.PriorityId);

            CreateTable(
                "dbo.Priorities",
                c => new
                    {
                        Id = c.Int(nullable: false),
                        Priority = c.String(nullable: false, maxLength: 24),
                    })
                .PrimaryKey(t => t.Id);

        }

        //this code is run if we decide that things have gone bad and
        //downgrade our
        //database to a previous version. It should be the inverse of the
        //changes
        //that are deployed in the Up() method.
```

```
    public override void Down()
    {
        DropForeignKey("dbo.Tasks", "AssignedToUserId", "dbo.AspNetUsers");
        DropForeignKey("dbo.Tasks", "PriorityId", "dbo.Priorities");
        DropIndex("dbo.Tasks", new[] { "PriorityId" });
        DropIndex("dbo.Tasks", new[] { "AssignedToUserId" });
        DropTable("dbo.Priorities");
        DropTable("dbo.Tasks");
        DropTable("dbo.AspNetUsers");
    }
  }
}
```

4. *Update our database connection string*: When we apply a
   Code First Migration, it will execute against the database
   specified in our DBContext subclass's database connection
   string. Therefore, we need to open the web.config file and
   update the TaskZillaContext and DefaultConnection
   node's connectionString property, which is located in the
   section.

   You can find your database's connection string by clicking the
   Show Database Connection Strings link in the Overview blade in
   the Azure Portal (Figure 4-16).

Figure 4-16. *You can find your database's connection string by clicking the Show Database Connection Strings link in the Overview blade in the Azure Portal*

5. *Add reference data to the Code First Migration*: Our Priorities table has priority records defined for Low, Medium, and High priorities. We want to push these reference records as part of our migration. To do so, open the Configuration.cs file in the Migrations folder and update the Seed method to match Listing 4-6.

Listing 4-6. The Configuration.cs File's Update Seed Method

```
protected override void Seed(TaskZilla.Persistence.TaskZillaContext context)
{
    context.Priorities.AddOrUpdate(
        new Persistence.Priority { Id = 1, Priority1 = "Low" },
        new Persistence.Priority { Id = 2, Priority1 = "Medium" },
        new Persistence.Priority { Id = 3, Priority1 = "High" }
    );
}
```

6. *Run TaskZilla to create the ASP.NET Identity tables*: Now that our web.config's DefaultConnection and TaskZillaContext's connection strings point to our new Azure SQL Database database, run the TaskZilla app locally from Visual Studio. This will create the ASP.NET Identity tables within our Azure SQL Database. You can see these tables as soon as TaskZilla launches (Figure 4-17). If your project isn't using ASP.NET Identity, you can skip this step.

Figure 4-17. *After running TaskZilla, you'll see that the ASP.NET Identity tables have been created*

7. *Perform the migration*: Now it's time to actually run the Entity Framework Code First Migration. At the Package Manager Console prompt, type Update-Database and press Enter. After the command executes, you'll see that the Tasks and Priorities tables have been successfully created in our Azure SQL Database TaskZilla database.

If you look at the tables in the TaskZilla database on Azure, you'll see a table called _MigrationHistory. This table is created by Entity Framework Code First Migrations. It tracks what migrations have been deployed to the database. This means that if you've defined five separate migrations locally, but only two have been deployed to the target database, the next time you run the Update-Database command against the target database, the remaining three migrations will be deployed in order.

Going forward, we'd like to use Code First Migrations to manage both our local development database schema and our Azure SQL Database instance. Therefore, we need to initialize our local database to use Code First Migrations.

We first need to change our `DefaultConnection` and `TaskZillaContext` connection strings in `web.config` to point to our local database. If we run the `Update-Database` command, though, Code First Migrations will try to create all database tables in our local database, which already exist.

To solve this problem, we can comment out all code in the `Up()` method of our `[timestamp]_InitialCreate.cs` class, then run the `Update-Database` command. This will create the __MigrationHistory table in our local TaskZilla database, and Code First Migrations will consider the `InitialCreate` migration to have been successfully deployed.

Publishing Schema Changes

We've successfully published our TaskZilla database to Azure using Entity Framework Code First Migrations, which we can also use to modify our database schema after the initial publish.

Let's assume that we need to add an AdditionalComments field to our Tasks table. To make this happen, we'll update our Tasks model, create a new migration, and push the migration to our target database. To do so, follow these steps:

1. *Update our Entity Framework model*: Open the `Task.cs` class in the Persistence folder. This is our Entity Framework model for the Tasks table. Add an `AdditionalComments` property by inserting the code in Listing 4-7 into the `Task` class.

Listing 4-7. The New AdditionalComments Property Definition in the Task Class

```
[StringLength(256)]
public string AdditionalComments { get; set; }
```

2. *Generate a new Entity Framework migration*: Now we need to direct the Code First Migration tool to examine our current Entity Framework model, compare it to the model from our last Entity Framework migration, and generate code to script the changes. At the Package Manager Console prompt, type `Add-Migration AdditionalComments` and press Enter.

When the command finishes executing, you'll notice a new file with a file name of [timestamp]_AdditionalComments.cs in your Migrations folder. Open this file, and you'll see that the Up() and Down() methods contain code to add and remove the AdditionalComments field (Listing 4-8).

Listing 4-8. Entity Framework Has Scripted the Creation of the Tasks. AdditionalComments Field in the Up()Method

```
namespace TaskZilla.Migrations
{
    using System;
    using System.Data.Entity.Migrations;

    public partial class AdditionalComments : DbMigration
    {
        public override void Up()
        {
            AddColumn("dbo.Tasks", "AdditionalComments",
            c => c.String(maxLength: 256));
        }

        public override void Down()
        {
            DropColumn("dbo.Tasks", "AdditionalComments");
        }
    }
}
```

3. *Publish the migration*: At the Package Manager Console command prompt, type Update-Database. When the command finishes executing, browse to your TaskZilla database and see that the AdditionalComments field has been added to the Tasks table (Figure 4-18). You'll need to make sure that you change your TaskZillaContext database connection string in the web.config file to point to your local database as well, then rerun the Update-Database command.

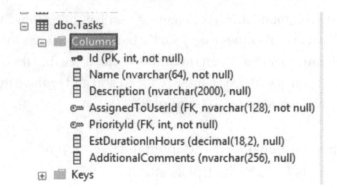

Figure 4-18. *The AdditionalComments column has been added successfully*

Rolling Back Schema Changes

You might push a new version of your web application to production and find that there are serious problems and you need to roll back to the previous version. Rolling back an Entity Framework Code First Migration is easy to do. You can use the command `Update-Database -TargetMigration [Name of Migration to roll back to]`. In our example, if we wanted to roll back to our initial publish and undo the creation of the AdditionalComments field, we would use the command `Update-Database -TargetMigration InitialCreate`.

I highly recommend testing both publish and rollback migrations in a staging environment before deploying a new version to production. Your day will go from bad to worse if you attempt to roll back a new version in your production environment, only to find out that there are problems with the rollback.

Backup and Restore

Backups and restores are an area where Azure really shines. To configure backups for your Azure SQL Database instance, you'll need to perform the following steps:

1.   Do nothing.

That's right: There's nothing for you to do. When a new database is provisioned, Azure automatically configures backups for you. Azure takes a full backup each week, differential backups each hour, and transaction log backups at five- to ten-minute intervals. The backups are stored for seven days for a Basic tier database, and 35 days for all databases in the Standard and Premium tiers.

Azure's backup strategy gives us the option for a point-in-time restore. You have the ability to restore a backup to:

- A point in time on the same logical server as the original database. This is great for those scenarios where users corrupt their own data, or if a developer forgets a "where" clause on a delete statement.

- The deletion time for a database that was deleted.

To restore a backup, do the following:

1. In the Azure Portal, navigate to your SQL Database's Overview blade. Click the Restore link (Figure 4-19).

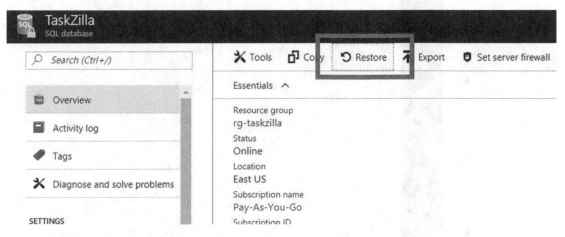

Figure 4-19. *The Restore link used to restore a backup*

2. The Restore blade is shown in Figure 4-20. On the Restore blade, you'll need to do the following:

   a. Enter a name for the new database that will be created from the restored backup.

   b. Next, enter the point in time you'd like to restore this database to. Pay special attention that the time is designated in UTC.

   c. Finally, specify the pricing tier for the restored database, or elect to place the database in an elastic pool.

   d. Click OK.

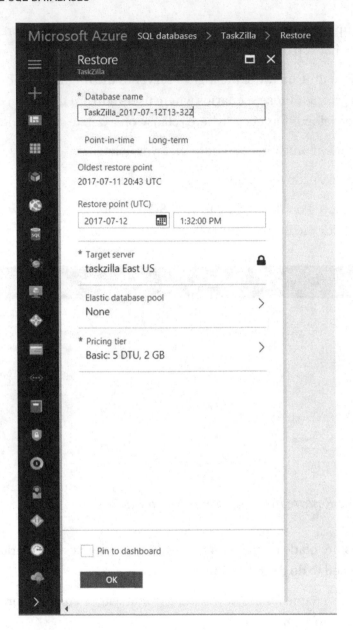

Figure 4-20. *The Restore blade allows you to restore a database to a point in time*

The new database will be created from the backup that covers the point in time that you specified.

Setting Up Alerts

If your SQL Database is experiencing problems, there are two ways for you to find out that something is going wrong:

1. Set up alerts, and receive e-mail notifications from Azure when the thresholds that you define are exceeded in a specified time period.

2. Hear about a problem from your customers.

Trust me, the first option is better.

You can set up alert rules to notify you on a wide range of metrics, such as DTU percentage, absolute DTU usage, CPU percentage, the number of deadlocks in a time period, the number of active connections to your database, and the list goes on and on.

To illustrate how configuring alerts works, let's create an alert rule that will send us an e-mail when DTUs for the TaskZilla database exceed 80% of the maximum DTUs available.

1. In the Azure Portal, navigate to the TaskZilla database management blade. On the left menu, click Alert Rules, located under the Monitoring heading. This will take you to the Alert Rules blade, which will list all of the alert rules that you've defined thus far. You'll need to click Add Alert to create a new rule.

2. On the Add an Alert Rule blade (Figure 4-21), you'll need to provide settings to configure the new alert. For our example, these are as follows:

    *   *Resource*: This allows you to select the database to monitor. Choose your TaskZilla database.

    *   *Name*: This is a friendly name for the new alert rule. It will appear on the Alert Rules blade. Name this rule DTUs.

    *   *Description*: This is a short description of the rule. Enter DTUs exceeds 80%.

- *Metric*: From this drop-down list, you can select a metric to monitor. Select DTU percentage. While you're here, expand the drop-down list to familiarize yourself with other metrics that are available for monitoring.

- *Condition*: Select Greater than.

- *Threshold*: Enter 80.

- *Period*: This is how long the metric must match the condition and threshold to trigger the alert. For our example, select Over the last 5 minutes.

- *Who to contact*: You can select the check box to e-mail owners, contributors, and readers. You can also include additional e-mails, or specify a web hook that will be called when the alert is triggered.

Click OK button to create the alert rule.

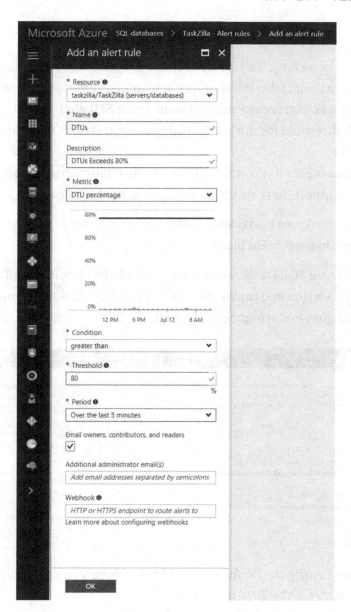

Figure 4-21. *The Add an Alert Rule blade allows us to create new alerts on a specified metric*

Scale Up

Several weeks after launching, TaskZilla has really caught on. Everyone at your company is using it to manage their tasks. While sitting at your desk enjoying a well-deserved afternoon coffee break, you receive an alert from Azure SQL that your DTUs have exceeded the 80% threshold for the last five minutes. You'll need to scale up the database to handle the load.

Fortunately, this is easy to do. Azure allows you to change instance sizes or service tiers without interruption. To scale up or scale down, do the following:

1. Log into the Azure Portal and navigate to your Azure SQL Database management blade.

2. On the Azure SQL Database management blade, click Pricing Tier (Scale DTUs) located under the Settings heading. This takes you to the Configure Performance blade (Figure 4-22).

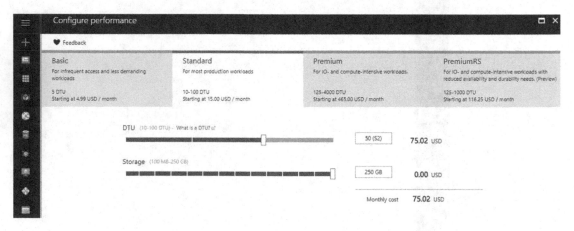

Figure 4-22. *The Configure Performance blade, where you can scale up or scale down your Azure SQL Database instance size*

3. Simply select the service tier from the tabs at the top (the tabs are labeled Basic, Standard, Premium, and PremiumRS). Within each tab, use the slider to select your desired amount of DTUs and storage. Your selection will correspond to an instance size within the tier. Based on your selection, Azure will show the service tier and estimated monthly spend. Click Apply to complete your scale up or scale down.

Remember that you're billed on an hourly basis for the number of hours that your database is provisioned. If you scale up or down midmonth, you'll be billed for the hours used at your original service tier, then for hours used during the remainder of the month at your new service tier.

Performance Tuning

Back in the old days (which means before Azure SQL Database), database performance tuning was a chore. It would usually start with a support ticket complaining about how an app was running slow. After some general debugging, you'd realize that there was a problem with database performance. If the culprit query wasn't immediately obvious, it was time to resort to the SQL Server Profiler to monitor usage and flag queries that took a long time to execute. Finally, you'd take a look at the naughty query's estimated execution plan to figure out where the bottleneck was and how it could be improved. At the end of the entire process, this often resulted in creating a new index.

With Azure SQL, the performance tuning process has been greatly simplified. Let's take a look at the Performance Recommendations and Query Performance Insight.

Performance Recommendations

Azure constantly monitors your app's queries and the resulting database performance. Over time, Azure will identify missing indexes and alert you that they should be added. To see all index recommendations, navigate to your Azure SQL Database management blade and click Performance Recommendations located under the Support + Troubleshooting heading. This will take you to the Performance Recommendations blade (Figure 4-23).

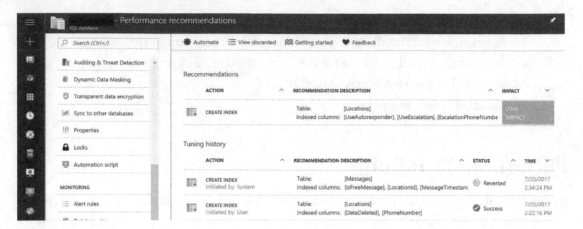

Figure 4-23. *The Performance Recommendations blade*

All recommended indexes are displayed in the Recommendations section. The Tuning History section will display all recommendations that have been applied. You'll note that in Figure 4-23, an index is listed as Reverted. If you apply a suggested index and Azure finds that it negatively affects performance, Azure will roll the index back.

Automating Performance Tuning

If you navigate to your Azure SQL Database management blade and click Automatic Tuning, you can specify whether Azure should automatically apply add and drop index recommendations (Figure 4-24). Whether you should enable automatic performance tuning is a matter of personal preference and the technology you've chosen for updating your database schema.

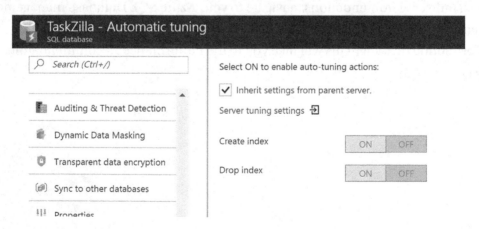

Figure 4-24. *Automatic tuning settings. You can inherit the auto tuning settings from the server, or override them at the database level*

If you are relying on a Database Project to publish changes to your database schema, you should not enable automatic performance tuning. Database Projects work by comparing your existing database schema to the defined database schema, then making changes to your database to bring it in line with the schema. If Azure automatically creates suggested indexes, and the new indexes are not present in your Database Project, your new indexes will be rolled back the next time that your Database Project is published. If you're using a Database Project, make sure that the recommended indexes get added to your database project to prevent rollback.

If you're using Entity Framework Code First Migrations, this isn't an issue. Code First Migrations don't reconcile your database schema to a defined model; it only publishes the changes that you've explicitly defined in your `DbMigration` subclass's `Up()` method. Therefore, it is safe to enable automatic performance tuning when using Entity Framework Code First Migrations.

Query Performance Insight

The Query Performance Insight blade shows you the most resource-intensive queries for a given time period. You can choose to see the most resource-intensive queries based on CPU, I/O, duration, or execution count. This is a great tool to find out what's driving your DTU consumption.

I like to check Query Performance Insight before applying Performance Recommendations to be sure that there aren't any suboptimal queries that trigger new index recommendations.

Geo-replication

When enabled, Geo-replication will asynchronously replicate transactions from your original database (called the primary) to a secondary copy. The secondary copy can be in the same region or in a different region. The secondary copy is read-only.

At any time, you can promote the secondary copy to become the primary. Once this occurs, the old primary becomes the new secondary and is also read-only.

There are several reasons we might want to enable Geo-replication and keep a secondary copy of our database, including these:

- *Disaster recovery*: For disaster recovery purposes, the secondary should live in a separate region. If the primary becomes unavailable, you can promote the secondary, then update your web application's database connection strings to point to the new primary.

- *Moving a database between regions*: If you need to migrate a web application between regions, consider enabling Geo-replication and defining your secondary database in the region to which you're migrating. Once the initial seeding is complete, Azure will asynchronously replicate transactions from your primary to your secondary, keeping the two in sync. When you are ready to complete the migration, promote your secondary to your primary.

- *Offload reporting*: If your application has DTU-intensive reporting requirements, create a secondary copy of your database to handle all reporting requests.

Let's enable Geo-replication for our TaskZilla database.

1. In the Azure Portal, navigate to your TaskZilla database management blade. Click Geo-replication menu under the Settings heading. This will take you to the Geo-replication management blade (Figure 4-25).

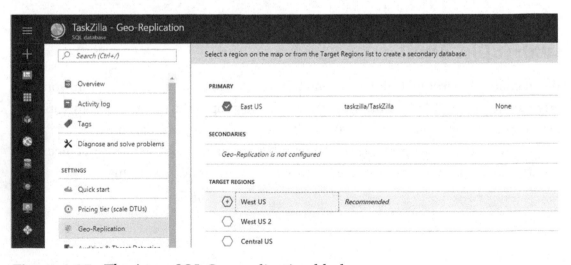

Figure 4-25. *The Azure SQL Geo-replication blade*

2. Your primary (which is your current TaskZilla database) and all
    secondary databases are listed. To add a new secondary, click a
    region in the Target Regions section. After clicking a region, you'll
    be taken to the Create Secondary blade (Figure 4-26).

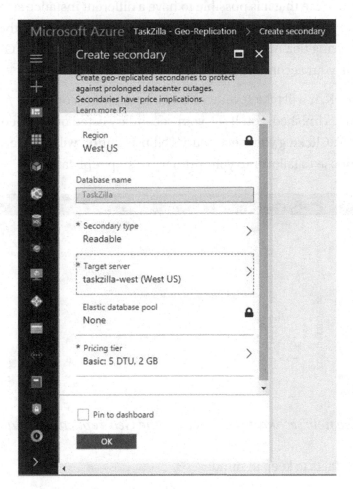

Figure 4-26. *The Create Secondary blade*

3. On the Create Secondary blade, we'll need to specify our server, indicate whether this secondary will be part of an elastic pool, and choose our pricing tier and instance size. The secondary's database name will be the same as the primary and cannot be changed. Note that it is possible to have a different instance size than the primary, but the primary and secondary must be in the same pricing tier. After configuring all required options, click OK to create your secondary database.

After clicking OK, it will take several minutes for Azure to configure your new secondary. When it's finished, you'll see your secondary listed on the Geo-replication blade (Figure 4-27). Clicking your secondary's ellipsis button will open a shortcut menu where you can choose to failover to your primary or stop replication.

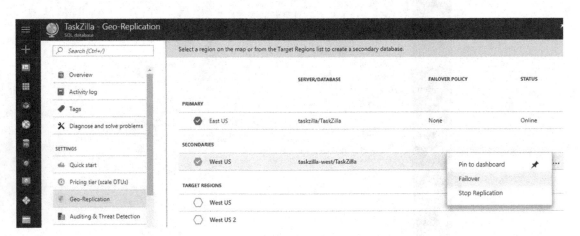

Figure 4-27. *The new secondary is listed on the Geo-replication blade*

Here are a few facts to keep in mind:

- Creating secondary replicas isn't free. Unless you add your secondary to an existing elastic pool, you'll pay for the instance size and pricing tier that you chose when setting up the secondary.

- In the event of an outage that makes your primary unavailable, you'll need to select the Failover option shown in Figure 4-27 to promote your secondary to become the primary. It's very important to realize that because your secondary database lives on another server, it will have a separate connection string. As part of the failover process, you'll need to update your web application's configuration string to point to the newly promoted primary.

- You're not restricted to a single secondary. You can have up to four secondary databases defined.

Summary

In this chapter, we introduced Azure SQL Database and discussed how to integrate it with a web application. In the next chapter, we begin exploring Azure's NoSQL offerings by diving into Azure Table Storage.

CHAPTER 5

Azure Table Storage

Azure Table Storage is a very fast, very cheap key/value storage service that can scale to hundreds of terabytes in size. It is part of the Azure Storage service, along with Azure Queues, Blobs, Files, and Disks. If you have very few keys that you will ever use in retrieving data, Table Storage might be exactly what you need.

How Table Storage Works

Azure Table Storage is a NoSQL key/value store. This means that when adding a new record to a Table Storage table, you'll specify a key. Whenever you want to retrieve a record, you pass in the key to a table and Azure Table Storage returns the record. You can think of each table in Table Storage as a giant, nearly infinitely scalable dictionary.

In Table Storage terminology, a record is called an entity. Azure stores entities in tables. An entity is simply a collection of properties, and properties are name and value pairs. Example of properties are First Name = Jim and Address = 100 Main Street. Each entity can have up to 255 properties.

Each entity in Azure Table Storage has three special properties called the partition key, the row key, and the timestamp. Entities within the same table that have the same partition keys will share the same partition, and the row key must be unique within a single partition. The partition key and row key together make up the single key that you use when looking up entities in a table. Both the partition and row keys are required to be strings. An empty string is a valid partition or row key. You get to specify which properties are used as the partition and row keys, and the choice is very important for scalability, as we'll see shortly. The timestamp is a special property that is set each time an entity is modified. You cannot update the timestamp property, as it is managed by Azure.

© Rob Reagan 2018
R. Reagan, *Web Applications on Azure*, https://doi.org/10.1007/978-1-4842-2976-7_5

If you are coming from a relational database background and haven't worked with NoSQL databases before, Azure Tables might initially seem a little strange. Although you can define multiple tables, these tables are not relational. Azure Tables does not support foreign keys or enforce relationships between tables. There are no joins, and you cannot access data within Azure Tables via SQL. In fact, a single table doesn't even have an enforced schema, meaning that you can mix entities with different property types within a single table.

Let's look at an example of three entities in an Azure Table (Table 5-1). We'll call this table Restaurants, and it will contain basic information on Taco Bell restaurants in Tennessee.

Table 5-1. *Restaurants*

Partition Key (City)	Row Key (City Business License Number)	Address	HasGorditas	Timestamp
Chattanooga	100	88 Broad Street	Yes	6/29/2016 12:04:39 AM
Chattanooga	110	1467 Market Street		8/15/2016 8:13:18 AM
Knoxville	100	41 Cumberland Blvd.	No	12/22/2016 12:10:01 PM

In this example, the first two records share a partition key of Chattanooga, meaning that they will both be stored as part of the Chattanooga partition. We can reference any of these records by querying the Restaurants table and providing the partition and row keys. The first and third records both have a row key of 100, and this is permissible because each of these records belongs to a different partition. Note that the first and third records have a property of HasGorditas, whereas the second record does not. This shows how it is possible to have different properties for entities that are stored in the same table. That might seem strange, but you will see how it can be advantageous when we discuss transactions.

Partitions

Relational databases are hard to scale because database files typically live on a single server, and every server has finite storage capacity. NoSQL databases such as Azure Tables are able to scale to hundreds of terabytes because they were designed to distribute data from a single table across many servers, and partitions are the mechanism for doing so.

All entities in a table that have the same partition key belong to the same partition. In our previous example, there are two partitions: one for Chattanooga and one for Knoxville. All data in a partition is stored on a single partition server, and one partition server may hold many different partitions.

For each partition, Azure has a scalability target of servicing 500 table operations per second. If a partition server is not experiencing heavy load, you could see higher throughput. To achieve this target, Azure might move partitions from a hot server to one that is currently receiving fewer requests.

Transaction Support and Batching

Table Storage allows you to submit up to 100 operations in a batch. Supported operations within a batch are insert, update, and delete. All entities within a batch must be part of the same partition. You cannot include a query within a batch operation, and an entity can only be modified once within a batch operation.

All operations within a batch are framed within a transaction. All operations succeed or fail together. If you require transaction support in your application, you must take this into consideration when choosing your partition keys and deciding what properties will be a part of each entity.

Types of Queries

Azure Tables only allow a single index, which is made up of the combination of the partition key and row key. This functions much like a primary key within a relational database. Table operations with a specified partition and row key are extremely speedy and allow Azure Tables to find the entity needed as fast as possible. This is called a point query.

Point queries are not the only type of query that you can perform. Other types of queries include the following:

- *Row range scan*: If you specify a partition key and a partial row key, Azure will scan the full range of possible matching entities within a single partition and return the results. The speed of this query depends on the number of records within the partition that must be scanned. Although not as performant as a point query, this is the second fastest query operation.

- *Partition range scan*: If you specify a partial partition key and an optional partial row key, you'll perform a partition range scan. Azure will scan all possible matching partitions and all possible matching rows within each partition and return the results. The speed depends on the number of partitions that must be touched, and the number of entities within each partition that must be examined. This is generally the third fastest type of query.

- *Full table scan*: This occurs if all partitions must be searched, and a subset or all entities within each partition must be examined. Performance depends on the number of partitions and entities that must be touched. This is generally the least performant type of query.

In a relational database, you can define as many secondary indexes as needed to ensure that queries can quickly find what's needed. In Azure Table Storage, though, you cannot define additional indexes within a table. This is important to understand when you're deciding if Azure Table Storage is the best fit for your project.

Working with Azure Table Storage

When choosing technologies, ease of use is extremely important. Azure Tables provide several ways to query and manipulate data.

REST API

You can call Azure Table Storage RESTful web services to perform any Table Services operation. Results are returned in JSON format or as an ATOM feed, depending on how you set the ACCEPT request header when making a request. Because the REST

API is a collection of HTTP/HTTPS endpoints, you can make use of the API with any language that is capable of making HTTP requests. This makes the REST API useful if you're programming in a language that doesn't yet have a Microsoft Azure Storage Client Library, or if you particularly enjoy tedium and pain.

Microsoft currently has libraries available for .NET, Java, Node.js, C++, Python, PHP, and Ruby. If you're using one of these languages, you should definitely use the appropriate SDK instead of the REST API.

Azure Storage Client Library

The Azure Storage Client Library provides easy-to-use methods to interact with Table Storage. You can do anything in the Client Library that you can with the REST API. The library is available via NuGet, and is also included in the Azure SDK for .NET. Even if you've installed the Azure SDK for .NET, it never hurts to check in NuGet to make sure that you have the most up-to-date version of the Storage Client Library.

Automatic retry is another compelling reason to make use of the Storage Client Library. We've discussed how Azure stores partitions on partition servers, and that there are service targets per server. It is possible that if you query a table that resides on a partition server that is experiencing a large volume of requests, your request might fail. Another possible cause of failure is querying a partition that is momentarily unavailable because it is in the process of being moved to another partition server. These issues can result in an HTTP 503 Server Busy or an HTTP 504 Timeout. Both of these failures are usually transient and short-lived. Retrying your request is usually successful.

If you're using the REST API, you can either tell users that is they are out of luck and their request failed, or you can write your own retry logic. If you're using the Azure Storage Client Library, there are several different retry policies that you can enable to automatically retry your request after failure.

As an added bonus, the Storage Client Library also supports querying Table Storage via LINQ.

Local Storage Emulator

Azure Table Storage is billed by average number of gigabytes stored per month, plus a fraction of a cent per 100,000 transactions. When developing a Table Storage solution, you can run your application locally and make use of Azure Table Storage. Unless you're dealing with hundreds of gigabytes or terabytes of data during development, the cost to use the live Azure Table Storage service is negligible. As of the time of this writing, locally redundant storage is billed at $0.07 per GB per month for the first TB of data stored. When developing locally and running against the live Azure Table Storage service, you will still have to deal with latency as data travels between your local machine and your chosen Azure datacenter.

If you don't care to incur charges during development or want to avoid network latency, you can develop using the Azure Storage Emulator. The Storage Emulator emulates Azure Blob, Queue, and Table services on your local machine. Although the Storage Emulator won't scale to the same level as the live Azure Table Storage service, it is perfectly acceptable to use in debug and testing.

The Storage Emulator is included in the Microsoft Azure SDK, and can also be installed via a separate download.

Table Design Guidelines

When designing relational databases, often little thought is given to indexing. We focus on bringing the database design to second or third normal form. Once we get there, we know that we can usually write queries to get the data that we need, and define indexes that cover our queries to ensure that we can get the data quickly. If application requirements change in the future (and they always do) and we need to add a new query that results in a large table scan, we can always define additional indexes as needed.

To design scalable solutions with Azure Table Storage, careful thought must be given to how data will be queried. The partition key and row key make up the only index at our disposal. Our goal is to choose how we split our data among tables and to choose appropriate partition and row keys for each table so that we make use of point queries as often as possible and to avoid heavy row range, partition range, and table scans.

Here is a set of design guidelines you can follow when making these decisions.

In general, choose partition keys that divide your data into smaller partitions instead of having one giant partition. This has several advantages. First, each partition has a scalability target of 500 table operations per second at the time of this writing. If you store all data on a single partition, your application could be throttled to a mere 500 table operations per second. If instead you split your data across 50 partitions, your theoretical minimum performance would be 25,000 table operations per second. Second, if you must resort to row range, partition range, or table scans, performance will be much better with smaller partitions to search and the ability to search partitions in parallel. Third, if you have large amounts of data and try to store it all on a single partition, you might be unsuccessful because your partition server's drive space has been exhausted. Microsoft has not yet published the maximum size of a single partition, but be aware that this is a possibility if you elect to use gigantic partitions.

When choosing a partition key, consider your need for transaction support. If multiple entities need to participate in a transaction to ensure all updates succeed or fail together, those entities must be stored in the same table and have the same partition key.

Carefully consider the queries that your application will execute to retrieve data and determine the keys required for those queries. If you only have a single key, use it as the partition key. If you have two keys, use one as the partition key and the other as the row key. If you have more than two keys, consider concatenating keys that will be queried together to form a compound key. For example, if you know that you'll query a person by first and last name, concatenate them together. Bill_Lumberg is a perfectly acceptable partition or row key.

Walkthrough: Restaurant Finder

Now that we've discussed theory, let's get down to practice and look at some code. To do so, we'll build an application called Restaurant Finder. The application serves an important purpose: It allows hungry developers to find a Taco Bell by a variety of search criteria.

To follow along with this example, you'll need to have installed either the Azure SDK for .NET or the Azure Storage Client Library and the Azure Storage Emulator. If you don't care to manually type the code, you can download the completed project from https://github.com/BuildingScalableWebAppsWithAzure/TacoBellFinder.git.

Restaurant Finder Requirements

The requirements for our application are listed here.

The application will have a search page. The searches that a user can perform are:

- By city, state, and restaurant ID number.

- By address, city, state, and zip code.

- By city, state, and zip code.

- By state and health rating.

- All restaurants that have Gorditas.

For any restaurant, users can update the health rating and whether or not the restaurant has Gorditas.

Users can delete a restaurant if it has been permanently closed.

Designing Our Data Storage

After looking at our requirements, the properties that we need to track for each restaurant are city and state, the restaurant ID number, street address, zip code, health rating, and whether or not the restaurant has Gorditas.

Our first step is to determine how many tables we will need in our solution. Because all data elements that we're tracking are related, let's store all of them in a single table called Restaurants.

Next, let's choose a partition key for the Restaurants table. Given the difficulty of changing partition and row keys, it's easy to panic when deciding how data will be stored in a Table Storage solution. Take a deep breath: Do the best you can on the first pass and iterate during development if necessary.

We want a partition key that will split our data up into many smaller partitions but will still allow us to execute as many point queries and potentially smaller row range scan queries as necessary given the queries that we plan to execute.

Let's examine our options. Whether a restaurant has Gorditas is a binary value, so we would have a maximum of two partitions. That would be the worst possible choice. Health rating is a poor choice because it would give us a theoretical maximum of 100 partitions and is only used in a single query. That's also a bad choice. Hopefully there are less than 100 maximum partitions based on health rating; if a county health department allows a restaurant with a health rating of 17 to stay in business, something is wrong. Restaurant ID looks interesting and uniquely identifies a single restaurant, but this would give us N partitions for N records, and Restaurant ID is only used in one query. State is used in four queries, but would give us just 50 partitions. If we concatenated City and State together, we would have many smaller partitions. This choice also restricts our queries to a row range scan on a single partition for the first three queries even if we choose our row key poorly. It also limits us to a partition scan on our fourth query. We will have to use a table scan to find restaurants that have Gorditas.

Next, let's choose our row key. Having Gorditas is not even a candidate for our row key because the combination of the partition and row keys must uniquely identify a record. The same problem exists for using health rating as our row key because it is certainly possible for two restaurants in the same city and state to have the same health rating. Zip code is not an acceptable choice for the same reason. Two restaurants having the same address within the same city seems highly unlikely, but possible. We do know that restaurant ID is guaranteed to be unique, however.

Choosing the restaurant ID as our row key will guarantee the uniqueness of an entity within a partition in our Restaurants table. It will also allow us to use a point query for our first query listed in the requirements. This means that the second and third queries will result in a row range scan across a single small partition of a few dozen entities at most. Our fourth query by state and health rating will be a partition scan across all partitions holding records for the specified state, and finding the restaurants with Gorditas will result in a full table scan. This seems like a good start, but perhaps we can find some optimizations once we get into the source.

Now that we've settled on our table design, let's write some code.

Setting Up the Project

We'll begin by creating our .NET Core project. Open Visual Studio and choose File ➤ New ➤ Project. Next, expand the Visual C# node and select .NET Core, then name your project TacoBellFinder (Figure 5-1).

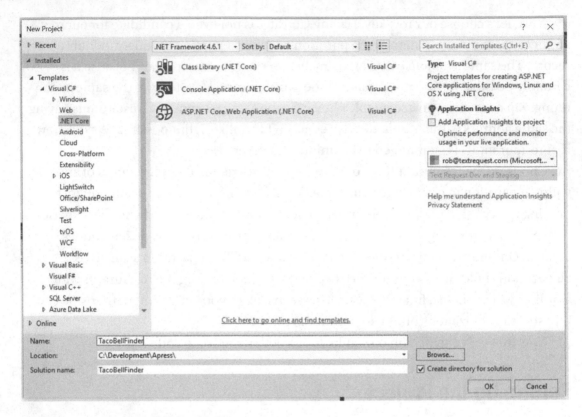

Figure 5-1. *Create the .NET Core project*

You'll then be prompted to select a template. Select Web Application and click OK.

Last but not least, let's add the necessary NuGet package. Right-click your project, select Manage NuGet Packages, select the Browse option, and search for the `WindowsAzure.Storage` package. Once you've located it, add it to your project.

Because our focus is on using Azure Table Storage, let's keep extraneous code that we'd normally write in production applications to a minimum. We won't worry about putting in place frameworks like AngularJS or React, or writing robust client-side validation.

Creating Our Restaurant Data Class

When working with relational databases, Entity Framework is kind enough to generate all data access classes for you. With Table Storage, we get to write them ourselves. The good news, though, is that the programming model is pretty simple and it's not hard to do.

For each table that we want to interact with, we need a single .NET class that derives from `Microsoft.WindowsAzure.Storage.Table.TableEntity`. The `TableEntity` class defines a few public properties that Table Storage requires, such as `PartitionKey`, `RowKey`, `Timestamp`, and `ETag`. The `ETag` property is a representation of an entity's last-modified timestamp and is used by Table Storage when updating entities. If you attempt to make updates to a table by passing a class that does not inherit from `TableEntity`, an exception will be thrown.

Make a new folder called Models in your project, then add a `Restaurants.cs` class. The complete code is listed here (Listing 5-1).

Listing 5-1. Restaurants.cs Class

```
namespace TacoBellFinder.Web.Models
{
    /// <summary>
    /// This class holds information about a single Taco Bell restaurant.
    /// Note that it
    /// inherits from TableEntity. All entities in a table that are manipulated
    /// through the Azure Table Storage SDK must inherit from TableEntity.
    /// </summary>
    public class Restaurant : TableEntity
    {
        public Restaurant()
        { }

        /// <summary>
        /// Constructor.
        /// </summary>
        /// <param name="city">The city where the restaurant is located. This will
        /// be half  of the partition key.</param>
        /// <param name="state">The state where the restaurant is located. This will
        /// be other half of the partition key.</param>
        /// <param name="restaurantNumber">The unique restaurant Id for this
        /// Taco Bell.
```

```
/// This will become the row key.</param>
public Restaurant(string city, string state, string restaurantId)
{
    string pKey = state + "_" + city;
    pKey = pKey.ToLower();
    this.PartitionKey = pKey;
    this.RowKey = restaurantId;
    this.City = city;
    this.State = state;
    this.RestaurantId = restaurantId;
}

/// <summary>
/// This is a convenience method so that we can initialize a
/// Restaurant record
/// in one line of code.
/// </summary>
public Restaurant(string city, string state, string restaurantId,
    string address, string zipCode, int healthRating, bool hasGorditas)
        : this(city, state, restaurantId)
{
    this.Address = address;
    this.Zipcode = zipCode;
    this.HealthRating = healthRating;
    this.HasGorditas = hasGorditas;
}

//Now we can define other properties that are not the row or
//partition key.
public string Address { get; set; }
public string Zipcode { get; set; }
public int HealthRating { get; set; }
public bool HasGorditas { get; set; }
```

```
        //We will repeat our city, state, and restaurantId properties so that
        //we do not
        //have to parse them from the row or partition keys.
          public string City { get; set; }
public string State { get; set; }
          public string RestaurantId { get; set; }
      }
}
```

Note that when we set our `PartitionKey` property, we are lowercasing the entire string value. This is because both the partition and row keys are case sensitive for comparison operations. The keys `TN_Chattanooga` and `tn_chattanooga` will refer to different entities. We are not lowercasing our `RowKey` property only because all restaurant ID numbers are always numeric.

The Data Service Class

We will use the Azure Storage Client Library to create our Restaurants table and populate, read, update, and delete its data. Let's wrap all calls to the Storage Client Library in a `RestaurantService` class. We'll then use .NET Core's dependency injection to inject an instance of `RestaurantService` into controllers that need it.

Because we're going to be using dependency injection, we'll need to first define an interface called `IRestaurantService.cs`. Create a new folder in the project called Services and add the interface. We'll start by defining a method for populating our demonstration data (Listing 5-2).

Listing 5-2. Populating Data

```
public interface IRestaurantService
{
    Task<bool> InitializeData();
}
```

The `InitializeData` method will connect to our Table Storage, check to see if the Restaurants table exists, and create it if it doesn't. It will then load all of our data for this example.

Let's create our `RestaurantService` class that implements the `IRestaurantService` interface. Right-click the Services folder that you just created and add the class. The code is provided in Listing 5-3.

Listing 5-3.   Create RestaurantService Class

```
using System;
using System.Collections.Generic;
using TacoBellFinder.Web.Models;
using Microsoft.Extensions.Options;
using Microsoft.WindowsAzure.Storage.Table;
using Microsoft.WindowsAzure.Storage;
using System.Threading.Tasks;

namespace TacoBellFinder.Web.Services
{
    public class RestaurantService : IRestaurantService
    {
        private AzureStorageConfig _config;

        /// <summary>
        /// Constructor. Our configuration file containing our account name
        /// and storage key
        /// are injected in.
        /// </summary>
        public RestaurantService(IOptions<AzureStorageConfig> config)
        {
            _config = config.Value;
        }
        /// <summary>
        /// Inserts or replaces all of our initial data for this project.
        /// </summary>
        /// <returns></returns>
        public async Task<bool> InitializeData()
        {
            CloudTable restaurantsTable = await GetRestaurantsTable();
```

```
//now, let's refresh our data using insert or replace. We'll frame
//all of
//our operations for a single partition together in a batch.
//This will give us transaction support, and will ensure that
//we're only
//charged for one storage operation per batch.

TableBatchOperation chattanoogaBatchOp = new
TableBatchOperation();
Restaurant chattanooga1 = new Restaurant("Chattanooga", "TN", "00001",
    "9918 Pennywood Lane", "37363", 98, true);
Restaurant chattanooga2 = new Restaurant("Chattanooga", "TN", "00002",
    "837 Stellar View", "37405", 100, true);
Restaurant chattanooga3 = new Restaurant("Chattanooga", "TN", "00019",
    "1467 Market Street", "37409", 97, false);
chattanoogaBatchOp.InsertOrReplace(chattanooga1);
chattanoogaBatchOp.InsertOrReplace(chattanooga2);
chattanoogaBatchOp.InsertOrReplace(chattanooga3);
await restaurantsTable.ExecuteBatchAsync(chattanoogaBatchOp);

TableBatchOperation knoxvilleBatchOp = new TableBatchOperation();
Restaurant knoxville1 = new Restaurant("Knoxville", "TN", "00119",
    "27 Cumberland Blvd", "37996", 88, true);
Restaurant knoxville2 = new Restaurant("Knoxville", "TN", "00128",
    "987 Scenic Highway", "37994", 88, false);
knoxvilleBatchOp.InsertOrReplace(knoxville1);
knoxvilleBatchOp.InsertOrReplace(knoxville2);
await restaurantsTable.ExecuteBatchAsync(knoxvilleBatchOp);

TableBatchOperation charlestonBatchOp = new TableBatchOperation();
Restaurant charleston1 = new Restaurant("Charleston", "TN", "02006",
    "100 Elm Street", "37310", 95, true);
```

153

```
Restaurant charleston2 = new Restaurant("Charleston", "TN", "02298",
    "15010 NE 36th Street", "37996", 97, false);
charlestonBatchOp.InsertOrReplace(charleston1);
charlestonBatchOp.InsertOrReplace(charleston2);
await restaurantsTable.ExecuteBatchAsync(charlestonBatchOp);

//let's throw in one Taco Bell outside of Tennessee so that we can
//verify a
//partition range scan is returning the correct results.
Restaurant birmingham = new Restaurant("Birmigham", "AL", "92763",
    "839 Sherman Oaks Drive", "35235", 70, true);
TableOperation insertBirminghamOp = TableOperation.
InsertOrReplace(birmingham);
await restaurantsTable.ExecuteAsync(insertBirminghamOp);

    return true;
}

/// <summary>
/// Returns a reference to the Restaurants table. Will create the table
///if the Restaurants table doesn't exist within the storage account.
 /// </summary>
 /// <returns></returns>
 private async Task<CloudTable> GetRestaurantsTable()
 {
    CloudStorageAccount storageAccount = GetCloudStorageAccount();
    CloudTableClient tableClient = storageAccount.
    CreateCloudTableClient();
    CloudTable restaurantsTable = tableClient.GetTableReference
    ("Restaurants");
    await restaurantsTable.CreateIfNotExistsAsync();
    return restaurantsTable;
}
```

```
/// <summary>
/// Attempts to connect to the Cloud Storage Account defined by the
/// storage account connection string specified in appsettings.json.
/// </summary>
/// <returns>A CloudStorageAccount instance if the connection is
/// successful. Otherwise throws an exception.</returns>
private CloudStorageAccount GetCloudStorageAccount()
{
    CloudStorageAccount storageAccount = null;
    if (!CloudStorageAccount.TryParse(_config.
    StorageConnectionString,
        out storageAccount))
    {
        throw new Exception("Could not connect to the cloud storage
        account.
            Please check the storage connection string.");
    }
    return storageAccount;
}
    }
}
```

Methods in `RestaurantService` that make calls to the Azure Storage Client are all marked as async and return a `Task<TResult>`. Note that if you return a `Task` instead of a `Task<TResult>` and an exception is thrown, the exception will be swallowed and will not appear in the stack trace. That's why we're returning `Task<bool>` instead of `Task` for several of these methods.

Also, note that if you fail to make use of async/await when making a call to Azure Storage, the thread will block and wait until the call returns. With a few thousand concurrent requests, this can lead to thread exhaustion and requests stacking up in your server's HTTP Request queue. That unfortunate situation will result in longer and longer wait times and eventually HTTP timeouts. Please make sure that you use async/await.

You will also notice that connecting to our `CloudStorageAccount` requires a connection string, which we are passing into the `RestaurantService` constructor within an `IOptions<AzureStorageConfig>` instance. The connection string contains your storage account name and key.

Finally, take a look at how each of our inserts is contained within a `TableBatchOperation` instance. Storage operations within a `TableBatchOperation` must all belong to the same partition and will succeed or fail together. This is the only mechanism for transaction support within Azure Table Storage. Each `TableBatchOperation` can contain up to 100 operations. As an added bonus, we are only billed one storage transaction per `TableBatchOperation`.

Project Settings

In .NET Core, Microsoft recommends creating a separate section per service within the `appsettings.json` file. Our `appsettings.json` file is shown in Listing 5-4.

Listing 5-4. Appsettings.json File

```json
{
    "Logging": {
        "IncludeScopes": false,
        "LogLevel": {
            "Default": "Debug",
            "System": "Information",
            "Microsoft": "Information"
        }
    },
    "AzureStorageConfig": {
      "StorageConnectionString": "UseDevelopmentStorage=true"
    }
}
```

We've defined a new section called `AzureStorageConfig`, and added a single key/value for our `StorageConnectionString`. Next, we need a way for our dependency injection system to read the `StorageConnectionString` and pass it into our `RestaurantService` class. To do so, we'll add the following `AzureStorageConfig` class to our Models folder (Listing 5-5).

Listing 5-5. Add AzureStorageConfig Class

```
namespace TacoBellFinder.Web.Models
{
    public class AzureStorageConfig
    {
        public string StorageConnectionString { get; set; }
    }
}
```

Next, let's wire up our dependency injection that will read and populate our AzureStorageConfig class and inject our RestaurantService class where it's needed.

Dependency Injection

To configure dependency injection, open the startup.cs file and jump to the Configure method. Change the code in the Configure method to match the code in Listing 5-6.

Listing 5-6. Configure Dependency Injection

```
// This method gets called by the runtime. Use this method to add
// services to the container.
public void ConfigureServices(IServiceCollection services)
{
    // Add framework services.
    services.AddMvc();

    // Add these services for TacoBellFinder.
    services.Configure<AzureStorageConfig>(Configuration.GetSection(
        "AzureStorageConfig"));
    services.AddTransient<IRestaurantService, RestaurantService>();
}
```

That's all there is to it. The IServiceCollection.Configure<TResult> method will read and populate the specified section of appsettings.json and make the resulting instance of type TResult available to inject into services that need it for configuration. IServiceCollection.AddTransient adds services that you define to the dependency injection container.

157

Loading Demo Data with the RestaurantData Controller

We've written our `RestaurantService.Initialize` method that will connect to the Azure Storage account specified in the `appsettings.json` file, but we've yet to decide how we will call this method. Let's add a `Controller` subclass to our `Controllers` folder. To do so, right-click the Controllers folder, select Add, and then select New Item. In the Add New Item dialog box, select the Web API Controller Class, name it `RestaurantDataController.cs`, and click Add.

Note   In ASP.NET Core, the MVC Controller Class and Web API Controller Class templates both inherit from `Microsoft.AspNetCore.MVC.Controller`. The only difference between the two options is the "using" statements and example methods that are generated. The class created by either template can be used for both WebAPI web service calls and for processing MVC requests.

The `RestaurantDataController` will have a single method called `Initialize`. This method will be called by an AJAX HTTP Post web service call, and will call our `RestaurantService`'s `InitializeData` method. The code for `RestaurantDataController.cs` is shown in Listing 5-7.

Listing 5-7. RestaurantDataController.cs

```
using Microsoft.AspNetCore.Mvc;
using TacoBellFinder.Web.Services;

namespace TacoBellFinder.Web.Controllers
{
    [Route("api/[controller]")]
    public class RestaurantDataController : Controller
    {
        private IRestaurantService _restaurantService;

        /// <summary>
        /// Dependency injection will inject the RestaurantService instance
        /// into our constructor.
        /// </summary>
```

```csharp
    public RestaurantDataController(IRestaurantService restaurantService)
    {
        _restaurantService = restaurantService;
    }

    /// <summary>
    /// When called, this method will set up our test data for the project.
    /// It will do the following:
    /// 1. Ensure that our table Restaurants is created.
    /// 2. Delete all entities in the Restaurants table.
    /// 3. Insert our handful of test records that we're using for
    /// illustration purposes.
    /// </summary>
    [HttpPost("initialize")]
    public async void Initialize()
    {
        await _restaurantService.InitializeData();
    }
}
}
```

We could call this web service endpoint to initialize our Restaurants table and populate our demo data from an HTTP request generating tool such as Postman or Fiddler4, but let's create a simple page with a single button that will allow us to do so from within the web application. To set up this page, we'll need to add the following method to our HomeController.cs class (Listing 5-8).

Listing 5-8. HomeController.cs Class

```csharp
[HttpGet("initialize-data")]
public IActionResult InitializeData()
{
    return View();
}
```

Now we're ready to create our View. Right-click on the Views/Home folder and select Add ➤ New Item. In the Add New Item dialog box, select MVC View Page and name it `InitializeData.cshtml`. The source for all Views in this project is found in the Git repo listed at the beginning of this section; adding the source for every view would make this book a bit too hefty. Figure 5-2 displays a screenshot of the resulting page. Note that you'll also need to swap out the contents of `Views/Shared/_Layout.cshtml`, which will contain our menu, stylesheet references, and JavaScript frameworks.

Figure 5-2. *Our InitializeData.cshtml view*

We're almost ready to click Populate. First, though, a word about where our table will actually live.

When developing an Azure Table Storage solution, you can either provision an Azure Storage service within an Azure datacenter and program directly against the live service, or you can install and use the Azure Storage Emulator on your local machine. The advantages of using the emulator are that there is zero network latency and it's totally free. If you develop against the live Azure Storage service, you will incur a charge and have to wait for the round trip from your local machine's development environment to the Azure datacenter. I personally prefer developing using the emulator, then deploying to staging and production environments that use the live Azure Storage service when I'm ready to test and publish.

Switching between the Azure Storage Emulator and the live version of the service is simple: You just swap out the `StorageConnectionString` property in the `appsettings.json` file. To use development storage, make sure that you've installed and started the Azure Storage Emulator, and set your `StorageConnectionString` to `"UseDevelopmentStorage=true"`.

The Azure Storage Emulator is included in the Azure SDK, and can also be downloaded separately from `https://azure.microsoft.com/en-us/downloads/`.

Now we're ready to create our first Azure Storage table and populate it with data. Run the application, navigate to the URL `http://localhost:[your_port]/initialize-data`, and then click Populate. If all went well, you should see a message below the Populate button that reads "The data was successfully loaded."

That was a bit anticlimactic. This application is asking you to take it on faith that it actually created a Restaurants table in your storage account and filled it with data. How can you know for sure? To verify that the application worked as it was supposed to, let's fire up Azure Storage Explorer.

Azure Storage Explorer

Azure Storage Explorer is a handy Windows application that you can use to inspect and manage the contents of an Azure Storage account that you have permissions to access. It lets us inspect the contents of tables; create and execute queries; add, edit, and delete data; and even import and export from a table in comma-separated value (CSV) format. You definitely need this tool, and it's totally free. You can download the installer for the latest version at `http://storageexplorer.com/`.

Once you've installed Storage Explorer, fire it up. A tree view on the left side of the application contains a list of all Azure Storage accounts you've added. By default, it includes a (Development) account for the local emulator. Drill down in the (Development) account to the Tables node, and you'll see the single Restaurants table (Figure 5-3). There should be a total of eight records.

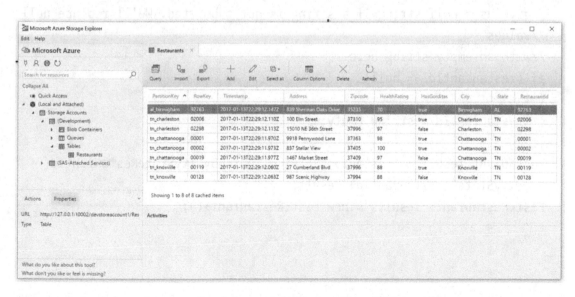

Figure 5-3. *Azure Storage Explorer, and all records within our Restaurants table*

We've now successfully created our Restaurants table and loaded demo data. Let's talk about the different ways we can query and retrieve it.

Point Queries

Point queries are queries that specify an exact partition key and row key. These types of queries will return a single record if a match is found. It is by far the fastest query to execute. When designing your tables, you should strive to make as many queries as possible run as point queries. In our example, we've chosen a partition key made up of the city and state, and a row key of the unique restaurant ID.

You'll need to modify the code for the View/Home/Index.cshtml view. Next, we'll add the method given in Listing 5-9 to HomeController.cs.

Listing 5-9. Modify HomeController.cs

```
[HttpGet]
public IActionResult SearchByCityStateRestaurantId(string cityState, string
restaurantId)
{
    //In table storage, an empty row or partition key is valid, but not a null.
    //Our MVC model binder will
    //give us a null string if a string is not submitted. We'll replace null
    //values
    //with an empty string here.
    if (restaurantId == null)
    {
        restaurantId = string.Empty;
    }
    Restaurant result = _restaurantService.SearchByCityStateRestaurantId(
        cityState, restaurantId).Result;
    List<Restaurant> results = new List<Restaurant>();
```

```
    if (result != null)
    {
        results.Add(result);
    }

    return View("Index", results);
}
```

Because all of our other search methods will return a List<Restaurant>, we're using List<Restaurant> as our ViewModel.

Now, let's add our SearchByCityStateRestaurantId to our IRestaurantService interface. This new method signature is:

```
Task<Restaurant> SearchByCityStateRestaurantId(string cityState, string
restaurantId);
```

Finally, you'll need to add the code shown in Listing 5-10 to RestaurantService.cs.

Listing 5-10. Add to Restaurant.cs

```
/// <summary>
/// This is a point query that will return the single restaurant identified by
/// the partition key cityState and
/// the row key restaurantId.
/// </summary>
public async Task<Restaurant> SearchByCityStateRestaurantId(string
cityState,
    string restaurantId)
{
    CloudTable restaurantsTable = await GetRestaurantsTable();
    TableOperation query = TableOperation.Retrieve<Restaurant>(cityState,
    restaurantId);
    TableResult retrievedResult = await restaurantsTable.
    ExecuteAsync(query);
```

```
if (retrievedResult != null)
{
    return (Restaurant)retrievedResult.Result;
}
else
{
    return null;
}
}
```

When we run our application with the updated View for Views/Home/Index.cshtml, we'll see the screen shown in Figure 5-4.

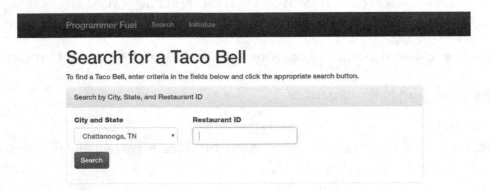

Figure 5-4. *Execute a point query by searching for a restaurant by city, state, and restaurant ID*

Executing the query for Chattanooga, TN and a restaurant ID of 00001 gives us the results in Figure 5-5.

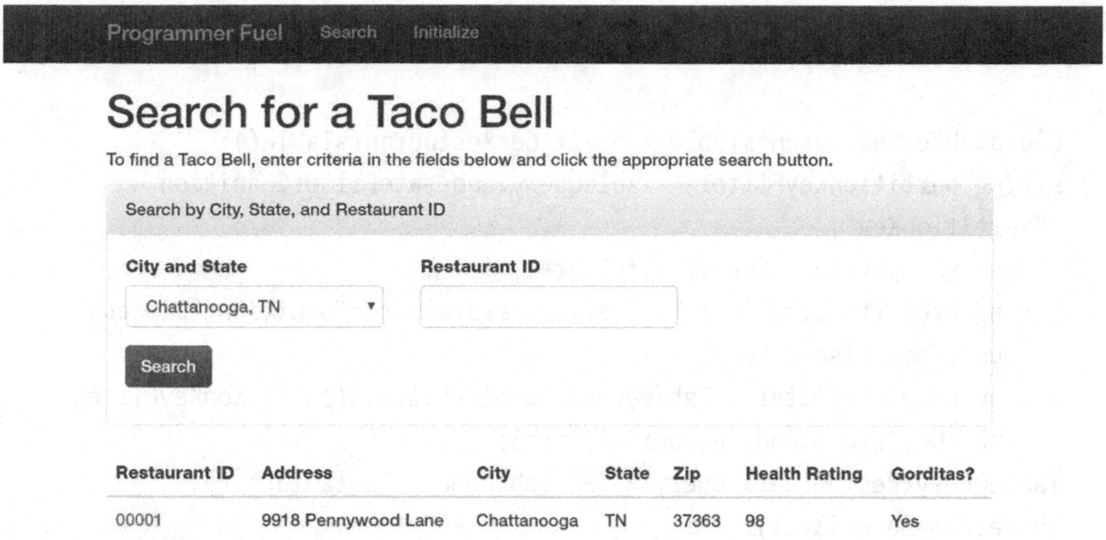

Programmer Fuel
Search
Initialize
Search for a Taco Bell
To find a Taco Bell, enter criteria in the fields below and click the appropriate search button.
Search by City, State, and Restaurant ID
City and State
Restaurant ID
Chattanooga, TN
Search
Restaurant ID Address City State Zip Health Rating Gorditas?
00001 9918 Pennywood Lane Chattanooga TN 37363 98 Yes

Figure 5-5. *The single result for our point query*

Row Range Scan Queries

Next, we'll query by city, state, and zip. The city and state will limit our search to a single partition, and we will have to look through a range of entities within that partition to find the restaurant records with a matching zip.

Add the following line of code to the `IRestaurantService` interface:

```
Task<List<Restaurant>> SearchByCityStateAndZip(string cityState, string zip);
```

Next, let's add the corresponding method shown in Listing 5-11 to execute our row range scan query to `RestaurantService.cs`.

Listing 5-11. Execute Row Range Scan Query to RestaurantService.cs

```
/// <summary>
/// Searches by a city, state, and zip. This will result in a row range scan
/// where we look at all potentially matching entities within a single partition.
/// Note that we are using a continuation token.
/// While it is extremely unlikely that there are more than a thousand restaurants
/// in a single zip code, it doesn't hurt to be prepare for the unexpected.
/// </summary>
```

```
public async Task<List<Restaurant>> SearchByCityStateAndZip(string
cityState, string zip)
{
    CloudTable restaurantsTable = await GetRestaurantsTable();
    string partitionKeyFilter = TableQuery.GenerateFilterCondition
    ("PartitionKey",
        QueryComparisons.Equal, cityState);
    string propertyFilter = TableQuery.GenerateFilterCondition("Zipcode",
        QueryComparisons.Equal, zip);
    string completeFilter = TableQuery.CombineFilters(partitionKeyFilter,
        TableOperators.And, propertyFilter);
    TableQuery<Restaurant> query = new TableQuery<Restaurant>().
    Where(completeFilter);
    List<Restaurant> restaurantsInZipCode = new List<Restaurant>();

    TableContinuationToken token = null;
    do
    {
        TableQuerySegment<Restaurant> results =
            await restaurantsTable.ExecuteQuerySegmentedAsync(query, token);
        token = results.ContinuationToken;

        foreach (Restaurant r in results.Results)
        {
            restaurantsInZipCode.Add(r);
        }
    } while (token != null);
    return restaurantsInZipCode;
}
```

Azure Table Storage limits the number of entities returned in a single query operation to 1,000. If there are more than 1,000 entities that match a query, Azure will issue a continuation token along with the results. You can then use the supplied continuation token to query for the next set of results. Azure will keep issuing continuation tokens until you reach the last set of 1,000 or fewer records.

I recommend placing continuation token logic in your apps even if you think that a particular query will never return more than 1,000 entities. Programs tend to do unexplained things, especially at 3:15 a.m. when it's your turn to be on call for support. Code defensively and avoid receiving those late-night support requests.

Next, add the code shown in Listing 5-12 to the HomeController class.

Listing 5-12. Add to HomeController Class

```
/// <summary>
/// Retrieves all restaurants in a given city, state, and zip. This will
/// execute a row range scan query against a single partition for matching
    records.
/// </summary>
[HttpGet]
public IActionResult SearchByCityStateZip(string cityState, string address,
    string zipCode)
{
    if (address == null) { address = string.Empty; }
    if (zipCode == null) { zipCode = string.Empty; }

    List<Restaurant> results = _restaurantService.SearchByCityStateAndZip
    (cityState,
        zipCode).Result;

    return View("Index", results);
}
```

Now we're able to run the application and search for restaurants in Chattanooga, TN in zip code 37363. The results are displayed in Figure 5-6.

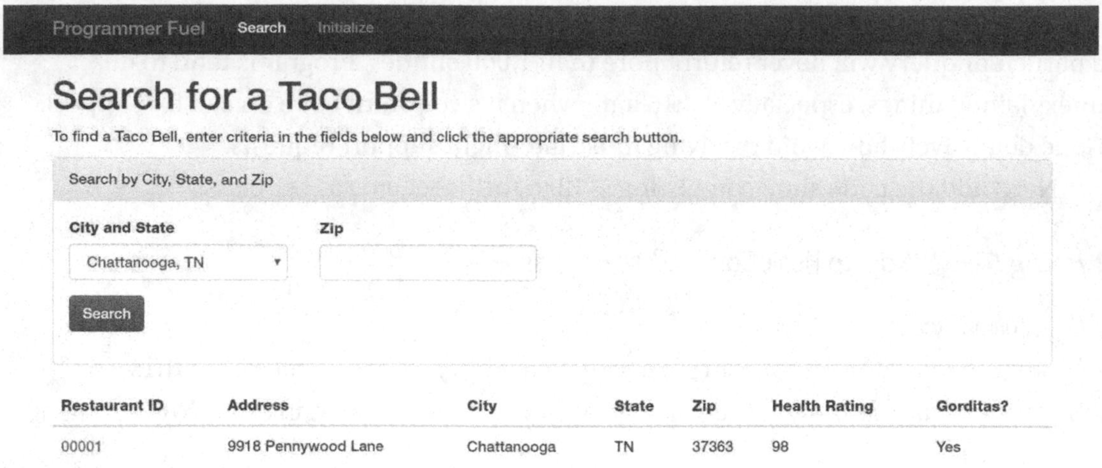

Figure 5-6. *Searching by city, state, and zip code*

Partition Range Scan Queries

A partition range scan query will examine a range of partitions that match a partial partition key and a range of rows within each partition that could match the row key. To illustrate this query, we'll search for all restaurants in a state that have a health rating greater than or equal to a specified value.

First, add the method signature to our IRestaurantService interface:

```
Task<List<Restaurant>> SearchByStateAndMinimumHealthRating(string state,
int healthRating);
```

Next, let's add the code in Listing 5-13 to our RestaurantService class. This code will perform the actual partition range scan query.

Listing 5-13. Perform Partition Range Scan Query

```
/// <summary>
/// Finds all restaurants in the given state that have the minimum specified
/// health rating. This will require
/// a partition range scan where we will find all partitions that match the
/// supplied state.
/// </summary>
```

```
public async Task<List<Restaurant>> SearchByStateAndMinimumHealthRating
(string state,
    int healthRating)
{
    //we are building our partition key with [state]_[city]. To do a partition
    ///range scan, we'll have to combine >= and <= operators, and append the
    ///underscore character and a letter to our state. This is because
    //Azure uses lexicographical order of strings when doing comparisons.
    //We do not need to worry with upper and lower case comparison issues because
    //all of our city and state values are lowercased before insert.
    CloudTable restaurantsTable = await GetRestaurantsTable();
    string partitionKeyGreaterThanOrEqualFilter =
        TableQuery.GenerateFilterCondition("PartitionKey",
        QueryComparisons.GreaterThanOrEqual, state + "_a");
    string partitionKeyLessThanOrEqualFilter =
        TableQuery.GenerateFilterCondition("PartitionKey",
        QueryComparisons.LessThanOrEqual, state + "_z");
    string healthRatingFilter = TableQuery.GenerateFilterConditionForInt
    ("HealthRating", QueryComparisons.GreaterThanOrEqual, healthRating);
    string completeFilter =
        TableQuery.CombineFilters(partitionKeyGreaterThanOrEqualFilter,
        TableOperators.And, partitionKeyLessThanOrEqualFilter);
    completeFilter = TableQuery.CombineFilters(completeFilter,
    TableOperators.And,
        healthRatingFilter);
    TableQuery<Restaurant> query = new TableQuery<Restaurant>().
    Where(completeFilter);
    List<Restaurant> restaurantsList = new List<Restaurant>();
```

```
TableContinuationToken token = null;
do
{
    TableQuerySegment<Restaurant> results =
        await restaurantsTable.ExecuteQuerySegmentedAsync(query, token);
    token = results.ContinuationToken;

    foreach (Restaurant r in results.Results)
    {
        restaurantsList.Add(r);
    }
} while (token != null);
return restaurantsList;
}
```

Recall that our partition key is in the format of [state name]_[city name]. We'd like to scan a subset of partitions that start with the state that we are searching for, but there are no "starts with" or "contains" query operators. Fortunately, we can construct something equivalent using greater than or equal to and less than or equal to operators. To do so, we need to remember that Azure uses a lexicographical ordering for string comparison when comparing partition and row keys. By creating a filter with the conditions that the partition key >= [state name]_a and partition key <= [state name]_z, we are guaranteed to search all partitions for the specified state. Note that this is true because we are storing all partition keys in lowercase. If not, we'd have to set our filters considering that in lexicographical ordering, all capital letters sort before all lowercase letters. If you need a refresher on lexicographical ordering, just consult an ASCII chart.

Now let's add the method from Listing 5-14 to HomeController.

Listing 5-14. Add Method to HomeController

```
/// <summary>
/// Searches by state and health rating. This will result in a partition
/// range scan with all matching states. To simplify this example, if the
/// user has supplied a nonnumeric healthRating, we will return no results.
/// </summary>
[HttpGet]
```

```
public IActionResult SearchByStateAndHealthRating(string state, string
healthRating)
{
    int intHealthRating = 0;
    if (! int.TryParse(healthRating, out intHealthRating))
    {
        return View("Index", new List<Restaurant>());
    }

    List<Restaurant> results =
        _restaurantService.SearchByStateAndMinimumHealthRating(state,
            intHealthRating).Result;
    return View("Index", results);
}
```

When we run the application and search for all restaurants with a health rating greater than or equal to 90 in Tennessee, we get the results shown in Figure 5-7.

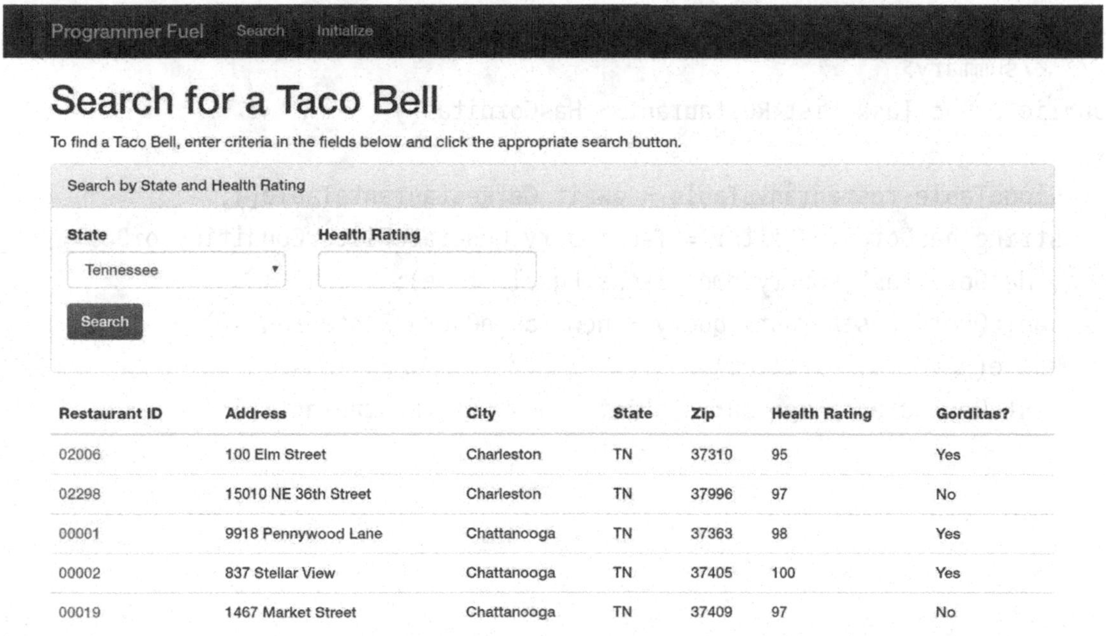
Programmer Fuel
Search
Initialize
Search for a Taco Bell
To find a Taco Bell, enter criteria in the fields below and click the appropriate search button.
Search by State and Health Rating
State
Health Rating
Tennessee
Search
Restaurant ID
Address
City
State
Zip
Health Rating
Gorditas?
02006 100 Elm Street Charleston TN 37310 95 Yes
02298 15010 NE 36th Street Charleston TN 37996 97 No
00001 9918 Pennywood Lane Chattanooga TN 37363 98 Yes
00002 837 Stellar View Chattanooga TN 37405 100 Yes
00019 1467 Market Street Chattanooga TN 37409 97 No

Figure 5-7. *All restaurants in Tennessee with a health rating greater than or equal to 90*

Full Table Scan Queries

Now for the most inefficient query of them all: the full table scan. For large tables, these should be avoided. A full table scan will examine every entity in a table, and it's caused by filtering on a property that is not part of the partition or row keys. In our example, we'll search for every entity in the Restaurants table that has Gorditas.

To see a full table scan in all of its ugliness, first add this method signature to IRestaurantService.cs:

```
Task<List<Restaurant>> HasGorditas();
```

Next, add the HasGorditas method shown in Listing 5-15 to RestaurantService.cs.

Listing 5-15. Add HasGorditas Method to RestaurantService.cs

```
/// <summary>
/// We're going to look at every record in the Restaurants table to see which
/// restaurants have Gorditas. This is the most expensive table operation.
/// Please,
/// do not try this at home. Or in a production system.
/// </summary>
public async Task<List<Restaurant>> HasGorditas()
{
    CloudTable restaurantsTable = await GetRestaurantsTable();
    string hasGorditasFilter = TableQuery.GenerateFilterConditionForBool
    ("HasGorditas", QueryComparisons.Equal, true);
    TableQuery<Restaurant> query = new TableQuery<Restaurant>().
    Where(hasGorditasFilter);
    List<Restaurant> restaurantsList = new List<Restaurant>();
```

```
TableContinuationToken token = null;
do
{
    TableQuerySegment<Restaurant> results = await
        restaurantsTable.ExecuteQuerySegmentedAsync(query, token);
    token = results.ContinuationToken;

    foreach (Restaurant r in results.Results)
    {
        restaurantsList.Add(r);
    }
} while (token != null);
return restaurantsList;
}
```

The code in Listing 5-16 for our Gordita search for the HomeController class is trivial.

Listing 5-16. Gordita Search for HomeController Class

```
/// <summary>
/// Retrieves all restaurants that have Gorditas on the menu.
/// </summary>
[HttpGet]
public IActionResult SearchForGorditas()
{
    List<Restaurant> results = _restaurantService.HasGorditas().Result;
    return View("Index", results);
}
```

When we run the application and click Search, we see the results shown in Figure 5-8.

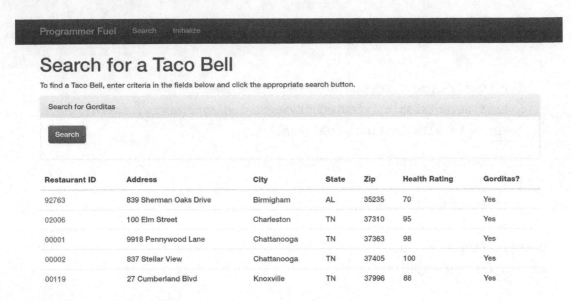

Figure 5-8. *The results of a full table scan to find all restaurants in all states that have Gorditas*

Editing a Restaurant

When making updates to an entity record, there are two methods for doing so: merge and replace. You'll also need to understand how Azure Storage manages concurrency using ETags.

ETags

When working with relational databases and issuing update statements, the last writer wins. With a relational database, the following interleaving of events is possible:

Tim and Sally both read restaurant record A.

Sally updates restaurant record A.

Tim updates restaurant record A without having seen Sally's changes. Sally's changes are overwritten and lost.

Azure Table Storage handles concurrency differently with the ETag. The ETag property belongs to the `TableEntity` class, from which all entity classes inherit. It contains the timestamp for the last time that an entity record was modified. When issuing an update, Azure will compare the current record's ETag to the ETag of the entity instance that you sent containing updates. If the ETags do not match, Azure will throw an exception.

If you want to ignore concurrency control and ensure that the last writer wins, you can set an entity's ETag to "*" before sending it to Azure Storage for an update. This will perform an update regardless of the value of the current entity's ETag.

Merge

The Merge method will compare the entity to merge against the entity residing in Azure Table Storage. Assuming that the ETags for both match or you have specified that the ETag should be ignored, Azure will copy the value of all properties that differ from the entity to merge to the entity already stored in Azure. Null properties in the entity to merge are ignored. Also, you cannot update a partition or row key with the merge operation.

The examples in Table 5-2 illustrate merge behavior.

Table 5-2. *Examples of Merge*

Property	Entity to Merge	Entity Within Azure Storage	Resulting Entity Within Azure Storage
Partition Key	tn_chattanooga	tn_chattanooga	tn_chattanooga
Row Key	00001	00001	00001
Timestamp/ETag	[timestamp]	[timestamp]	[timestamp]
Address	803 Chamberlain Blvd	9918 Pennywood Lane	803 Chamberlain Blvd
Zipcode	NULL	37404	37404
HealthRating	NULL	99	99
HasGorditas	NULL	True	True

Notice that the entity to merge only updated the Address property because all other property values were left null.

Replace

As the name implies, the replace operation replaces all values for a given entity. Unlike merge, replace does not ignore null values in the entity to replace and will overwrite nonnull values for the entity within Azure Storage with null values. Let's look at examples of replace in Table 5-3.

Table 5-3. *Examples of Replace*

Property	Entity to Merge	Entity Within Azure Storage	Resulting Entity Within Azure Storage
Partition Key	tn_chattanooga	tn_chattanooga	tn_chattanooga
Row Key	00001	00001	00001
Timestamp/ETag	[timestamp]	[timestamp]	[timestamp]
Address	803 Chamberlain Blvd	9918 Pennywood Lane	803 Chamberlain Blvd
Zipcode	37406	37404	37406
HealthRating	NULL	99	NULL
HasGorditas	False	True	False

Updating a Restaurant

For our application, we'll use the replace method. By this point, you know the drill: Let's start by adding in the necessary method signature to our IRestaurantService interface.

```
Task<bool> UpdateRestaurant(Restaurant r);
```

Next, let's add the concrete implementation in our RestaurantService class, as shown in Listing 5-17.

Listing 5-17. Add Implementation to RestaurantService Class

```
/// <summary>
/// Updates the specified restaurant by replacing the record. The replace will be
/// performed based on the row and partition key, and all properties within
/// Table storage for the existing restaurant will be overwritten with
```

```
/// the values stored in r.
/// </summary>
public async Task<bool> UpdateRestaurant(Restaurant r)
{
    CloudTable restaurantsTable = await GetRestaurantsTable();
    TableOperation updateOperation = TableOperation.Replace(r);
    await restaurantsTable.ExecuteAsync(updateOperation);
    return true;
}
```

Finally, let's add the method shown in Listing 5-18 to our HomeController.cs file.

Listing 5-18. Add Method to HomeController.cs

```
[HttpPost]
public IActionResult UpdateRestaurant(Restaurant restaurantToUpdate)
{
    bool wasSuccessful = _restaurantService.UpdateRestaurant(restaurantTo
    Update).Result;
    return View("RestaurantUpdated");
}
```

You'll also need to add the EditRestaurant.cshtml file to this project. In EditRestaurant.cshtml, you'll notice that we have hidden fields for ETag, PartitionKey, RowKey, City, State, and RestaurantId. This is because these values cannot be updated, so we don't even bother showing them in the form. We do need their values, however, when we call replace and send a Restaurant instance back to the server.

The Edit Restaurant screen is shown in Figure 5-9. After updating, the app shows a message letting you know that the update succeeded.

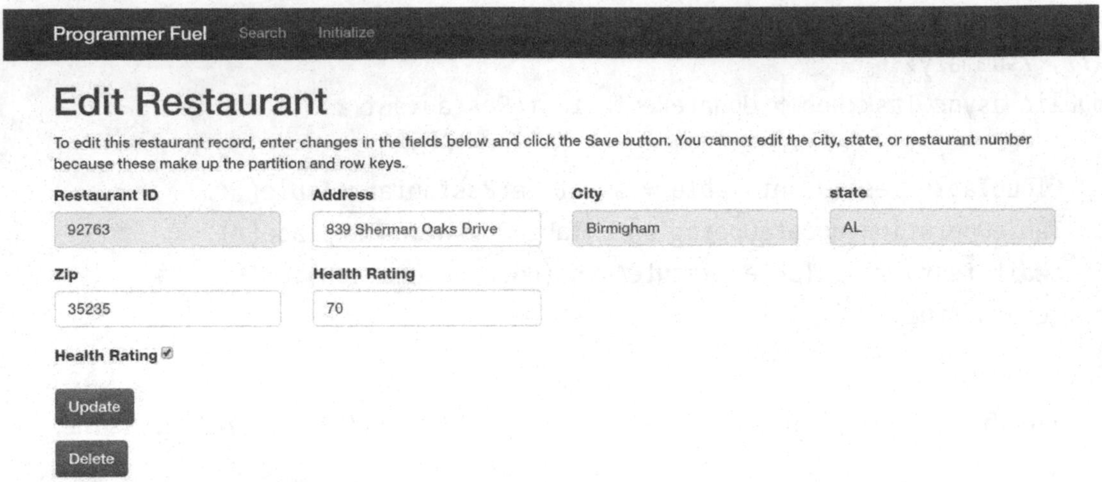

Figure 5-9. *The Edit Restaurant screen*

Deleting a Restaurant

We've already placed a Delete button on the Edit Restaurant page that we built in the last section. All that remains is to write a few lines of code to enable the delete.

Let's start with our HomeController class. Add the method given in Listing 5-19.

Listing 5-19. Enable a Delete

```
[HttpPost]
public IActionResult DeleteRestaurant(Restaurant restaurantToDelete)
{
   bool wasSuccessful = _restaurantService.DeleteRestaurant(restaurantTo
   Delete).Result;
   return View("RestaurantDeleted");
}
```

Next, we add the following method signature to IRestaurantService:

```
Task<bool> DeleteRestaurant(Restaurant r);
```

For our short and sweet grand finale, the code from Listing 5-20 goes in RestaurantService.cs.

Listing 5-20. RestaurantService.cs

```
/// <summary>
/// Deletes the supplied restaurant. Remember that Restaurant r must have a
/// partition key and row key defined, and no other properties matter.
/// </summary>
public async Task<bool> DeleteRestaurant(Restaurant r)
{
    CloudTable restaurantsTable = await GetRestaurantsTable();
    TableOperation deleteOperation = TableOperation.Delete(r);
    await restaurantsTable.ExecuteAsync(deleteOperation);
    return true;
}
```

Clicking Delete on the Edit Restaurant screen will remove the Restaurant from the Restaurants table. If you'd like to restore the demo data, just click Initialize and click Populate once again.

Provisioning an Azure Storage Service

Now that our application is developed, it's time to move from our local Azure Storage Emulator to an actual live Azure Storage Service. To do so, log into your Azure account, then choose New ➤ Storage ➤ Storage Account (Figure 5-10).

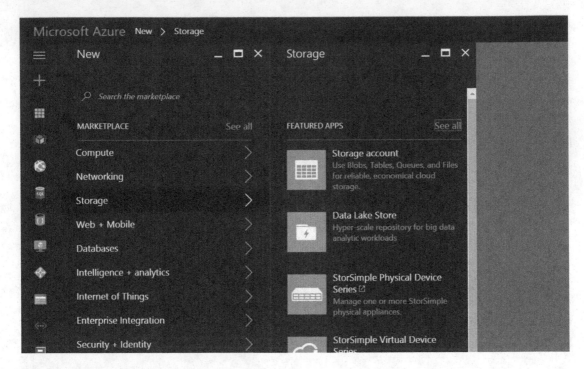

Figure 5-10. *Creating a new Storage account*

Next, you'll see a screenful of settings that you must specify to provision a new Storage resource (Figure 5-11).

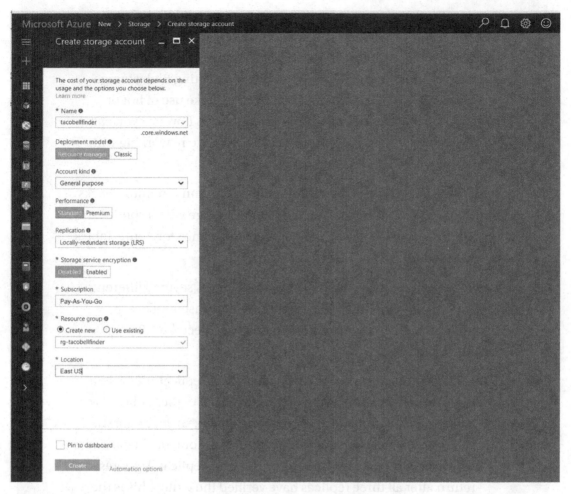

Figure 5-11. *Specify settings for a new Azure Storage service*

There are a few settings that you must specify. Let's look at them one by one.

- *Name*: This is the name of your Storage account. It will be used in your connection string and must be unique across all Azure Storage accounts.

- *Deployment model*: The Resource manager deployment model lets you specify a resource group that your new Storage account will belong to. Placing multiple services that make up an application into the same resource group allows you to manage them together. Choosing a Classic deployment model means that you'll have to manage each service individually. Choose Resource manager for all new services.

- *Account Kind*: Your options are General purpose and Blob storage. General purpose accounts will allow you to create all storage services: Queues, Tables, Blobs, and File Storage. A Blob storage account only allows you to provision Blobs. Selecting Blob storage will allow you to choose whether you want to make use of hot or cool tiers for storing your data. This choice affects how fast you can retrieve blob data and cost for storage. Because we're working with Table Storage, select General purpose.

- *Performance*: You can choose Standard or Premium. Premium backs any Azure VM disks that are moved to blob storage with a solid-state disk for fast access. It has no impact on performance for Azure Tables. Select Standard.

- *Replication*: To protect your data, Microsoft offers several different replication options. This is also important for disaster recovery planning. The different replication options all affect the GB per month storage cost.

  - *Locally-redundant storage (LRS)*: Azure will replicate your data three times within the same datacenter. Each of the replicas is on a different fault domain and upgrade domain, so your data will still be available as service updates are rolled out, or if a hardware failure occurs on a rack holding one of your replicas. Updates return after all three replicas have verified the write. This is the cheapest option, but doesn't help you with disaster recovery if the datacenter hosting your tables goes offline.

  - *Zone-redundant storage (ZRS)*: This option replicates data to two or more datacenters within the same region. However, it only applies to block blobs in general-purpose storage accounts. When using Table Storage, this option does you no good.

- *Geo-redundant storage (GRS)*: With GRS, your data is written to three different replicas within the same datacenter, just as is done with LRS. In addition, your data is asynchronously replicated to a datacenter in another region, where it is again replicated three times. This protects your data in the event of a catastrophic failure at your chosen primary datacenter, such as if the datacenter floods with ten feet of water and then catches fire during an earthquake. In the event of a catastrophic failure, Microsoft will failover to the secondary data center. You cannot read from the replicas in the secondary datacenter until this explicit failover. You also have no control over when the failover occurs. The failover datacenter is fixed and cannot be changed. For example, North Central US will always fail over to South Central US.

- *Read-access geo-redundant storage (RA-GRS)*: RA-GRS works just as GRS but with an added bonus: You can read from replicas in the secondary datacenter. When you provision with RA-GRS, you will be provided with a second endpoint that you can use in a connection string for reading only.

  Even though finding the nearest Taco Bell can be considered mission-critical to some developers, we have the ability to click a button and restore our data as needed. Therefore, choose LRS to keep costs down.

- *Storage service encryption*: Storage service encryption (SSE) only applies to Azure Blob Storage, so it's of no use to you when working with Azure Tables. For completeness, though, SSE encrypts Blob storage data at rest using 256-bit AES encryption, which is very secure. Key management is transparent. At the time of this writing, there is no way for you to even see your key, revoke keys, or change your keys. If you are using Blob storage, there is no additional cost to make use of encryption. You will, however, take a small performance penalty for doing so.

- *Subscription*: Choose the subscription you want to use for this new Storage service.

- *Resource group*: If you're going to also deploy the TacoBellFinder application to an App Services Web App, you'll want to put both the Storage and Web App services in the same Resource group so that they can be managed together.

- *Location*: This determines the datacenter that your Storage service will reside in. I always pick a location that is central to my expected user base. In general, if you're launching an application that will primarily be used in the United States, choose a U.S. data center and not Japan West.

After entering all settings, click Create.

Using Your Azure Storage Service

To get started with your newly provisioned Storage account, you only need to replace your local emulator's connection string in `appsettings.json` with the new connection string for your Azure Storage account.

To find your new connection string, browse to your new Storage service in the Azure Portal. Under Settings, click Access Keys. This launches the Access Keys management blade. Finally, click on the ellipsis icon next to key1 and select View Connection String (Figure 5-12). Copy and paste the connection string into your `appsettings.json`'s `StorageConnectionString` property, and rerun your web application.

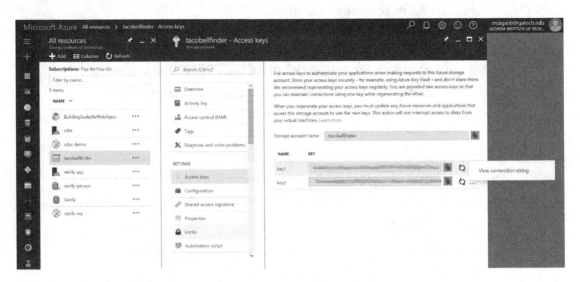

Figure 5-12. Copying the Azure Storage connection string

Pricing

Azure Table Storage pricing is calculated based on the average GB per month stored, and on the number of transactions executed.

Storage costs are based on the replication tier chosen. Prices decrease per GB stored after you reach 1 TB. At the time of this writing, locally redundant storage is the cheapest at $0.07/GB per month, and read-access geo-redundant storage is the most expensive at $0.12/GB per month.

Transactions are priced at $0.0036 per 100,000. A transaction includes any read or write operation. Remember that a single batch containing up to 100 storage operations is still only billed as one transaction.

As you can see, this technology is extremely cost effective.

Summary

This wraps up our discussion of Azure Table Storage. We've discussed what it is, how it works, design strategies and guidelines, and walked through an example application.

In the next chapter, we discuss Cosmos DB, Azure's other NoSQL technology that's of interest to web application developers.

CHAPTER 6

Cosmos DB

For nearly four decades, developers have been using relational databases such as SQL Server as a data store. Relational databases have many advantages: They save space and prevent data duplication through normalization. Perhaps most important, they're well understood. If you've been building software in the past 20 years, you are likely intimately familiar with at least one commercial relational database system.

As useful as relational databases are, they have some shortcomings. Relational schemas are fixed and somewhat difficult to change. The end result is that modeling nonuniform data is difficult. Pause for a minute and consider how difficult it would be to design a relational schema that would efficiently handle all products on Amazon.com. Amazon carries electronics such as audio speakers, which have attributes such as impedance, minimum and maximum frequency response, and maximum watts. Amazon also carries running shoes, which have attributes such as heel drop, material, and weight.

Should we create one giant Products table that has an attribute for every conceivable property of each product? This would result in a Products table with tens of thousands of columns, and each product would only have values for a dozen or so. We'd have a very sparsely populated Products table with lots of wasted space. We could also store all product details in a ProductAttributes table that consists of ProductId, Property, and Value columns. Both of these approaches are suboptimal.

A second shortcoming for relational databases is scalability. Once your database outgrows the processing power of a single server, you're forced to scale horizontally by partitioning your data and splitting it across two or more servers. Doing so makes backups, schema updates, and system-wide queries more difficult. Scalability is becoming a concern as we build software with global reach and massive data storage requirements.

© Rob Reagan 2018
R. Reagan, *Web Applications on Azure*, https://doi.org/10.1007/978-1-4842-2976-7_6

Developers weren't the only ones struggling with these limitations. Microsoft was also wrestling with how to store data for global-scale applications. Microsoft set out to design a new NoSQL database that is lightning fast, globally scalable, and can handle workloads of any size. After several years of development and internal use, in 2014 Microsoft released DocumentDB as an Azure PaaS offering. In 2017, Microsoft rolled out additional features for DocumentDB and changed its name to Cosmos DB.

Introducing Cosmos DB

Cosmos DB is a planet-scale NoSQL database. It has the following main strengths.

- *Global scale*: With a few mouse clicks, you can replicate your data to other Azure regions around the globe. Each replica is read-enabled. Although you can have as many read-enabled replicas as you wish, only one region will be write-enabled. Cosmos also includes multi-homing APIs, enabling instances of your web application running in different datacenters to always read from the closest replica. This enables you to reduce latency for reads.

- *Multimodel support*: When you create a Cosmos DB database, you can choose among four different data models and associated APIs. The available data models are DocumentDB, MongoDB, Table, and Graph. Choosing the appropriate data model for your project can greatly reduce complexity. For example, choosing the Graph API to model social relationships would be easier than attempting to represent the same data using DocumentDB. In this chapter, we focus exclusively on the DocumentDB model.

- *NoSQL*: Like other NoSQL solutions, Cosmos DB doesn't enforce a schema. This allows you to store data with completely different schemas. We'll discuss documents and data modeling in an upcoming section.

- *Automatic indexing of all data*: By default, Cosmos DB indexes all of your data. This results in lightning-fast retrieval. In fact, Cosmos's SLA guarantees that the end-to-end latency for reads in the same region for a 1 KB document will be under 10 ms at the 99th percentile.

- *Limitless throughput*: Cosmos DB is billed by the total amount of data stored plus the number of request units per second (RU/s) that you have allocated. An RU is a measure of database power. Although the exact metrics that go into an RU are not publicly defined, we do know that one RU will read a 1 KB document in one second. Pulling more performance from Cosmos DB is simply a matter of allocating more RU/s. Within the Azure Portal, you can allocate up to 250,000 RU/s. To scale further, call Azure Support and ask them to raise the limit.

- *Limitless storage*: There is no upper limit on the amount of data that Cosmos DB can store.

  To give you a sense of what is possible, Microsoft uses Cosmos DB as the data store for their Windows Data and Analytics service that handles crash reporting for Windows. Cosmos DB is also the backing data store for parts of the Windows Store and Xbox.

In the rest of the chapter, we cover the Cosmos DB resource model, what a Cosmos document is, and how documents are accessed. We then talk about partitions and how Cosmos DB scales. We illustrate all of these concepts while working through building out an e-commerce platform for a new fictitious online retailer.

Congo, the (Hopefully) Up-and-Coming Online Retail Giant

Jeff Bezos has made a tremendous amount of money with Amazon by selling all sorts of items online. How hard could it possibly be to become the world's most dominant online retailer? Let's create another e-commerce platform called Congo, which will undoubtedly bring Amazon to its knees. While we build out Congo, we'll cover Cosmos DB concepts and write some code.

Congo Requirements

For this example app, we'll create a web application that meets the following requirements:

- We will carry products with varying attributes.

- Each product will belong to a single product category.

- Products can have 0 to N reviews. Each review will have the reviewer's name, the review text, and a product rating on a scale of 1 to 5.

- There is no limit to the number of reviews that a product can have.

- On the home page, visitors will be able to search for products by name. Visitors can search across all product categories, or limit their search to a single product category.

- In the product search results, we will show the average rating based on reviews.

- When a visitor views the product details page, we'll show the product information and the first review. The visitor can then elect to see all reviews if interested.

We won't worry about creating an account, logging in, or placing orders because it's not pertinent to our discussion of Cosmos DB. We'll also omit other nonpertinent code such as checking input for errors.

Congo Tech Stack

We'll use ASP.NET MVC for our web application framework, Bootstrap version 3.3.7 for our grid system and base CSS, and Cosmos DB for our data store.

Cosmos DB is an excellent choice for this application for the following reasons.

- *It's schema-less*: Various products will have various attributes. For example, we'll need to track different properties for automobile tires and lipstick. For the former, we'll need to store information about tread patterns, expected mileage, and size. For the latter, we'll need to store color, ingredients, and sheen. Whereas it would be a challenge to store such disparate information in a relational database, Cosmos doesn't enforce a schema and we can store any properties we please within a document.

- *Scalable throughput*: We expect Congo to handle tens of millions of page views and transactions per day. Scaling a relational database to handle such traffic would be extremely difficult. With Cosmos, we'll simply reserve more RU/s to handle the load.

- *Near limitless storage*: We plan to eventually carry a million products, store millions of orders, and track analytics to better understand customer behavior. This will translate into many terabytes of information. At the time of this writing, the maximum size of an Azure SQL DB instance is 4 TB. With Cosmos, we have unlimited storage.

Note   Wondering when you should choose Cosmos DB as a data store? You should consider Cosmos when you expect your application will handle huge volumes of data, high data velocity, or data that doesn't conform to a schema. Data volume is straightforward: If you expect to store and access more data than will fit in a relational database offering, consider Cosmos. High data velocity means that you're reading and writing data at such throughput that relational databases might struggle with keeping up. As we've seen, throughput with Cosmos is simply a matter of increasing the reserved RUs. Finally, any application that has data that is difficult to map to a fixed schema is a candidate for Cosmos.

The Cosmos DB Resource Model

Before you can work with Cosmos, you must first create a Cosmos DB database account. A database account is a container for zero or more databases. Provisioning a database account doesn't have billing implications.

A Cosmos DB Database is a logical container for one or more collections. A database also holds users and their associated user permissions.

A collection holds JSON documents and associated JavaScript logic such as stored procedures, user-defined functions, and triggers. Each collection also has an assigned throughput capacity that is measured in RU/s. The minimum number of RU/s that can be assigned to a collection is 400. Because Cosmos DB is billed by the total amount of data stored and the total reserved RU/s, provisioning a collection has billing implications.

A document is JSON content that holds your data. There's nothing proprietary about the JSON document format used by Cosmos. Listing 6-1 shows two separate valid JSON documents, one for a product category and one for a product.

Listing 6-1. Two Examples of JSON Documents

```
{
    "categoryname": "Mobile Phones",
    "categorydescription": "Will that be an Android or iOS device?",
    "id": "2",
    "doctype": "category",
}
{

    "categoryid": "1",
    "productname": "American Stratocaster",
    "attributes": [
        {
            "attribute": "Manufacturer",
            "value": "Fender"
        },
        {
            "attribute": "Model",
            "value": "American Stratocaster"
        }],
    "reviews": null,
    "averagerating": 0,
    "description": "If you watch Jimmy Hendrix play the Star Spangled Banner
        at Woodstock, you'll want one of these guitars.",
    "price": 1350,
    "id": "STRAT-AM-S",
    "doctype": "product"
}
```

There are several advantages to using JSON documents to store data. JavaScript is ubiquitous, and nearly every modern programming language has provisions for parsing and working with JSON. Because most developers are already very familiar with JSON, using JSON reduces what developers must learn to be productive with Cosmos.

Partitions: How Cosmos DB Scales to Unlimited Storage

Azure SQL Database is limited to a database size of 4 TB, so how does Cosmos infinitely scale? The answer is by using partitions.

Collections are composed of logical partitions, and logical partitions contain documents. When you define a new collection, you must specify a partition key for the collection. When you store a document within a collection, Cosmos hashes the value of the document's partition key to map the document to a logical partition within the collection.

Logical partitions are stored in physical partitions. Each physical partition is 10 GB in size and is stored on highly available SSDs. One physical partition will contain one or more logical partitions. If your collection contains logical partitions A and B that are each 3 GB in size, Cosmos might store both logical partitions on a single physical partition. When a logical partition exceeds 10 GB in size, Cosmos will split the logical partition and move one or parts both to a new physical partition.

The good news is that aside from specifying a partition key, partition management is completely transparent to developers.

To meet the SLA, Cosmos places throughput limits on logical partitions for reads and writes, and ACID transactions are bounded within a single logical partition. This has several implications that we discuss in greater detail in the next section.

Data Modeling

Experienced relational database developers can look at the aforementioned requirements for Congo and have a pretty good idea of how to translate those requirements into a relational schema. How do we go about translating requirements into Cosmos DB's data model?

Being a NoSQL database, Cosmos DB doesn't enforce a schema at the database level. Schema enforcement is left up to developers. Before we begin developing Congo, we'll need to decide on the types of documents we'll store and the schema for each.

When designing relational data models, we normalize so that data isn't repeated. With Cosmos, duplicating data across documents isn't necessarily a cardinal sin. Our goals when designing how data will be stored in Cosmos are to do the following:

- *Minimize the number of retrievals in our application*: If we can grab all data necessary in a single trip to the database, our application will be more performant than if we have to make many trips to the database.

- *Ensure that document growth is bounded*: Documents cannot be larger than 2 MB. As document size increases, read and write performance decreases.

- *Spread data across partitions to increase write throughput and performance*: If our application is write-intensive, we want to ensure that data is spread somewhat evenly across partitions to prevent write bottlenecks.

- *Store data that is retrieved together on the same partition*: Queries that retrieve data from multiple partitions are more expensive to perform.

- *Store data that participates in the same transaction on the same partition*: ACID transactions cannot span partitions unless you are using a single partition collection.

The first two design goals pertain to how we divide our application data into documents. The last three pertain to our choice of partition keys for each document.

Determining Document Schemas

Our first step is to determine how we'll divide our application's data into documents. The main questions when doing so are when to embed child data, and when to break child data out into a separate document. For example, Congo has multiple product categories, each containing multiple products. Should we create one large product category document that embeds an array of its products (Listing 6-2), or should we create a small product category document and N separate product documents that reference the parent product category document (Listing 6-3)?

Listing 6-2. We Could Create a Single Product Category Document That Embeds All Products Within the Category

```
{
  "categoryname": "Guitars",
  "products": [
    {
      "productname": "American Stratocaster",
      ... other product properties ...
    },
    {
      "productname": "Gibson Les Paul",
      ... other product properties ...
    }
  ]
}
```

Listing 6-3. We Could Create a Product Category Document, a Separate Document for Each Product Within the Category, and Reference the Category Document from Within Each of Its Products

```
{
  "id": "1",
  "categoryname": "Guitars"
}

{
  "productname": "American Stratocaster",
  "categoryid": "1",
  ... other properties ...
}

{
  "productname": "Gibson Les Paul",
  "categoryid": "1",
  ... other properties ...
}
```

Here are rules of thumb to consider when determining document schemas and whether to embed or reference.

1. Consider how data will be queried. If data is queried together, consider embedding it. This allows us to make a single trip to the database rather than multiple trips.

2. If child records are dependent on the parent record and will not be queried separately, consider embedding the child records. Otherwise, consider referencing.

3. If there's a one-to-one relationship, consider embedding.

4. If child records will be zero to few, consider embedding. If child records can grow to an unbounded size, consider referencing instead of embedding. Unbounded growth of a document can bump against the 2 MB document size limit, and reads and writes against larger documents are less performant.

5. If child records have different write volatilities than parent records, consider referencing. For example, consider a stock trading application. If you embedded the stocks that everyone owns within their account document, you'd have to update each account document for every tick of every stock.

Let's return to our example application and revisit our requirements.

-   Product categories will be queried together to feed our category drop-down list.

-   Users can search for products across all categories, or limit their search to a single category.

-   On the product page, we'll display all information for a single product. We will also show the first product review.

-   Once the user is on a product page, he or she can request to see all reviews for the product.

Now let's apply our rules of thumb to our requirements.

Product categories contain products. Rule 4 applies: Because there is no upper limit to the number of products in a category, it's a bad idea to embed products within a category document. Therefore, we'll have separate documents for products and product categories. Rule 2 comes into play as well because products will definitely be queried apart from their category.

What about reviews? When a visitor browses a product, we'll show the first review by default. However, reviews can be unbounded as well. We'll have a separate document for each review, and keep a reference in each review to its parent product.

Because we have to show the first review for a product on the product details page, we'll be forced to make two queries to do so: one for the product document and a second for the first review. We also know that reviews will rarely, if ever, be edited. Taking Rule 1 into consideration, we can actually embed a copy of the first review for a product within the product document as well as write the first review to a separate product review document. This will allow us to retrieve data for the product page in a single trip to the database.

Determining Partition Keys

Before finalizing our data model, we need to consider how we'll spread documents across partitions to optimize performance. We do this by specifying a property as the partition key when we create a collection. This partition key should be present in all documents. Documents with the same partition key will be stored in the same partition. The following rules of thumb apply when choosing a partition key for documents in a collection:

1. Transactions are scoped to a single partition. Documents that will participate in the same transaction need to be on the same partition.

2. When querying documents, you'll need to include the partition key within a query. This allows Cosmos DB to jump directly to the appropriate partition to perform the query. It is possible to include multiple partitions within a query, but this is accomplished via parallel queries and consumes resources. Data that will be queried together should live on the same partition

or should be limited to a few partitions. Without specifying a partition key, Cosmos will have to scan all partitions, which is analogous to a full table scan in relational databases.

3. Although it's best to keep data that will be queried together on the same partition, we want to distribute writes as evenly as possible across partitions. This is because Cosmos has RU/s limitations on a single logical partition. If all of our data lives on a single partition and we hit those limitations, we'll be throttled and write performance will suffer.

Categories, products, and reviews will be created once and infrequently, if ever, updated. Because our documents will be read-heavy but not write-heavy, we want to make sure that we optimize for fast querying.

Creating and updating products, reviews, and categories doesn't require transaction support. Therefore, it's not required that categories, products, or reviews live on the same partition for transaction support.

Because visitors can query across all products when performing a product search, it is beneficial that all product documents live in the same partition. All categories will be queried together to populate our categories drop-down list. It's useful if all category documents live on the same partition.

All reviews for a single product will be retrieved together. There's nothing wrong with having smaller partitions. We will group all reviews for a single product into the same partition.

Because there's not a natural property that exists across all three of our document schemas, we will introduce a new property called `partitionkey`. For all category documents, the `partitionkey` will be `"category"`. For all product documents, the partition key will be `"product"`. For all reviews, it will be `"review"` + the product ID.

Examples of category, product, and review documents are shown in Listing 6-4.

Listing 6-4. Examples of Our Final Category, Product, and Review Documents

```
{
    "id": "1",
    "doctype": "category",
    "partitionkey": "category",
    "categoryname": "Guitars",
    "categorydescription": "Fine six stringed instruments for sale."
}
{

    "id": "tay214ced",
    "doctype": "product",
    "partitionkey": "product",
    "categoryid": "1",
    "productname": "Taylor 214 Cutaway Deluxe",
    "attributes": [
      {
        "attribute": "Manufacturer",
        "value": "Taylor"
      },
      {
        "attribute": "Model",
        "value": "214 CE Deluxe"
      },
      {
        "attribute": "Guitar Type",
        "value": "Acoustic"
      },
      {
        "attribute": "Back and Sides",
        "value": "Mahogany"
      }
    ],
    "firstreview": {
      "reviewername": "D. Dykes",
```

```
        "rating": 5,
        "review": "I've played Taylor guitars for years, and wouldn't play
        anything else.
                This six-string is well-balanced and a beauty for the price.",
        "createdat": "2017-09-03T11:03:37.34291-04:00",
        "productid": "tay214ced",
        "id": "review_d_dykes",
        "doctype": "product_review",
        "partitionkey": "review-tay214ce"
    },
    "averagerating": 4,
    "description": "Great for playing in coffee shops and serenading the
    people present,
                whether they want to hear you or not.",
    "price": 1699
}

{

    "id": "REVIEW_D_DYKES",
    "doctype": "product_review",
    "partitionkey": "review-tay214ce",
    "productid": "TAY214CED",
    "reviewername": "D. Dykes",
    "rating": 5,
    "review": "I've played Taylor guitars for years, and wouldn't play
    anything else.
                This six-string is well-balanced and a beauty for the price.",
    "createdat": "2017-09-03T11:03:37.34291-04:00"
}
```

A Single Collection or Multiple Collections

With relational databases, data is stored in tables. Developers who are new to Cosmos DB sometimes ask if there should be one collection created per document schema. For example, is it a good idea for us to create a collection for category documents, a second collection for product documents, and a third for reviews?

It is perfectly acceptable, and often preferable to store different document types in the same collection. Recall that when creating a new collection, you must allocate at least the minimum number of RU/s. Splitting different document types into separate collections can then become an expensive proposition.

Also recall that transactions are limited to the same partition. Placing documents in two separate collections guarantees that they cannot participate in the same transaction.

An easy way to ensure that your queries are limited to a particular document type is to include a doctype property on each document. If you refer back to Listing 6-4, you'll see this strategy in action. All category documents have a doctype property with a "category" value. If we want to only retrieve category documents, we can include the doctype in our filter criteria. You'll see this done in example code shortly.

Using the Cosmos DB Emulator for Local Development

Rather than create an Azure Cosmos DB collection and incur charges during development, we can use the Azure Cosmos DB Emulator. The Azure Cosmos DB Emulator is a service that runs on your local computer and provides nearly the same functionality as Cosmos DB. Because the Emulator makes use of your machine's local file system to store documents, you won't see the same performance or scalability as Cosmos DB, and global replication is not available.

The Emulator is an excellent way to develop and test the correctness of your application before deploying it to Azure for final testing and production. We'll begin our Congo development using the Emulator, then publish to Cosmos DB at the end of the project.

To download the Cosmos DB Emulator, visit https://aka.ms/cosmosdb-emulator.

Creating a Collection in the Emulator

After installing the Emulator, you'll find a new Azure Cosmos Emulator icon in your system tray (Figure 6-1). Click the Emulator icon and select Open Data Explorer to launch the Emulator in your browser (Figure 6-2).

Figure 6-1. *After installing the Azure Cosmos DB Emulator, you'll find a new Emulator icon in your system tray*

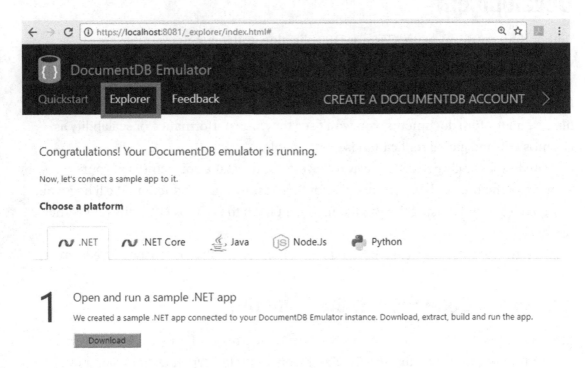

Figure 6-2. *The main screen in the Emulator interface*

Let's create a collection in the Emulator that we can use for developing Congo. To create a new collection, do the following:

1. On the Emulator's main page, click Explorer (Figure 6-2). This navigates you to the Explorer page.

2. On the Explorer page (Figure 6-3) click New Collection to open the Add Collection drawer. You'll be prompted for the following settings:

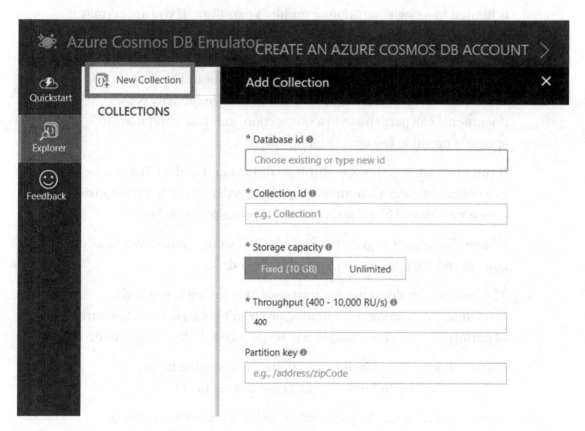

Figure 6-3. *On the Explorer page, click New Collection to open the Add Collection drawer.*

- *Database id*: This is the Database ID of the database that will host this new collection. You can have as many separate databases defined in the Emulator as needed. Enter `congo-db` for the Database id. This will be used along with the Collection Id when querying the collection.

- *Collection Id*: This is the unique identifier for your new collection. The Collection Id will be used when creating a connection to the collection to perform queries. Enter `congo-collection`.

- *Storage capacity*: This allows you to specify whether your collection is limited to a single partition or multiple partitions. If you are certain that your collection will never grow past 10 GB of data, select the Fixed (10 GB) option. Doing so will mean that all of the documents in this collection will be stored on a single partition. The main advantages of choosing the Fixed (10 GB) storage capacity is that all documents can participate in a transaction, and you won't need to specify a partition key when making queries.

  If you don't want to impose a limit on the amount of data that can be stored in a collection, select Unlimited. This means that you'll have to consider how data is partitioned by choosing an appropriate partition key.

  Because we expect to grow beyond 10 GB of storage and have already considered our partitioning, select Unlimited.

- *Throughput*: For development purposes, this setting is somewhat academic. Because we're emulating, we won't get an accurate picture of performance and no charges will be incurred. Accept the default.

- *RU/s*: This specifies RUs per second. It's a feature that helps collections deal with bursty loads. Leave this set to Off.

- *Partition key*: This is the path within each document to its partition key. Enter `/partitionkey`.

  Click OK to create the new collection in the Emulator.

3. After creating our new collection, you'll see the congo-collection listed beneath the Collections heading.

Next, let's load some data into our new collection.

Importing Congo Data Using the DocumentDB Data Migration Tool

To load our initial Congo documents, we could enter them one by one in the Emulator's UI. A faster way, though, is to import documents using the DocumentDB Data Migration Tool.

The DocumentDB Data Migration tool is an open source desktop application that will import data into a Cosmos DB collection from a variety of sources such as SQL Server, MongoDB, CSV files, or JSON documents. It's a very handy tool, especially if you're migrating from another database to Cosmos. To load our application's data, we'll first create a JSON file containing the initial example documents.

Congo's Initial Data

The initial data for Congo is specified in Listing 6-5. You can also find this file in the /Data directory of the completed project on GitHub.

Listing 6-5. Our Example Data Contains Two Category Documents, Three Product Documents, and a Couple of Reviews

```
[
  {
    "id": "1",
    "doctype": "category",
    "partitionkey": "category",
    "categoryname": "Guitars",
    "categorydescription": "Fine six stringed instruments for sale."
  },

  {
    "id": "2",
    "doctype": "category",
    "partitionkey": "category",
    "categoryname": "Mobile Phones",
    "categorydescription": "Will that be an Android or iOS device?"
  },
```

```json
{
  "id": "tay214ced",
  "doctype": "product",
  "partitionkey": "product",
  "categoryid": "1",
  "productname": "Taylor 214 Cutaway Deluxe",
  "averagerating": 4,
  "description": "Great for playing in coffee shops and serenading the
people present,
                  whether they want to hear you or not.",
  "price": 1699,
  "attributes": [
    {
      "attribute": "Manufacturer",
      "value": "Taylor"
    },
    {
      "attribute": "Model",
      "value": "214 CE Deluxe"
    },
    {
      "attribute": "Guitar Type",
      "value": "Acoustic"
    },
    {
      "attribute": "Back and Sides",
      "value": "Mahogany"
    }
  ],
  "firstreview": {
    "reviewername": "D. Dykes",
    "rating": 5,
    "review": "I've played Taylor guitars for years, and wouldn't play
anything else.
```

```
            This six-string is well-balanced and a beauty for the price.",
      "createdat": "2017-09-03T11:03:37.34291-04:00",
      "productid": "tay214ced",
      "id": "review_d_dykes",
      "doctype": "product_review",
      "partitionkey": "review-tay214ce"
   }
},

{
   "id": "review_d_dykes",
   "doctype": "product_review",
   "partitionkey": "review-tay214ced",
   "productid": "tay214ced",
   "reviewername": "D. Dykes",
   "rating": 5,
   "review": "I've played Taylor guitars for years, and wouldn't play
   anything else.
                This six-string is well-balanced and a beauty for the price.",
                "createdat": "2017-09-03T11:03:37.34291-04:00"
},

{
   "id": "review_cfmartin",
   "doctype": "product_review",
   "partitionkey": "review-tay214ced",
   "productid": "tay214ced",
   "reviewername": "CF Martin",
   "rating": 3,
   "review": "I mean, it's Ok. But give me a Martin D-28 any day of the week.",
   "createdat": "2017-09-03T11:03:37.4206531-04:00"
},

{
   "id": "strat-am-s",
   "doctype": "product",
```

```
    "partitionkey": "product",
    "categoryid": "1",
    "productname": "American Stratocaster",
    "averagerating": 0,
    "description": "If you watch Jimmy Hendrix play the Star-Spangled
    Banner at Woodstock, you'll want one of these guitars.",
    "price": 1350,
    "attributes": [
      {
        "attribute": "Manufacturer",
        "value": "Fender"
      },
      {
        "attribute": "Model",
        "value": "American Stratocaster"
      },
      {
        "attribute": "Guitar Type",
        "value": "Electric"
      },
      {
        "attribute": "Body",
        "value": "Alder"
      }
    ]
  },

  {
    "id": "lame",
    "doctype": "product",
    "partitionkey": "product",
    "categoryid": "2",
    "productname": "Apple iPhone",
    "averagerating": 0,
```

```json
  "description": "Apple's flagship phone. Can make calls, browse the web,
  get email,
                   and annoy you into submission when it wants to install an
                   update.",
  "price": 699,
  "attributes": [
    {
      "attribute": "Manufacturer",
      "value": "Apple"
    },
    {
      "attribute": "Model",
      "value": "iPhone 7"
    },
    {
      "attribute": "Radio",
      "value": "GSM"
    },
    {
      "attribute": "Network",
      "value": "Verizon"
    },
    {
      "attribute": "Total Storage",
      "value": "256GB"
    },
    {
      "attribute": "Color",
      "value": "Space Gray"
    }
  ]
  }
]
```

Note that all JSON documents are stored within an array. Save this JSON data in a document on your local machine in preparation for the import.

You can download the binaries here: `https://www.microsoft.com/en-us/` `download/details.aspx?id=46436`. You can also browse the code or build from source by visiting the project's GitHub repo at `https://github.com/Azure/azure-documentdb-` `datamigrationtool`.

After downloading the binaries or building the project, do the following to import our example data into our new collection in the local Cosmos DB Emulator.

1. Launch the DocumentDB Data Migration Tool.

2. On the Source Information screen, click Add Files and choose the file containing the JSON from the previous section. Click Next to continue.

3. Next, we'll tell the Migration Tool where to send our data on the Target Information screen. You'll be prompted for the following settings (Figure 6-4):

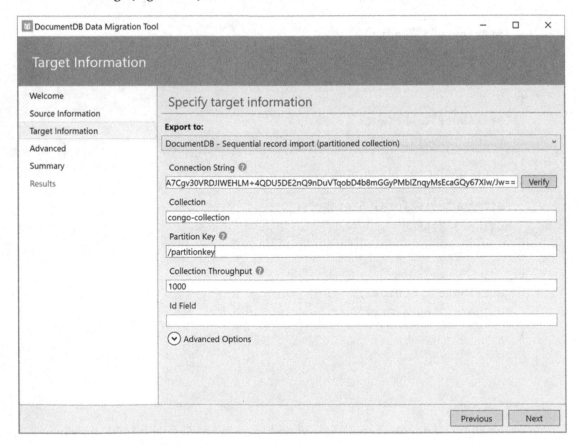

Figure 6-4. *Specifying where to import information*

- *Connection String*: The connection string is composed of the database name, account endpoint, and account key. For the Emulator, the account endpoint is by default `https://localhost:8081`. The Emulator's account key is always . If you're following this tutorial, your database name should be congo-db. Therefore the full connection string will be `database=congo-db;AccountEndpoint=https://localhost:8081/;AccountKey=C2y6yDjf5/R+ob0N8A7Cgv30VRDJIWEHLM+4QDU5DE2nQ9nDuVTqobD4b8mGGyPMbIZnqyMsEcaGQy67XIw/Jw==`. Click Verify to confirm that you are able to successfully connect to your local Emulator.

- *Collection*: This is the Collection Id that we will load documents into. Enter `congo-collection`.

- *Partition Key*: This is the path within each document where the partition key is found. Enter `/partitionkey`.

- *Collection Throughput*: This is only applicable if the Migration Tool is creating a new collection. You can leave this at the default value.

4. The Advanced Options pane lets you specify an error log file. Click Next again to see a summary of the import that's about to take place. Finally, click Import to execute the import process.

If all goes well, you'll see a success message. You can then jump back into the Azure Cosmos DB Emulator, click the Explorer tab, and drill down to the Documents menu item in congo-collection. You should see a list of all documents that were imported (Figure 6-5).

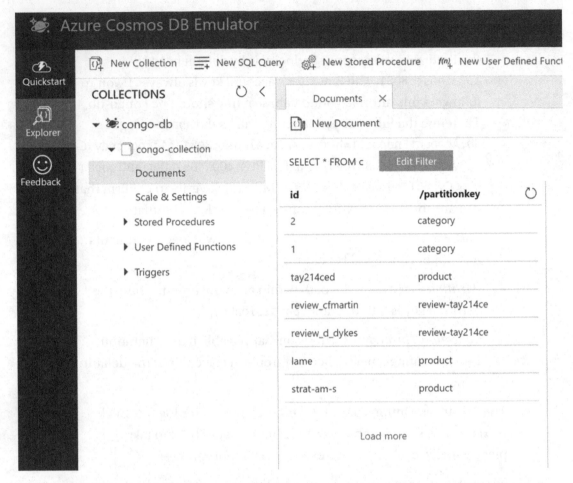

Figure 6-5. *After running the DocumentDB Data Migration Tool and returning to the local Azure Cosmos DB Emulator, we see that our documents were imported successfully*

Querying a Collection

Developers can query Cosmos DB using Cosmos DB SQL. Cosmos DB SQL is a subset of ANSI SQL, and will look very familiar to relational database developers. It supports filtering, projections, aggregations, and ordering of results. Instead of querying tables, all Cosmos DB queries are executed against a collection.

The biggest difference between ANSI SQL and Cosmos DB SQL is that Cosmos DB doesn't support relational joins.

Let's execute a few queries against the data that we loaded into our Emulator.

After opening the Emulator, navigate to the Explorer tab. You'll need to expand the `congo-db` and `congo-collection` nodes, then click Documents (Figure 6-5).

On the Documents screen, click New SQL Query to open a query window. The query window prepopopulates with `SELECT * FROM c`. If you execute this query, you'll see that all documents within the collection are returned.

Let's retrieve a specific document by its unique ID. Enter the query `SELECT * FROM c` where `c.id = "1"`. Note that the ID is actually in quotation marks because it is a string type. When you execute this query, you'll see that our Guitars category document was returned.

Next, let's return all product documents. To do so, use the query `SELECT * FROM c` where `c.doctype = "product"`. Our three product documents will be returned.

We can also perform projections and reshape our results or take a subset of fields. We can retrieve only the product name and price for all product documents with the query `SELECT c.productname, c.price FROM c WHERE c.doctype = "product"`.

Note   Complete coverage of Cosmos DB SQL is beyond the scope of this book. You can view the full SQL syntax reference at `https://docs.microsoft.com/en-us/azure/cosmos-db/documentdb-sql-query-reference`.

If you'd like to try queries without having to set up the emulator or create a Cosmos DB collection, you can use Microsoft's Query Playground to execute queries against a prepopulated data set from a browser. The Query Playground is at `https://www.documentdb.com/sql/demo`.

Creating the Congo Example Application

Our example application will have several pages:

- A home page that allows users to search for products and view all search results.

- A product details page that can optionally show all reviews.

- An edit product details page that allows an administrator to update a product's name, description, and price.

- A page that allows a user to create a new product review.

If you'd rather avoid the chore of typing, you can clone the final project from GitHub at `https://github.com/BuildingScalableWebAppsWithAzure/congo.git`.

Creating the Project and Solution

Let's get our hands dirty and write some code. We'll start by setting up our basic solution and project.

1. Open Visual Studio and select File ➤ New ➤ Project.

    Select the ASP.NET Web Application (.NET Framework) template located under the Installed ➤ Templates ➤ Visual C# ➤ Web category (Figure 6-6). Name the solution Congo. Name the project Congo.Web. Click OK to continue.

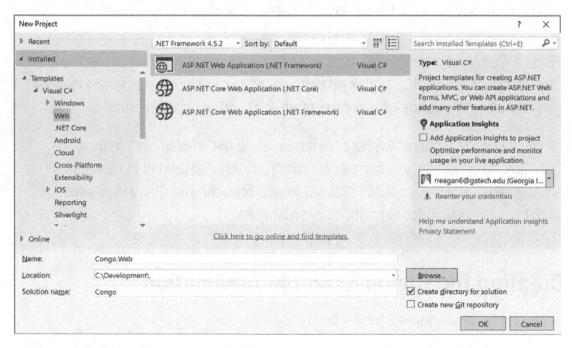

Figure 6-6. *Select the ASP.NET Web Application (.NET Framework) template*

2. Next, you'll be asked to choose an ASP.NET Template for your project. Select MVC, then click OK.

Creating the Model Classes

Our model classes are used to hold a representation of categories, products, and reviews. We'll also use the model classes to ferry information back and forth between our application and our Cosmos DB collection.

To keep things organized in the project, I recommend creating a `Models` folder in the `Congo.Web` project to hold all model classes. The code for all of our model classes is shown in Listing 6-6.

Listing 6-6. The Code for Our Model Classes

```
namespace Congo.Web.Models
{
    using Newtonsoft.Json;

    /// <summary>
    /// this is the parent class for all of our Cosmos DB documents.
    /// Since we're storing documents with different schemas, the DocType
    /// property
    /// will let us specify the document type. In this project, that will
    /// be either be
    /// "product", "review", or "category".
    /// </summary>
    public class CongoDocument
    {
        [JsonProperty("id")]
        public string Id { get; set; }

        [JsonProperty("doctype")]
        public string DocType { get; set; }

        [JsonProperty("partitionkey")]
        public string PartitionKey { get; set; }
    }
}
namespace Congo.Web.Models
{
    /// <summary>
```

```csharp
        /// Our doctype constants as is stored in the parent class CongoDocument.
        /// </summary>
        public class Constants
        {
            public const string DOCTYPE_CATEGORY = "category";
            public const string DOCTYPE_PRODUCT = "product";
            public const string DOCTYPE_REVIEW = "product_review";
        }
}
namespace Congo.Web.Models
{
    using Newtonsoft.Json;

    /// <summary>
    /// products have differing attributes based on the type of product.
    /// This acts as a key/value pair for a single attribute. Note that
    /// this doesn't
    /// inherit from CongoDocument because it will always be part of a
    /// Product document.
    /// </summary>
    public class ProductAttribute
    {
        [JsonProperty("attribute")]
        public string Attribute { get; set; }

        [JsonProperty("value")]
        public string Value { get; set; }
    }
}
namespace Congo.Web.Models
{
    using System;
    using Newtonsoft.Json;
    using System.ComponentModel.DataAnnotations;

    /// <summary>
    /// Models a single product review.
```

```
        /// </summary>
        public class ProductReview : CongoDocument
        {
            [Required]
            [JsonProperty("reviewername")]
            public string ReviewerName { get; set; }

            [Required]
            [JsonProperty("rating")]
            public decimal Rating { get; set; }

            [Required]
            [JsonProperty("review")]
            public string Review { get; set; }

            [JsonProperty("createdat")]
            public DateTime CreatedAt { get; set; }

            [JsonProperty("productid")]
            public string ProductId { get; set; }

        }
}
namespace Congo.Web.Models
{
    using Newtonsoft.Json;

    /// <summary>
    /// Models a single product category.
    /// </summary>
    public class ProductCategory : CongoDocument
    {
        [JsonProperty("categoryname")]
        public string CategoryName { get; set; }

        [JsonProperty("categorydescription")]
        public string CategoryDescription { get; set; }
    }
}
```

```
namespace Congo.Web.Models
{
    using Newtonsoft.Json;

    /// <summary>
    /// Models a single product.
    /// </summary>
    public class Product : CongoDocument
    {
        [JsonProperty("categoryid")]
        public string CategoryId { get; set; }

        [JsonProperty("productname")]
        public string ProductName { get; set; }

        [JsonProperty("attributes")]
        public ProductAttribute [] Attributes { get; set; }

        [JsonProperty("reviews")]
        public ProductReview [] TopReviews { get; set; }

        [JsonProperty("firstreview")]
        public ProductReview FirstReview { get; set; }

        [JsonProperty("averagerating")]
        public decimal AverageRating { get; set; }

        [JsonProperty("description")]
        public string Description { get; set; }

        [JsonProperty("price")]
        public decimal Price { get; set; }
    }
}
```

Note how we can change the name of a property when it is serialized to JSON by using the Newtonsoft.Json.JsonPropertyAttribute. In this example, we're following convention that .NET property names are capitalized, and JavaScript property names are lowercased.

Creating View Model Classes

Our view model classes are used to represent information as it moves back and forth between our views and controllers and our service tier. Create a folder called `ViewModels` and place all of the code from Listing 6-7 within it.

Listing 6-7. Congo's View Model Classes

```
namespace Congo.Web.ViewModels
{
    /// <summary>
    /// Our view model for a single product category.
    /// </summary>
    public class CategoryVM
    {
        public CategoryVM() { }

        /// <summary>
        /// Convenience method for copying from a ProductCategory model to
        /// a CategoryVM.
        /// </summary>
        /// <param name="categoryName"></param>
        /// <param name="categoryDescription"></param>
        public CategoryVM(string id, string categoryName, string
        categoryDescription)
        {
            this.Id = id;
            this.CategoryName = categoryName;
            this.CategoryDescription = categoryDescription;
        }

        public string Id { get; set; }
        public string CategoryName { get; set; }
        public string CategoryDescription { get; set; }
    }
}
```

```
namespace Congo.Web.ViewModels
{
    using System;

    public class ProductReviewVM
    {
        public string Id { get; set; }
        public string ProductId { get; set; }
        public string ReviewerName { get; set; }
        public decimal Rating { get; set; }
        public string Review { get; set; }
        public DateTime CreatedAt { get; set; }
    }
}
namespace Congo.Web.ViewModels
{
    /// <summary>
    /// Used for submitting information for a new review.
    /// </summary>
    public class WriteReviewVM
    {
        public ProductReviewVM Review { get; set; }
        public string ProductName { get; set; }
        public string ProductId { get; set; }
        public string WriteReviewResult { get; set; }
    }
}
namespace Congo.Web.ViewModels
{
    /// <summary>
    /// The view model for a single product attribute.
    /// </summary>
    public class AttributeVM
    {
```

```csharp
        public string Attribute { get; set; }
        public string Value { get; set; }
    }
}
namespace Congo.Web.ViewModels
{
    using System.Collections.Generic;

    /// <summary>
    /// Holds information about a single product. This includes reviews and
    /// attributes.
    /// </summary>
    public class ProductVM
    {
        public ProductVM()
        {
            this.Reviews = new List<ProductReviewVM>();
            this.Attributes = new List<AttributeVM>();
        }

        public string Id { get; set; }
        public string ProductName { get; set; }
        public string Description { get; set; }
        public decimal Price { get; set; }
        public decimal? AverageRating { get; set; }
        public List<ProductReviewVM> Reviews { get; set; }
        public List<AttributeVM> Attributes { get; set; }
    }
}
namespace Congo.Web.ViewModels
{
    /// <summary>
    /// Encapsulates a product search request.
    /// </summary>
    public class ProductSearchRequestVM
    {
```

```
        public string ProductName { get; set; }
        public string CategoryId { get; set; }
    }
}
namespace Congo.Web.ViewModels
{
    using System.Collections.Generic;

    /// <summary>
    /// Holds a list of all products returned by a query.
    /// </summary>
    public class ProductSearchResultsVM
    {
        public List<ProductVM> ProductResults { get; set; }
    }
}
```

Creating the Home Page

Our home page lets visitors query by product name and category, then displays the search results.

Let's start by creating our `ProductRepository` class. This class is responsible for all interaction with our Cosmos DB collection. To support the home page, we'll need a method that retrieves all category documents, and also queries by product name and category. To create the `ProductRepository` class, do the following:

1. Create a new folder in the Congo.Web project called `Persistence`. Place a new class file called `ProductRepository.cs` within this new folder.

2. The code for the `ProductRepository` class is given in Listing 6-8.

Listing 6-8. The ProductRepository Class

```
namespace Congo.Web.Persistence
{
    using System;
    using System.Collections.Generic;
```

```csharp
using Congo.Web.Models;
using Microsoft.Azure.Documents;
using Microsoft.Azure.Documents.Client;
using System.Threading.Tasks;
using Microsoft.Azure.Documents.Linq;

public class ProductRepository
{
    //a single DocumentClient instance that is shared across all instances
    //of ProductRepository. We can set up the DocumentClient once and reuse
    //since this is a static member variable.
    private static DocumentClient _client;
    private static Uri _collectionUri;
    private static string _databaseId;
    private static string _collectionId;

    /// <summary>
    /// Should be called before any other methods. We'll call this method in
    /// our Global.asax when
    /// the app launches. This will set up our static member variables.
    /// </summary>
    public static void Initialize(string databaseId, string collectionId,
        string endPoint, string primaryKey)
    {
        if (_client == null)
        {
            _client = new DocumentClient(new Uri(endPoint), primaryKey);
        }
        //all of our documents for this application live in the same
        //collection. We'll go ahead and create the collection's Uri
        //here and hang
        //on to it for all future requests.
        _collectionUri = UriFactory.CreateDocumentCollectionUri(databaseId,
            collectionId);
        _databaseId = databaseId;
        _collectionId = collectionId;
    }
```

```
/// <summary>
/// Searches the product name field and returns all matching products.
/// If the categoryId is null, we'll include all categories.
/// Note that we're using a parameterized query to product against
/// injection attacks since we're working
/// with strings provided by users.
/// </summary>
/// <param name="categoryId">The ID of the category where we should limit
/// our product search. If null, search all categories.</param>
/// <param name="productName">The name of the product to search
for.</param>
public async Task<List<Product>> SearchForProducts(string categoryId,
    string productName)
{
    SqlParameterCollection sqlParams = new SqlParameterCollection();
    //construct our SQL statement. Note the inclusion of the
    //partition key.
    //If you fail to include the partition key in a query against a
    //partitioned
    //collection, you will receive an error.
    string sqlQuery = $"select * from c where c.doctype = 'product' and
        c.partitionkey = '{Constants.PARTITIONKEY_PRODUCT}'";
    if (! string.IsNullOrEmpty(categoryId))
    {
        sqlQuery += " and (c.categoryid = @categoryId)";
        sqlParams.Add(new SqlParameter("@categoryId", categoryId));
    }
    if (! string.IsNullOrEmpty(productName))
    {
        sqlQuery += " and contains(lower(c.productname), lower
        (@productName))";
        sqlParams.Add(new SqlParameter("@productName", productName));
    }
```

```
//create our SqlQuerySpec parameterized query
SqlQuerySpec querySpec = new SqlQuerySpec(sqlQuery, sqlParams);

IDocumentQuery<Product> productsQuery = _client.
CreateDocumentQuery<Product>(
        _collectionUri, querySpec,
        new FeedOptions { MaxItemCount = -1 }).AsDocumentQuery();

List<Product> results = new List<Product>();
while (productsQuery.HasMoreResults)
{
    results.AddRange(await productsQuery.
    ExecuteNextAsync<Product>());
}

return results;
}

/// <summary>
/// Returns all product categories defined in the system. We do not
/// have to
/// worry about injection
/// attacks with this query since we aren't accepting input from
/// the user.
/// </summary>
public async Task<List<ProductCategory>> GetAllCategories()
{
    IDocumentQuery<ProductCategory> categoriesQuery =
        _client.CreateDocumentQuery<ProductCategory>(
        _collectionUri, "select * from c where c.doctype =
        'category' and
        c.partitionkey = 'category'",
        new FeedOptions { MaxItemCount = -1 }).AsDocumentQuery();
```

```
        List<ProductCategory> results = new List<ProductCategory>();
        while (categoriesQuery.HasMoreResults)
        {
            results.AddRange(await
                categoriesQuery.ExecuteNextAsync<ProductCategory>());
        }

        return results;
    }
  }
}
```

The `Microsoft.Azure.Documents.Client.DocumentClient` class is used to execute requests against a Cosmos DB service. Because it is costly to create, we're storing a reference as a static member variable so that it's only created once, then shared across all `ProductRepository` instances. To create this instance and perform other initialization, we'll call the `ProductRepository`'s `Initialize` method from the `Application_Start` method in our `Global.asax`.

For simplicity, we're executing SQL statements to perform our categories and products queries. The `DocumentClient` class includes overloaded methods to query via LINQ to Cosmos DB SQL.

3. Next, we'll create our `ProductService` class, which is our business logic layer. Given the simplicity of this application, its main job will be to pass requests from our `HomeController` class to our `ProductRepository` class and map the results to view model instances.

    Create a folder within the Congo.Web project called `Services`, and place a new `ProductService` class within the folder. The code for the `ProductService` class is shown in Listing 6-9.

Listing 6-9. The ProductService Class

```
namespace Congo.Web.Services
{
    using System.Collections.Generic;
    using Congo.Web.ViewModels;
    using System.Threading.Tasks;
    using Congo.Web.Persistence;
    using Congo.Web.Models;

    /// <summary>
    /// Business logic for interacting with products, categories, and reviews.
    /// </summary>
    public class ProductService
    {
        private ProductRepository _repository;

        /// <summary>
        /// Constructor
        /// </summary>
        public ProductService()
        {
            _repository = new ProductRepository();
        }
        /// <summary>
        /// Returns all product categories defined in the system.
        /// </summary>
        /// <returns></returns>
        public async Task<List<CategoryVM>> GetAllCategories()
        {
            List<ProductCategory> allCategories = await _repository.
            GetAllCategories();
            List<CategoryVM> results = CopyCategoriesToViewModel(allCategories);
            return results;
        }
```

```
/// <summary>
/// Searches for all products whose productName property contains the
/// value specified in productName. If a categoryId is specified, we will
/// restrict the search to products within the specified category.
/// </summary>
public async Task<ProductSearchResultsVM> SearchForProducts(string
categoryId,
    string productName)
{
    List<Product> retrievedProducts = await
        _repository.SearchForProducts(categoryId, productName);
    ProductSearchResultsVM results =
        CopyProductSearchResultsToViewModel(retrievedProducts);
    return results;
}
private ProductSearchResultsVM CopyProductSearchResultsToViewModel(
    List<Product> products)
{
    ProductSearchResultsVM resultsVM = new ProductSearchResultsVM();
    resultsVM.ProductResults = new List<ProductVM>();
    foreach (Product p in products)
    {
        resultsVM.ProductResults.Add(CopyProductToViewModel(p));
    }
    return resultsVM;
}

private ProductVM CopyProductToViewModel(Product p)
{
    ProductVM productVm = new ProductVM()
    {
        Id = p.Id,
        ProductName = p.ProductName,
        Description = p.Description,
```

```
            Price = p.Price,
            AverageRating = p.AverageRating
        };

        foreach (ProductAttribute attribute in p.Attributes)
        {
            productVm.Attributes.Add(new AttributeVM()
            {
                Attribute = attribute.Attribute,
                Value = attribute.Value
            });
        }

        //see if there's a first review. If so, add it.
        if (p.FirstReview != null)
        {
            ProductReviewVM reviewVM = CopyProductReviewToViewModel
            (p.FirstReview);
            productVm.Reviews.Add(reviewVM);
        }
        return productVm;
    }

    private List<CategoryVM> CopyCategoriesToViewModel(
        List<ProductCategory> categories)
    {
        List<CategoryVM> categoriesVM = new List<CategoryVM>();
        foreach (ProductCategory c in categories)
        {
            categoriesVM.Add(new CategoryVM(c.Id, c.CategoryName,
                c.CategoryDescription));
        }
        return categoriesVM;
    }
  }
}
```

4.   The HomeController class answers HTTP requests and delegates
     processing to the ProductService class. You can delete the
     contents of the HomeController class that were created by the
     MVC template and add the code in Listing 6-10.

Listing 6-10. The HomeController Class

```
namespace Congo.Web.Controllers
{
    using System.Web.Mvc;
    using System.Threading.Tasks;
    using Congo.Web.ViewModels;
    using Congo.Web.Services;
    using System.Collections.Generic;
    using System;

    public class HomeController : Controller
    {
        private ProductService _productService = new ProductService();

        /// <summary>
        /// Returns the home page that includes the product search fields.
        /// </summary>
        public async Task<ActionResult> Index()
        {
            ViewBag.Categories = await _productService.GetAllCategories();
            return View();
        }

        /// <summary>
        /// Searches our Cosmos DB collection for all product documents matching
        /// </summary>
        [HttpPost]
        public async Task<ActionResult> SearchForProducts(
            ProductSearchRequestVM searchRequest)
        {
            ViewBag.Categories = await _productService.GetAllCategories();

            //get our search results...
```

```
ProductSearchResultsVM searchResults = await
    _productService.SearchForProducts(searchRequest.CategoryId,
    searchRequest.ProductName);
ViewBag.SearchResults = searchResults;
return View("Index");
        }
    }
}
```

For the sake of brevity, we'll skip printing the content Index.
cshtml, but it is available within the Git repository.

5. Before we run our application, we still need to provide the
    information for how to connect to our Cosmos DB service.
    This involves modifying the <appSettings> section in
    our project's web.config file with our Cosmos DB service's
    details, and then altering the global.asax.cs file so that our
    ProductRepository's Initialize method is called on startup.
    Add the code in Listing 6-11 to your web.config file, and replace
    the contents of global.asax.cs with the code in Listing 6-12.

Listing 6-11. The Additions That You Must Make to Your web.config File's
<appSettings> Section

```
<appSettings>
    [... other settings in this section ...]
    <!-- Our Cosmos DB settings. Note that these settings are for the
    Cosmos DB Emulator. You will need to make sure that
    you have the Emulator running, or swap these out with your Azure Cosmos
    DB database
    Id, collection Id, endpoint, and primary key. -->
    <add key="DatabaseId" value="congo-db" />
    <add key="CollectionId" value="congo-collection" />
    <add key="EndPoint" value="https://localhost:8081/" />
    <add key="PrimaryKey" value="C2y6yDjf5/R+obON8A7Cgv30VRDJIWEHLM+4QDU5DE
    2nQ9nDuVTqobD4b8mGGyPMbIZnqyMsEcaGQy67XIw/Jw==" />
</appSettings>
```

Listing 6-12. The Contents of the global.asax.cs File

```
namespace Congo.Web
{
    using System.Web.Mvc;
    using System.Web.Optimization;
    using System.Web.Routing;
    using Congo.Web.Persistence;
    using System.Configuration;

    public class MvcApplication : System.Web.HttpApplication
    {
        protected void Application_Start()
        {
            AreaRegistration.RegisterAllAreas();
            FilterConfig.RegisterGlobalFilters(GlobalFilters.Filters);
            RouteConfig.RegisterRoutes(RouteTable.Routes);

            BundleConfig.RegisterBundles(BundleTable.Bundles);
            string databaseId = ConfigurationManager.
            AppSettings["DatabaseId"];
            string collectionId = ConfigurationManager.
            AppSettings["CollectionId"];
            string endPoint = ConfigurationManager.AppSettings["EndPoint"];
            string primaryKey = ConfigurationManager.AppSettings["PrimaryKey"];
            ProductRepository.Initialize(databaseId, collectionId,
            endPoint, primaryKey);
        }
    }
}
```

Our final step is to make sure that you start the Azure Cosmos DB Emulator if it's not already running. After doing so, run the application. You should see the screen shown in Figure 6-7.

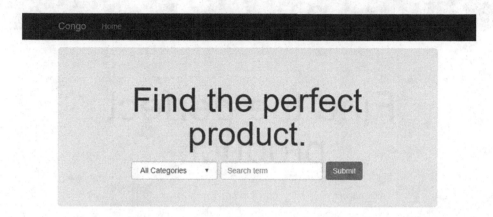

Figure 6-7. *The Congo home screen allows visitors to search for a product by name*

Try searching for "Stratocaster" in All Categories. You'll see the single result shown in Figure 6-8.

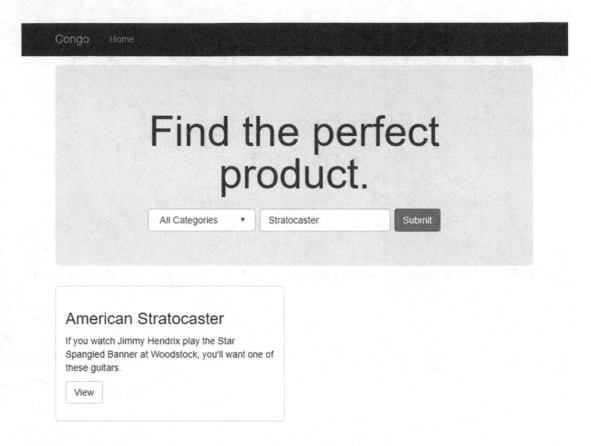

Figure 6-8.   *Searching for a Stratocaster in All Categories*

The Product Details Page

The Product Details page shows all information about a product, as well as the first review.

We'll start with the additions to our data access layer. Add the GetProductById method in Listing 6-13 to the ProductRepository class.

Listing 6-13. The GetProductById Method, Which Is Used to Retrieve a Specific Product Document by ID

```
/// <summary>
/// Retrieves a product document by id.
/// </summary>
public async Task<Product> GetProductById(string productId)
{
    //If you need a single document and you have the id, you don't have to
    //perform a query. Instead, you can read it directly via its unique
    //URI. Note that
    //since this is a partitioned collection, we still have to include the
    //partition
    //key value in the RequestOptions.
    Uri productDocumentUri = UriFactory.CreateDocumentUri(_databaseId,
    _collectionId, productId);
    Document productDocument = await _client.ReadDocumentAsync
    (productDocumentUri,
        new RequestOptions { PartitionKey =
        new PartitionKey(Constants.PARTITIONKEY_PRODUCT) });
    if (productDocument != null)
    {
        return (Product)(dynamic)productDocument;
    }
    return null;
}
```

When we have the ID of a document, we don't have to resort to a SQL query. Instead, we can construct a URI that directly references the document. Because this is a partitioned collection, we still must include the partition key for the document that we're referencing in the RequestOptions parameter.

Next, we'll add the code in Listing 6-14 to the ProductService class.

Listing 6-14. The GetProductById Method

```
/// <summary>
/// Searches for a product by productId. Will return a productVM instance
/// if found.
/// Otherwise returns null.
/// </summary>
public async Task<ProductVM> GetProductById(string productId)
{
    Product p = await _repository.GetProductById(productId);
    if (p != null)
    {
        ProductVM result = CopyProductToViewModel(p);
        return result;
    }
    return null;
}
```

Finally, add the method given in Listing 6-15 to the HomeController class.

Listing 6-15. The Product Method in the HomeController Class

```
/// <summary>
/// displays the details for a single product.
/// </summary>
[HttpGet]
public async Task<ActionResult> Product(string id)
{
    ProductVM product = await _productService.GetProductById(id);
    return View(product);
}
```

To test, run the application and search for "Stratocaster". Click View to see the retrieved product's details. The product details screen for the American Stratocaster is shown in Figure 6-9.

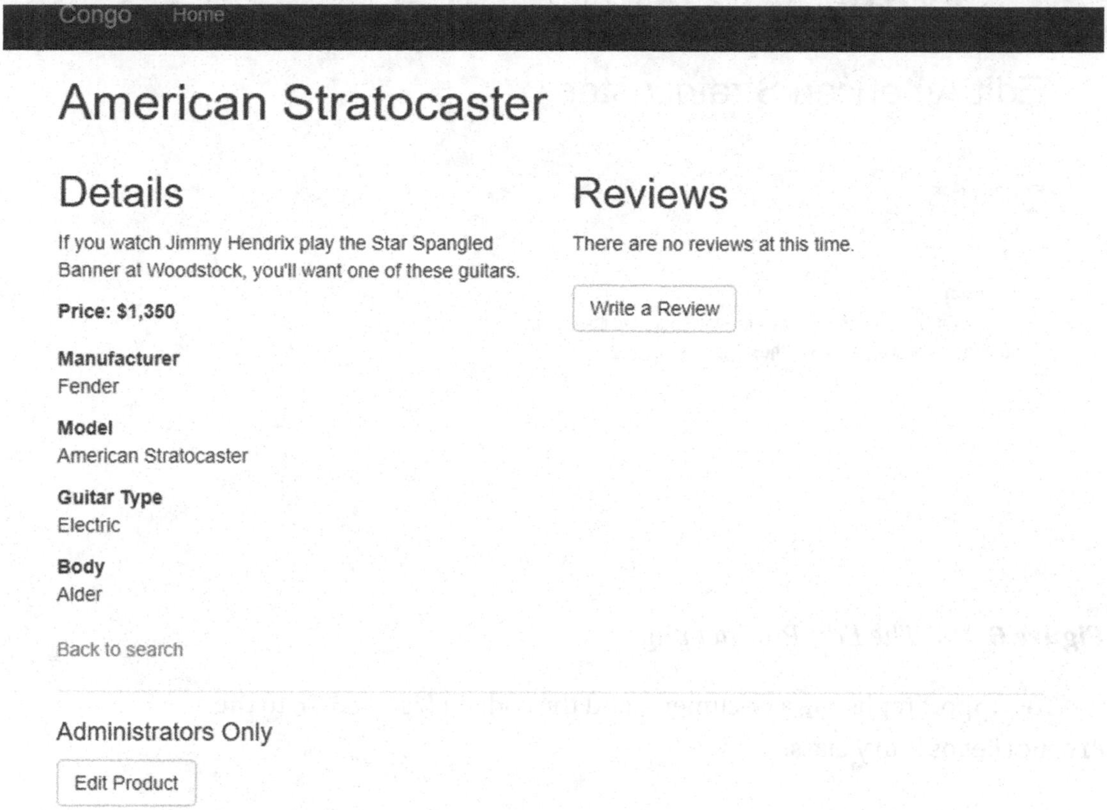

Congo   Home

American Stratocaster

Details

If you watch Jimmy Hendrix play the Star Spangled
Banner at Woodstock, you'll want one of these guitars.

Price: $1,350

Manufacturer
Fender

Model
American Stratocaster

Guitar Type
Electric

Body
Alder

Back to search

Administrators Only

Edit Product

Reviews

There are no reviews at this time.

Write a Review

Figure 6-9. *The product details page for the American Stratocaster product*

Editing a Product

We've successfully queried for product documents and retrieved a single document
by ID. Let's look at how to update a document in Cosmos DB. Updating is a bit of a
misnomer. Instead of updating portions of a document, Cosmos DB replaces the entire
document in the collection.

If you browse to a product in the Congo application, you'll see an Edit Product
button at the bottom of the screen. Clicking Edit Product navigates you to the Edit
Product page (Figure 6-10).

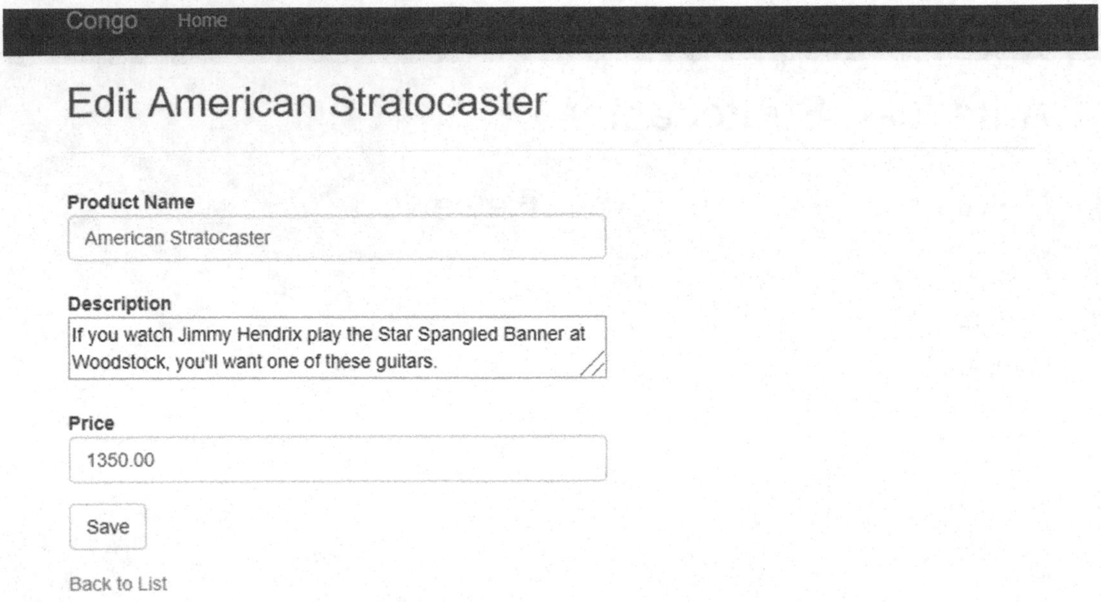

Congo   Home

Edit American Stratocaster

Product Name

American Stratocaster

Description

If you watch Jimmy Hendrix play the Star Spangled Banner at
Woodstock, you'll want one of these guitars.

Price

1350.00

Save

Back to List

Figure 6-10. *The Edit Product page*

To support replacing a document, add the code in Listing 6-16 to the
ProductRepository class.

Listing 6-16. Updates to the ProductRepository Class to Support Updating a
Product Document

```
/// <summary>
/// There is no concept of updating an existing document. Instead, we
/// replace documents.
/// This method replaces the document with the specified id.
/// </summary>
public static async Task<Document> UpdateItemAsync<T>(string id,
    string partitionKey, T item)
{
    Uri documentUri = UriFactory.CreateDocumentUri(_databaseId,
        _collectionId, documentId);
    return await _client.ReplaceDocumentAsync(documentUri, item,
        new RequestOptions { PartitionKey = new PartitionKey(partitionKey)
});
}
```

238

The code in Listing 6-17 should be added to the `ProductService` class. It retrieves the latest version of the product document, copies updates from a view model class to the current version, then hands the updated model instance to the `ProductRepository` to complete the update.

Listing 6-17. The UpdateProduct Method That Should Be Added to the ProductService Class

```
/// <summary>
/// Writes the values found in vm back to our Cosmos DB collection.
/// </summary>
/// <param name="vm"></param>
/// <returns></returns>
public async Task UpdateProduct(ProductVM vm)
{
    //first, retrieve the product from the database. We're doing so because
    //we are allowing only a subset of fields to be updated, and we are ultimately
    //replacing the document in Cosmos DB.
    Product p = await _repository.GetProductById(vm.Id);

    p.ProductName = vm.ProductName;
    p.Description = vm.Description;
    p.Price = vm.Price;

    await _repository.UpdateItemAsync(p.Id, Constants.PARTITIONKEY_PRODUCT, p);
}
```

To complete the Edit Product page, add the methods in Listing 6-18 to the `HomeController` class.

Listing 6-18. The EditProduct Methods in the HomeController Class That Support the Edit Product Page

```
/// <summary>
/// Shows the edit product page for the specified product.
/// </summary>
[HttpGet]
```

```
public async Task<ActionResult> EditProduct(string id)
{
    ProductVM product = await _productService.GetProductById(id);
    return View(product);
}

/// <summary>
/// Handles the postback that contains edits made to a product. This will
/// write edits to our Collection, then redirect the caller back to the
/// product details
/// page.
/// </summary>
[HttpPost]
public async Task<ActionResult> EditProduct(ProductVM vm)
{
    await _productService.UpdateProduct(vm);
    return RedirectToAction("Product", new { id = vm.Id });
}
```

Retrieving All Reviews

When a product details page loads, we only display the first review. You'll recall that we embedded the first review within the product document so that we'd only have to perform a single query to materialize the product details page. If a user wants to see all reviews, he or she will need to click the See All Reviews link. We'll make an AJAX call within the view to retrieve all reviews, then display them to the user.

To retrieve all reviews for a product, add the code shown in Listing 6-19 to the ProductRepository class.

Listing 6-19. Add the GetReviewsForProduct Method to the ProductRepository Class

```
/// <summary>
/// Queries the Cosmos DB collection for all reviews for a specific product.
/// </summary>
```

```
public async Task<List<ProductReview>> GetReviewsForProduct(string productId)
{
    string sqlQuery = $"select * from c where c.doctype = 'product_review'
        and c.productid = '{productId}' and c.partitionkey = 'review-
        {productId}'";

    IDocumentQuery<ProductReview> reviewsQuery =
        _client.CreateDocumentQuery<ProductReview>(_collectionUri, sqlQuery,
        new FeedOptions { MaxItemCount = -1 }).AsDocumentQuery();
    List<ProductReview> results = new List<ProductReview>();
    while (reviewsQuery.HasMoreResults)
    {
        results.AddRange(await reviewsQuery.ExecuteNextAsync<ProductReview>());
    }
    return results;
}
```

The additional methods needed in the `ProductService` are shown in Listing 6-20.

Listing 6-20. Additional Methods Needed in the ProductService Class to Support Loading All Reviews for a Product

```
/// <summary>
/// Retrieves all reviews for a given product.
/// </summary>
public async Task<List<ProductReviewVM>> GetAllReviewsForProduct(string
productId)
{
    List<ProductReview> allReviews = await _repository.GetReviewsForProduct
    (productId);
    List<ProductReviewVM> allReviewsVM = new List<ProductReviewVM>();
    foreach (ProductReview pr in allReviews)
    {
        ProductReviewVM vm = CopyProductReviewToViewModel(pr);
        allReviewsVM.Add(vm);
    }
```

```
    return allReviewsVM;
}
private ProductReviewVM CopyProductReviewToViewModel(ProductReview pr)
{
    ProductReviewVM reviewVm = new ProductReviewVM()
    {
        Id = pr.Id,
        ReviewerName = pr.ReviewerName,
        Rating = pr.Rating,
        Review = pr.Review,
        CreatedAt = pr.CreatedAt
    };
    return reviewVm;
}
```

To wrap this section up, add the code in Listing 6-21 to the HomeController.cs file.

Listing 6-21. The AllReviews Method Should Be Added to the HomeController Class

```
/// <summary>
/// Returns a partial view populated with all reviews for a product.
/// </summary>
[HttpGet]
public async Task<ActionResult> AllReviews(string id)
{
    List<ProductReviewVM> allReviews = await _productService.
    GetAllReviewsForProduct(id);
    return View(allReviews);
}
```

Creating a New Review

Let's turn our attention to adding a new document to Cosmos. On the product details screen, visitors can click Write a Review to navigate to the Write a Review page (Figure 6-11).

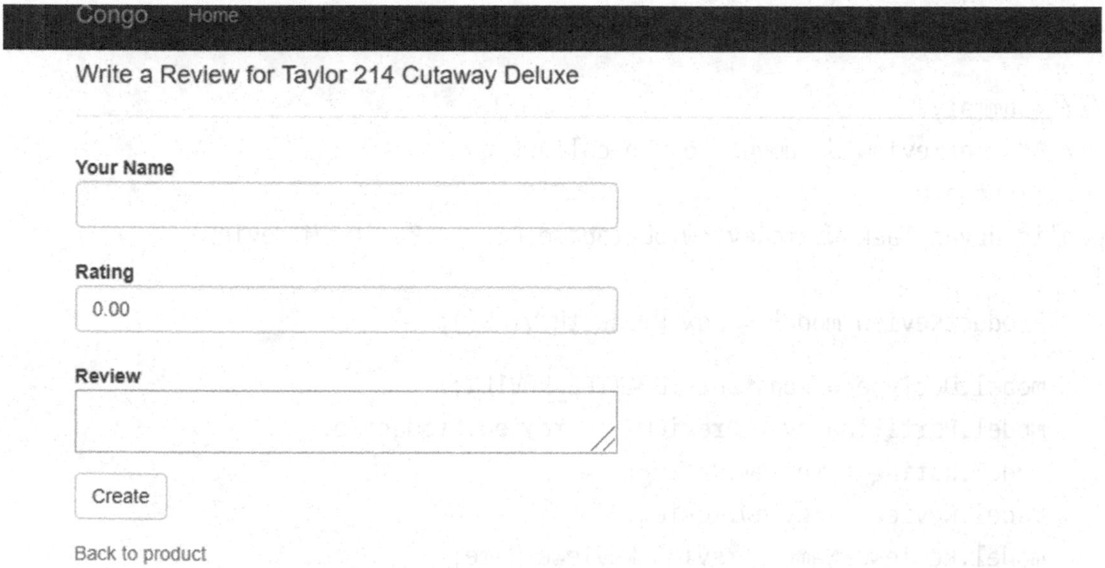

Figure 6-11. *The Write a Review page lets visitors create a new product review*

The method to write a new document to our Cosmos DB collection is trivial. The DocumentDB API doesn't care about the contents of the document; it just needs a valid JSON document and the URI of the collection that should be written to. The code to create a new document is shown in Listing 6-22 and should be added to the ProductRepository class. Note the generic document argument. This method can be used to add any type of document to the collection.

Listing 6-22. This Method Adds a Document to Our Cosmos DB Collection

```
/// <summary>
/// writes the supplied document to the database
/// </summary>
public async Task<Document> CreateDocumentAsync<T>(T document)
{
    return await _client.CreateDocumentAsync(_collectionUri, document);
}
```

Our ProductService needs the code in Listing 6-23. Notice that after a review is added, we'll query the associated product document and check to see if a review exists. If not, we'll update the product document by setting its FirstReview property to the newly created review.

Listing 6-23. The ProductService Class's WriteReviewToDatabase Method

```
/// <summary>
/// Adds a review document to the collection.
/// </summary>
public async Task WriteReviewToDatabase(ProductReviewVM review)
{
    ProductReview model = new ProductReview();

    model.DocType = Constants.DOCTYPE_REVIEW;
    model.PartitionKey = "review-" + review.ProductId;
    model.Rating = review.Rating;
    model.Review = review.Review;
    model.ReviewerName = review.ReviewerName;
    model.ProductId = review.ProductId;
    //we'll have the document that was just inserted returned so that we can
    //get the new id.
    model = (ProductReview)(dynamic)await _repository.CreateDocumentAsync(model);

    //next, check to see if there is already a first review for the
    //product. If not, update the product document to include
    //this new review.
    Product p = await _repository.GetProductById(review.ProductId);
    if (p.FirstReview == null)
    {
        p.FirstReview = model;
        await _repository.UpdateProduct(p);
    }
}
```

All that's left to do is add the methods in Listing 6-24 to the HomeController class.

Listing 6-24. The New Methods for the HomeController Class That Are Required for the Write a Review Page

```
/// <summary>
/// Renders a page where the user can write a review for the requested
/// product.
/// </summary>
[HttpGet]
public async Task<ActionResult> WriteReview(string id)
{
    ProductReviewVM reviewVm = new ProductReviewVM();
    ProductVM product = await _productService.GetProductById(id);
    WriteReviewVM vm = new WriteReviewVM();
    vm.Review = reviewVm;
    vm.ProductId = id;
    vm.ProductName = product.ProductName;
    return View(vm);
}

/// <summary>
/// Submits a new review from a user. After saving the review, this method will
/// redirect the user back to the product page.
/// </summary>
[HttpPost]
public async Task<ActionResult> WriteReview(WriteReviewVM model)
{
    try
    {
        model.Review.ProductId = model.ProductId;
        await _productService.WriteReviewToDatabase(model.Review);
        model.WriteReviewResult = "Your review was successfully added.";
    }
    catch (Exception)
    {
```

```
        model.WriteReviewResult = "There was a problem adding your review.";
    }
    return View(model);
}
```

Deleting a Review

To delete a document, Cosmos DB requires the document ID, the collection from which to delete the document, and the document's partition key.

Remember that Cosmos DB doesn't enforce relationships between documents; all relationships must be maintained by the application. Because we're storing a copy of the first product review within the product document, we'll have to handle the following scenarios.

- If a user deletes a review that is not the first review, we can safely delete the review's document and be done.

- If a user deletes the first review, we'll need to remove the review's document, then remove the copy of the first review that is stored in the product's document. We'll also have to check to see if there are any other reviews for the product. If so, we'll need to store a copy of the next review in the product's document.

Add the code shown in Listing 6-25 to the ProductRepository class.

Listing 6-25. The DeleteDocumentAsync Method

```
/// <summary>
/// Removes a document from the collection.
/// </summary>
/// <returns></returns>
public async Task DeleteDocumentAsync(string documentId, string
partitionKey)
{
    Uri documentUri = UriFactory.CreateDocumentUri(_databaseId,
        _collectionId, documentId);
```

```
    await _client.DeleteDocumentAsync(documentUri,
        new RequestOptions { PartitionKey = new PartitionKey(partitionKey)
});
}
```

The logic to enforce referential integrity is in the `ProductService` class, shown in Listing 6-26.

Listing 6-26. Deleting a Review Requires That We Enforce Referential Integrity at the Application Level

```
/// <summary>
/// Removes the specified review from the Cosmos DB collection. Also checks
/// to see
/// if the deleted review is the first review for its associated product. If so,
/// remove the product's first review as well.
/// </summary>
/// <returns></returns>
public async Task DeleteReview(string reviewId, string productId)
{
    await _repository.DeleteDocumentAsync(reviewId, $"review-{productId}");

    //retrieve the associated product. We'll check to see if it includes the
    //deleted review.
    Product p = await _repository.GetProductById(productId);
    if (p.FirstReview.Id == reviewId)
    {
        //we are deleting the first review. Find the next review and set it
        //as the first, if applicable.
        List<ProductReview> allReviews =
            await _repository.GetReviewsForProduct(productId);
        ProductReview nextReview = null;
        if (allReviews.Count > 0)
```

```
        {
            nextReview = allReviews[0];
        }
        p.FirstReview = nextReview;
        await _repository.UpdateItemAsync(p.Id, Constants.PARTITIONKEY_
        PRODUCT, p);
    }
}
```

The code that must be added to the HomeController class to support deleting reviews is shown in Listing 6-27.

Listing 6-27. The HomeController Class's DeleteReview Method

```
/// <summary>
/// Deletes the specified review.
/// </summary>
/// <param name="reviewId">The id of the review to delete.</param>
/// <param name="productId">The id of the product that the review belongs
/// to</param>
/// <returns></returns>
public async Task<ActionResult> DeleteReview(string reviewId, string
productId)
{
    await _productService.DeleteReview(reviewId, productId);
    return RedirectToAction("Product", new { id = productId });
}
```

Creating a Cosmos DB Account, Database, and Collection

We've finished with our Congo example and have it running successfully on our local Azure Cosmos DB Emulator. Now it's time to create an Azure Cosmos DB service in the cloud.

To do so, follow these steps.

1. Log into the Azure Portal. Click the New Resource icon in the upper left corner of the portal to create a new Resource. Search for "Azure Cosmos DB," then click Create (Figure 6-12).

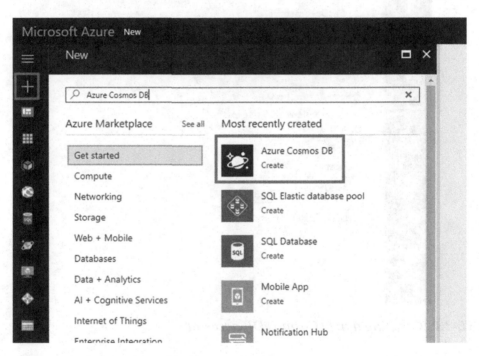

Figure 6-12. *Creating a Cosmos DB account*

2. On the New Account blade, you'll need to fill in the following
    fields (Figure 6-13).

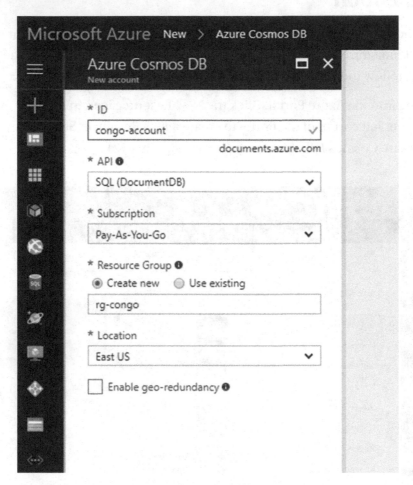

Figure 6-13. *Creating a new Cosmos DB account*

- *ID*: This is your account identifier. It must be unique across all
  Cosmos DB instances.

- *API*: This sets the API that all databases within this account
  will use. You have the choice of SQL (DocumentDB),
  MongoDB, Gremlin (graph), or Table (key-value). Select SQL
  (DocumentDB).

- *Subscription*: The Azure subscription that should be billed for this
  Cosmos DB's account usage.

- *Resource Group*: The resource group that will hold this Cosmos DB account. Create a new group called `rg-congo`.

- *Location*: You can place this new Cosmos DB account in any Azure region. For best results, choose the region closest to you. We'll also want to make sure that when we deploy our Congo Web App, we place it in the same region as our Cosmos DB account.

Click Create to create your Cosmos DB account.

3. Now that we've created an account, let's create our first batabase and collection. Navigate to the Cosmos DB management blade, and click Add Collection in the header (Figure 6-14).

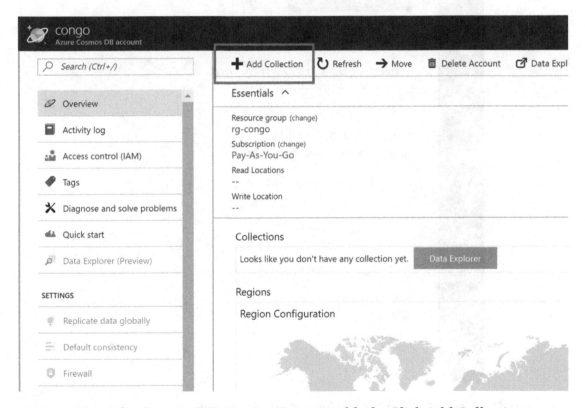

Figure 6-14. *The Cosmos DB Account Overview blade. Click Add Collection to create a new collection*

On the Create Collection blade, you'll need to enter values for the following fields (Figure 6-15).

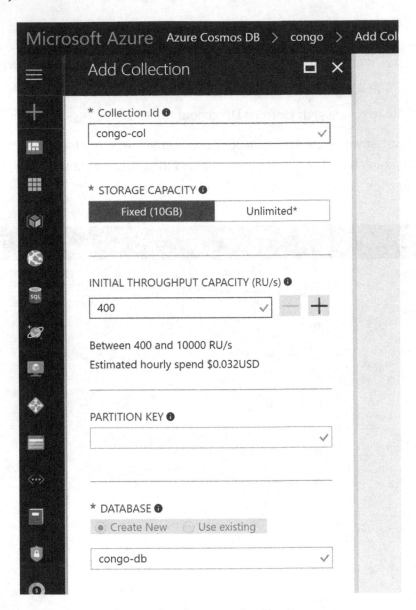

Figure 6-15. *Creating an Azure database and collection*

Collection Id: This is the unique identifier for your new collection. The Collection Id will be used when creating a connection to the collection to perform queries. Enter `congo-collection`.

Storage Capacity: This is where you'll choose between creating a collection that is limited to a single physical partition, or one that allows multiple physical partitions. If you are certain that your collection will never grow past 10 GB of data, select the Fixed (10 GB) option. Doing so will mean that all of your documents in this collection will be stored on a single partition. The main advantage of choosing Fixed (10 GB) is that the minimum number of RU/s is 400, which is approximately $25.00 per month. Also, you aren't required to specify a partition key when interacting via the DocumentDB API if you choose the Fixed (10 GB) option.

If you don't want to impose a limit on the amount of data that can be stored in a collection, select Unlimited.

You can choose either option for our Congo example application. To keep costs to a minimum, I recommend selecting Fixed (10 GB).

Initial Throughput Capacity (RU/s): This is the amount of provisioned throughput per second as measured in RUs. For the Fixed (10 GB) storage capacity, this setting defaults to 5,000, which has a monthly cost of approximately $288.00. For this example, please specify 400 RU/s, which is the minimum amount of RU/s allowed. You can change the number of provisioned RU/s as needed with no downtime.

Partition Key: This is the path within each document to the value that will be used as the partition key. If you leave this field blank, all documents will be stored in the same logical partition. For our Congo example application, enter `/doctype`.

Database: This is the Database ID of the database that will host this new collection. Enter `congo-db` for the database name. This will be used along with the Collection ID when querying the collection.

Click OK to create the database and collection.

The final step is to update the `web.config` file to make use of our Azure Cosmos DB URI and primary key. To find the URI and primary key, log into the Azure Portal, navigate to your Cosmos DB management blade, and click Keys located in the Settings section.

After updating your `web.config` file, you'll need to push the Congo example data into your Azure Cosmos DB Collection using the DocumentDB Data Migration Tool. You can then run Congo locally against your newly provisioned collection. Optionally, you can also deploy Congo to an Azure Web App instance located in the same region as your Congo DB account.

Scaling

Scaling throughput is simple: Simply add more RU/s to your collection. You can do this by browsing to your Cosmos DB account in the Azure Portal and selecting Scale. On the Scale blade, you can set RU/s up and down as needed (Figure 6-16).

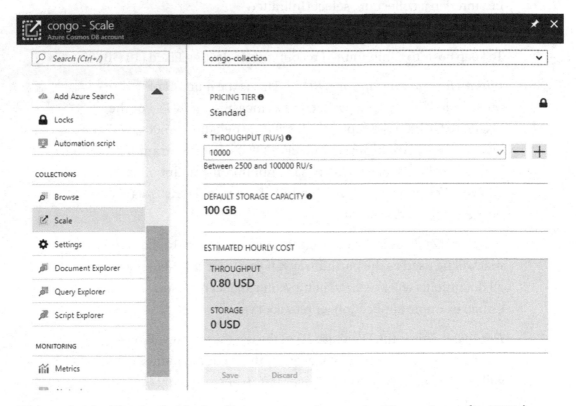

Figure 6-16. *The Scale blade allows you to change the Throughput (in RU/s) setting for the selected collection*

If you chose the Fixed (10 GB) storage option when you created your collection, your only option for scaling is to add more RU/s. A fixed (10 GB) collection is limited to a maximum of 10,000 RU/s. To scale further, you'll need to migrate your data to an unlimited storage collection.

If you provisioned a collection with unlimited storage capacity, you're limited to a maximum of 100,000 RU/s. If you need more than this, call Azure support and they will raise your account's limit.

Summary

We've discussed what Cosmos DB offers, when it makes sense to use Cosmos, and best practices for creating data models. We then put theory into practice by building out a portion of an e-commerce platform. While working through our example app, we also discussed how to use the Azure Cosmos DB Emulator, the DocumentDB Data Migration Tool, and how to scale a Cosmos DB collection.

In the next chapter, we'll introduce Azure's managed Redis Cache, which can be used to build a caching layer for frequently accessed data. By serving data from Redis instead of making expensive trips to a data store, you can turbocharge your web applications' performance.

CHAPTER 7

Redis Cache

Memory caching is the act of storing data that an application needs in memory where it can be quickly retrieved. Under certain circumstances, doing so can dramatically increase both an application's throughput and performance. Caching data in memory is especially effective when an application needs to repeatedly access the same data that is expensive to retrieve or calculate. Let's take a look at an example where an application can benefit from memory caching.

TechStore is a fictitious online retailer that sells the latest and greatest gadgets. Once a week, TechStore reviews its product catalog and adds new products, removes old products, and updates pricing.

TechStore is built on Azure and has a very simple architecture consisting of three Web App instances that read and write data to an Azure SQL Database. Their Web Apps are currently handling several hundred requests per second, and most of these requests are for product pages. Let's take a look at how TechStore fulfills a request to serve a product information page. The high-level steps are illustrated in Figure 7-1.

1. An HTTP request is received and the Azure network load balancer routes the request to one of the Web App instances.

2. The application running on the Web App instance receives the request and determines which product the user wants to see. The application then issues requests to the Azure SQL Database to retrieve the product's information from various tables.

3. The Azure SQL Database receives the query, creates an execution plan, and retrieves the product data. The requested data is read from the Azure SQL data file that resides on a physical hard drive.

© Rob Reagan 2018
R. Reagan, *Web Applications on Azure*, https://doi.org/10.1007/978-1-4842-2976-7_7

4. The Azure SQL Database returns the data to the application running on the Web App.

5. The application materializes the page using the product data, and returns the page to the caller.

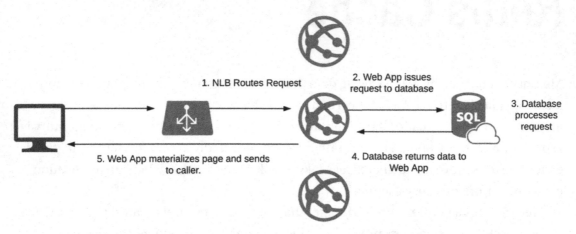

Figure 7-1. *A request where the Web App must retrieve information from an Azure SQL Database*

If we profile a request for a product page, we'd see that the majority of time is spent waiting on the results from the database query. The reason is that often Azure SQL must retrieve data from a hard disk, and disk reads are several orders of magnitude slower than accessing data that's already in memory.

Consider what would happen if Apple actually released an innovative product after a five-year drought. Yes, I realize that this is a highly unlikely scenario, but please quit laughing and bear with me. On the day that this new product is released, TechStore's servers would be slammed with tens of thousands of product page requests for Apple's amazing new product. Each request would result in a query to the Azure SQL Database or the same product data.

The Cache Aside Pattern

In such situations, we can use a memory cache to both scale and decrease response time. The Cache Aside pattern works as follows:

1. Identify data that is frequently requested and choose to cache the data. Note that you'll rarely cache all data in your application because not all data is frequently requested and cache sizes are limited compared to a data store backed by disks.

2. When your application needs data that is cached, first check to see if the data is currently in cache. If so, use the data from cache. If it is not in cache, retrieve the data from the data store and cache it.

3. If cached data is updated, first write the updated data to your data store, then remove the record that was just updated from the cache. The next time that the data is requested, it will be read from the data store and cached.

That's all there is to it! Figure 7-2 shows the same request in the previous illustration that is serviced from the cache instead of from a relational database.

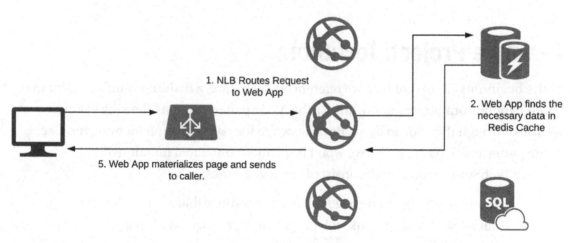

Figure 7-2. *Servicing a request from a cache instead of from a relational database*

Azure Redis Cache

Azure Redis Cache is a NoSQL key/value database that can be used to implement the Cache Aside pattern. Azure Redis Cache is a PaaS that you can provision within the Azure Portal, then connect to from your code using a connection string and your chosen Redis client library. Microsoft didn't create Redis from scratch. Redis is actually a mature, open source software package that's been around since 2010. The Microsoft Azure Redis service is based on the open source version. You can think of Redis as a giant `System.Collections.Generic.Dictionary` instance. Each data value within Redis is set and retrieved with a key of type `string`. Data values can be strings, serialized .NET objects, hashes, lists, sets, or sorted sets.

To interact with Redis Cache, you'll need to use a client library. Because Redis is extremely popular and there are already multiple client libraries available, Microsoft elected not to create their own. To interact with Redis from a .NET application, I highly recommend using the `StackExchange.Redis` library. This is an open source project created and maintained by the good folks at StackExchange, who are also the creators of StackOverflow.com. `StackExchange.Redis` implements all Redis commands and can be installed as a NuGet package. We'll make use of the `StackExchange.Redis` library in our example project.

Example Project: TechStore

At the beginning of this chapter, we referenced TechStore, a fictitious online retailer that could benefit from implementing the Cache Aside pattern. In the following example, we walk through the code to do so. Because we're focusing on implementing the Cache Aside pattern with Azure Redis, we won't implement unrelated functionality.

Our TechStore example will consist of just three pages:

- *Home page*: The home page will list all products that are listed in the database. Clicking a link will navigate to a product details page.

- *Product details page*: This displays product and specification information.

- *Edit product page.* This page allows administrators to update product details.

Our tech stack is equally simple and consists of an ASP.NET MVC application that talks to a SQL Server database using Entity Framework.

We begin by building a basic version of the TechStore web application that relies solely on Entity Framework to interact with the database. Then we update the project to add a caching layer.

Creating the Project

To create the solution, do the following:

1. Open Visual Studio and select File ➤ New ➤ Project.

2. In the New Project dialog box, select the ASP.NET Web Application (.NET Framework) template located under the Installed ➤ Visual C# ➤ Web section.

3. Name the new project TechStore.Web, name the solution TechStore (see Figure 7-3), then click OK.

4. You'll then be asked to choose an ASP.NET template. Select MVC, then click OK.

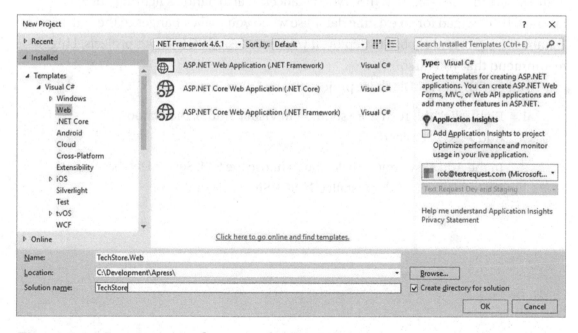

Figure 7-3. *Creating our solution and ASP.NET MVC project*

Now that our project has been created, let's create our database and populate it with test data.

Creating the Database

We'll use a SQL Server database with a simple two-table schema. The tables and attributes are listed in Figure 7-4.

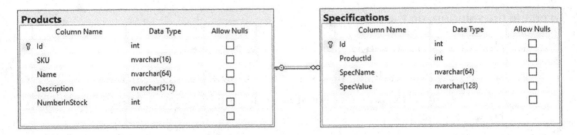

Figure 7-4. *Our TechStore database schema*

I find it easiest to create and maintain a SQL Server database via a SQL Server Database project. SQL Server Database projects will script and execute TSQL for both Azure SQL and stand-alone SQL Server instances. It also handles figuring out what needs to be changed for an existing database when you make changes to the SQL Server Database project and choose to deploy. If you're not using SQL Server projects, I highly recommend that you do so.

To add a SQL Server Database project, do the following:

1. Right-click the TechStore solution in Visual Studio, then choose Add ➤ New Project.

2. In the Add New Project dialog box, choose the SQL Server Database Project located under Installed ➤ SQL Server (Figure 7-5).

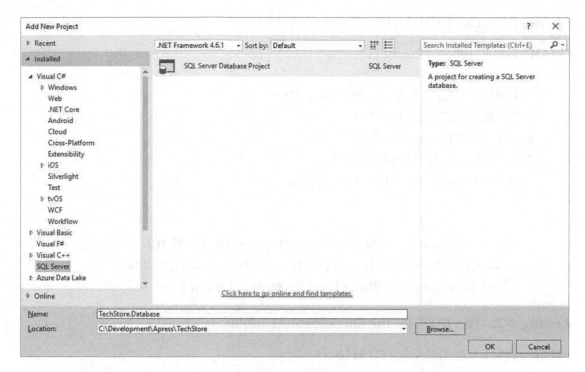

Figure 7-5. Adding a SQL Server Database project to the solution

 3. Name the new project TechStore.Database, then click OK.

After creating the project, we need to add our tables.

 1. Right-click the TechStore.Database project and select Add ➤
     Table.

 2. In the Add New Item dialog box, select the Table template located
     under Installed ➤ SQL Server. Name this new table Products,
     then click Add.

 3. Click the new Products.sql item that has been added to your
     project. This will open the table designer. Here you'll see the
     design surface that lets you add and edit table columns. The TSQL
     view is listed below the design surface. Enter the TSQL given in
     Listing 7-1 into the TSQL view, then save the Products.sql file.

Listing 7-1. The TSQL for Our Products Table

```
CREATE TABLE [dbo].[Products]
(
      [Id] INT NOT NULL PRIMARY KEY IDENTITY,
    [SKU] NVARCHAR(16) NOT NULL,
    [Name] NVARCHAR(64) NOT NULL,
    [Description] NVARCHAR(512) NOT NULL,
    [NumberInStock] INT NOT NULL DEFAULT 0
)
```

4. Next, we'll add our Specifications table. As we did in Step 2, add a new Specifications.sql script to this project. Open the Specifications.sql file and add the code in Listing 7-2.

Listing 7-2. The TSQL for the Specifications Table

```
CREATE TABLE [dbo].[Specifications]
(
    [Id] INT NOT NULL PRIMARY KEY IDENTITY,
    [ProductId] INT NOT NULL,
    [SpecName] NVARCHAR(64) NOT NULL,
    [SpecValue] NVARCHAR(128) NOT NULL,
    CONSTRAINT [FK_Specifications_Products] FOREIGN KEY (ProductId)
        REFERENCES [Products]([Id])
)
```

5. Now it's time to provision an Azure SQL Database resource. To do so, log into your Azure account and provision one as described in Chapter 4. Because this is a small example, you can choose the 5 DTU database from the Basic pricing tier. Don't forget to set the Firewall Rules for your new database so that you can connect from your PC.

6.   We now need to publish our SQL Server Database project to our
      new Azure SQL Database. First, we need to tell our database
      project that we want to publish to an Azure database. Right-click
      the `TechStore.Database` project and select Properties. On the
      Project Settings screen, set the Target Platform to Microsoft Azure
      SQL Database V12. Click Save.

7.   It's time to publish. Right-click TechStore.Database and select
      Publish to open the Publish Database dialog box (Figure 7-6). You'll
      need to click Edit and enter the connection string information for
      your Azure SQL Database. Name the database `TechStore`, then
      click Publish. Your database will be published to Azure.

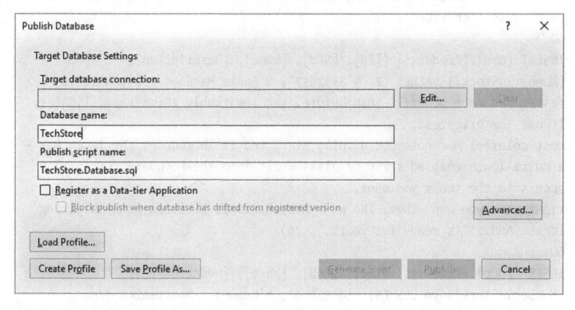

Figure 7-6. *The Publish Database dialog box*

8.   Now let's populate our database with test data. Connect to your
      Azure SQL Database using SQL Server Management Studio and
      open a new query pane. Execute the TSQL code in Listing 7-3 to
      populate your tables with test data. Rather than type this code,
      I recommend downloading it from the project's GitHub repo at
      `https://github.com/BuildingScalableWebAppsWithAzure/`
      `TaskZilla.git`. The following product descriptions were sourced
      from BestBuy.com to lend a bit of authenticity to our example.

Listing 7-3. Our TSQL Test Data

```
USE [TechStore]
GO
SET IDENTITY_INSERT [dbo].[Products] ON

GO
INSERT [dbo].[Products] ([Id], [SKU], [Name], [Description],
[NumberInStock]) VALUES (1, N'5656023', N'Google Pixel 4G LTE2', N'Bring
the power of Google directly to your fingertips with the Google Pixel.
A large 32GB of storage keep data secure, while unlimited cloud storage
transfers data as needed, and it''s completely automatic. The large 5-inch
screen is protected by Corning Gorilla Glass 4 to ensure the Google Pixel
remains scratch-free.', 5)
GO
INSERT [dbo].[Products] ([Id], [SKU], [Name], [Description],
[NumberInStock]) VALUES (2, N'8532557', N'Apple MacBook Pro', N'It''s
faster and more powerful than before, yet remarkably thinner and lighter.
It has the brightest,
most colorful Mac notebook display ever. And it introduces the Touch Bar -
a Multi-Touch enabled strip of glass built into the keyboard for instant
access to the tools you want,
right when you want them. The new MacBook Pro is built on groundbreaking
ideas. And it''s ready for yours.', 26)
GO
INSERT [dbo].[Products] ([Id], [SKU], [Name], [Description],
[NumberInStock]) VALUES (3, N'4457500', N'Huawei - Smartwatch 42mm
Stainless Steel - Silver Leather', N'With its Bluetooth interface, this
smartwatch easily pairs with your
compatible Apple® iOS or Android device and delivers call, text and app
notifications to keep you informed. Just say "OK Google" to control
functions using spoken commands.
Plus, stay on top of fitness goals with a built-in activity tracker with
heart rate monitor.', 7)
```

```
GO
SET IDENTITY_INSERT [dbo].[Products] OFF
GO
SET IDENTITY_INSERT [dbo].[Specifications] ON

GO
INSERT [dbo].[Specifications] ([Id], [ProductId], [SpecName], [SpecValue])
VALUES (1, 1, N'Carrier', N'Verizon')
GO
INSERT [dbo].[Specifications] ([Id], [ProductId], [SpecName], [SpecValue])
VALUES (2, 1, N'Wireless Technology', N'4G LTE, CDMA, GSM, WCDMA')
GO
INSERT [dbo].[Specifications] ([Id], [ProductId], [SpecName], [SpecValue])
VALUES (3, 1, N'Operating System', N'Android 7.0 Nougat')
GO
INSERT [dbo].[Specifications] ([Id], [ProductId], [SpecName], [SpecValue])
VALUES (4, 1, N'Maximum Usage Time', N'26 hours')
GO
INSERT [dbo].[Specifications] ([Id], [ProductId], [SpecName], [SpecValue])
VALUES (5, 1, N'Screen Size', N'5 inches')
GO
INSERT [dbo].[Specifications] ([Id], [ProductId], [SpecName], [SpecValue])
VALUES (6, 2, N'Hard Drive Capacity', N'128 GB')
GO
INSERT [dbo].[Specifications] ([Id], [ProductId], [SpecName], [SpecValue])
VALUES (7, 2, N'Hard Drive Type', N'Other')
GO
INSERT [dbo].[Specifications] ([Id], [ProductId], [SpecName], [SpecValue])
VALUES (8, 2, N'Operating System', N'Mac OS X 10.9 Mavericks')
GO
INSERT [dbo].[Specifications] ([Id], [ProductId], [SpecName], [SpecValue])
VALUES (9, 2, N'Processor Speed', N'2.7 gigahertz')
GO
INSERT [dbo].[Specifications] ([Id], [ProductId], [SpecName], [SpecValue])
VALUES (10, 2, N'System Memory', N'8 GB')
```

```
GO
INSERT [dbo].[Specifications] ([Id], [ProductId], [SpecName], [SpecValue])
VALUES (11, 3, N'Operating System', N'Android')
GO
INSERT [dbo].[Specifications] ([Id], [ProductId], [SpecName], [SpecValue])
VALUES (12, 3, N'Water Resistant', N'Yes')
GO
INSERT [dbo].[Specifications] ([Id], [ProductId], [SpecName], [SpecValue])
VALUES (13, 3, N'Screen Size', N'36 millimeters')
GO
INSERT [dbo].[Specifications] ([Id], [ProductId], [SpecName], [SpecValue])
VALUES (14, 3, N'Band Material', N'Leather')
GO
INSERT [dbo].[Specifications] ([Id], [ProductId], [SpecName], [SpecValue])
VALUES (15, 3, N'Internal Memory', N'4GB')
GO
SET IDENTITY_INSERT [dbo].[Specifications]  OFF
GO
```

Adding Entity Framework

We'll now add Entity Framework to our application. We could use ADO.NET or another ORM package such as Dapper, but Entity Framework 6 has built-in support for handling transient faults such as a temporary loss of network connectivity and retrying queries. This functionality is needed when working with Azure SQL Databases. To add Entity Framework to the project, do the following:

1. First, we need to add the NuGet package for Entity Framework. Right-click on the TechStore.Web project and select Manage NuGet Packages. Click the Browse tab and search for EntityFramework. Select the latest version, then click Install to add it to your project.

2. Next, we need to add our DbContext subclass and associated model classes. We'll place these files in a Persistence folder in the TechStore.Web project.

   a. Add the Persistence folder by right-clicking the TechStore. Web project and selecting Add ➤ New Folder. Rename the new folder Persistence.

   b. After adding the Persistence folder, right-click the folder and select Add ➤ New Item. In the Add New Item dialog box, select the ADO.NET Entity Data Model located under the Installed ➤ Visual C# ➤ Data category. Name this new item TechStoreContext and click Add.

   c. Next, the Entity Data Model Wizard will launch and ask how you'd like to configure our new Entity Framework model. Select Code First from database, then click Next.

   d. You'll now need to tell the Entity Data Model Wizard to which database you'd like to connect to generate our DbContext subclass and models (see Figure 7-7). You'll need to click New Connection and enter the necessary information to connect to your Azure SQL Database instance. Also, select the Save Connection Settings in Web.Config As check box, and enter TechStoreContext as the key. Click Next to continue.

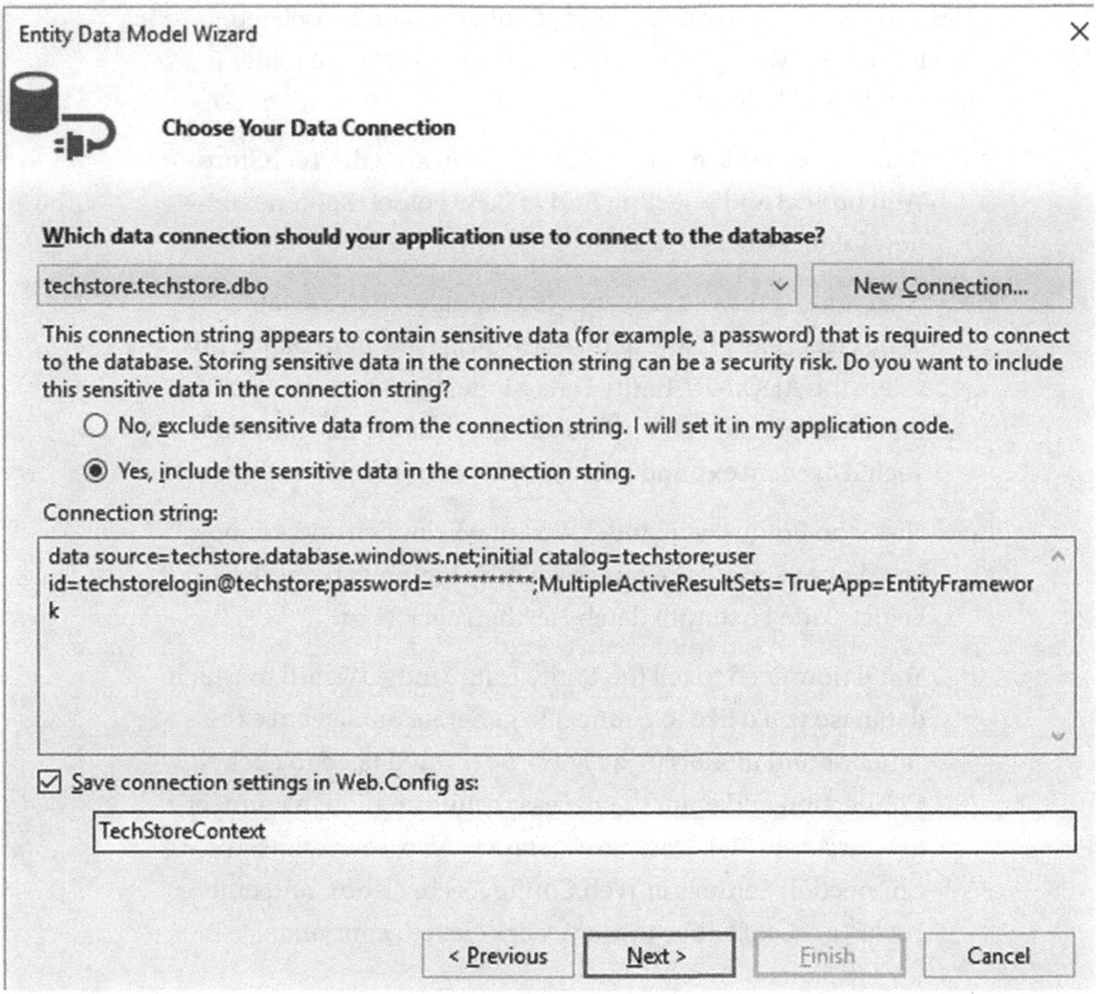

Figure 7-7. *The Entity Data Model Wizard asks to which database you'd like to connect to generate the DbContext and models*

e. For our last step, you must select the database objects and settings you'd like to include. Select the Tables treeview items, then click Finish. You should see `Product.cs`, `Specification.cs`, and `TechStoreContext.cs` files added to your `Persistence` folder.

Entity Framework has now been added to our project. Now it's time to create our view models.

Adding View Models

I'm not a fan of reusing model classes that are generated by Entity Framework. Because there's rarely a one-to-one match between the data model and what needs to be displayed on pages, it's architecturally cleaner to have a separate set of view models, and use a service layer to populate them. We'll now create the view models that we'll need for this application.

For demonstration purposes, we want to display the number of microseconds that it takes for our server to process requests. When we add our caching layer, we also want to display to the user whether the request was served from cache or from the database. Therefore, we'll have our view model classes inherit from the BaseModel class, shown in Listing 7-4.

Listing 7-4. Our BaseModel Class

```
namespace TechStore.Web.Models
{
    /// <summary>
    /// All of our View Models will inherit from this class. It will contain
    /// the retrieval method
    /// and retrieval time for servicing the request.
    /// </summary>
    public class BaseModel
    {
        public string RetrievalMethod { get; set; }
        public decimal RetrievalTime { get; set; }

        /// <summary>
        /// Used only when we update an entity. This will transmit any
        /// notifications
        /// from our service class to the view.
        /// </summary>
        public string LastUpdatedMessage { get; set; }
    }
}
```

Each product in the system will have a variable number of specifications. Because different types of products will have different attributes, we're storing specifications as labels and values. An example of a specification might be Processor speed for a laptop, or Screen size for a mobile phone. The SpecificationDetails class is shown in Listing 7-5.

Listing 7-5. The SpecificationDetails Class

```
namespace TechStore.Web.Models
{
    public class SpecificationDetails
    {
        public string SpecName { get; set; }
        public string SpecValue { get; set; }
    }
}
```

Our product details and edit product pages will need all of the information for a single product. A product will have zero or more specifications. Our ProductDetails class is shown in Listing 7-6.

Listing 7-6. The ProductDetails View Model Class

```
using System.Collections.Generic;

namespace TechStore.Web.Models
{
    /// <summary>
    /// This class is our MVC ViewModel for a product.
    /// </summary>
    public class ProductDetails : BaseModel
    {
        public ProductDetails()
        {
            this.Specifications = new List<SpecificationDetails>();
        }

        public int Id { get; set; }
```

```
        /// <summary>
        /// A list of all specifications for this product.
        /// </summary>
        public List<SpecificationDetails> Specifications { get; }
        public string SKU { get; set; }
        public string Name { get; set; }
        public string Description { get; set; }
        public int NumberInStock { get; set; }
    }
}
```

Our home page will list all products in the system. Our ProductList class will inherit from BaseModel and have a list of ProductDetails. It's shown in Listing 7-7.

Listing 7-7. The ProductList Class

```
using System.Collections.Generic;

namespace TechStore.Web.Models
{
    public class ProductList : BaseModel
    {
        public ProductList()
        {
            this.Products = new List<ProductDetails>();
        }

        public List<ProductDetails> Products { get; set; }
    }
}
```

Let's move on to our service layer.

Creating the Service Layer

Our Entity Framework TechStoreContext class will act as our application's persistence layer. Now let's build our service layer. This layer will be responsible for the application's business logic. Our business logic in this application is very simple: We'll retrieve and update information from the database. When we add Redis to this solution and introduce a cache, the service layer will coordinate checking the cache for requested product information before resorting to looking in the database.

As usual, let's first define an interface for our service class to implement. Create a Services folder in the TechStore.Web project to hold our service class and accompanying interface, then add the IProductService interface as shown in Listing 7-8.

Listing 7-8. Title Here

```
namespace TechStore.Web.Services
{
    public interface IProductService
    {
        Task<ProductList> RetrieveAllProducts();
        Task<ProductDetails> RetrieveProductDetails(int productId);
        Task UpdateProductDetails(ProductDetails product);
    }
}
```

Next is for our actual ProductService implementation. The code is shown in Listing 7-9.

Listing 7-9. The ProductService Class

```
using System;
using System.Threading.Tasks;
using TechStore.Web.Models;
using TechStore.Web.Persistence;
using System.Data.Entity;
using System.Configuration;
using System.Linq;
```

```
namespace TechStore.Web.Services
{
    /// <summary>
    /// This class is responsible for retrieving and updating product information.
    /// </summary>
    public class ProductService : IProductService
    {

        private const string DATABASE_RETRIEVAL = "SQL Server Database";
        private const string REDIS_RETRIEVAL = "Redis Cache";
        private static ConnectionMultiplexer _redisConnection;

        /// <summary>
        /// Retrieves a list of all products from the database. Note that we
        /// are not getting the Specifications since we're just listing products
        /// and not viewing product details.
        /// </summary>
        public async Task<ProductList> RetrieveAllProducts()
        {
            ProductList allProducts = await RetrieveAllProductsFromDatabase();
            return allProducts;
        }

        /// <summary>
        /// Retrieves a single product from the database.
        /// </summary>
        public async Task<ProductDetails> RetrieveProductDetails(int productId)
        {
            ProductDetails product = await RetrieveProductFromDatabase
            (productId);
            return product;
        }

        /// <summary>
        /// Updates a product in the database
        /// </summary>
```

```
public async Task UpdateProductDetails(ProductDetails product)
{
    await UpdateProductInDatabase(product);
}

/// <summary>
/// Retrieves a product from the database using the supplied primary
/// key.
/// </summary>
private async Task<ProductDetails> RetrieveProductFromDatabase(int
productId)
{
    ProductDetails product = null;
    using (var db = new TechStoreContext())
    {
        var productFromDb = await db.Products.Where(b => b.Id ==
        productId)
            .Include(b => b.Specifications).FirstOrDefaultAsync();
        if (productFromDb != null)
        {
            product = CreateProductDetails(productFromDb);
            product.RetrievalMethod = DATABASE_RETRIEVAL;
        }
    }
    return product;
}

/// <summary>
/// Updates a Products record in the database.
/// </summary>
private async Task UpdateProductInDatabase(ProductDetails product)
{
    using (var db = new TechStoreContext())
    {
        var productFromDb = await db.Products.FindAsync(product.Id);
        if (productFromDb == null)
```

```
        {
            throw new Exception("We couldn't find a product for Id " +
            product.Id);
        }

        productFromDb.Name = product.Name;
        productFromDb.Description = product.Description;
        productFromDb.SKU = product.SKU;
        productFromDb.NumberInStock = product.NumberInStock;

        await db.SaveChangesAsync();
        product.LastUpdatedMessage =
            "Successfully updated at " + DateTime.Now.ToString("o");
    }
}

/// <summary>
/// Retrieves all products from the database, stores them in a
/// ProductList
/// instance, and returns them to the caller.
/// </summary>
private async Task<ProductList> RetrieveAllProductsFromDatabase()
{
    ProductList allProducts = new ProductList();
    allProducts.RetrievalMethod = DATABASE_RETRIEVAL;
    using (var db = new TechStoreContext())
    {
        var productsFromDb = await db.Products.ToListAsync();
        foreach (Product p in productsFromDb)
        {
            allProducts.Products.Add(CreateProductDetails(p));
        }
    }
    return allProducts;
}
```

```
/// <summary>
/// Copies data from our Entity Framework-generated Product class to our
/// ProductDetails view model class.
/// </summary>
private ProductDetails CreateProductDetails(Product p)
{
    ProductDetails details = new ProductDetails();
    details.Id = p.Id;
    details.Name = p.Name;
    details.Description = p.Description;
    details.SKU = p.SKU;
    details.NumberInStock = p.NumberInStock;

    //now let's set up our specifications
    foreach (Specification s in p.Specifications)
    {
        SpecificationDetails specDetail = new SpecificationDetails();
        specDetail.SpecName = s.SpecName;
        specDetail.SpecValue = s.SpecValue;
        details.Specifications.Add(specDetail);
    }
    return details;
}
}
}
```

Creating the Controller and Views

Now that our service layer is complete, we're ready to implement our controller. To do so, let's open the HomeController.cs file and delete its contents. You can also delete all other controller classes that were created as part of the project template; they are not needed.

Because this is such a small project and we're working to keep the example simple, we'll place all code within our HomeController.cs file. The contents of HomeController. cs are given in Listing 7-10.

Listing 7-10. The HomeController Class

```
using System.Web.Mvc;
using TechStore.Web.Services;
using TechStore.Web.Models;
using System.Threading.Tasks;
using System.Diagnostics;

namespace TechStore.Web.Controllers
{
    public class HomeController : Controller
    {
        private IProductService _productService;
        private const long NANOSECONDS_PER_SECOND = 1000L * 1000L * 1000L;

        /// <summary>
        /// Constructor. In a production application, the IProductService
        /// instance
        /// should be injected by a Dependency Injection container.
        /// To keep this illustration simple, we'll instantiate our
        /// IProductService
        /// in the constructor.
        /// </summary>
        public HomeController()
        {
            _productService = new ProductService();
        }

        /// <summary>
        /// Returns the home page that lists all products in the database.
        /// </summary>
        [HttpGet]
        public async Task<ActionResult> Index()
        {
            Stopwatch timer = new Stopwatch();
```

```
    timer.Start();
    ProductList allProducts = await _productService.
    RetrieveAllProducts();
    timer.Stop();

    long requestDuration =
        CalculateRequestDurationInMicroseconds(Stopwatch.Frequency,
        timer.ElapsedTicks);
    allProducts.RetrievalTime = requestDuration;
    return View(allProducts);
}

/// <summary>
/// Returns a product details page for the requested product.
/// </summary>
/// <param name="id">The ID for the products record that we'd like to
/// view. </param>
[HttpGet]
public async Task<ActionResult> Product(int id)
{
    Stopwatch timer = new Stopwatch();
    timer.Start();
    ProductDetails product = await _productService.
    RetrieveProductDetails(id);
    timer.Stop();

    long requestDuration =
        CalculateRequestDurationInMicroseconds(Stopwatch.Frequency,
        timer.ElapsedTicks);
    product.RetrievalTime = requestDuration;
    return View(product);
}

/// <summary>
/// Created the edit product page for the requested product.
/// </summary>
```

```
[HttpGet]
public async Task<ActionResult> EditProduct(int id)
{
    Stopwatch timer = new Stopwatch();
    timer.Start();
    ProductDetails product = await _productService.
    RetrieveProductDetails(id);
    timer.Stop();

    long requestDuration =
        CalculateRequestDurationInMicroseconds(Stopwatch.Frequency,
        timer.ElapsedTicks);
    product.RetrievalTime = requestDuration;
    return View(product);
}

/// <summary>
/// Updates the product's information. This will update the database
/// and evict any cache
/// record for the edited product so that our cache won't serve stale data.
/// </summary>
[HttpPost]
public async Task<ActionResult> EditProduct(ProductDetails product)
{
    await _productService.UpdateProductDetails(product);
    return View(product);
}

/// <summary>
/// Helper method that will take our timer's frequency and elapsed
/// time in ticks,
/// and calculate the number of microseconds that the request took.
/// </summary>
private long CalculateRequestDurationInMicroseconds(long
stopWatchFrequency,
    long elapsedTicks)
```

```
    {
        long nanosecondsPerTick = NANOSECONDS_PER_SECOND / Stopwatch.
        Frequency;
        long requestLength = elapsedTicks * nanosecondsPerTick;
        return requestLength;
    }
  }
}
```

The HomeController class delegates the work of retrieving and updating product information to the ProductService class. The most interesting aspect is the use of the Stopwatch class to time how long it takes for the service layer to process a request.

For brevity, we'll skip each page's markup. You can find the markup along with the completed example at https://github.com/BuildingScalableWebAppsWithAzure/ TaskZilla.git.

Running the TechStore Application

We're now ready to run our application, but to get a true picture of how long it takes to retrieve product information from the database, you'll need to provision a Web App resource and deploy to Azure. If you run the web application locally against a SQL Azure Database, the majority of page processing time will be due to network latency. When you create your Web App, make sure that you do so in the same region where you provisioned your SQL Azure Database. If you'd like to look at a detailed walkthrough for deploying a Web App to Azure, return to Chapter 2.

After deploying the web application to Azure, you should see the index page shown in Figure 7-8.

Welcome to TechStore!

We have an extensive selection of products. Click on the product you'd like to view.

- Google Pixel 4G LTE2
- Apple MacBook Pro
- Huawei - Smartwatch 42mm Stainless Steel - Silver Leather

Retrieved via **SQL Server Database.**
Total retrieval time: **9,889.70** microseconds

Figure 7-8. *The TechStore index page that lists all products*

You'll notice a large drop in total retrieval time from the initial load to all subsequent page loads. This is because Azure SQL implements its own caching. The initial page load runs approximately 400 ms, and subsequent page loads are taking around 10 ms on an Azure Free Tier Web App.

Let's click a product link to view a product details page. The product page for the Google Pixel phone is shown in Figure 7-9.

TechStore

Google Pixel 4G LTE2

SKU	5656023
Name	Google Pixel 4G LTE2
Description	Bring the power of Google directly to your fingertips with the Google Pixel. A large 32GB of storage keep data secure, while unlimited cloud storage transfers data as needed, and it's completely automatic. The large 5-inch screen is protected by Corning Gorilla Glass 4 to ensure the Google Pixel remains scratch-free.
NumberInStock	5

Specifications

Carrier	Verizon
Wireless Technology	4G LTE, CDMA, GSM, WCDMA
Operating System	Android 7.0 Nougat
Maximum Usage Time	26 hours
Screen Size	5 inches

Edit | Back to List

Retrieved via **SQL Server Database.**
Total retrieval time: **442,631.40** microseconds

Figure 7-9. *The product details page for the Google Pixel*

The initial page load ran 442 ms.

Clicking the Edit link will take you to the edit page for this product. The edit product page will also retrieve the product record from the database, and will also write it back to the database if the user saves his or her edits.

Create an Azure Redis Cache Resource

Let's see if we can improve on our product details page load performance by introducing the Cache Aside pattern using a Redis Cache instance.

Currently, there is no local emulator for Azure Redis, so we'll need to provision an Azure Redis Cache instance within the portal. For other projects that use Redis, you'll have to do the same.

To create an Azure Redis Cache resource, do the following:

1. Log into the Azure Portal and click New Resource to create a new resource.

2. On the New Resource blade, select Redis Cache, located on the Databases menu.

3. On the New Redis Cache blade, you'll need to fill out information on your new cache instance. The fields are described as follows:

   - *DNS Name*: Enter a unique name for your cache. This name will become part of the resource's URI and must be unique. I named mine TechStore, but because I've used that name, you cannot use it.

   - *Subscription*: Choose the subscription you'd like to bill for this new cache instance from the drop-down list.

   - *Resource Group*: I recommend placing all of your resources for a solution in a single resource group. Select the same resource group you used when provisioning the TechStore database.

- *Location*: This is the region in which your Redis Cache will be provisioned. It is very important that you locate your Redis Cache resource in the same region where your Web App(s) host your web application. If you host your Web Apps in one region and your Redis Cache in another, all performance benefits of caching will be lost due to network latency between your web application and the cache. In fact, doing so will make your application much slower.

- *Pricing Tier*: There are three separate pricing tiers: Basic, Standard, and Premium. Each tier adds more performance and features. We discuss these in more detail in the "Scaling Out" section later in this chapter. For our exercise, choose the cheapest option, which is C0 Basic. At the time of this writing, this will cost $16.37 per month.

All of the other features will be disabled when you choose the Basic tier, and are only enabled if you choose an instance from the Premium tier. Click Create to provision your new cache instance.

Implementing the Cache Aside Pattern with Redis Cache

We're now ready to add a caching layer to our application. Let's start by caching product records that we're currently retrieving from the database.

First, we need to add the necessary NuGet packages to our project. There are several Redis clients that you could use to work with a Redis instance. We're going to use `StackExchange.Redis`, which is the library that Microsoft recommends. When we store a `ProductDetails` instance in our Redis Cache, we need to first serialize it to JSON format. To do so, use the `Newtonsoft.Json` library. To add these packages, right-click the TechStore.Web project and select Manage NuGet Packages. Click the Browse tab, search for `Newtonsoft.Json` and `StackExchange.Redis` and add each of these packages to the project.

We now need to add our Redis Cache connection string to our `web.config` file. To get your Redis Cache connection string, log into the Azure Portal, navigate to your Redis Cache resource, and click Overview. Under the Keys heading, click the Show Access Keys link (Figure 7-10).

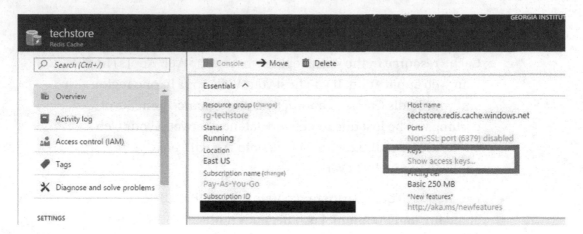

Figure 7-10. *Click the Show Access Leys link to find your Redis Cache connection string*

This opens the Manage Keys blade. Copy the connection string listed under the Primary connection string (StackExchange.Redis). Add this as an entry in the `<appsettings>` section in your `web.config`. The entry will look similar to the following:

```
<add key="redisCacheConnectionString" value="[cache name].redis.cache.
windows.net:6380,password=[your password],ssl=True,abortConnect=False" />
```

Next, we need to modify our `ProductService` class. Before retrieving a product from the database, we'll check to see if it exists within our cache. If so, we'll return the requested `ProductDetails` instance. If not, we'll retrieve it from the database, add it to our cache, and return it to the caller. The next time that the same product information is requested, it will already be loaded in our cache from the previous request.

The modified `ProductService` class is shown in Listing 7-11. Changes that incorporate Redis for our Cache Aside pattern are shown in bold.

Listing 7-11. The Modified ProductService Class That Includes a Cache Aside Pattern Implementation Using Redis Cache

```
using System;
using System.Threading.Tasks;
using TechStore.Web.Models;
using TechStore.Web.Persistence;
using System.Data.Entity;
using System.Configuration;
```

```csharp
using System.Linq;
using StackExchange.Redis;
using Newtonsoft.Json;

namespace TechStore.Web.Services
{
    /// <summary>
    /// This class is responsible for retrieving and updating product
    /// information.
    /// </summary>
     public class ProductService : IProductService
     {
        private const string DATABASE_RETRIEVAL = "SQL Server Database";
        private const string REDIS_RETRIEVAL = "Redis Cache";
        private static ConnectionMultiplexer _redisConnection;

        /// <summary>
        /// Constructor that is only called once, no matter how many times this
        /// class is instantiated. The ConnectionMultiplexer class is
        /// expensive,
        /// and we do not want to re-create it for each request.
        /// </summary>
        static ProductService()
        {
            string redisConnectionString =
                ConfigurationManager.AppSettings["redisCacheConnectionString"];
            _redisConnection = ConnectionMultiplexer.Connect(redisConnection
            String);
        }

        /// <summary>
        /// Retrieves a list of all products from the database. Note that we are
        /// not getting the Specifications since we're just listing products and
        /// not viewing product details.
        /// </summary>
```

```
public async Task<ProductList> RetrieveAllProducts()
{
    ProductList allProducts = await RetrieveAllProductsFromDatabase();
    return allProducts;
}

/// <summary>
/// Retrieves a single product. We'll first look to see if the product is
/// in cache. If so, serve it. If not, retrieve it from the database,
/// add to cache, and then serve it.
/// </summary>
public async Task<ProductDetails> RetrieveProductDetails(int productId)
{
    ProductDetails product = await RetrieveProductFromCache(productId);
    if (product == null)
    {
        //we've had a cache miss. We're going to have to retrieve the
        product
        //from the database, then add it to cache before returning.
        product = await RetrieveProductFromDatabase(productId);
        await AddProductToCache(product);
    }

    return product;
}

/// <summary>
/// Updates the product in our database
/// </summary>
public async Task UpdateProductDetails(ProductDetails product)
{
    //first, update the product in our system of record.
    await UpdateProductInDatabase(product);
}
```

```csharp
/// <summary>
/// Convenience method for creating a Redis Cache key for a product.
/// </summary>
private string CreateProductCacheKey(int productId)
{
    return "product:" + productId;
}

/// <summary>
/// Checks our Redis Cache for the requested product. If found, we
/// return the
/// ProductDetails record. If not, we return null.
/// </summary>
private async Task<ProductDetails> RetrieveProductFromCache(int
productId)
{
    string productKey = "product:" + productId;
    IDatabase cache = _redisConnection.GetDatabase();
    string val = await cache.StringGetAsync(productKey);
    if (val == null)
    {
        //cache miss. We don't have this product cached yet.
        return null;
    }

    ProductDetails product = JsonConvert.DeserializeObject<Product
    Details>(val);
    product.RetrievalMethod = REDIS_RETRIEVAL;
    return product;
}

/// <summary>
/// Adds a product to our Redis Cache.
/// </summary>
private async Task AddProductToCache(ProductDetails product)
{
    string productKey = CreateProductCacheKey(product.Id);
```

```
        IDatabase cache = _redisConnection.GetDatabase();
        string serializedProduct = JsonConvert.SerializeObject(product);
        await cache.StringSetAsync(productKey, serializedProduct);
    }

    /// <summary>
    /// Retrieves a product from the database using the supplied primary
    /// key.
    /// </summary>
    private async Task<ProductDetails> RetrieveProductFromDatabase(int
    productId)
    {
        ProductDetails product = null;
        using (var db = new TechStoreContext())
        {
            var productFromDb = await db.Products.Where(b =>
                b.Id == productId).Include(b => b.Specifications).
                FirstOrDefaultAsync();
            if (productFromDb != null)
            {
                product = CreateProductDetails(productFromDb);
                product.RetrievalMethod = DATABASE_RETRIEVAL;
            }
        }
        return product;
    }

    /// <summary>
    /// Updates a Products record in the database.
    /// </summary>
    private async Task UpdateProductInDatabase(ProductDetails product)
    {
        using (var db = new TechStoreContext())
        {
            var productFromDb = await db.Products.FindAsync(product.Id);
            if (productFromDb == null)
```

```
    {
        throw new Exception("We couldn't find a product for Id " +
        product.Id);
    }

    productFromDb.Name = product.Name;
    productFromDb.Description = product.Description;
    productFromDb.SKU = product.SKU;
    productFromDb.NumberInStock = product.NumberInStock;

    await db.SaveChangesAsync();
    product.LastUpdatedMessage = "Successfully updated at " +
        DateTime.Now.ToString("o");
    }
}

/// <summary>
/// Retrieves all products from the database, stores them in a
/// ProductList
/// instance, and returns them to the caller.
/// </summary>
/// <returns></returns>
private async Task<ProductList> RetrieveAllProductsFromDatabase()
{
    ProductList allProducts = new ProductList();
    allProducts.RetrievalMethod = DATABASE_RETRIEVAL;
    using (var db = new TechStoreContext())
    {
        var productsFromDb = await db.Products.ToListAsync();
        foreach (Product p in productsFromDb)
        {
            allProducts.Products.Add(CreateProductDetails(p));
        }
    }
    return allProducts;
}
```

```
/// <summary>
/// Copies data from our Entity Framework-generated Product class to our
/// ProductDetails view model class.
/// </summary>
private ProductDetails CreateProductDetails(Product p)
{
    ProductDetails details = new ProductDetails();
    details.Id = p.Id;
    details.Name = p.Name;
    details.Description = p.Description;
    details.SKU = p.SKU;
    details.NumberInStock = p.NumberInStock;

    //now let's set up our specifications
    foreach (Specification s in p.Specifications)
    {
        SpecificationDetails specDetail = new SpecificationDetails();
        specDetail.SpecName = s.SpecName;
        specDetail.SpecValue = s.SpecValue;
        details.Specifications.Add(specDetail);
    }
    return details;
}
}
}
```

There are a few points I'd like to bring to your attention in our new `ProductServices` class.

- When using the `StackExchange.Redis` library, we use the `ConnectionMultiplexor` class to connect to a Redis Cache. This is a heavyweight object and should be reused between requests. In our example, we defined our `ConnectionMultiplexor` as a static member variable and set it in a static constructor. This ensures that no matter how many instances of `ProductService` are created, all instances will use the same `ConnectionMultiplexor` instance.

- The read portion of the Cache Aside pattern is implemented in the `RetrieveProductDetails` method. We first check the cache for the requested product. If it doesn't exist, we retrieve the Product record from the database, then add it to the cache.

- Note that when adding a `ProductDetails` instance to our cache, we defined our key for the product as `"product:[:productid]"`. I recommend prefacing your keys with a string for each different type of class you store within the cache. This will avoid collisions and make debugging easier when you are looking at keys currently stored within a cache.

- Each `ProductDetails` instance that we store within the cache must be serialized to a string. Serializing to JSON using Newtonsoft.Json will be your best bet. Remember to deserialize when you retrieve an object instance from the Redis Cache.

Publish the updated version of TechStore to your Azure Web App, then rerun. Once the index page loads, click a product link to navigate to a product page. After publishing, I navigated to the Apple Macbook Pro product page. The product record was retrieved from Azure SQL and was likely not present within the database's page cache. The total request processing time was 530 ms. I requested the page again, and the total request processing time was 2.9 ms (see Figure 7-11). That, my friend, is the power of memory caching.

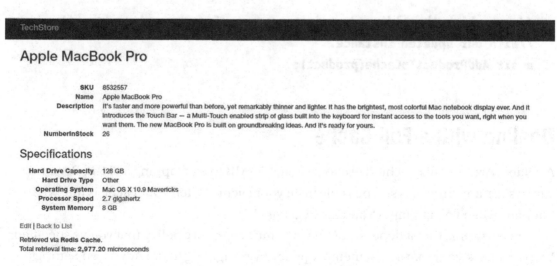

Figure 7-11. *Our total request processing time using Redis Cache was 2.9 ms*

Handling Stale Cache Records

Reads from Redis are lightning fast, but our app still has a problem. What happens if we edit a product record? If you read through the ProductService class, you'll see that updates to a product record are written directly to the database. The original unaltered record remains in cache, blissfully unaware that it's been changed in the database. To fix this, we need to make sure that after updating a product record in the database, we remove the corresponding product record from the cache and add the updated version. In the AddProductToCache method, calling StringSetAsync will add or replace a value for a given key.

Adding this functionality is simple; in fact, it's only a single line of code. Take a look at Listing 7-12 to see the ProductService's modified UpdateProductDetails method.

Listing 7-12.

```
/// <summary>
/// Updates the product in our database, then evicts the old stale record
/// from cache.
/// </summary>
public async Task UpdateProductDetails(ProductDetails product)
{
    //first, update the product in our system of record.
    await UpdateProductInDatabase(product);

    //next, kick the old product instance out of cache and replace it
    //with our updated instance.
    await AddProductToCache(product);
}
```

Dealing with a Full Cache

Available Azure Redis Cache sizes range from 250 MB to a whopping 530 GB. Because cache sizes are finite, it is still possible to fill your cache. When your cache is full, what happens when you attempt to add the next item?

The answer is that it depends on the maximum memory policy that you've specified. You can check your maximum memory policy by navigating to the Advanced Settings blade of your Redis resource. By default, Redis uses a volatile least recently used (LRU) policy. This means that items within the cache that have been used the least recently will be evicted from the cache to make room for newly added items. This policy works well for our application. Suppose that TechStore's cache was full and we needed to add a new entry for the iPhone 8. We could safely evict product information for the iPhone 4S, which likely hasn't been requested in quite some time. Unless you have a good reason for doing so, I recommend accepting the default of volatile-lru. Other options include evicting key/value pairs at random, not evicting and throwing an exception instead, and evicting a key that has the shortest time-to-live remaining.

This brings us to our next topic, which is explicitly setting time-to-live for a key.

Setting Time-to-Live

Your application's data might be temporally sensitive: Data is needed for a given period of time, then is rarely used afterward. Imagine how we might implement caching on Reddit.com. New posts are hot and experience many reads. After a few days when a post has scrolled off of the first few pages, it is rarely accessed. We don't want old cat meme posts from five days ago clogging up our valuable cache when we have brand new cat memes that are experiencing thousands of requests per second. In situations such as this, it's best to cache data and tell Redis to evict data from the cache after a set period of time.

Setting a time-to-live is simple: We just use an overload for the `StringSetAsync` method. If we wanted to change TechStore's `AddProductToCache` method to expire a `ProductDetails` record from cache after one day, we'd use the following line of code:

```
await cache.StringSetAsync (productKey, serializedProduct, TimeSpan.
FromDays(1));
```

Viewing Redis Cache Contents

When developing with Redis Cache, it's often helpful to view the contents of the cache or flush its contents. To do so, I recommend a handy tool called Redis Desktop Manager (RDM). You can download RDM from `https://redisdesktop.com`. RDM is an open source project that was created by Igor Malinovskiy and is supported by a host of contributors.

Connect to a Redis Cache

After installing Redis Desktop Manager, you'll need to create a connection to your Redis instance. Click Connect to Redis Server (see Figure 7-12) to open the Connection dialog box. In the Connection dialog box, you'll need to supply the following data:

- *Name*: This is the name that will be displayed in the instance list of available servers. You can name your cache anything you like.

- *Host*: This is the URI of the Redis cache. It will be in the form of [your cache instance name].redis.cache.windows.net.

- *Port*: Set this to port 6380 for Secure Sockets Layer (SSL).

- *Auth*: This is the primary access key listed on your Redis Cache's Access Keys blade in the Azure Portal. To get there, navigate to your Redis Cache's management blade, click Access Keys.

We're not quite done. By default, Azure Redis requires a connection over SSL. Click the SSL tab in the Connection dialog box, then select the Use SSL Protocol check box. You can now test your connection, then click OK to add your cache instance to the list of available caches in Redis Desktop Manager.

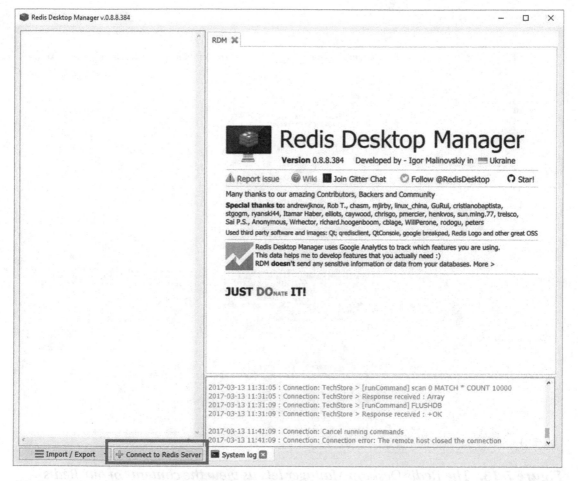

Figure 7-12. *The Redis Desktop Manager program. Click Connect to Redis Server to create a connection to your Azure Redis Cache*

Viewing Cache Contents

After connecting to a Redis server, your connection will appear in the left pane. To view the contents of the cache, double-click your connection and expand nodes as needed. Keys will be displayed as terminal nodes in the tree view. Click a key to view the value. Notice that in Figure 7-13, we've selected the key of product:1. Our ProductDetails class that has been serialized to JSON appears in the Value panel to the right. This is another great reason to use JSON as your serialization format.

Figure 7-13. *The Redis Desktop Manager lets us view the contents of our Redis Cache*

Flushing the Cache

To flush the entire contents of a cache, right-click a database node within a cache and select Flush Cache from the shortcut menu. All keys within the database will be removed.

Scaling Azure Redis Cache

There are several options for scaling Redis Cache.

Scaling Up

Redis has three different pricing tiers: Basic, Standard, and Premium. Within each tier, there are various cache sizes. As the cache size within a tier increases, the maximum number of allowed connections and network performance increases as well. The simplest way to scale is to move to a more powerful plan. When you do so, the data within your cache is automatically migrated.

Scaling Out

All caches within the Basic tier are single instance and have no SLA. These are not recommended for critical jobs where data cannot be lost. Caches within the Standard tier allow master/slave replication and automatic failover along with a 99.9% uptime SLA. Even within the Standard tier, though, you cannot scale beyond 53 GB in size.

Caches within the Premium tier allow clustering and sharding of your data. You can have up to ten caches participate in a cluster, allowing a maximum combined cache size of up to 530 GB. You can configure the number of caches in your cluster by clicking the Redis Cluster Size menu option. Note that if your current cache is not within the Premium tier, this feature is disabled.

When you enable clustering, Azure will handle distributing your data throughout the cluster via sharding. This process is transparent to you, and you don't have to do anything additional to your code.

Using Multiple Caches

For the Cache Aside pattern, you do not have to put all of your data within a single cache. You can create two or more cache instances, and separate your data by type. For example, TechStore might elect to keep all product data in `techstore1.redis.cache.windows.net`, and all customer reviews in `techstore2.redis.cache.windows.net`. Your application will have to point to the correct cache to store and retrieve data.

Summary

This chapter covered:

- How accessing data in memory is much faster than accessing data stored on disk.

- The Cache Aside pattern. Frequently used data can be stored in a Redis Cache instance. Your application will first look in the cache to find the data. If it is not found, it's retrieved from disk and stored within the cache.

- TechStore, which illustrated the Cache Aside pattern with Redis.

- How to view data within a Redis Cache using Redis Desktop Manager.

- How to scale Redis Cache.

In the next chapter, we'll dive into WebJobs.

CHAPTER 8

WebJobs

Thus far, we've discussed creating Web Apps and several options for data storage. When building a web application, it's not just about creating web methods and answering page requests, though. Sometimes, processes need to run on a schedule, or you need to respond to events that occur. Examples include sending daily e-mails, texting users a welcome message when they sign up, creating daily reports, and archiving data.

How can we handle these requirements? We could spin up a VM, then write a set of console applications to periodically wake up and do some work. We'd also need to write a monitoring service to check the health of our console applications and restart them if they crash. We'd also need to set up logging to help us troubleshoot if things go wrong. Last but not least, we'd need to configure Windows Task Scheduler to execute our processes at a periodic interval.

Setting up a VM and writing such infrastructure is both tedious and difficult to support. This is exactly why WebJobs were invented.

So what exactly is a WebJob? A WebJob is a console application that makes use of the WebJob API. A WebJob runs as a separate process inside an Azure Web App and can execute functions on a set schedule or respond to events such as the creation of new Storage Queue messages, Service Bus messages, Azure Table entries, or Azure Blob entries.

If you're already running a Web App, WebJobs cost nothing to run. That's right: zero, zilch, nada! Inside of a Web App, WebJobs share resources with your main web application and any other WebJobs living on the same Web App instance. Aside from your Web App's physical resources such as CPU and memory, there is no limit to the number of WebJobs that can live on a single Web App.

© Rob Reagan 2018
R. Reagan, *Web Applications on Azure*, https://doi.org/10.1007/978-1-4842-2976-7_8

Invoking WebJob Methods

A WebJob will execute one or more methods in response to events that you specify. Some of the more common events that can trigger the execution of a WebJob method include the following:

- *A schedule*: You can tell a WebJob to execute a method at a given time interval. For example, you can specify that a method should be called every 30 minutes, perhaps to aggregate sales lead data and e-mail a summary to a sales team leader.

- *A new Storage Queue message*: WebJobs will periodically check a Storage Queue for new messages. If new messages are found, they will be deserialized and handed to a method you designate for processing.

- *A new Service Bus Queue message*: Much like responding to Storage Queue messages, your WebJob will execute when a new Service Bus Queue message is created and added to a queue. The message will be deserialized and passed to your method for processing.

- *A new Storage Blob*: When a new Storage Blob is created, your designated method will execute.

- *Blob updates*: Similarly, when a Blob is updated, your WebJob method will be called.

- *Being explicitly invoked*: You can call WebJob methods via an HTTP Post, much like calling a RESTful web service.

We've talked about how WebJobs are simply console applications that run inside of a Web App, and that methods can be called when certain events occur. How do we tell a WebJob which method should be called when a specified event takes place? The answer is that we decorate methods with attributes. For example, in Listing 8-1, we've decorated the `ProcessQueueMessage` method with the `QueueTriggerAttribute` and passed the name of the Storage Queue that we're monitoring as an argument. This tells our WebJob that whenever a new message is inserted into the `webjobmessages` queue, the `ProcessQueueMessage` method should be called.

Listing 8-1. We've Decorated a WebJob Method so That It Will Be Called When a New Storage Queue Message Is Inserted into the Specified Queue

```
public static void ProcessQueueMessage([QueueTrigger("webjobmessages")]
string message, TextWriter log)
{
    log.WriteLine(message);
}
```

There are a host of other attributes you can use to instruct Azure to call a method when certain events occur, such as `BlobTrigger` and `ServiceBusTrigger`.

Microsoft has open sourced the entire WebJob API and given developers the ability to create their own triggers to respond to various events by writing against the Azure WebJobs SDK Extensions API. Microsoft and other developers have done just that, and given us additional triggers such as these:

- *TimerTrigger*: This works as a chron job and will execute a method on a schedule. Before `TimerTrigger`, we had to use the Azure Scheduler service or specify a schedule in an external `settings.job` JSON file.

- *FileTrigger*: `FileTrigger` will monitor a given directory in your Web App for new or updated files, and will call the specified method when those changes occur.

- *ErrorTrigger*: `ErrorTrigger` is like a WebJob-wide catch block for exceptions. A method decorated with the `ErrorTrigger` attribute will be called when an unhandled exception occurs. This is a great way to send out alerts to the poor soul on call for support.

- *TwilioTrigger*: `TwilioTrigger` was written by the communications juggernaut Twilio. `TwilioTrigger` will send an SMS message to a designated number when a WebJob method is called. It's useful for combining with other triggers, such as `ErrorTrigger`.

This is not an exhaustive list of extension triggers, and the list will continue to grow as Microsoft and other vendors publish more. To see what's available, visit the GitHub repo at `https://github.com/Azure/azure-webjobs-sdk-extensions`.

The WebJob Demo Application

Now that we've had an overview of what WebJobs are and what they can do for you, let's walk through an example app and look at some code.

We'll create an application called WebJob Demo. The WebJob Demo solution will consist of a WebJob, a shared Models project, and an ASP.NET MVC Core web application that will allow us to create various events for our WebJob methods to respond to. We'll look at several common cases such as responding to queued messages, executing on a given schedule, and how to handle errors. Throughout this example, we'll talk about how to develop WebJobs locally. We'll end the discussion with deploying our WebJob to Azure.

Note   You can download the completed solution at `https://github.com/BuildingScalableWebAppsWithAzure/WebJobDemo.git`

Creating Our Solution and WebJob Project

Let's jump right in by creating our WebJob.

1. Open Visual Studio and select File ➤ New ➤ Project. This opens the New Project dialog box.

2. On the New Project dialog box, select the Azure WebJob template located under Templates ➤ Windows ➤ Cloud. Let's name the project `WebJobDemo.WebJob`, and name the solution `WebJobDemo` (Figure 8-1). Click OK to create the solution and project.

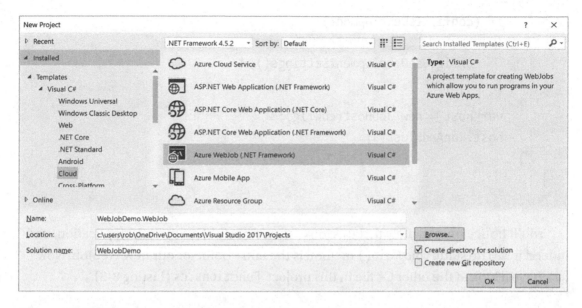

Figure 8-1. *Creating our solution and Azure WebJob project*

3. Right-click the WebJobDemo.WebJob project, then select Manage
   NuGet Packages Add the NuGet packages `Microsoft.Azure.`
   `WebJobs`, `Microsoft.Azure.WebJobs.Core`, and `Microsoft.`
   `Azure.WebJobs.Extensions`.

The Azure WebJob template will create two C# files for us in our new project:
`Program.cs` and `Functions.cs`. Let's start by taking a look at `Program.cs` (Listing 8-2).

Listing 8-2. The Program.cs File Provided by the Azure WebJob Project Template

```
using Microsoft.Azure.WebJobs;

namespace WebJobDemo.WebJob
{
    class Program
    {
        // Please set the following connection strings in app.config for this
        // WebJob to run: AzureWebJobsDashboard and AzureWebJobsStorage
        static void Main()
        {
            var config = new JobHostConfiguration();
```

```
        if (config.IsDevelopment)
        {
            config.UseDevelopmentSettings();
        }

        var host = new JobHost(config);
        host.RunAndBlock();
    }
  }
}
```

You'll notice immediately that this looks suspiciously like a console application, and indeed it is. The static void Main() method is the entry point for our new WebJob. Now let's have a look at the other C# file in this project, Functions.cs (Listing 8-3).

Listing 8-3. The Functions.cs File Generated by the Azure WebJob Project Template

```
using System.IO;
using Microsoft.Azure.WebJobs;

namespace WebJobDemo.WebJob
{
    public class Functions
    {
        // This function will get triggered/executed when a new message is
        written
        // on an Azure Queue called queue.
        public static void ProcessQueueMessage([QueueTrigger("queue")] string
        message,
            TextWriter log)
        {
            log.WriteLine(message);
        }
    }
}
```

`Functions.cs` is traditionally where you'll place all triggered methods for your WebJob. You can see that we have a single method called `ProcessQueueMessages`, and it's decorated with a `QueueTriggerAttribute`. The `QueueTriggerAttribute` instructs Azure to call our `ProcessQueueMessage` method whenever a new message is placed on the Azure Storage Queue named "queue".

So how does this work behind the scenes? The `JobHost` class that is instantiated in the `Program` class's `Main` method is part of the Azure WebJobs SDK. Its purpose is to manage all of the functions and their associated triggers within a WebJob. When `JobHost` is instantiated, it will find all public methods within the project that are decorated with trigger attributes that respond to events. `JobHost` will then monitor the specified queues, blob containers, or file directories to watch for triggering events. When events that we're interested in occur, `JobHost` will call the appropriate methods.

Running Our WebJob Locally

Let's run our WebJob locally and see what happens. First, though, we need to do a bit more configuration. If we open the `app.config` file, we can see the code shown in Listing 8-4.

Listing 8-4. The app.config File for Our WebJobDemo.WebJob WebJob

```
<connectionStrings>
    <add name="AzureWebJobsDashboard" connectionString=""/>
    <add name="AzureWebJobsStorage" connectionString=""/>
</connectionStrings>
```

Azure uses the Storage account referenced by `AzureWebJobsDashboard` to write diagnostic logs for WebJobs that have been deployed to Azure. We discuss logging in further detail an upcoming section. The Storage account referred to by `AzureWebJobsStorage` is used by Azure to store runtime and configuration information about your WebJob. For example, if your WebJob is deployed to a Web App that has been scaled out to multiple instances, and your WebJob has a method that is scheduled to run using a `TimerTrigger` attribute, Azure will ensure that there is only one copy of your WebJob running. Azure records which Web App instance is hosting your WebJob by using the Storage account specified by `AzureWebJobStorage`. You don't have to worry about any of the bookkeeping that Azure does in the `AzureWebJobStorage` Storage account, but you do have to provide a Storage account for Azure to use to do so.

Because we're going to initially test our WebJob locally, you can enter
`UseDevelopmentStorage=true` for both the `AzureWebJobsDashboard` and
`AzureWebJobsStorage` properties in the `app.config` file.

After updating `app.config`, run the application. You'll see a console window appear
with our WebJob's output (Figure 8-2).

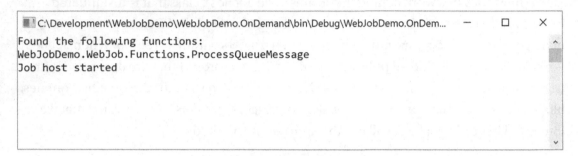

Figure 8-2. *The output of running our WebJobDemo.WebJob*

We can see that Azure has successfully located our `ProcessQueueMessage` method
and is waiting for a message to appear in the queue. To make this demo more exciting,
let's build a web application that will insert messages into the queue so that our WebJob
can consume them.

Creating Our WebJobDemo Web Application

Let's add a new ASP.NET Core Web Application to our project. To add the new project, do
the following:

1. Right-click the solution in Visual Studio Solution Explorer, select
    Add, then select New Project.

2. In the Add New Project dialog box, select the ASP.NET Core Web
    Application (.NET Framework) under the Installed ➤ Visual
    C# ➤ Web section. This will run our ASP.NET Core project on the
    full .NET Framework rather than using ASP.NET Core 1.0. This is
    important because it will allow us to use packages written for the
    full .NET Framework that haven't yet been ported to .NET Core.

3.   Name your new project WebJobDemo.Web, then click OK (Figure 8-3).

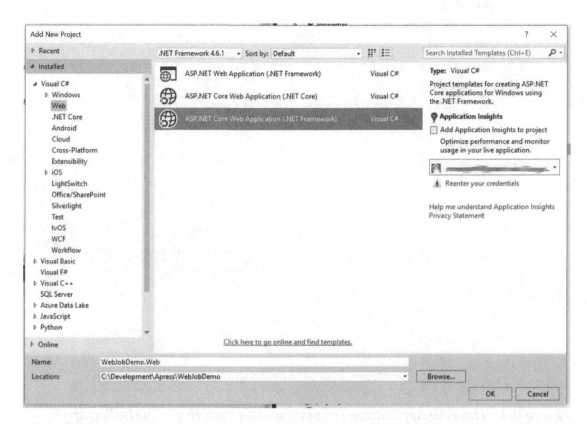

Figure 8-3.   *Selecting the ASP.NET Core Web Application (.NET Framework) template*

4. Finally, select the Web Application template and click OK
    (Figure 8-4).

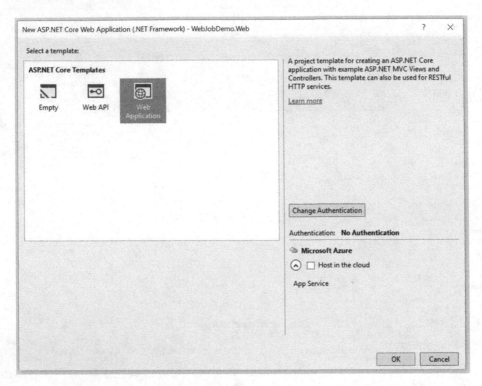

Figure 8-4. *The Web Application template will set up a HomeController, an
associated view, and routing. It'll save us some typing.*

Creating Our Model

Our goal is to use our new web application to create a Storage Queue message, then have
our WebJob's ProcessQueueMessage method consume the new message. We could pass
a string as the message, but that's boring. A better real-world example is to send a class
instance as the payload for the queue message. Let's create a QueueMessage class that
we'll use to do so.

Because we're going to use the same class in both our WebJobsDemo.Web and
WebJobsDemo.WebJob projects, we'll need to create a new project called WebJobsDemo.
Models that is referenced by both.

1. Right-click the WebJobDemo solution in the Solution Explorer window, select Add, and then select New Project.

2. In the Add New Project dialog box, choose the Class Library that is located under Installed ➤ Visual C# ➤ Windows ➤ Classic Desktop (Figure 8-5). Name the class library `WebJobDemo.Models`, and click OK.

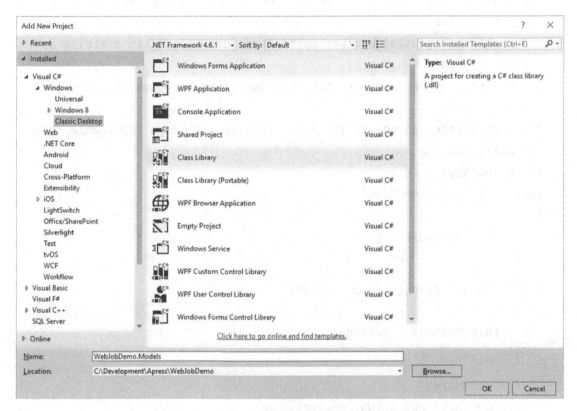

Figure 8-5. *Add a new Class Library called WebJobDemo.Models to the solution*

3. Next, we need to add our `QueueMessage.cs` class to our new `WebJobDemo.Models` project. Our Class Library template already gave us a `Class1.cs class`. Rename the file `QueueMessage.cs`, then replace its contents with the code in Listing 8-5.

Listing 8-5. The QueueMessage.cs Class

```
namespace WebJobDemo.Models
{
    /// <summary>
    /// This class contains information sent as a queue message. We are
    /// using this
    /// class as the model for both Service Bus Queues and Azure Storage
    /// Queues. The
    /// reason we're using a class instead of just passing in a string as
    /// the payload
    /// for both queue types is that it's useful to know how to serialize,
    /// pass, and
    /// deserialized an object instance. This is much more applicable real
    /// world example.
    /// </summary>
    public class QueueMessage
    {
        public QueueMessage()
        { }

    public QueueMessage(string message)
        {
            this.Message = message;
        }

        /// <summary>
        /// Contains our actual message.
        /// </summary>
        public string Message { get; set; }
    }
}
```

4. Finally, add a reference to the new WebJobDemo.Models project
    from both the WebJobDemo.Web and WebJobDemo.WebJob projects.

Creating Our Services for WebJobDemo.Web

We now need code that will place a message in a Storage Queue so that it can be read by our WebJob. To make that magic happen, let's create a StorageQueueService.cs class and place the logic there. Because we're using dependency injection, we'll create our IStorageQueueService.cs interface first.

1. Add a new folder to the WebJobDemo.Web project by right- clicking it in the Solution Explorer, selecting Add, and then selecting New Folder. Name the new folder Services.

2. Right-click the new Services folder, select Add, and then select New Item.

    When the Add New Item dialog box opens, select Interface, name it IStorageQueueService.cs, and click Add.

3. Replace the contents of IStorageQueueService.cs with the code in Listing 8-6.

Listing 8-6. Our IStorageQueueService.cs Interface Implemented by StorageQueueService.cs

```
using System.Threading.Tasks;
using WebJobDemo.Models;

namespace WebJobDemo.Web.Services
{
    public interface IStorageQueueService
    {
      Task EnqueueMessage(QueueMessage queueMessage);
    }
}
```

4. To connect to an Azure Storage Queue, we'll need to reference a few libraries. Right-click WebJobDemo.Web and select Manage NuGet Packages. You'll need to add WindowsAzure.Storage to the project.

5. For the final step, let's create our StorageQueueService.cs class.
    Right-click the Services folder once again, select Add, and then
    select Class. Name the new class StorageQueueService.cs, then
    replace the contents of this new class with the code found in
    Listing 8-7.

Listing 8-7. The QueueService.cs Class: The EnqueueMessage Method Will
Enqueue a QueueMessage on the Specified Storage Queue

```
using System.Threading.Tasks;
using WebJobDemo.Models;
using Newtonsoft.Json;
using Microsoft.WindowsAzure.Storage.Queue;
using Microsoft.WindowsAzure.Storage;

namespace WebJobDemo.Web.Services
{
    public class StorageQueueService : IStorageQueueService
    {
        private readonly string _connectionString;
        /// <summary>
        /// Constructor.
        /// </summary>
        /// <param name="connectionString">The connection string to the
        /// Storage account that
        /// we're using.</param>
        public StorageQueueService(string connectionString)
        {
            _connectionString = connectionString;
        }
        /// <summary>
        /// Serializes queueMessage and adds it to the Storage queue
        /// webjobmessages.
        /// </summary>
        public async Task EnqueueMessage(QueueMessage queueMessage)
        {
```

```
        CloudStorageAccount storageAccount = CloudStorageAccount.Parse(_
        connectionString);
        CloudQueueClient queueClient = storageAccount.
        CreateCloudQueueClient();
        //queue names MUST be all lowercase and can only contain letters,
        //numbers, and the
        //dash character. if you do not follow these rules, Azure will bop
        //you over the
        ///head with a 400 Bad Request.
        CloudQueue queue = queueClient.GetQueueReference("webjobmessages");
        await queue.CreateIfNotExistsAsync();
        //to send a class instance as a Storage Queue message payload, we
        //must first serialize it.
        //to JSON. Newtonsoft's JsonConvert class will do the trick.
        string serializedMsg = JsonConvert.SerializeObject(queueMessage);
        CloudQueueMessage queueMsg = new CloudQueueMessage(serializedMsg);
        await queue.AddMessageAsync(queueMsg);
    }
  }
}
```

Creating Our MVC Web Controller and View

Now that our service containing the Storage Queue logic is in place, let's turn our attention to setting up our web project's UI. We'll make changes to the HomeController.cs file and its accompanying view. The end result of our efforts will be the screen shown in Figure 8-6. The UI is pretty simple: Type a message in the Message text box, then click Send.

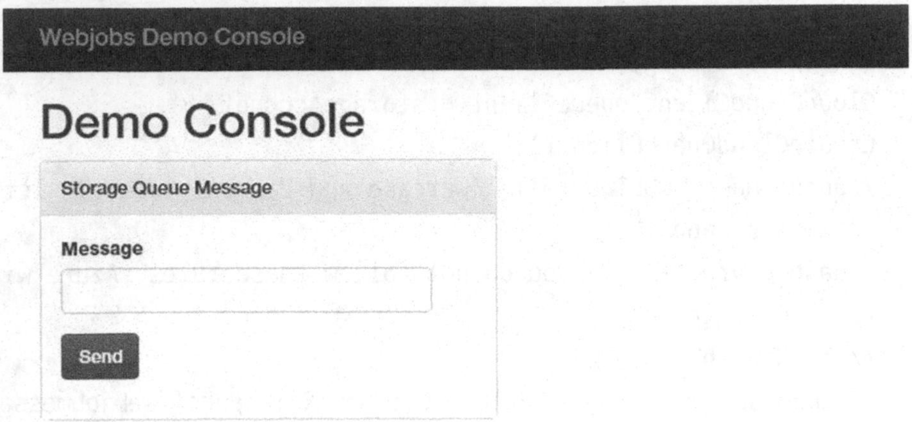

Figure 8-6. *The UI for our web project will allow us to send a message to our Storage Queue*

Let's make the changes listed here.

1. In WebJobDemo.Web, expand the Views ➤ Home folder. Delete the About.cshtml and Contact.cshtml files; we don't need them for this demo.

2. We are going to need a model class to transport information back and forth between our HomeController and its view. Right-click the WebJobDemo.Web project and select Add ➤ New Folder. Name the new folder ViewModels. Add a new class to the ViewModels folder called QueueMessageViewModel.cs. Replace its code with the code in Listing 8-8.

Listing 8-8. The QueueMessageViewModel Class

```
namespace WebJobDemo.Web.ViewModels
{
    /// <summary>
    /// This class carries data back and forth between our HomeController
    /// methods
    /// and our strongly typed view.
    /// </summary>
    public class QueueMessageViewModel
    {
```

```
        public string StorageQueueMessage { get; set; }
        public string LastPostStatus { get; set; }
    }
}
```

3. Open the HomeController.cs file in the WebJobDemo.Web ➤
    Controllers folder. Replace the code in HomeController.cs with
    the code in Listing 8-9.

Listing 8-9. The HomeController Class Code

```
using System;
using Microsoft.AspNetCore.Mvc;
using WebJobDemo.Web.ViewModels;
using WebJobDemo.Web.Services;
using WebJobDemo.Models;

namespace WebJobDemo.Web.Controllers
{
    public class HomeController : Controller
    {
        private readonly IStorageQueueService _storageQueueSvc;

        /// <summary>
        /// Constructor
        /// </summary>
        public HomeController(IStorageQueueService storageQueueSvc)
        {
            _storageQueueSvc = storageQueueSvc;
        }

        [HttpGet]
        public IActionResult Index()
        {
            return View();
        }
```

```
/// <summary>
/// Called when the user submits a message to send to our WebJob.
/// This method
/// passes the message to our StorageQueueService for enqueueing.
/// </summary>
[HttpPost]
public IActionResult Index(QueueMessageViewModel model)
{
    model.LastPostStatus = string.Empty;
    if (!string.IsNullOrEmpty(model.StorageQueueMessage))
    {
        //the user has supplied a message. Place the message inside a
        //QueueMessage
        //instance and pass it to our StorageQueueService for enqueueing.
        QueueMessage queueMsg = new QueueMessage(model.
        StorageQueueMessage);
        _storageQueueSvc.EnqueueMessage(queueMsg);

        //tell the user that the message was successfully processed.
        model.LastPostStatus = "Posted the message \"" + model.
        StorageQueueMessage +
            "\" to the Storage Queue at " + DateTime.Now.ToString();
    }
    model.StorageQueueMessage = string.Empty;
    return View(model);
    }
  }
}
```

4. Next, let's update the code for our view. You'll need to update
   the contents of the WebJobDemo.Web ➤ Views ➤ Home ➤
   Index.cshtml and the WebJobDemo.Web ➤ Views ➤ Shared
   ➤ _Layout.cshtml files. To save space, we won't list the HTML
   markup, but you can view the markup or download the completed
   project at our GitHub repository.

5. Our application needs to know what Storage account it's going to use to send a queue message, so let's add that configuration info to WebJobDemo.Web's `appsettings.json` file (Listing 8-10). We're initially using the local Azure Storage Emulator to test our application, so update the `StorageConnectionString` property to `"UseDevelopmentStorage=true"`.

Listing 8-10. The WebJobDemo.Web's appsettings.json File

```
{
    "Logging": {
    "IncludeScopes": false,
    "LogLevel": {
        "Default": "Debug",
        "System": "Information",
        "Microsoft": "Information"
        }
    },
    "AzureStorageConfig": {
    "StorageConnectionString: "UseDevelopmentStorage=true"
    }
}
```

6. Finally, we need to set up our dependency injection so that our `StorageQueueService` will be injected into the `HomeController`'s constructor. Open WebJobDemo.Web's `Startup.cs` file. Make sure that you add the `"using WebJobDemo.Web.Services"` statement. Then modify the `ConfigureServices` method so that it matches Listing 8-11.

Listing 8-11. The Contents of Startup.cs's ConfigureServices Method

```
// This method gets called by the runtime. Use this method to add services
// to the container.
public void ConfigureServices(IServiceCollection services)
{
    // Add framework services.
    services.AddMvc();
    //configure our dependency injection for our StorageQueueService.
    IConfiguration storageConfig = Configuration.GetSection("AzureStorageConfig");
    string storageConnectionString =
        storageConfig.GetValue<string>("StorageConnectionString");
    //rather than using IOptions and a custom class for config settings for
    //our Storage
    //connection string, we can read the connection string as a string
    //value, then set up
    //a factory to perform our actual instantiation.
    Func<IServiceProvider, IStorageQueueService> queueStorageFactory = m =>
        new StorageQueueService(storageConnectionString);
    services.AddTransient<IStorageQueueService>(queueStorageFactory);
}
```

Running Our Web Application

The moment of truth has arrived: Let's run our web application and create some Storage Queue messages. Right-click the WebJobDemo.Web project, select Set as Startup Project, then run the application. You should see the screen in Figure 8-6 in your browser. Enter a message in the Message text box and click Send. You should then see a confirmation alert letting you know that the message was successfully sent (Figure 8-7).

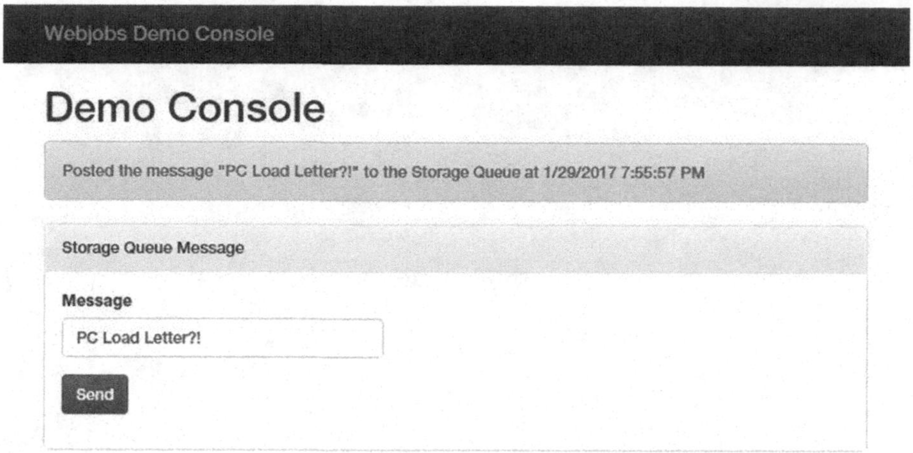
Webjobs Demo Console
Demo Console
Posted the message "PC Load Letter?!" to the Storage Queue at 1/29/2017 7:55:57 PM
Storage Queue Message
Message
PC Load Letter?!
Send

Figure 8-7. *Our Queue message was posted successfully to our Storage Queue*

But was it? Programmers are a skeptical bunch, especially when code runs correctly on the first try. Let's open Azure Storage Explorer and check to make sure that the queue message is actually waiting in the Storage Queue.

Note Azure Storage Explorer is a free tool that allows you to inspect Storage Queues, Blobs, and Tables. You can download the latest version at `http://storageexplorer.com/`

Within Azure Storage Explorer, browse to the local emulator and expand the resources treeview until you find your Storage account's Queues. You should then see your webjobmessages queue. Clicking the queue will show that your message was written successfully (Figure 8-8).

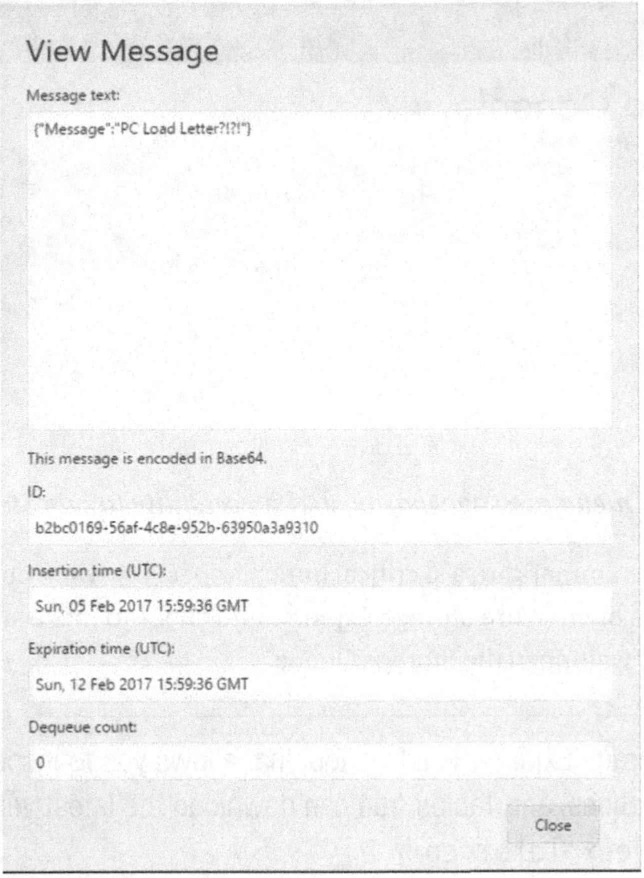

Figure 8-8. *Clicking the queue message in Azure Storage Explorer shows the message's details and confirms that it was successfully written to the queue*

Running Our WebJob Locally: Part II

Now that there's a message waiting in our queue, let's launch our WebJob locally and see what happens. Before we do, we need to make sure that our WebJob knows exactly which queue it should be monitoring.

First, our WebJob's `QueueTrigger` needs to know what account it should connect to. There are two ways to specify a Storage account.

1. By default, the `QueueTrigger` will monitor the Storage account referenced by the `AzureWebJobsStorage` connection string in `app.config`.

2. You can override the default settings in `Program.cs` setting the
    `JobConfiguration`'s `StorageConnectionString` property.

For simplicity, let's go ahead and set the `AzureWebJobsStorage` connection string
in our WebJobDemo.WebJob's `app.config` file. Make sure you use the same connection
string that's set in our WebJobDemo.Web project's `appsettings.json` file.

Now that we've got the Storage account set properly, we need to tell our WebJob
which queue within the Storage account it should monitor. We do this by specifying an
argument to the method's `QueueTriggerAttribute`. Open `Functions.cs`, and set the
queue name in the `QueueTriggerAttribute` to `webjobmessages`.

Now we're ready to run our application. To make things easier to test, let's tell Visual
Studio that we want to run our WebJob and our web application simultaneously. To do
so, right-click the solution in Solution Explorer and select Properties. In the Solution
Properties dialog box, expand Common Properties and select Startup Project. Select
the Multiple Startup Projects option (Figure 8-9) and set WebJobDemo.Web and
WebJobDemo.WebJob to start.

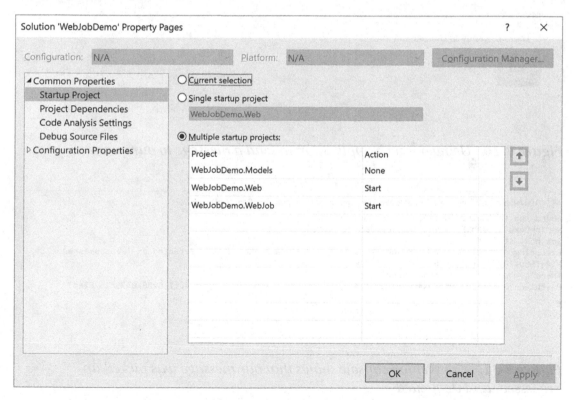

Figure 8-9. *The solution's Properties dialog box allows you to set multiple
startup projects*

Finally, run the application in debug mode. You'll see both the web and WebJob projects launch.

In the web application, add a message to the Message text box and click Send (Figure 8-10). In a few seconds, you should see a log message in the console when our WebJob picks up the message from the queue and processes it (Figure 8-11).

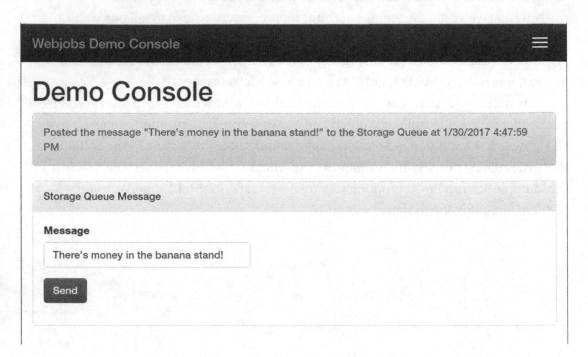

Figure 8-10. *Using our web application to send a message to our queue*

Figure 8-11. *The WebJob console shows that our message was picked up, processed, and dequeued*

You will notice that there is a time lag from when you send a message in the web application to when the WebJob picks up and processes the message. The reason is that under the covers, the QueueTriggerAttribute is polling the underlying Storage queue. Recall that there are two parts to the cost of Azure Storage Queues: average GB stored per month and transaction costs. At the time of this writing, Microsoft charges $0.0036 per 100,000 transactions. A transaction is a queue read or write operation. If our QueueTrigger polled the Storage Queue for new messages as fast as it could, transaction costs per month could add up to real money. To keep your transaction costs negligible, the QueueTrigger implements a random exponential back-off algorithm to determine how often it checks for new messages. As long as the QueueTrigger keeps finding an empty queue, it will increase the time between checks until it reaches the maximum wait time. You can configure this maximum wait time using JobHostConfiguration's Queues.MaxPollingInterval property. By default, the maximum polling interval is one minute.

Running a WebJob on a Schedule

We often need to write code that will run on a set schedule. Perhaps your code needs to execute every 15 minutes and check your database for new sales leads. Or perhaps you need to run a nightly job that will wake up at 2:00 a.m. and bill customers' credit cards. Microsoft has given us a handy tool to run recurring logic, and it's called the TimerTriggerAttribute.

The TimerTriggerAttribute is very easy to use. First, you have to call the JobHost Configuration class's UseTimers() method in your WebJob's Program.cs. If you neglect to do so, no timers will run. After that, simply decorate the WebJob method that you'd like to execute, and pass the schedule to the TimerTriggerAttribute as an argument.

Chrontab or Timespan Expressions

There are two separate overloads for the TimerTriggerAttribute. The first overload is TimerTriggerAttribute(string scheduleExpression). The scheduleExpression argument is a standard chrontab expression or a time interval. The TimerTriggerAttribute can distinguish between the two because a chrontab expression is in the format of {second} {minute} {hour} {day} {month} {day of the week}, whereas a timespan is in the format of hh:mm:ss. Examples of chrontab expressions are given in Table 8-1, and timespan examples are listed in Table 8-2.

Table 8-1. *Valid Chrontab Expressions*

Expression	Meaning
0 30 20 * * *	Run every day at 8:30 p.m.
0 0 2 * * MON	Run every Monday at 2:00 a.m.
0 0 2 * * MON-FRI	Run every weekday (Monday through Friday) at 2:00 a.m.
0 */5 * * * *	Run every five minutes

Table 8-2. *Valid Timespan Expressions*

Expression	Meaning
1:00:00	Run every hour from startup
0:30:00	Run every half-hour from startup
0:00:45	Run every 45 seconds

Note that all chrontab expressions use the server's local time zone. Therefore, a server located in the East datacenter will have a clock set to UTC – 5:00 for Eastern Standard Time, whereas the West datacenter will have a clock set to UTC – 8:00 for Pacific Standard Time.

Note   For a detailed explanation of chrontab syntax, visit
`https://en.wikipedia.org/wiki/Cron#CRON_expression`

An example is in order. First, open the `Program.cs` file in the WebJobDemo.WebJob project. You'll need to add the line `config.UseTimers()` before creating the `JobHost` instance. Next, open the `Functions.cs` file. Add the method in Listing 8-12.

Listing 8-12. The ScheduledMethodUsingTimespanExpression Uses a TimerTriggerAttribute Initialized Using a Timespan Expression

```
public static void ScheduledMethodUsingTimespanExpression(
    [TimerTrigger("00:00:30")] TimerInfo timer)
{

    Console.WriteLine("Timer triggered at " + DateTime.Now);
}
```

This method uses a timespan expression that will fire the `TimerTrigger` and call the method every 30 seconds. Set the WebJobDemo.WebJob project as the only startup project and run the application. You'll see log messages in the console showing that the trigger does indeed fire every half-minute (Figure 8-12).

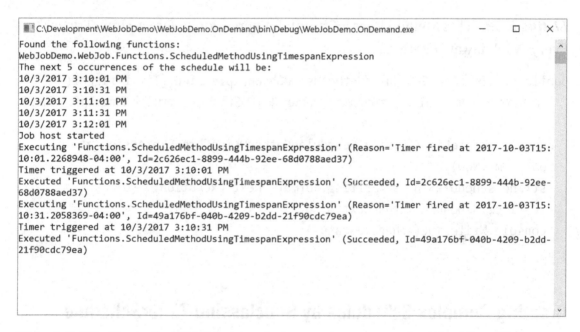

```
C:\Development\WebJobDemo\WebJobDemo.OnDemand\bin\Debug\WebJobDemo.OnDemand.exe          —    □    ×
Found the following functions:
WebJobDemo.WebJob.Functions.ScheduledMethodUsingTimespanExpression
The next 5 occurrences of the schedule will be:
10/3/2017 3:10:01 PM
10/3/2017 3:10:31 PM
10/3/2017 3:11:01 PM
10/3/2017 3:11:31 PM
10/3/2017 3:12:01 PM
Job host started
Executing 'Functions.ScheduledMethodUsingTimespanExpression' (Reason='Timer fired at 2017-10-03T15:
10:01.2268948-04:00', Id=2c626ec1-8899-444b-92ee-68d0788aed37)
Timer triggered at 10/3/2017 3:10:01 PM
Executed 'Functions.ScheduledMethodUsingTimespanExpression' (Succeeded, Id=2c626ec1-8899-444b-92ee-
68d0788aed37)
Executing 'Functions.ScheduledMethodUsingTimespanExpression' (Reason='Timer fired at 2017-10-03T15:
10:31.2058369-04:00', Id=49a176bf-040b-4209-b2dd-21f90cdc79ea)
Timer triggered at 10/3/2017 3:10:31 PM
Executed 'Functions.ScheduledMethodUsingTimespanExpression' (Succeeded, Id=49a176bf-040b-4209-b2dd-
21f90cdc79ea)
```

Figure 8-12. *From the WebJob console output, we can see that the TimerTrigger invoked the method every 30 seconds as expected*

We can also use the same `TimerTriggerAttribute` overload, but specify a chrontab expression. Listing 8-13 shows a method that will execute every weekday at 10:00 a.m. To run this method, comment out the previous example, paste this code into `Functions.cs`, and run the application. Although it is unlikely that you're actually executing this code on a weekday at 9:57 a.m., this method will print its execution schedule, as shown in Figure 8-13.

```
C:\Development\WebJobDemo\WebJobDemo.OnDemand\bin\Debug\WebJobDemo.OnDemand.exe          —   □   ×
Found the following functions:
WebJobDemo.WebJob.Functions.ProcessQueueMessage
WebJobDemo.WebJob.Functions.ScheduledMethodUsingTimespanExpression
The next 5 occurrences of the schedule will be:
10/3/2017 2:25:34 PM
10/3/2017 2:26:04 PM
10/3/2017 2:26:34 PM
10/3/2017 2:27:04 PM
10/3/2017 2:27:34 PM
Job host started
Executing 'Functions.ScheduledMethodUsingTimespanExpression' (Reason='Timer fired at 2017-10-03T14:25:34.0540535-04:00',
 Id=84821b6e-357d-497d-b6c6-7339fa6c7606)
Timer triggered at 10/3/2017 2:25:34 PM
Executed 'Functions.ScheduledMethodUsingTimespanExpression' (Succeeded, Id=84821b6e-357d-497d-b6c6-7339fa6c7606)
```

Figure 8-13. *The ScheduledMethodUsingChronExpression method's execution schedule is printed to the console*

Listing 8-13. This Method Uses a Chrontab Expression to Fire a TimerTrigger Every Weekday at 10:00 a.m.

```
public static void ScheduledMethodUsingChronExpression([TimerTrigger(
    "0 0 10 * * MON-FRI", UseMonitor = true, RunOnStartup = true)] TimerInfo timer)
{
    Console.WriteLine("Firing ScheduledMethodUsingChronExpression at {0}",
    DateTime.Now);
    string scheduleStatus = string.Format("Next Execution: '{0}'",
        timer.ScheduleStatus.Next);
    Console.WriteLine(scheduleStatus);
}
```

Creating Complex Schedules by Subclassing TimerSchedule

If you need to create an extremely oddball schedule that you cannot express in a chrontab expression, you can use the second `TimerTriggerAttribute` overload, `TimerTriggerAttribute(Type scheduleType)`. For the `Type`, you'll need to create a subclass of one of the following classes that are found in the `Microsoft.Azure.WebJobs.Extensions.Timers` namespace and initialize the schedule in your inherited class's constructor. Each of these classes inherits from the `TimerSchedule` class.

- *DailySchedule*: This allows you to specify one or more times within a day. The `TimerTriggerAttribute` will fire each day on the specified times. For example, you might want to specify that a method will execute daily at 3:27:18 a.m. and 1:09:01 p.m. If you actually do need to execute a method daily at these times, please e-mail me and tell me what in the world you're doing!

- *ConstantSchedule*: This allows you to execute a task for a fixed interval. For example, you can create a schedule that will execute a method every 20 minutes. This is not very useful, as it's much easier to use a timespan or chrontab expression to accomplish the same thing.

- *ChronSchedule* This subclass allows you to specify multiple chrontab expressions. The trigger will then fire for each chrontab expression that the `ChronSchedule` contains. This is useful for combining multiple chrontab expressions. For example, you could specify that a trigger should fire every weekday at 5:00 p.m. and on Saturday and Sunday at 3:00 p.m.

- *WeeklySchedule*: This allows you to specify a day of the week and time of day that a trigger should fire. You can add multiple values. For example, you might specify that the trigger should fire every Monday at noon, Tuesday at 5:00 p.m., and Saturday at 10:00 a.m.

Now let's look at an example. The usage is a little strange because we need to create a subclass of one of the above classes and initialize the schedule in the subclass's constructor. Open `Functions.cs`, comment out all methods, and add the code in Listing 8-14.

Listing 8-14. Code That Should Be Placed Inside the Functions Class to Demonstrate a Complex TimerTrigger Schedule

```
/// <summary>
/// We inherit from the DailySchedule class if we want to create our own
/// daily schedule.
/// This will set up a TimerTriggerAttribute to call a method at 2:30 a.m.,
/// 4:45 a.m., and
/// 11:10:15 p.m. every day.
/// </summary>
```

```
public class TimerDailySchedule : DailySchedule
{
    public TimerDailySchedule() : base("2:30:00", "4:45:00", "23:10:15")
    { }
}
/// <summary>
/// Takes a type that derives from DailySchedule as an argument. You can do
/// the same
/// thing with a class that inherits from WeeklySchedule, ConstantSchedule,
/// ChronSchedule, or WeeklySchedule.
/// </summary>
public static void ScheduledMethodUsingDailySchedule(
    [TimerTrigger(typeof(TimerDailySchedule), RunOnStartup = true)]
    TimerInfo timer)
{

    Console.WriteLine("Firing ScheduledMethodUsingChronExpression at {0}",
    DateTime.Now);
    string scheduleStatus = string.Format("Next Execution: '{0}'",
        timer.ScheduleStatus.Next);
    Console.WriteLine(scheduleStatus);
}
```

That's not a typo: We did just define an inner class within the Functions class called TimerDailySchedule. In the ScheduleMethodUsingDailySchedule method, we pass the TimerDailySchedule type as an argument to the TimerTriggerAttribute. When we run our WebJob, we see that the execution times are in fact what we specified in our oddball schedule that was defined in the TimerDailySchedule constructor (Figure 8-14).

```
■ C:\Development\WebJobDemo\WebJobDemo.OnDemand\bin\Debug\WebJobDemo.OnDemand.exe        —    □    ×
Found the following functions:
WebJobDemo.WebJob.Functions.ProcessQueueMessage
WebJobDemo.WebJob.Functions.ScheduledMethodUsingDailySchedule
Executing 'Functions.ScheduledMethodUsingDailySchedule' (Reason='Timer fired at 2017-10-03T14:27:49.9732587-04:00', Id=6
1a93c21-537f-4259-a3d7-713d72cf5898)
Firing ScheduledMethodUsingChronExpression at 10/3/2017 2:27:50 PM
Next Execution: '10/3/2017 11:10:15 PM'
Executed 'Functions.ScheduledMethodUsingDailySchedule' (Succeeded, Id=61a93c21-537f-4259-a3d7-713d72cf5898)
The next 5 occurrences of the schedule will be:
10/3/2017 11:10:15 PM
10/4/2017 2:30:00 AM
10/4/2017 4:45:00 AM
10/4/2017 11:10:15 PM
10/5/2017 2:30:00 AM
Job host started
```

Figure 8-14. *After executing our WebJob, we see the expected execution schedule for our TimerDailySchedule subclass has been written to the console*

Handling Exceptions with the ErrorTriggerAttribute

In life, we must handle terrible situations such as unhandled exceptions in our code or Tom Brady winning yet another Super Bowl. While the ErrorTriggerAttribute can't help in stopping the New England Patriots offense, it can notify you when an unhandled exception occurs in your WebJob's job functions.

Using the ErrorTriggerAttribute is simple. All that you have to do is this:

1. Enable the use of the ErrorTriggerAttribute by calling the JobHostConfiguration's UseCore() method in your WebJob's Program class. If you don't call this method when your WebJob starts up, the ErrorTriggerAttribute will never fire when an unhandled exception occurs.

2. Decorate the method that you'd like called when an unhandled exception occurs. Listing 8-15 shows a method that has been decorated with ErrorTriggerAttribute and will be called on each unhandled exception.

Listing 8-15. A Method Decorated with the ErrorTriggerAttribute

```
/// <summary>
/// This method be called for uncaught exceptions thrown in this WebJob. This
/// method will be called for each exception that occurs.
/// </summary>
public static void SimpleErrorHandler([ErrorTrigger()] TraceFilter filter)
{
    Console.WriteLine("SimpleErrorHandler: " + filter.Message);
}
```

Now let's test and make sure that our method works as expected. To do so, let's revisit our ProcessQueueMessage method in the Functions class.

We already have the ability to send a Storage Queue message from our demo web application to our WebJob. When we do so, the QueueTriggerAttribute trigger that decorates our ProcessQueueMessage method will fire, and our method will be called. Let's add some additional code to the ProcessQueueMessage method that will examine our queue message text and throw an exception if that text equals error (see Listing 8-16).

Listing 8-16. We've Added Code to Check Our Incoming Message and Throw an Exception if the Message Is Equal to Error

```
public static void ProcessQueueMessage(
    [QueueTrigger("webjobmessages")] QueueMessage message, TextWriter log)
{
    if (message.Message == "error")
    {
        throw new Exception("Houston, we have a problem!");
    }
    Console.WriteLine(message.Message);
}
```

Once more, let's right-click our solution, select Properties, and change our settings so that we start both the WebJobDemo.Web and WebJobDemo.WebJob projects simultaneously. Once the web application fires up, enter `error` in the message field and click Send. Next, check the WebJobDemo.WebJob console and take a look at the output (Figure 8-15).

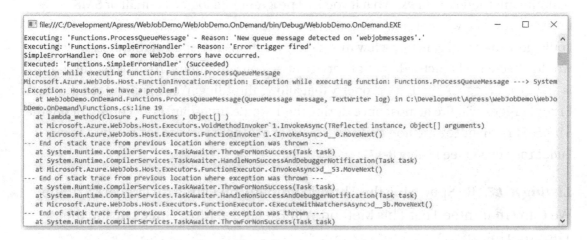

Figure 8-15. *We can see that our ErrorTrigger did fire when an unhandled exception occurred*

As you can see, the `ErrorTrigger` did fire, and our `SimpleErrorHandler` method was called. In fact, it was called five times. What happened?

When our `QueueTrigger` receives a message, it hides the message from other readers for a short period of time. This prevents a queue message from being processed multiple times if there are multiple readers monitoring a queue. When our `ProcessQueueMessage` completes successfully, the `QueueTrigger` will remove the message from the Storage Queue. If an exception occurs, our `QueueTrigger` will make the queue message visible to other readers once again. This is why you see the error message five times; as an exception is thrown, our `ProcessQueueMessage` marks the message as visible. Once the message is visible, our `QueueTrigger` fires and reads the message again.

Why five times, though? Storage Queues have the concept of poison messages and a maximum dequeue count, which we discuss further in Chapter 9. A poison message is a message that has been dequeued a maximum number of times and has thus been deemed undeliverable. Once a message is considered poison, it is placed in a separate queue within the same Storage account. The poison message queue is named [original queue name]-poison. You can view the contents of the poison message queue using Azure Storage Explorer.

Throttling the ErrorTriggerAttribute

In the previous section, we saw how a single poison message triggered our error handling method five times. What if you had programmed logic to e-mail or SMS message yourself whenever an exception occurred? You can imagine how something could go wrong and generate a few thousand exceptions in a span of minutes, which would effectively launch a denial-of-service attack on your inbox. To prevent this, there is an ErrorTriggerAttribute property that allows throttling. We're guaranteed that the ErrorTrigger will fire at most once during the Throttle timespan. Let's comment out the SimpleErrorHandler method and add a new ThrottledErrorHandler method to our Functions class (see Listing 8-17).

Listing 8-17. By Specifying the Throttle Property on Our ErrorTriggerAttribute, We Can Guarantee That This Method Will Execute at Most Once During the Throttle Timespan

```
/// <summary>
/// By setting the ErrorTriggerAttribute's Throttle property, we can limit the
/// number of times this method can be triggered to a maximum of once
/// within the
/// Throttle timespan.
/// </summary>
public static void ThrottledErrorHandler([ErrorTrigger(Throttle = "0:2:00")]
    TraceFilter filter)
{
    Console.WriteLine ("ThrottledErrorHandler: " + filter.Message);
}
```

Running our previous example again, we can see that our ErrorTrigger only fires once even though five exceptions are thrown by our poison queue message.

Deploying WebJobs to Azure

Our WebJob is running successfully locally. Now let's publish it to Azure.

Hosting Requirements

WebJobs are deployed to Azure Web Apps. If you already have a Web App provisioned, there's no additional cost to adding a WebJob to an existing Web App. There are a few caveats to take into consideration.

- Enable your Web App's Always On setting. Web App instances in the Free and Shared tiers will be unloaded from memory to conserve resources if the web application that's hosted on the Web App doesn't receive a request for 20 minutes. If your WebJob is hosted on a Free or Shared tier Web App instance that gets unloaded, your WebJob will be unloaded as well and will cease functioning. To prevent this from happening, host your WebJobs on a Web App instance in the Basic, Standard, or Premium tiers.

- Azure has a configuration setting called WEBJOBS_IDLE_TIMEOUT that is denoted in seconds and defaults to two minutes. If your on-demand WebJob isn't triggered within the WEBJOBS_IDLE_TIMEOUT interval, Azure will kill your WebJob. I recommend setting your Web App's WEBJOBS_IDLE_TIMEOUT variable to a healthy number of seconds to prevent this from happening. You can set this variable on the Web App's Application Settings screen by adding it to the App Settings section.

- Within a Web App instance, each WebJob has its own process. However, all web applications and WebJobs on the instance will share system resources. It is possible for a WebJob to gobble memory and starve other WebJobs or web applications residing on the same instance. Be cognizant of shared resources when you're conducting capacity planning.

Deploying a WebJob

There are two methods for deploying a WebJob: via File Transfer Protocol (FTP) or by publishing directly from Visual Studio.

FTP

If you log into your account on the Azure Portal and navigate to your Web App's Overview blade, you can download your Web App's publish profile (Figure 8-16). The publish profile is an XML document that contains an FTP address, username, and password that you can use to FTP into your Web App. Note that if you have more than one instance of your Web App running, they all share the same files.

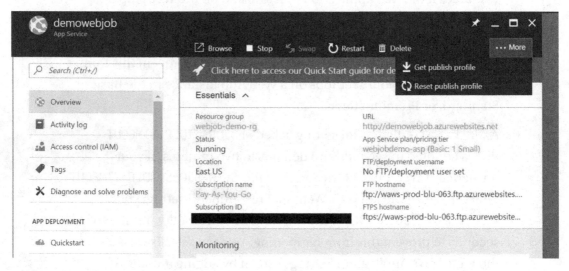

Figure 8-16. *Download your Web App's publish profile by clicking More and selecting Get Publish Profile*

You can even use Windows Explorer as your FTP client. Just open Windows Explorer and paste your FTP address directly into the location bar.

Once you've FTPed into your Web App, you can xcopy the files from your WebJob's `bin\debug` or `bin\release` directory into the appropriate directory, and your WebJob will begin running. For continuous WebJobs such as our example, the directory is `D:\home\site\wwwroot\app_data\jobs\continuous\{job name}`. Let's give that a try now with our continuous WebJob.

1. Right-click on the WebJobDemo.WebJob in Visual Studio's Solution Explorer and select Rebuild.

2. Log into the Azure Portal, navigate to the Web App that we want to deploy to, and download the publish profile.

3. While on the Web App's management blade, select Application Settings and make sure that Always On is set to On.

    Let's also make sure that our `WEBJOBS_IDLE_TIMEOUT` variable is set. Scroll down to the App Settings section. Add the key `WEBJOBS_IDLE_TIMEOUT`, and set the value to something outlandish, like 86,400, to prevent your on-demand WebJobs from ever timing out.

    Next, scroll down further on the Application Settings panel to the Connection Strings section and add the key `AzureWebJobsDashboard` and the value for your Storage account's connection string. Unfortunately, Azure cannot read this value from your `app.config` file, and you must manually enter it here if you want to take advantage of the WebJobs Dashboard in Azure.

    Don't forget to click Save at the top of the blade before navigating away, or your changes will be lost.

4. Use the credentials from the publish profile to FTP into our Web App.

5. Navigate to the folder `site/wwwroot/app_data/jobs/continuous`. You might have to create folders from `app_data` down. Once in the continuous folder, create a new folder called `WebJobDemo` to host your WebJob.

6. Copy the contents from your WebJobDemo.WebJob project's `bin\debug` folder to the WebJobDemo folder that you just created on the Web App. Congratulations: You've just published your WebJob!

Publishing via Visual Studio

Publishing via Visual Studio is simple. Let's demonstrate by publishing our WebJobDemo.WebJob project using Visual Studio's tooling.

1. Right-click the WebJobDemo.WebJob project. Select Publish as Azure WebJob from the shortcut menu.

2. In the Add Azure WebJob dialog box, update the WebJob name to WebJobDemo. Azure will not allow periods or other special characters in the WebJob name. Set the WebJob run mode to Run Continuously, then click OK (Figure 8-17).

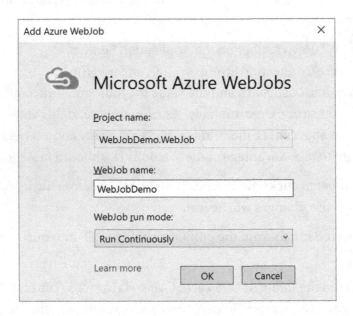

Figure 8-17. *Specifying a WebJob name and run mode. You will only see this dialog box the first time you publish from Visual Studio. To change these settings on subsequent publishes, edit the webjob-publish-settings.json file found in your WebJobDemo.WebJob's Properties folder.*

3. In the Publish dialog box, you'll first need to specify which Azure Web App you want to deploy to. You can either click Microsoft Azure App Service to log into your Azure account from Visual Studio and choose a Web App, or you can click Import and choose a previously downloaded publish profile (Figure 8-18).

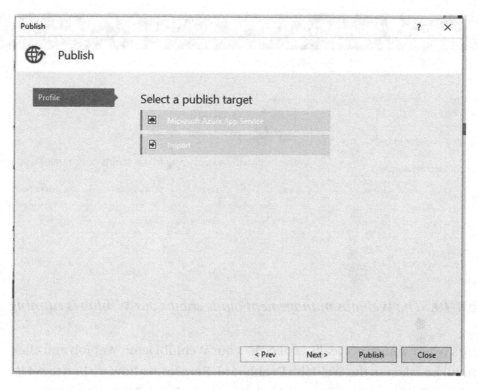

Figure 8-18. *Choosing a Web App as a publish target for our WebJob*

4. After choosing a publish target, click Next to verify any connection strings that your WebJob might use. Because we're not making use of a database in our on-demand WebJob, click Next to advance to the Settings screen.

5. On the Settings screen, choose your build configuration and click Publish. You've now successfully published the WebJob via Visual Studio.

Monitoring a WebJob in the Cloud

We can verify that our WebJobs were actually published by returning to our Web App's management screen in the Azure Portal. If you look through the available menu options, you'll see an option labeled Web Jobs. Clicking it will take you to the WebJobs management blade. This screen will list all WebJobs running on the Web App. You should see the entry for WebJobDemo (Figure 8-19).

Figure 8-19. *The WebJobs management blade shows our WebJob is running*

Here's where things get really cool. Select our WebJobDemo WebJob and click Logs. You'll be taken to the WebJob's Dashboard. Remember how we had to set the AzureWebJobsDashboard key in our Web App's properties and specify our Storage account's connection string? That was so that Azure could write runtime information for our WebJobs to a Storage Blob, and this is where the dashboard data that was written appears (Figure 8-20).

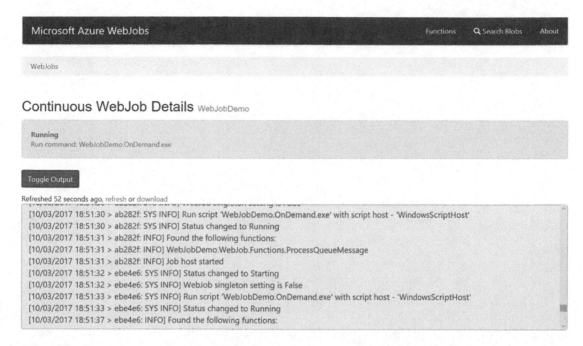

Figure 8-20. *The Azure dashboard. For continuous WebJobs, we can see the function that is running, how long it's been running, and Toggle Output to view logs. These logs are useful as a starting point for troubleshooting issues in deployment.*

For continuous WebJobs, we can see the function that is running continuously and how long it's been running. We can also click Toggle Output to see logs written by Azure in addition to any statements that we wrote to Console.

Summary

We've discussed what WebJobs are, built an example, and ran our WebJob locally and in Azure. In the next chapter, we discuss queues in detail and how they can be used to build highly scalable web applications.

CHAPTER 9

Message Queues

A message queue is a service that allows two processes to communicate asynchronously. Message queues are conceptually very simple. A process that we'll call the sender creates a message and adds it to a message queue. A process that we'll call the receiver periodically checks the queue for new messages. If a new message is found, the receiver will process the message and remove it from the queue. Queue implementations will typically guarantee receivers a first-in-first-out (FIFO) ordering of messages. In other words, if a sender inserts messages A, B, and C into the queue, messages will be dequeued by a receiver in the order of A, B, and then C.

Folks who have never worked with messaging queues might be asking "So, what exactly *is* a message?" A message is simply information in an agreed-on format that needs to be communicated to another process. Typically, it's information that the receiver needs to do something with. For example, our sender might send a class instance containing data that needs to be processed. Messages can also be binary data and could consist of an uploaded image that needs to be filtered, resized, and saved to disk.

Notice that because a sender process is inserting messages into a queue, and a receiver process is retrieving messages from the queue, the sender and receiver processes don't have to know anything about each other to work together. This raises some interesting possibilities. A sender process could be a .NET Core MVC web application running inside an Azure Web App, and the receiver could be a WebJob running in an entirely different Web App. The receiver could be a Node.js application running inside an Azure VM. The receiver could be a Python app living inside a corporate network behind a firewall. As you can see, message queues offer you a tremendous amount of architectural freedom. The important takeaway is that message queues allow you to break up and decouple your application. This is very useful in certain scenarios, which we discuss later in this chapter.

When a message queue receives a message, it will save it to persistent storage. Once a sender inserts a message, it will live in the queue until it is dequeued by a receiver or

© Rob Reagan 2018
R. Reagan, *Web Applications on Azure*, https://doi.org/10.1007/978-1-4842-2976-7_9

exceeds a specified message expiration date and is automatically deleted. The persistent storage of messages means that the sender and receiver processes don't even need to be online at the same time to communicate. A sender process could enqueue a message at 9:00 a.m., and a receiver process running on a schedule could wake up an hour later, dequeue the message, and process it. Allowing processes to communicate even when they are not running concurrently is called temporal decoupling.

The final feature we need to discuss in this overview is how receivers read messages from a message queue. In most implementations, there are two options: read and dequeue, and read and lock.

With read and dequeue, a receiver will remove a message from the queue when it's read. Read and dequeue is usually an atomic operation. Consider what happens, though, if an exception occurs while the message is being processed. Unless additional steps are taken, the contents of the message will be lost and the message will never be fully processed. For some types of messages, occasional message loss is not a big deal. For other types, lost messages can be catastrophic and get people fired.

When used properly, read and lock will ensure that messages are not lost. When a message is read, it remains in the message queue but is invisible to all receivers until the message lock is abandoned, the lock times out, or the message is explicitly dequeued after successful processing. We can structure our code so that message locks are released in the event of an exception. When a lock is abandoned or expires, the message will become visible to any and all receivers, and another attempt can be made to process the message.

In a read and lock scenario, what happens if we end up with a message that cannot be processed due to being malformed or an application error? Won't the message remain trapped in the message queue, endlessly cycling? Not quite! Most message queues (including all Azure message queue implementations) have the concept of poison messages. Each time a receiver dequeues a message, the message's dequeue count is incremented. When a maximum dequeue count is reached, the message is removed from the queue automatically.

Benefits of Using Message Queues

We've talked in general about how message queues work, but what are the benefits of using them? Here are the main benefits of using them.

- *Scalability*: Thus far, we've discussed how message queues have a sender and a receiver, but there's no reason that we couldn't have multiple receivers processing messages from the same queue. Imagine if our sender is a web application that sends messages that require lots of work to process. We could have a single instance of our web application sending messages, and multiple instances of our receiver process to do the work required. Decoupling using a message queue allows us to scale parts of our application separately. If queue length continues to grow because messages are being added faster than they can be processed, we can simply add more receivers to process messages faster. In fact, Azure Web Apps' Autoscale feature can use a message queue's length as a trigger for when to scale up or scale out. Scaling out receivers to handle the work needed is called load balancing.

- *Elasticity*: Message queues can help absorb a burst in workload and keep your application from collapsing due to a surge in traffic. Twilio.com's outbound SMS messaging API is a good real-world example. When a customer calls Twilio's outbound SMS API to send a text message, Twilio receives the message and then immediately enqueues it. Multiple worker processes receive the messages and handle the actual sending of the SMS messages. If Twilio tried to send SMS messages from within their API's code, their servers could quickly reach capacity and fail due to a large and unexpected spike in traffic. A message queue ensures that work will eventually be done, even if the system lacks the resources to perform the work immediately. This is also called load leveling.

- *Temporal decoupling*: Because senders and receivers are only communicating through a message queue, and because messages within a message queue will remain until they are dequeued or expire, the sender and receiver do not even need to be running at the same time to work together. You could design a receiver that wakes up at a given interval, processes messages until no more messages remain, then goes to sleep for another hour.

- *Resiliency*: Resiliency is made possible by temporal decoupling. If a receiver process fails and goes down like a glass-jawed prizefighter, messages within a message queue are not lost. They can be processed when the receiver comes back online.

Types of Azure Message Queues

Azure offers two flavors of messaging queues: Service Bus Messaging Queues and Azure Storage Queues.

Service Bus Queues

Azure Service Bus is a messaging service that allows apps to communicate in various ways. Service Bus encompasses three separate technologies: queues, topics and subscriptions, and relays. Although we won't discuss topics and subscriptions or relays in depth, I do want to make you aware of them and what they're used for.

Service Bus topics and subscriptions are an implementation of the publish and subscribe pattern. An application can create one or more topics, and publishers create messages and add them to individual topics. One or more subscribers can subscribe to a topic and will receive any messages sent to the topic. Subscribers don't have to receive all messages sent to a topic; they can declare filters to determine exactly what types of messages they're interested in receiving. Topics and subscriptions are the way to go if you need to publish messages that need to be sent to N different receivers simultaneously. This contrasts with message queues, where only one receiver can process a message sent to a message queue.

Service Bus relays allow two applications that might live behind firewalls to communicate securely without modifying firewall rules. With Service Bus relays, two separate applications make outbound connections (which are allowed by most firewalls) to a defined Service Bus relay. The Service Bus relay then opens a bidirectional socket that both applications can use to send and receive data.

Now comes our main event: discussing Service Bus queues. Service Bus queues are a robust implementation of the messaging queue concept. One or more senders create and insert messages into a Service Bus queue, and one or more receivers read and remove messages. Here are some of the more interesting and useful functionalities that Service Bus queues offer.

- Message ordering is guaranteed. If the temporal ordering of three sent messages is A, B, and then C, the messages will be read in the order of A, B, and then C.

- Receivers can read messages through two different receive modes: Peek & Lock or Receive & Delete. Peek & Lock allows the receiver to read a message while locking the message to prevent it from being read by any other receivers. The Peek & Lock operation is atomic. The message will remain inaccessible to other receivers until the receiver explicitly calls the message's `Complete()`, `Abandon()`, or `Deadletter()` methods, or until the message lock expires. Calling `Complete()` on the message after it is successfully processed will remove the message from the queue. The `Deadletter()` method will remove a message from the queue and place it in the dead letter subqueue. The dead letter subqueue is a separate queue that holds messages that cannot be processed. Calling `Abandon()` will release the lock on the message and make it visible once again to all receivers. The `Abandon()` method is useful to place in the catch portion of a try/catch block in case something goes wrong during processing.

   Receive & Delete removes a message from the message queue when it is read. This is the more efficient of the two read modes. However, if problems occur while processing your message, the message will be lost and not automatically added back to the queue.

- Messages will remain in the message queue until their Message Time to Live is reached; at that point they will be automatically removed. There is no maximum on the Message Time to Live.

- You can guarantee that a message will be delivered at least once. You can also guarantee that a message will be delivered at most once.

- There is support for automatic dead lettering. If a message's dequeue count exceeds a threshold, it will automatically be moved to the dead letter queue. This ensures that your app will not try to continually try to process a message that has errored out multiple times.

- The maximum size of a queue cannot exceed 80 GB.

Azure Storage Queues

Azure Storage Queues are part of the Azure Storage service, along with Tables, Blobs, and Files. Storage Queues are an older technology and not as full-featured. These are the main differences between Storage Queues and Service Bus queues.

- Although Storage Queue message ordering is typically FIFO, ordering when dequeueing is not guaranteed. Messages that are placed in the queue in the order of A, B, and then C could be dequeued in the order of B, A, and then C.

- The only receive mode for reading from a Storage Queue is Peek & Lease. When a message is read, it is made invisible to other receivers until the lease expires or the message is explicitly deleted.

- Messages can live in the queue up to a maximum of seven days before they are automatically removed.

- You can guarantee that a message will be delivered at least once. In certain circumstances, messages might also be delivered more than once. You must write additional logic in your receiver to recognize and handle messages that are dequeued more than once if double processing is unacceptable in your application.

- There is no built-in support for dead lettering messages that exceed the maximum dequeue count.

- The maximum size of a Storage Queue cannot exceed the maximum size of a Storage account, which is 200 TB.

You should choose Service Bus queues over Storage Queues unless you need a queue size more than 80 GB in size, messages will live for seven days or less, and your message size is less than 64 KB.

Demo Project: QueueDemo

We'll now walk through an example of some of the most common features you'll need when adding messaging queue functionality to your applications. We'll build a set of console applications that will demonstrate sending and receiving messages, scaling out with multiple receivers, Peek & Lock versus Receive & Delete read modes, exception handling, and dead lettering.

At the time of this writing, .NET Core Service Bus libraries have not yet been released. We'll create this console application using the full .NET Framework 4.6.1.

Provisioning a Service Bus Resource

Currently, there isn't a local emulator for any of the Azure Service Bus services. Therefore, you'll need to create a Service Bus resource within the Azure Portal to do any development with Service Bus message queues. So, let's start by provisioning our Service Bus resource in the portal.

1. Log into the Azure Portal. Click the + icon to provision a new resource. The Service Bus option is located under Enterprise Integration (Figure 9-1).

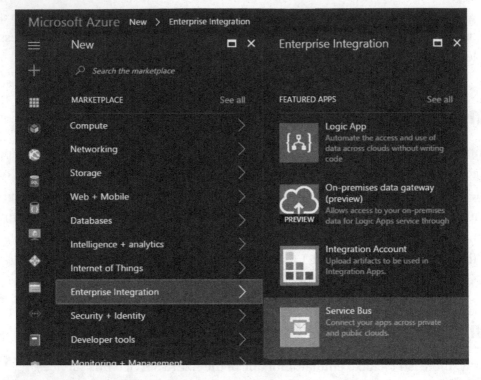

Figure 9-1. *Provisioning a new Service Bus resource*

2. Next, we need to fill in a few Service Bus specific settings. The
    settings you'll be prompted for are as follows:

    • *Name*: This is the name of your Service Bus namespace. You can
      group multiple Queues, Topics and Subscriptions, and Relays
      within a single namespace. Enter a name of your choice.

    • *Pricing Tier*: Because we're only working with message queues, the
      Basic tier is sufficient for this demo. The Basic tier charges $0.05
      per million operations, so this demo will only cost you a nickel.

    • *Subscription*: Simply choose your subscription from the drop-
      down list. This is the subscription that will be billed for usage.

    • *Resource Group*: As discussed in Chapter 2, a resource
      group allows you to group multiple services together for
      management purposes. Let's create a new resource group called
      servicebusqueue-rg.

- *Location*: This is the datacenter where your Service Bus resource will be located. Choose the datacenter closest to you to reduce network latency.

When you've entered this information, click Create.

3. Thus far, we've only created a Service Bus namespace, which is the container that holds message queues, Topics and Subscriptions, and Relays. We still need to actually provision our queue within Service Bus. To do so, navigate to your newly created Service Bus resource. Click Queues, then click the + icon on the Queue management blade to create a new Queue. You'll be prompted for the settings in Figure 9-2.

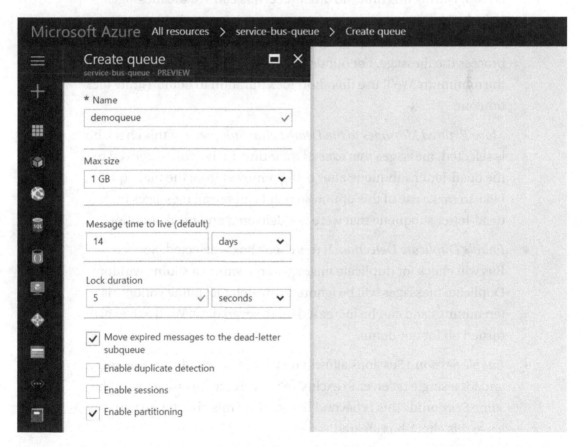

Figure 9-2. *Settings required to create a new message queue within a Service Bus namespace*

- *Name*: This is the name of your new message queue.

- *Max size*: This is the max queue size. You can choose 1 GB to 5 GB in size, in 1 GB increments. After a queue fills up with messages, any caller attempting to insert a new message will receive an exception. Interestingly enough, Microsoft does not charge based on max size, so you are free to choose the maximum of 5 GB.

- *Message Time to Live*: This is how long messages will remain in the message queue unprocessed before being automatically deleted.

- *Lock Duration*: When using Peek & Lock as the receive mode, a lock will be issued on a message for the lock duration when the message is read. During this time, no other receivers can see the message. If the lock expires and the message has not been explicitly marked as completed or dead lettered, all receivers will be able to see and process the message. For our demo, set this to five seconds, which is the minimum. We'll use this short lock duration to demonstrate lock timeout.

- *Move Expired Messages to the Dead-Letter Subqueue*: If this check box is selected, messages that exceed their time to live will be moved to the dead-letter subqueue after being removed from the main queue. I like to make use of this option so that I can see all messages in the dead-letter subqueue that were not delivered and need attention.

- *Enable Duplicate Detection*: If this check box is selected, Service Bus will check for duplicate messages sent within a sliding window. Duplicate messages will be ignored. The default sliding window is ten minutes and can be increased up to seven days. We'll leave this turned off for our demo.

- *Enable Sessions*: Sessions allows you to set a SessionId per message, and for a single receiver to exclusively receive all messages with the same SessionId. This is beyond the scope of this chapter, so you can leave this check box cleared.

- *Enable partitioning*: Without partitioning enabled, all messages are written to a single message store, which is the persistent storage for messages. The implementation details of the message store are both hidden and unimportant to us. An unpartitioned queue will also use a single message broker, which is the worker process that handles all message queue requests. If partitioning is enabled, Azure will spread your queue across 16 partitions, which gives you multiple message stores and message brokers. Incoming messages are distributed to one of the 16 message stores based on the presence of an explicit partition key, the presence of a session key, or a round-robin assignment. This entire process is transparent to receivers. Making use of partitioning doesn't add additional cost and gives you greater reliability. I recommend always enabling it.

Once you have finished entering data in the required fields, click Create to create your queue.

Creating the Sender Console Application

Now that we've created our Service Bus resource and accompanying message queue, let's create our console application to create messages and then drop them in our queue.

First, let's create a new project and solution in Visual Studio. In Visual Studio, select File ➤ New ➤ Project. In the New Project dialog box, choose the Console Application template located under Installed ➤ Templates ➤ Visual C# ➤ Windows. Name the project ServiceBusQueue.Sender, then enter QueueDemo for the Solution Name (Figure 9-3). After choosing a location for this solution and project, click OK.

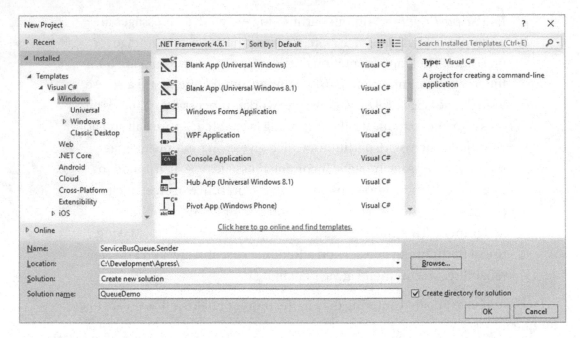

Figure 9-3. *Create a solution and new console application for this example*

Last but not least, let's add the `Microsoft.ServiceBus` and `Newtonsoft.Json` NuGet packages to this project. To do so, right-click the ServiceBusQueue.Sender project and select Manage NuGet Packages. On the NuGet package management screen, select the Browse tab, search for, and then add each one.

Creating Our Common Models Project

When sending messages, you'll often want to serialize a class instance with various properties. Because we're going to have several console applications in this demo, let's create a shared models project to hold our common data class. Right-click the QueueDemo solution, then choose Add ➤ New Project to open the Add New Project dialog box. We'll want to choose the Class Library template, which is located beneath the Installed ➤ Visual C# ➤ Windows treeview item. Name this project `QueueDemo.Models` and click OK.

The Class Library template was kind enough to give us a single code file named `Class1.cs`. That's not a very descriptive name, so let's rename it `QueueMessage.cs`. Then open the `QueueMessage.cs` file and add the contents in Listing 9-1.

Listing 9-1. Our QueueMessage Class, Which Will Be the Payload of Our Queue Messages

```
namespace QueueDemo.Models
{
    public class QueueMessage
    {
        public string Message { get; set; }
    }
}
```

Our `ServiceBusQueue.Sender` console app requires a reference to this project. Right-click the `ServiceBusQueue.Sender`'s `References` node in the Solution Explorer, select Add Reference, and add a reference to this project.

Getting a Service Bus Connection String

The simplest way to connect to a Service Bus is to use a connection string. To find your Service Bus connection string, log into the Azure Portal, navigate to your Service Bus's management blade, and click Shared Access Policies located under Settings (Figure 9-4).

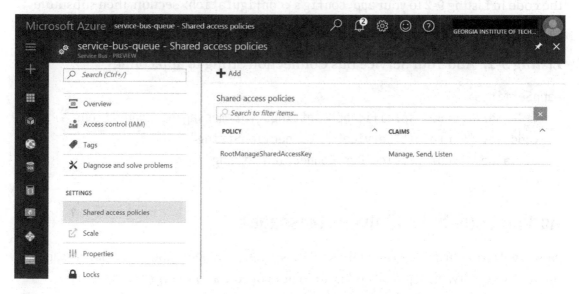

Figure 9-4. The RootManageSharedAccessKey is the default shared access policy that allows clients to send, listen, and manage Service Bus resources

Click the RootManageSharedAccessKey to navigate to the Policy management blade. Copy the CONNECTION STRING-PRIMARY KEY connection string. We'll need this for our ServiceBusQueue.Sender's app.config file.

The RootManageSharedAccessKey is the default access policy that is created when a Service Bus resource is provisioned, but you can create multiple policies to tighten security and fit your needs. Each policy you create can have its own combination of manage, send, and listen claims. Following the principle of least permissions, it's good practice to grant as few claims as needed. For example, if an application is going to only read messages, you can create a separate access policy for the reader application and only grant the listen claim. You would then use the new claim's CONNECTION STRING-PRIMARY KEY as the connection string when connecting to the service bus from your reader application. For the sake of simplicity, we'll use the same RootManageSharedAccessKey access policy for all applications in our demo.

Updating the ServiceBusQueue.Sender's app.config File

Our console app will read the Service Bus connection string from our app.config file. Remember the connection string that you copied from your Service Bus's RootManageSharedAccessKey access policy in the previous section? You'll need to add the code in Listing 9-2 to your app.config's <configuration> section, then substitute your connection string.

Listing 9-2. Add Your Service Bus Connection String to app.config

```
<appSettings>
    <!-- Service Bus specific app settings for messaging connections -->
    <add key="Microsoft.ServiceBus.ConnectionString"
       value="[Your Service Bus Connection String"/>
</appSettings>
```

Adding Code to Send Queue Messages

Now we'll write the code to actually send messages through our Service Bus message queue. For clarity, we'll put all code within our console app's Program.cs file. The complete source code for Program.cs is shown in Listing 9-3.

Listing 9-3. The ServiceBusQueue.Sender's Program.cs File

```csharp
using System;
using System.Threading.Tasks;
using Microsoft.ServiceBus;
using Microsoft.ServiceBus.Messaging;
using System.Configuration;
using QueueDemo.Models;
using Newtonsoft.Json;

namespace ServiceBusQueue.Sender
{
    class Program
    {
        static async Task Run()
        {
            //we'll create our MessageSender only once. You should NOT re-create a
            //connection to your Service Bus for each message; that is a
            //very expensive operation!
            string serviceBusConnectionString =
                ConfigurationManager.AppSettings["Microsoft.ServiceBus.
                ConnectionString"];
            string queueName = "demoqueue";
            MessagingFactory senderFactory =
                MessagingFactory.CreateFromConnectionString
                (serviceBusConnectionString);

            //our MessagingFactory has retry logic in case there's a transient error.
            //We'll specify an exponential backoff retry policy.
            senderFactory.RetryPolicy = new RetryExponential
            (TimeSpan.FromSeconds(1),
                TimeSpan.FromMinutes(5), 10);

            //our MessageSender instance is what actually sends messages to
            //the queue.
            var sender = await senderFactory.CreateMessageSenderAsync(queueName);
```

```
    //type out some instructions for our user...
    Console.WriteLine("Service Bus message queue sender started. Enter
    a message and press enter to send it via the message queue.");
    Console.WriteLine("Type 'exit' to quit");
    Console.Write(">");

    //we'll keep waiting on the user to type in a new message until
    //they enter "exit" and hit Enter
    //at our command prompt.
    string message = Console.ReadLine();
    while (message.ToLower() != "exit")
    {
      //BrokeredMessage instances are what we can send to our Service Bus
      //message queue.
      BrokeredMessage msg = CreateMessage(message);
      await sender.SendAsync(msg);

      Console.WriteLine("Message sent.");
      Console.Write(">");
      message = Console.ReadLine();
    }
  }

  /// <summary>
  /// This will create a class instance and set the string message as a
  /// property. We'll then serialize the QueueMessage class instance
  /// and set
  /// the serialized instance as the BrokeredMessage message body.
  /// BrokeredMessages are what Service Bus message queues send and receive.
  /// </summary>
  private static BrokeredMessage CreateMessage(string message)
  {
    QueueMessage msgPayload = new QueueMessage();
    msgPayload.Message = message;
```

```
    BrokeredMessage brokeredMsg =
        new BrokeredMessage(JsonConvert.SerializeObject(msgPayload));
    return brokeredMsg;
}

/// <summary>
/// Our console app entry point.
/// </summary>
static void Main(string[] args)
{
    Run().GetAwaiter().GetResult();
}
}
}
```

This is a simple console program that will read a line of input from the user, then send the text entered as a message on our Service Bus message queue. When the user types exit, the program will end. It will also end if you hit your computer's power button, but I've been told that's bad form by our company's hardware support team on more than one occasion.

A few things to note:

- To send messages to our Service Bus queue, we instantiate a MessagingFactory class named senderFactory in our Run() method. You might see several examples online of sending messages using a Microsoft.ServiceBus.Messaging.QueueClient instance. Although this is a slightly simpler approach, it will only work for communicating with message queues. If you use a MessagingFactory instead, it is trivial to switch from messaging queues to topics and subscriptions if you ever need to move to a publish/subscribe architecture.

- When we call our MessagingFactory's sendAsync method to send a message, we're passing it a BrokeredMessage instance. You can only send BrokeredMessage instances through a Service Bus queue. You'll notice in our CreateMessage method, however, that we serialize our QueueMessage instance to JSON, then pass the serialized output to the BrokeredMessage constructor to be used as our payload. You can also use binary data as the BrokeredMessage payload, which can be a little more compact. However, I prefer serializing to JSON because it's a cross-platform standard and is readable when you're trying to troubleshoot issues.

- We are using the async version of methods such as `MessagingFactory.CreateMessageSenderAsync` and `MessageSender.SendAsync`. These both make remote calls to our Azure Service Bus and are traversing the network to do so. As we've discussed in previous chapters, failure to use async methods will tie up threads and can lead to thread starvation for your application when it's under load.

Let's run this thing and make sure that it works. Make sure that your ServiceBusQueue.Sender project is set as the startup project in your solution, then run it with debugging. You should see the console window and output shown in Figure 9-5.

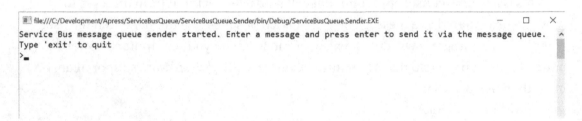

Figure 9-5. *The output from running the ServiceBusQueue.Sender console application*

Type any random message, such as "Hello from the other side (of the queue)," then press Enter. You'll then receive a confirmation that your message has been successfully sent to our Service Bus message queue.

Viewing Service Bus Message Queue Messages with Service Bus Explorer

I've asked you to take it on faith that our message was actually enqueued. Now it's time to prove it.

In previous chapters, we talked about Azure Storage Explorer, the handy open source tool that allows you to view the contents of Storage Blobs, Queues, and Tables. There is a similar tool called Service Bus Explorer for viewing the contents of Service Bus queues as well as other services such as topics, event hubs, notification hubs, and relays. Unfortunately, there isn't a convenient binary and installer; you'll have to clone the Git repo and build it from source. The GitHub project repo can be found at `https://github.com/paolosalvatori/ServiceBusExplorer`. Even though building this utility from source is a few more steps, it's definitely worth it. This application is an invaluable tool for developing with Service Bus.

After downloading and building Service Bus Explorer, launch the resulting executable. Once it opens, select File ➤ Connect from the top-level menu. This will open a dialog box that will let you create a connection to a Service Bus (Figure 9-6).

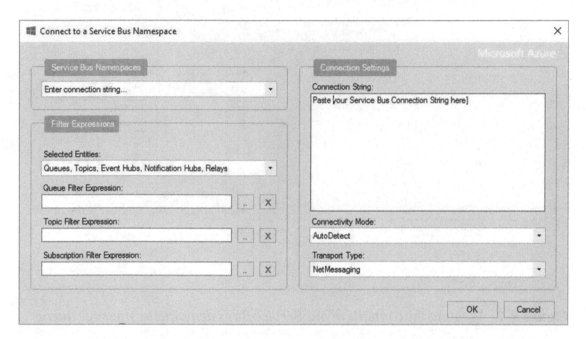

Figure 9-6. *Connecting to a Service Bus from the Service Bus Explorer application*

Under Service Bus Namespaces, select Enter Connection String as your method of connecting. You'll then need to paste your Service Bus connection string in the text area to the right. This is the same connection string that we set in our `app.config`'s `Microsoft.ServiceBus.ConnectionString` property in the previous section. Finally, click OK to create the connection.

After connecting, expand the Queues treeview node under your Service Bus's name, then click the demoqueue queue node. The content panel of the application will change to display information about the demoqueue. Click Messages on the content panel to view a list of all messages sitting in the queue. Make sure to choose Peek mode when prompted and not Receive and Delete. Peek allows us to look at messages without actually dequeueing them.

The message that we just sent through our console application should be the only one in the queue. When you select it, you'll see the JSON for our serialized QueueMessage class containing the text of the message that we just sent (Figure 9-7).

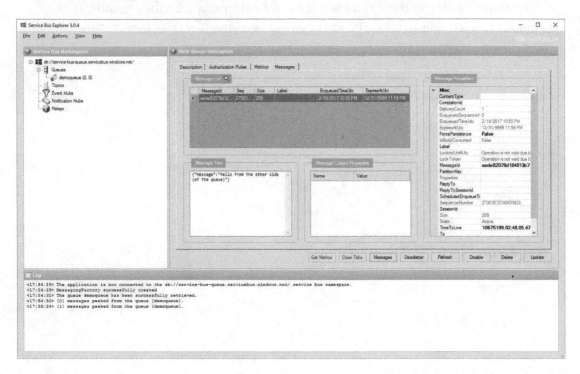

Figure 9-7. Viewing the contents of our Service Bus's demoqueue message queue

Building Our Service Bus Queue Message Receiver

We've successfully sent a message to our Service Bus queue and verified that it is indeed there. Now let's look at how to receive messages. To so do, we'll build a second console application that polls for new messages within the queue and processes each of them in turn. For demonstration purposes, our message processing will consist of writing the contents of each message to the console window.

To create our receiver, let's add a new console application to the project. Right-click the QueueDemo solution, then select Add, and select New Project. Just like we did for our ServiceBusQueue.Sender project, choose the Console Application template

located under Installed ➤ Templates ➤ Visual C# ➤ Windows. Name the new project
ServiceBusQueue.Receiver, then click OK.

Next, we'll need to add the necessary packages and references to our new
ServiceBusQueue.Receiver project. In the Solution Explorer, right-click the project and
select Manage NuGet Packages. In the NuGet package manager, add the Microsoft.
ServiceBus and Newtonsoft.Json packages. Then add a reference to the QueueDemo.
Models project.

Now we're ready for the code. Open the ServiceBusQueue.Receiver's Program.cs file,
and add the code in Listing 9-4.

Listing 9-4. Our Queue Message Receiver Code in the ServiceBusQueue.
Receiver's Program.cs File

```
using System;
using System.Threading;
using System.Threading.Tasks;
using Microsoft.ServiceBus.Messaging;
using System.Configuration;
using QueueDemo.Models;
using Newtonsoft.Json;

namespace ServiceBusQueue.Receiver
{
   class Program
   {
      /// <summary>
      /// A convenience method for writing to the console
      /// </summary>
      private static void WriteToConsole(string message, ConsoleColor color)
      {
         lock (Console.Out)
         {
            Console.WriteLine(message, color);
         }
      }

      /// <summary>
```

```csharp
/// Our async method that will listen for incoming queue messages and
/// process them.
/// </summary>
static async Task Run(CancellationToken cancellationToken)
{
    string serviceBusConnectionString =
        ConfigurationManager.AppSettings["Microsoft.ServiceBus.
        ConnectionString"];
    string queueName = "DemoQueue";

    MessagingFactory receiverFactory =
        MessagingFactory.CreateFromConnectionString(serviceBus
        ConnectionString);
    var receiver = await receiverFactory.CreateMessageReceiverAsync
    (queueName,
        ReceiveMode.PeekLock);

    var doneReceiving = new TaskCompletionSource<bool>();


    //when our cancellation token's Cancel method is called, we'll run the
    //asynchronous anonymous function below, which will tell our
    //MessageReceiver
    //to quit listening for messages, and exit this method.
    cancellationToken.Register(
        async () =>
        {
            await receiver.CloseAsync();
            await receiverFactory.CloseAsync();
            doneReceiving.SetResult(true);
        });

    receiver.OnMessageAsync(
        async message =>
        {
            QueueMessage queueMsg = null;
            var jsonBody = message.GetBody<string>();
```

```
            queueMsg = JsonConvert.DeserializeObject<QueueMessage>(jsonBody);

            //we "processed" this message successfully. Let's dequeue it!
            await message.CompleteAsync();
            WriteToConsole("Message successfully received and dequeued: " +
                queueMsg.Message, ConsoleColor.DarkBlue);

        },
        new OnMessageOptions { AutoComplete = false, MaxConcurrentCalls = 1 });

        //don't exit this method until we signal to do so from our
        //cancellationToken instance.
        await doneReceiving.Task;
    }

//Our entry point to the console application
static void Main(string[] args)
{
    Console.WriteLine("Receiver started. Listening for messages...");

    // close the receiver and factory when the CancellationToken fires
    var cts = new CancellationTokenSource();
    var runTask = Run(cts.Token);
    Console.ReadKey();
    cts.Cancel();
    runTask.GetAwaiter().GetResult();
    }
  }
}
```

There's a bit of threading code such as the CancellationToken and
TaskCompletionSource instances that are intended to keep this console application from
exiting until the user presses a key. This threading code isn't important to our discussion
on Service Bus queues.

Let's walk through our `Run` method, which is where messages are processed.

- Just like in our sender example, we create a `MessagingFactory` instance. This class handles authenticating with Azure and connecting to our Service Bus resource based on the supplied connection string.

- To actually receive messages, we need an instance of the `MessageReceiver` class. We get this by calling our `MessagingFactory` instance's `CreateMessageReceiverAsync` method. As arguments, we must pass in the name of the queue within our Service Bus's namespace that we'd like to monitor, as well as the receive mode. Our receive mode options are `PeekLock` and `ReceiveAndDelete`. For this example, we'll specify `PeekLock`, which means that we need to explicitly acknowledge that a message has finished processing by calling the `Complete` method, which will dequeue the message.

- Now that we've set up a `MessageReceiver` instance called receiver, we'll call the `OnMessageAsync` method to begin receiving messages. Instead of having to poll to see if new messages are available, the framework will call the anonymous async method that you specify whenever a new message is received.

- `OnMessageAsync` also takes an `OnMessageOptions` instance as an argument that defines how the framework will handle passing messages to your anonymous method. `OnMessageOptions` properties include the following:

  - *AutoComplete*: This should be set to true if you want the `OnMessageAsync` method to automatically call `Complete()` when a message has finished processing without an exception being thrown. If you set this to false, you'll have to explicitly call the message's `Complete()` method to remove it from the queue. If you fail to do so, the message will become visible again after the message lock has expired and will be reprocessed. Note that this property only applies if the receive mode is set to `PeekLock`.

  - *MaxConcurrentCalls*: This is an integer value that tells the framework the maximum number of concurrent threads it can use to process messages.

For our example, we'll set AutoComplete to false so that we can demonstrate calling Complete(). We'll also set the MaxConcurrentCalls to 1.

- Within our OnMessageAsync's anonymous method, we receive a BrokeredMessage instance called message. We then get the BrokeredMessage's body, which is a QueueMessage instance that has been serialized to JSON format. By calling JsonConvert. DeserializeObject on the message's body, we receive back the QueueMessage that was originally enqueued by our ServiceBusQueue.Sender console application.

- Finally, we call our BrokeredMessage's Complete() method to dequeue the message, and we write the message to the console.

Testing Our Service Bus Queue Message Receiver

Let's run the full demonstration. To make things more interesting, set both the ServiceBusQueue.Receiver and ServiceBusQueue.Sender to start simultaneously. We can then send messages and watch as they are received. To do so, right-click on the QueueDemo solution in the Solution Explorer and select Properties. In the Solution Property Pages dialog box, select Multiple Startup Projects, and select both the ServiceBusQueue.Receiver and ServiceBusQueue.Sender's action to Start (Figure 9-8).

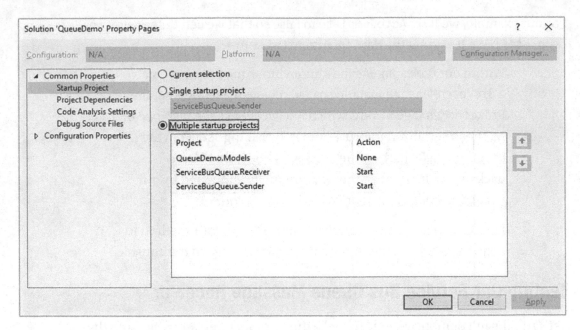

Figure 9-8. *Setting both the sender and receiver console app to start simultaneously*

Once you've configured both projects to start simultaneously, run with debugging. You should see both console windows launch. Enter messages in the ServiceBusQueue. Sender's console window and press Enter. You should see the message echoed to the ServiceBusQueue.Receiver's console window (see Figures 9-9 and 9-10).

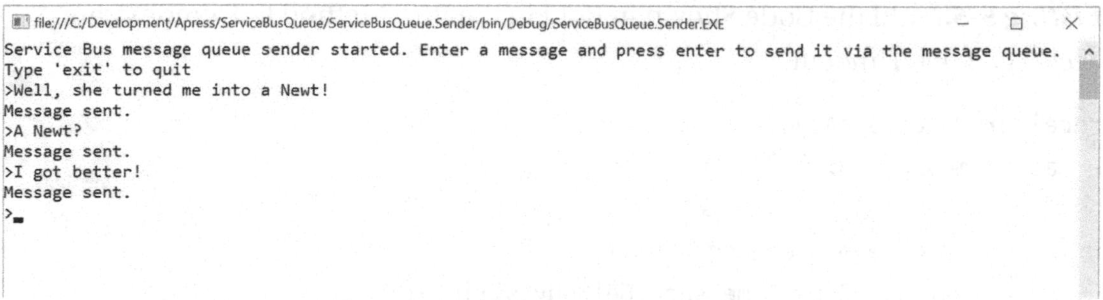

Figure 9-9. *Enter messages and press Enter. These will be sent to our Service Bus queue.*

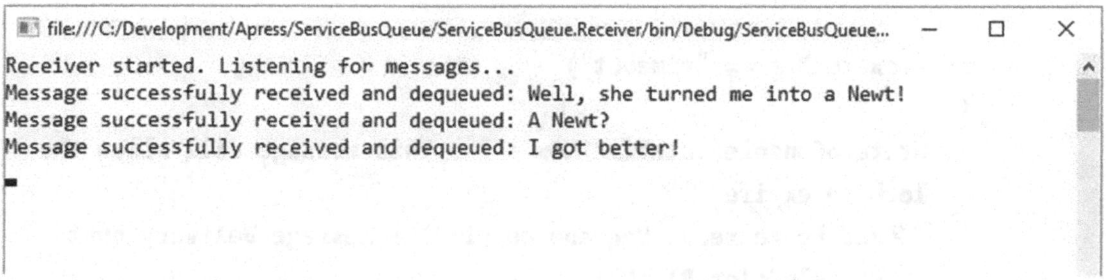

Figure 9-10. *Messages that you send will be echoed to the ServiceBusQueue. Receiver's console window.*

Message Lock Timeout

When a message is received in PeekLock receive mode, a lock is applied to the message when it is read from the queue. If the receiver doesn't explicitly call the message's Complete(), Abandon(), or Deadletter() methods, the lock will expire and the message will once again become visible to any receivers who are monitoring the queue. The lock duration is specified at the queue level, and can be changed via the queue's Properties blade in the Azure Portal.

Recall that when we created our queue in the Azure Portal, we set the lock duration to five seconds, which is the minimum allowed value. Let's make some changes to our Program class in our ServiceBusQueue.Receiver project. Add the code shown in bold in Listing 9-5 to your Program class's Run method.

Listing 9-5. Add the Code Shown in Bold to the Run Method to Demonstrate
Message Lock Timeout

```
receiver.OnMessageAsync(
    async message =>
    {
        QueueMessage queueMsg = null;
            var jsonBody = message.GetBody<string>();
            queueMsg = JsonConvert.DeserializeObject<QueueMessage>(jsonBody);

            string loweredMsg = queueMsg.Message.ToLower();

            if (loweredMsg == "timeout")
            {
                WriteToConsole(DateTime.Now + " : This message will allow the
                lock to expire
                    and be re-read. Dequeue count: " + message.DeliveryCount,
                    ConsoleColor.Black);
            }
            else
            {
                //we processed this message successfully. Let's dequeue it!
                await message.CompleteAsync();
                WriteToConsole("Message successfully received and dequeued: " +
                    queueMsg.Message, ConsoleColor.DarkBlue);
            }
    },
        new OnMessageOptions { AutoComplete = false, MaxConcurrentCalls = 1 });
```

We've added code that will check to see if the text of a message is `"timeout"`. If so, we
will not call `Complete()` on the message and will allow the message lock to expire. Once
the message's lock expires, it will become visible and be reread. This will continue until
the maximum delivery count for the message is reached, at which point the message will
be moved to the dead letter subqueue.

Once you've made the changes just listed, run both the ServiceBusQueue.Sender
and ServiceBusQueue.Receiver projects in debug mode. Enter `"timeout"` in the sender's
console window and watch the output in the receiver's console (Figure 9-11).

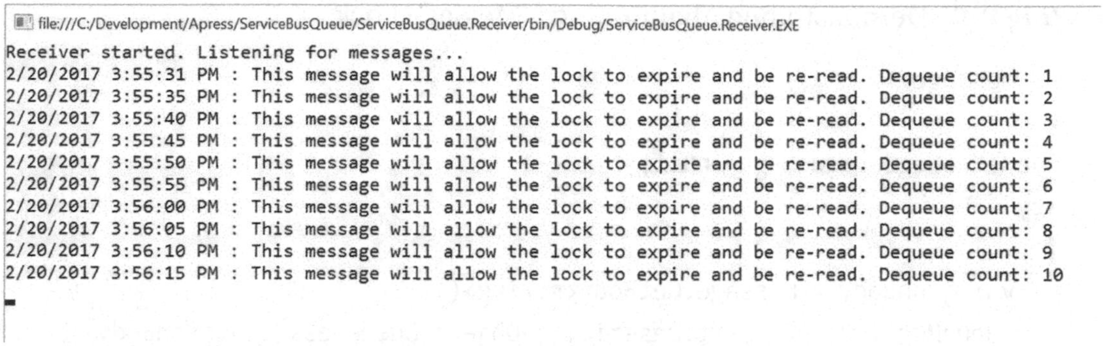

```
file:///C:/Development/Apress/ServiceBusQueue/ServiceBusQueue.Receiver/bin/Debug/ServiceBusQueue.Receiver.EXE
Receiver started. Listening for messages...
2/20/2017 3:55:31 PM : This message will allow the lock to expire and be re-read. Dequeue count: 1
2/20/2017 3:55:35 PM : This message will allow the lock to expire and be re-read. Dequeue count: 2
2/20/2017 3:55:40 PM : This message will allow the lock to expire and be re-read. Dequeue count: 3
2/20/2017 3:55:45 PM : This message will allow the lock to expire and be re-read. Dequeue count: 4
2/20/2017 3:55:50 PM : This message will allow the lock to expire and be re-read. Dequeue count: 5
2/20/2017 3:55:55 PM : This message will allow the lock to expire and be re-read. Dequeue count: 6
2/20/2017 3:56:00 PM : This message will allow the lock to expire and be re-read. Dequeue count: 7
2/20/2017 3:56:05 PM : This message will allow the lock to expire and be re-read. Dequeue count: 8
2/20/2017 3:56:10 PM : This message will allow the lock to expire and be re-read. Dequeue count: 9
2/20/2017 3:56:15 PM : This message will allow the lock to expire and be re-read. Dequeue count: 10
```

Figure 9-11. *Demonstrating message lock expiration*

Notice that after our five-second message lock expired, the message became visible and was dequeued once again. Our timestamps show that the lock is indeed five seconds.

It's important to point out that when using PeekLock, your queue's lock duration should be set long enough to cover processing under heavy load. Otherwise, your message could be processed twice or more due to the following interleaving of events:

1. A receiver reads a message with PeekLock and begins processing.

2. While the original receiver is still processing, the message lock expires. The message is once again unlocked and visible in the queue. Another receiver thread dequeues the message a second time.

3. The original receiver finishes processing the message.

4. The second receiver finishes processing the message.

To complete this exercise, open the Service Bus Explorer app once again and select the demoqueue. Click Deadletter in the View Queue panel to verify that after our message's dequeue count exceeded the maximum dequeue count, the message was in fact moved to the dead letter queue.

Abandoning a Message Lock

Instead of allowing a message's lock to expire, we can immediately release a lock by calling the BrokeredMessage's Abandon() method. This allows any listening receiver to immediately reread the message. It's useful to place in a catch block after an exception has occurred due to some transient set of circumstances. To demonstrate, add the code shown in bold in Listing 9-6 to the Run method in the ServiceBusQueue.Receiver's Program class.

Listing 9-6. Demonstrating Abandoning a Message Lock

```
async message =>
{
    QueueMessage queueMsg = null;
    try
    {
        var jsonBody = message.GetBody<string>();
        queueMsg = JsonConvert.DeserializeObject<QueueMessage>(jsonBody);

        string loweredMsg = queueMsg.Message.ToLower();
        if (loweredMsg == "timeout")
        {
            WriteToConsole(DateTime.Now + " : This message will allow the lock to
                expire and be re-read. Dequeue count: " + message.DeliveryCount,
                ConsoleColor.Black);
        }

        else if (loweredMsg == "exception")
        {
            throw new Exception("Exception thrown for demonstration purposes.");
        }
        else
        {
            //we processed this message successfully. Let's dequeue it!
            await message.CompleteAsync();
            WriteToConsole("Message successfully received and dequeued: " +
                queueMsg.Message, ConsoleColor.DarkBlue);
        }
    }
    catch (Exception ex)
    {
        await message.AbandonAsync();
```

```
        WriteToConsole(DateTime.Now + " : Abandoning message lock due to
        exception.
            Delivery count: " + message.DeliveryCount + " Exception: " +
            ex.Message,
            ConsoleColor.Red);
    }
},
new OnMessageOptions { AutoComplete = false, MaxConcurrentCalls = 1 });
```

After making the changes, run both the ServiceBusQueue.Sender and ServiceBusQueue.Receiver projects in debug mode. Enter "exception" in the sender's console window. The receiver's output is shown in Figure 9-12.

```
file:///C:/Development/Apress/ServiceBusQueue/ServiceBusQueue.Receiver/bin/Debug/ServiceBusQueue.Receiver.EXE
Receiver started. Listening for messages...
2/20/2017 7:38:55 PM : Abandoning message lock due to exception. Delivery count: 1 Exception: Exception thrown for demonstration purposes.
2/20/2017 7:38:55 PM : Abandoning message lock due to exception. Delivery count: 2 Exception: Exception thrown for demonstration purposes.
2/20/2017 7:38:56 PM : Abandoning message lock due to exception. Delivery count: 3 Exception: Exception thrown for demonstration purposes.
2/20/2017 7:38:56 PM : Abandoning message lock due to exception. Delivery count: 4 Exception: Exception thrown for demonstration purposes.
2/20/2017 7:38:56 PM : Abandoning message lock due to exception. Delivery count: 5 Exception: Exception thrown for demonstration purposes.
2/20/2017 7:38:56 PM : Abandoning message lock due to exception. Delivery count: 6 Exception: Exception thrown for demonstration purposes.
2/20/2017 7:38:56 PM : Abandoning message lock due to exception. Delivery count: 7 Exception: Exception thrown for demonstration purposes.
2/20/2017 7:38:56 PM : Abandoning message lock due to exception. Delivery count: 8 Exception: Exception thrown for demonstration purposes.
2/20/2017 7:38:56 PM : Abandoning message lock due to exception. Delivery count: 9 Exception: Exception thrown for demonstration purposes.
2/20/2017 7:38:56 PM : Abandoning message lock due to exception. Delivery count: 10 Exception: Exception thrown for demonstration purposes.
```

Figure 9-12.   *The output from our ServiceBusQueue.Receiver when abandoning a message lock*

As soon as a message lock is abandoned, the receiver will reread and lock the message. This continues until the maximum dequeue count is reached and the message is dead lettered. You'll notice that from the timestamps, there is very little delay from when a lock is released and the message becomes visible to when the message is reread and locked again.

Dead Lettering a Message

When processing a queue message, you don't have to wait for the maximum dequeue count to be reached to quit attempting to process a message. If you know that you no longer need to attempt to process a message, you can call the BrokeredMessage's DeadLetter() or DeadLetterAsync() methods. These methods will immediately dequeue the message and move it to the dead letter subqueue.

Scaling Out

One of the major benefits of using message queues is the ability to decouple parts of your application and scale them independently. If you find that a queue is increasing in length because the receiver is falling behind and messages are being added to the queue faster than they can be processed, you can remedy the situation by adding more receivers.

Here's an analogy that we're all familiar with in the real world. When you go to the post office during lunch to mail a package, there's usually a single clerk working at 11:45 a.m. Under normal circumstances, a single counter clerk is able to handle all customers' needs in a timely fashion without any single customer having to wait for a long time. As the number of customers visiting the post office during their lunch breaks increases, though, the line of customers begins to lengthen.

We could leave our single clerk at the counter to serve a growing number of customers; eventually the clerk would get to everyone. Alternatively, a second clerk could work the counter to service the line of customers twice as fast. The moral of the story is this: You can add additional receivers to drain a queue as load increases, and remove receivers as load decreases. In fact, this is an option for Web App Autoscale as discussed in Chapter 2. Instead of keying on CPU utilization or memory pressure, you can scale up or scale out a Web App instance that hosts WebJobs that are monitoring a Service Bus queue based on the Service Bus queue length.

To demonstrate this, we'll launch a single instance of our sender application, and a couple of instances of our receiver. To make this demo more compelling, let's add a `Thread.Sleep(5000)` call immediately after calling `CompleteAsync()` on our `BrokeredMessage`. This will simulate a heavy workload for queue message processing.

After adding the `Thread.Sleep(5000)` call, launch both the sender and receiver console apps. You'll need to navigate to the ServiceBusQueue.Receiver's `\bin\debug` directory and manually launch a second instance of `ServiceBusQueue.Receiver.exe`.

When all apps are launched, start entering messages every few seconds into the sender's console window to fill up the queue. For my demo, I entered each letter of the alphabet as a message. Notice how some messages are grabbed and processed by the first receiver, and others are processed by the second (Figure 9-13).

```
C:\Development\Apress\QueueDemo\ServiceBusQueue.Receiver\bin\Debug\ServiceBusQueue.Receiver.
PID 20788 receiver started. Listening for messages...
2/21/2017 3:07:05 PM Message successfully received and dequeued: c
2/21/2017 3:07:14 PM Message successfully received and dequeued: f
2/21/2017 3:07:20 PM Message successfully received and dequeued: h
2/21/2017 3:07:26 PM Message successfully received and dequeued: j
2/21/2017 3:07:31 PM Message successfully received and dequeued: l
2/21/2017 3:07:41 PM Message successfully received and dequeued: o
2/21/2017 3:07:47 PM Message successfully received and dequeued: q
2/21/2017 3:07:52 PM Message successfully received and dequeued: s
2/21/2017 3:07:57 PM Message successfully received and dequeued: t
2/21/2017 3:08:02 PM Message successfully received and dequeued: v
2/21/2017 3:08:07 PM Message successfully received and dequeued: x
2/21/2017 3:08:12 PM Message successfully received and dequeued: z
```

```
file:///C:/Development/Apress/QueueDemo/ServiceBusQueue.Receiver/bin/Debug/ServiceBusQueue.Receiver.
PID 29892 receiver started. Listening for messages...
2/21/2017 3:06:56 PM Message successfully received and dequeued: a
2/21/2017 3:07:01 PM Message successfully received and dequeued: b
2/21/2017 3:07:06 PM Message successfully received and dequeued: d
2/21/2017 3:07:12 PM Message successfully received and dequeued: e
2/21/2017 3:07:17 PM Message successfully received and dequeued: g
2/21/2017 3:07:22 PM Message successfully received and dequeued: i
2/21/2017 3:07:27 PM Message successfully received and dequeued: k
2/21/2017 3:07:32 PM Message successfully received and dequeued: m
2/21/2017 3:07:37 PM Message successfully received and dequeued: n
2/21/2017 3:07:42 PM Message successfully received and dequeued: p
2/21/2017 3:07:48 PM Message successfully received and dequeued: r
2/21/2017 3:08:00 PM Message successfully received and dequeued: u
2/21/2017 3:08:06 PM Message successfully received and dequeued: w
2/21/2017 3:08:12 PM Message successfully received and dequeued: y
```

Figure 9-13. *Both of our receiver console app instances. Messages were typed in alphabetical order with a five-second wait after receiving each message*

Note   If you enter several messages a second, you might notice that the dequeue seems out of order. Message A might be delivered before message B if they are entered almost simultaneously. This is due to differing network latency when making calls to the Azure queue. B was actually enqueued before A. Rest assured that the FIFO ordering of messages is preserved.

Using Message Queues to Build Azure Web Applications

When developing web applications, you probably won't make use of console apps. Instead, you'll likely send messages from a web application, then receive and process messages from a WebJob. Microsoft has taken much of the work out of receiving Service Bus queue messages by providing a `ServiceBusTriggerAttribute` class that we can use to mark methods with in triggered WebJobs. The `ServiceBusTriggerAttribute` handles all of the bookkeeping required to monitor a Service Bus queue and call our designated method when new messages arrive.

To demonstrate, let's add a new WebJob project to our QueueDemo solution. To do so, right-click the QueueDemo solution, select Add, and then select New Project. Select the

Azure WebJob template located under the Visual C# ➤ Cloud category. Let's name this new project ServiceBusQueue.WebJob. Click OK to create the new project (Figure 9-14).

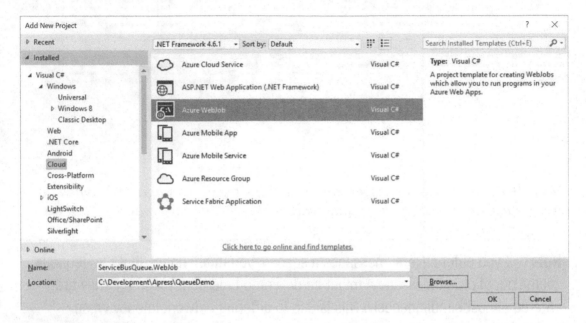

Figure 9-14. *Creating a new WebJob project called ServiceBusQueue.WebJob*

Next, we need to add the appropriate NuGet packages to our new WebJob. Right-click the ServiceBusQueue.WebJob project and select Manage NuGet Packages. On the NuGet package management screen, select the Browse tab, then search for and install both the Microsoft.Azure.WebJobs.ServiceBus and Newtonsoft.Json packages. The former is required to reference the ServiceBusTriggerAttribute, which we will use to mark a method to be called when new messages arrive. The latter will be used to deserialize our QueueMessage class instance that we receive. To finish our project setup, right-click the ServiceBusQueue.WebJob project's References, select Add Reference, and add a reference to the QueueDemo.Models project. We'll need the QueueDemo.Models so that we can reference the QueueMessage class, which we'll deserialize from all of our received messages.

Next, let's add the required settings to our app.config file. We'll need to do three things. First, we need to set Storage connection string values for our AzureWebJobsDashboard and AzureWebJobsStorage values. As mentioned in the previous chapter, these are used to log events so that they appear on the Azure Portal's

WebJobs Dashboard, and for internal bookkeeping. Second, we need to set the value of the `AzureWebJobsServiceBus` connection string. This is what our WebJob's `ServiceBusTriggerAttribute` will use to determine which Service Bus to monitor for messages. Finally, we'll need to add an `AppContextSwitchOverrides` node to our runtime section. This is required for authentication to work correctly using the latest version of the `Microsoft.ServiceBus` package when running with .NET Framework 4.6.1. This might or might not be applicable to future versions. See the example sections in Listing 9-7.

Listing 9-7. Settings That Must Be Added to Your WebJob's app.config File

```xml
<?xml version="1.0" encoding="utf-8"?>
<configuration>
    <connectionStrings>

        <add name="AzureWebJobsDashboard" connectionString="[Your Storage account
        connection string "/>
        <add name="AzureWebJobsStorage connectionString="[Your Storage account
        connection string "/>
        <add name="AzureWebJobsServiceBus" connectionString="[Your Service Bus
        connection string"/>
    </connectionStrings>
    ... a bunch of other boilerplate settings elided for brevity...
    <runtime>
        <AppContextSwitchOverrides value="Switch.System.IdentityModel.Disable
        MultipleDNSEntriesInSANCertificate=true" />
    </runtime>
</configuration>
```

Now, let's create the code for our WebJob's `Program` class. It's just a few lines, shown in Listing 9-8. If you've read Chapter 8, which focused on WebJobs, this code will be very familiar. Note that you have to call the `JobHostConfiguration` instance's `UseServiceBus()` method. If you fail to do so, new messages to your Service Bus queue will not trigger the marked method in your `Functions` class.

Listing 9-8. The Entirety of the ServiceBusQueue.WebJob Project's Program.cs File

```
using Microsoft.Azure.WebJobs;

namespace ServiceBusQueue.WebJob
{
    class Program
    {
        static void Main()
        {
            var config = new JobHostConfiguration();
            config.UseServiceBus();
            var host = new JobHost(config);
            host.RunAndBlock();
        }
    }
}
```

Let's jump over to the Functions class in our Functions.cs file. The contents of the file are shown in Listing 9-9.

Listing 9-9. Our Functions Cclass Definition

```
using Microsoft.Azure.WebJobs;
using Microsoft.ServiceBus.Messaging;
using QueueDemo.Models;
using Newtonsoft.Json;
using System;

namespace ServiceBusQueue.WebJob
{
    public class Functions
    {
        // This function will get triggered/executed when a new message is
        // written
        // on an Azure Service Bus queue called demoqueue.
        public static void ProcessQueueMessage([ServiceBusTrigger("demoqueue")]
            BrokeredMessage message)
```

```
    {
        //first, we need to deserialize our QueueMessage class.
        var jsonBody = message.GetBody<string>();
        QueueMessage queueMsg = JsonConvert.DeserializeObject<QueueMessage>
        (jsonBody);
        //Write the message to the console for demonstration purposes.
        Console.WriteLine("Message : " + queueMsg.Message);
    }
  }
}
```

The ProcessQueueMessage method will be called whenever a new message is posted to the demoqueue Service Bus queue. The ServiceBusTriggerAttribute that we used to mark our ProcessQueueMessage method with gives us the following functionality:

- Whenever a new message is posted to the demoqueue, our trigger will read the message using the PeekLock read mode. The message is given to us as a method argument of type BrokeredMessage.

- If the function completes without throwing an exception, the ServiceBusTriggerAttribute will automatically call the BrokeredMessage's Complete() method.

- If the function throws an exception, the ServiceBusTriggerAttribute will automatically call the method's Abandon() method.

- If the function runs longer than the Queue's lock duration, the ServiceBusTriggerAttribute will automatically renew the message lock.

As you can see, using the ServiceBusTriggerAttribute takes a great deal of work out of processing Service Bus queue messages.

We can run our WebJob locally along with our ServiceBusQueue.Sender console application for demonstration purposes. Just as we did previously, right-click the QueueDemo solution in the Solution Explorer window and select Properties to open the solution's Properties dialog box. On the Startup Project screen, select the Multiple Startup Projects option and set both the ServiceBusQueue.Sender and ServiceBusQueue. WebJob projects to start. Make sure that you set the ServiceBusQueue.Receiver's startup action to None, or else our receiver console app could snatch messages before the WebJob gets a chance to see them. When finished, click OK and run the application in debug. As before, send messages through our sender console app, and you'll see sent messages written to the WebJob's console (Figure 9-15).

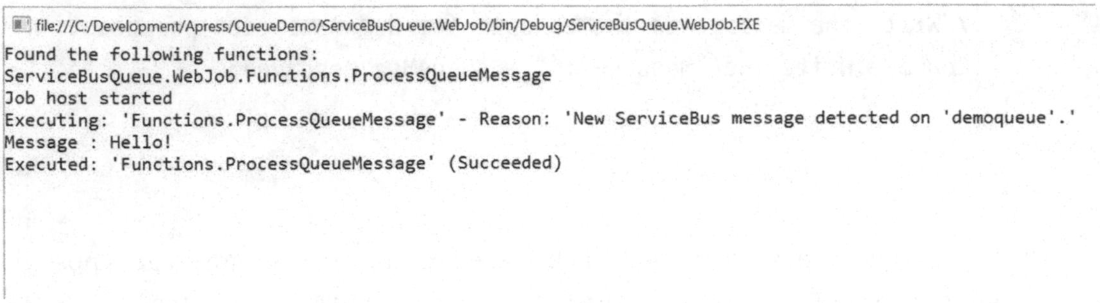

```
file:///C:/Development/Apress/QueueDemo/ServiceBusQueue.WebJob/bin/Debug/ServiceBusQueue.WebJob.EXE
Found the following functions:
ServiceBusQueue.WebJob.Functions.ProcessQueueMessage
Job host started
Executing: 'Functions.ProcessQueueMessage' - Reason: 'New ServiceBus message detected on 'demoqueue'.'
Message : Hello!
Executed: 'Functions.ProcessQueueMessage' (Succeeded)
```

Figure 9-15. *Our WebJob's console window after starting up and receiving a message from our Service Bus queue*

Summary

We've discussed basic message queue concepts and looked at Service Bus and Storage queues. We then walked through a demonstration of Service Bus queue concepts such as provisioning a Service Bus resource, sending and receiving messages, message lock timeout, dead lettering, and abandoning messages. We ended the chapter with an example of how you could use Service Bus queues in a production web application. In the next chapter, we'll take a look at other tips and tricks that are useful for scaling web applications.

CHAPTER 10

Other Tips and Tricks

We've all experienced web sites that take several seconds to load. Fifteen years ago, when DSL connections where considered fast, a page load that took several seconds was acceptable. This is no longer the case. In fact, since 2010, Google has used page speed as a ranking factor for search results. A nontrivial percentage of users will abandon slow sites and skip to the next search result. Given these facts, I strongly believe that performance should be a feature of every web application.

Throughout this book, we've talked in detail about how to use various Azure services to scale and speed up web apps. There are several tips and tricks, however, that are not specific to Azure that can help you squeeze performance from your web application. In some cases, these performance increases can be dramatic. Most of these tips and tricks are also very easy to implement.

This chapter is structured as a cookbook. We'll look at each individual optimization and explain it in detail. We'll illustrate several of our optimizations by looking at an example app called Turtles. Let's get started.

The Turtles Web Application

With most examples throughout this book, we've built the application over time and added functionality as we went. In this chapter, though, we'll start with a fully built application that runs poorly and optimize it throughout the chapter.

The Turtles web application is extremely simple: It's a single-page MVC application that uses Bootstrap and doesn't even have a database. The single page is displayed in Figure 10-1.

© Rob Reagan 2018
R. Reagan, *Web Applications on Azure*, https://doi.org/10.1007/978-1-4842-2976-7_10

Turtles have been around for a very long time. They first emerged some 157 million years ago. There are currently 327 known species.

Turtles vary widely in size. Leatherback Sea Turtles have been measured at six feet in length with a total weight of over 2,000 pounds. The tiniest species is the speckled padloper tortoise. It is roughly three inches in length and weighs less than a roll of pennies.

Turtles defend themselves by withdrawing into their shells. Their shells are made of bone, and are near impenetrable to most predators.

A relatively new species of turtles in Manhattan are known to live underground and have become bipedal. While these particular turtles are omnivorous, they've shown a particular fondness for pizza of any type. After forming a symbiotic relationship with a large anthropomorphic rat, these turtles have fashioned an elaborate self-defense mechanism which is much more sophisticated than withdrawing into their shells. With the help of Casey Jones and April O'Neil, these rambunctious tortoises fight crime and defend New York against the Foot Clan.

Figure 10-1. *The completed Turtles web application home page*

Let's run through the code needed to set this application up.

Creating the Solution and Project

We'll start with creating our solution.

1. Open Visual Studio 2015 and select File ➤ New Project.

2. In the New Project dialog box, select the ASP.NET Web Application (.NET Framework) template. It is located under the Installed ➤ Templates ➤ Visual C# ➤ Web category (Figure 10-2).

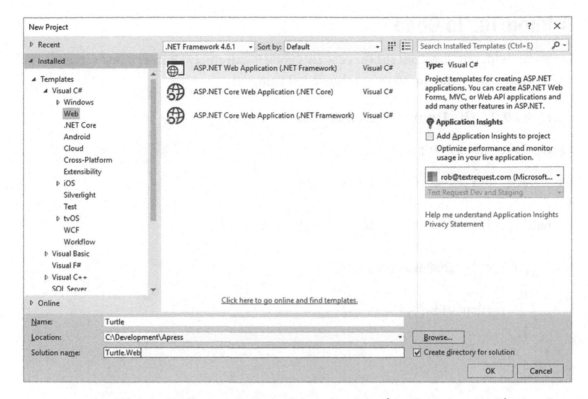

Figure 10-2. *Choosing the ASP.NET Web Application (.NET Framework) template*

3. Name the new web application `Turtle`, and the solution
    `Turtle.Web`. Click OK to continue.

4. On the next screen, you'll be prompted to select an ASP.NET
    template. Select the MVC template and click OK. Your project is
    now created.

This template includes some extraneous files that we won't need. Go ahead and
delete the following from the project:

*   The `AccountController.cs` and `ManageController.cs` in the
    `Controllers` folder.

*   All classes in the `Models` folder.

*   The `Account` and `Manage` subfolders located in the `View` folder.

*   The `Project_Readme.html` file.

Now that we've tidied up, let's move on to the code.

Adding Turtle Code

Let's start with our HomeController.cs. This code is extremely simple; it just serves a single view. The complete source is shown in Listing 10-1.

Listing 10-1. The HomeController.cs Code

```
using System.Web.Mvc;

namespace Turtle.Web.Controllers
{
    public class HomeController : Controller
    {
        public ActionResult Index()
        {
            return View();
        }
    }
}
```

Next, let's look in the Views\Shared folder and update our _Layout.cshtml page. The source for _Layout.cshtml is shown in Listing 10-2.

Listing 10-2. The Contents of the _Layout.cshtml File

```
<!DOCTYPE html>
<html>
<head>
    <meta charset="utf-8"/>
    <meta name="viewport" content="width=device-width, initial-scale=1.0">
    <title>Turtles</title>
    <script src="/Scripts/jquery-1.10.2.js"></script>

    <script src="/Scripts/bootstrap.js"></script>
    <script src="/Scripts/respond.js"></script>
    <script src="/Scripts/modernizr-2.6.2.js"></script>
    <link href="/Content/bootstrap.css" rel="stylesheet"/>
```

```
<style type="text/css">
    body {
        padding-top: 50px;
        padding-bottom: 20px;
    }

    /* Set padding to keep content from hitting the edges */
    .body-content {
        padding-left: 15px;
        padding-right: 15px;
    }

    /* Override the default bootstrap behavior where horizontal
    description lists will truncate terms that are too long to fit in the
    left column */
    .dl-horizontal dt {
        white-space: normal;
    }

    /* Set width on the form input elements since they're 100% wide by
    default */
    input,
    select,
    textarea {
        max-width: 280px;
    }

    .main-image {
        max-width: 100%;
    }
</style>
</head>
<body>
    <div class="navbar navbar-inverse navbar-fixed-top">
        <div class="container">
            <div class="navbar-header">
                <button type="button" class="navbar-toggle" data-toggle="collapse"
```

```
                data-target=".navbar-collapse">
                <span class="icon-bar"></span>
                <span class="icon-bar"></span>
                <span class="icon-bar"></span>
            </button>
            @Html.ActionLink("All About Turtles", "Index", "Home",
            new { area = "" },
                new { @class = "navbar-brand" })
        </div>
        <div class="navbar-collapse collapse">
            <ul class="nav navbar-nav">
                <li>@Html.ActionLink("Home", "Index", "Home")</li>
            </ul>
        </div>
    </div>
  </div>
  <div class="container body-content">
      @RenderBody()
  </div>
</body>
</html>
```

There are all sorts of bad things going on in _Layout.cshtml, but we'll get to them in short order.

Next, let's update the contents of the \Views\Home\Index.cshtml file. The complete source is displayed in Listing 10-3.

Listing 10-3. The \Views\Home\Index.cshtml Source

```
<h1>Turtles</h1>
<div class="jumbotron">
    <img src="~/Content/Images/Turtle.jpg" class="main-image"/>
</div>

<div class="panel panel-default">
    <div class="panel-body">
```

```
    <p>
        Turtles have been around for a very long time. They first
        emerged some 157
        million years ago. There are currently 327 known species.
    </p>
    <p>
        Turtles vary widely in size. Leatherback Sea Turtles have been
        measured at six
        feet in length with a total weight of over 2,000 pounds. The
        tiniest species is
        the speckled padloper tortoise. It is roughly three inches in
        length and
        weighs less than a roll of pennies.
    </p>
    <p>
        Turtles defend themselves by withdrawing into their shells.
        Their shells
        are made of bone, and are near impenetrable to most predators.
    </p>
    <p>
        A relatively new species of turtles in Manhattan are known to
        live underground and have become bipedal. While these
        particular turtles
        are omnivorous, they've shown a particular fondness for pizza
        of any type.
        After forming a symbiotic relationship with a large
        anthropomorphic rat,
        these turtles have fashioned an elaborate self-defense mechanism which
        is much more sophisticated than withdrawing into their shells.
        With the help
        of Casey Jones and April O'Neil, these rambunctious tortoises
        fight crime and
        defend New York against the Foot Clan.
    </p>
    </div>
</div>
```

Last but not least, we need to add our main image to the project. Because it would be extremely hard for you to type the contents of a large image into your favorite hex editor, I recommend that you download the image from this chapter's Git repo. In honesty, any large image you have laying around will do. The example image that we're using for this chapter is 4601 × 3200 in size at 400 dpi resolution. It weighs in at a hefty size of 10.1 MB. Place this image, called `Turtle.jpg`, in the `\content\images` folder.

Publishing to Azure

For our performance tuning, I prefer to look at real numbers from our actual hosting environment. Although not required for your continued enjoyment of this chapter, I recommend setting up an Azure Web App F1 Free tier instance, then publish the Turtles app there. If you'd like a detailed walkthrough for setting up a Web App instance and publishing, review Chapter 2.

How Pages Are Rendered

As developers, we spend a lot of time on back-end development to optimize performance. Once a request hits our .NET code, we worry about efficient algorithms, finely tuned databases, and caching to make sure that our servers deliver a response in minimal time. However, it is quite possible to have a finely tuned back end and a poorly performing web application that leaves users sighing and tapping their fingers while waiting for your pages to load. A fast back end is only one component of performance. Before we look at various tips and tricks to decrease page load time, let's run through a high-level overview of what happens when users request a page in their browser.

Initial Page Request

When a user navigates to your web application, there are a few steps involved before their browser can even request the initial page. These steps include a potential Domain Name System (DNS) lookup to get your site's address, opening the initial connection with your server, and potentially negotiating an SSL connection if your site supports SSL. After these initial steps complete, the user's browser sends a request and then waits for the response. While the browser waits, the page request is traversing the network to reach your site, your servers are processing the request and sending a response, and the response traverses back through the network to the user's browser. We call the time that is spent traversing the network network latency, or just latency for short. Once the user's browser receives the response, it begins parsing the page.

Page Parsing and Rendering

Now that the browser has the initial page, it starts parsing the HTML from beginning to end. As HTML elements are read, they are converted into DOM elements and become part of the DOM tree. As CSS elements are encountered, they are also parsed and become part of the page's CSS Object Model (CSSOM). After all HTML and CSS has been parsed and the DOM and CSSOM have been constructed, they are combined into a render tree, which is then used to calculate the layout of individual elements and then painted to the screen.

I've glossed over a few important details. When the browser is parsing a page's HTML, if it encounters a reference to an external stylesheet, it will suspend DOM construction and immediately request, wait for, and parse the external CSS before continuing. It gets even worse, though. If inline JavaScript is encountered, the parser will be suspended while the JavaScript is executed. Whenever a `<script>` tag that points to an external JavaScript file is found, the browser suspends parsing, downloads, and executes the external JavaScript file.

Measuring Page Performance

There are various online tools and services such as Yahoo's yslow.org and Google's PageSpeed toolset (`https://developers.google.com/speed/pagespeed`) that will take a look at individual pages and make recommendations for improving performance based on a ruleset. These are excellent tools for diagnosing performance issues due to front-end code or suboptimal server configuration, and I encourage you to check them both out. For illustrations throughout this chapter, though, we'll use Chrome DevTools's Network tab. If you aren't already using it, Chrome DevTools is the Swiss Army knife for front-end development and debugging.

Let's use Chrome DevTools to see how our Turtles site is performing.

1. Open Chrome and navigate to the URL for your Turtles web application on Azure.

2. Right-click anywhere on the page in Chrome and select Inspect to open DevTools.

3. Once DevTools is open, select the Network tab. To see how the page would perform with no caching, make sure to select the Disable Cache check box at the top of the page. You'll then need to refresh the main page for Turtles in your browser to gather statistics. The results will then be displayed (Figure 10-3).

Name	Status	Type	Initiator	Size	Time
Turtle.jpg	200	jpeg	(index)	10.2 MB	6.22 s
respond.js	200	script	(index)	5.1 KB	235 ms
modernizr-2.6.2.js	200	script	(index)	19.9 KB	350 ms
jquery-1.10.2.js	200	script	(index)	106 KB	911 ms
eltortuga.azurewebs...	200	document	Other	4.1 KB	1.10 s
bootstrap.js	200	script	(index)	16.3 KB	310 ms
bootstrap.css	200	stylesheet	(index)	25.8 KB	545 ms

7 requests | 10.4 MB transferred | Finish: 7.87 s | DOMContentLoaded: 2.11 s | Load: 7.88 s

Figure 10-3. *The initial performance results for our Turtles site hosted in Azure*

There is much performance information available on this screen. Let's run through the highlights.

- Requested resources that make up the page are listed in the Name column on the far left of the screen. Resources are listed in the order in which they are requested. You can see that we began with `eltortuga.azurewebsites.net`, then proceeded to request six additional files. These include four JavaScript files, one CSS file, and an image.

- The Status column tells us the result of each request. Because we see 200 OK for each request, we know that all files were downloaded successfully. We'll revisit this column in future optimizations.

- The Time column tells us the total elapsed time from the initial resource request to when the content was completely downloaded. Note that this number doesn't include time spent while the request was queued. We'll discuss queued requests and why they occur later in the chapter.

- At the very bottom of the screen, we see the total number of requests, total size of all content downloaded, and how long it took to completely render the entire page.

Looking at the bottom of the page, we can see that our simple page took 7.88 seconds to fully load. For such a simple page, this is fairly awful. Let's see what we can do to improve it.

Combining and Minifying JavaScript and CSS Files

When a page is loaded, the majority of time is typically spent waiting for content to download from the server. If you hover over a cell in the Waterfall column on the DevTools' Network tab, you can see a pop-up that displays the various components that make up a resource's load time. Figure 10-4 shows the total time to load our main HTML page.

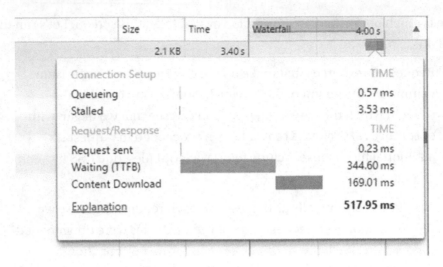

Figure 10-4. *Hover over a cell in the Waterfall column to view the breakout of how long a resource took to download*

Let's revisit what happens when a page is parsed. Each external JavaScript and CSS file must be fully downloaded before the page can be rendered. You might think that because external files can be downloaded in parallel, having multiple JavaScript and CSS files isn't such a big deal. However, browsers limit the number of concurrent connections to a single domain. Chrome's limitation is six concurrent connections. Therefore, if your site includes a dozen JavaScript frameworks and CSS files that are all downloaded separately, the first six can be downloaded concurrently, and the remaining six will be queued and await an available connection.

The answer is to combine JavaScript files into a single JavaScript file. Likewise, CSS files need to be combined as well. In ASP.NET MVC, we can make use of ScriptBundles and StyleBundles to do so. After combining files, the browser will only need to make one request to retrieve all JavaScript for your site.

Creating Bundles

Let's combine the JavaScript files and CSS files in the Turtles app into their respective bundles.

1. In the Turtles.Web project, expand the App_Start folder. You should see a file called BundleConfig.cs, which contains a class called BundleConfig. The BundleConfig class contains a single static method called RegisterBundles, which takes a

BundleCollection as an argument. There's nothing magic about this class's name, location in the project, or method name; these are all just conventions. You could even incorporate all bundle creation directly into your Application_Start method if you chose to do so.

2. Inside the BundleConfig class's RegisterBundles method, delete the existing code. Replace the method with the contents of Listing 10-4.

Listing 10-4. The RegisterBundles Method That Creates our ScriptBundle and StyleBundle

```
public static void RegisterBundles(BundleCollection bundles)
{
        bundles.Add(new ScriptBundle("~/scripts/js").Include(
           "~/Scripts/jquery-{version}.js",
            "~/Scripts/modernizr-*",
           "~/Scripts/bootstrap.js",
           "~/Scripts/respond.js"));

   bundles.Add(new StyleBundle("~/Content/css").Include(
      "~/Content/bootstrap.css",
      "~/Content/site.css"));
}
```

3. Next, open the project's Global.asax.cs file. We'll need to make sure that the method includes the line "BundleConfig. RegisterBundles(BundleTable.Bundles);" (see Listing 10-5). The BundleTable class holds the default BundleCollection, which stores all defined ScriptBundles and StyleBundles.

Listing 10-5. The Application_Start() Method in the Global.asax.cs File Must Contain the BundleConfig.RegisterBundles(BundleTable.Bundles) Method Call

```
protected void Application_Start()
    {
        AreaRegistration.RegisterAllAreas();
        FilterConfig.RegisterGlobalFilters(GlobalFilters.Filters);
        RouteConfig.RegisterRoutes(RouteTable.Routes);
        BundleConfig.RegisterBundles(BundleTable.Bundles);
}
```

4. To finish things up, we need to link to our newly created JavaScript and CSS bundles. Open the _Layout.cshtml file located in the \Views\Shared folder. Remove all <script> and CSS <link> tags linking to individual JavaScript and CSS files. Add "@Scripts. Render("~/Scripts/js");" immediately before the closing </body> tag. Add "@Styles.Render("~/Content/css")" as the last line before the closing </head> tag.

5. Redeploy the application to Azure. When we load the Turtles web application's main page and look at the Network tab in Chrome DevTools, we'll see that we're no longer downloading separate JavaScript or CSS files. Instead, we're downloading a combined JavaScript file called js, and a combined CSS file called css (see Figure 10-5).

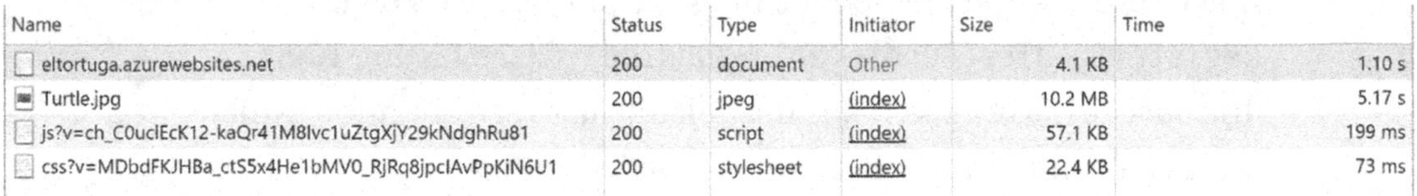

Name	Status	Type	Initiator	Size	Time
eltortuga.azurewebsites.net	200	document	Other	4.1 KB	1.10 s
Turtle.jpg	200	jpeg	(index)	10.2 MB	5.17 s
js?v=ch_C0uclEcK12-kaQr41M8lvc1uZtgXjY29kNdghRu81	200	script	(index)	57.1 KB	199 ms
css?v=MDbdFKJHBa_ctS5x4He1bMV0_RjRq8jpclAvPpKiN6U1	200	stylesheet	(index)	22.4 KB	73 ms

4 requests | 10.3 MB transferred | Finish: 6.29 s | DOMContentLoaded: 1.43 s | Load: 6.32 s

Figure 10-5. *All JS and CSS files have been bundled*

By combining JS and CSS files into bundles, we've cut our total downloads for this page from seven to four, and dropped our page load time from 7.88 seconds to 6.32 seconds. Not too shabby for a few minutes of work!

Minification

Minification is the removal of extraneous whitespace and the renaming of JavaScript variables to shrink the size of a CSS or JavaScript file. By decreasing the size of files, we can decrease each file's download time and ultimately our page load time. With bundling, you get minification for free as long as you are building with the release configuration.

To see for yourself, navigate to the bundled JS file. You'll see that whitespace has been removed and variables have been renamed. The JS bundle weighs in at just 57.1 KB.

As you might imagine, debugging minified JavaScript files is virtually impossible. If you build and run using the debug configuration, CSS and JS files are not combined or minified, making debugging possible.

GZip Compression

File transfer time is a component of page load time. We can decrease file transfer time by compressing files that our server sends back to browsers, and browsers can decompress the received files before processing them.

Fortunately, the use of GZip (which stands for GNU Zip, an open source compression algorithm) has been standard in browsers for years. Azure enables GZip compression for Web Apps by default, so there's nothing more for you to do. I mention GZip compression only to make you aware that it is an optimization that is already occurring.

You can verify that GZip compression is used by examining the response header of a file downloaded from an Azure Web App. When GZip compression is in use, you'll see a response header of `Content-Encoding: gzip`.

Using Async/Await

Using asynchronous programming in your web applications will not decrease response time, but it will allow your application to scale under load. Asynchronous calls are typically used for long-running requests to external services. When you use the await keyword, you're instructing the .NET Runtime that the current thread can be returned to the thread pool while waiting on the asynchronous operation to complete. In the meantime, the thread can do other useful work. When the operation completes, a new thread will be assigned from the thread pool to continue execution.

What happens if you do not use asynchronous programming for asynchronous long-running operations? Failure to use await will result in the current thread blocking and waiting on the operation to complete. In the event of heavy traffic, this can quickly lead to a bad situation. When all worker threads are busy, new HTTP requests are queued and wait for available threads. If requests build in the HTTP request queue faster than they are serviced, the queue length increases and leads to longer response times. Eventually, requests will time out and will receive an HTTP 503 Service Unavailable response.

Here's a real-life illustration that we're all familiar with that I'll shamelessly reuse. Imagine going to the paint counter at the local hardware store to buy a couple of gallons of paint for your living room. When you arrive, you see that a long line has already formed. Curious as to what's causing the holdup, you peer around the corner to the front of the line. The clerk, Mr. Blocking Thread, takes a single customer's order, meanders over to the paint mixer, starts it, and stares at the mixer for the entire five-minute mixing process. When the paint mixer finishes, he returns to the customer to finish the transaction. Because there are already 20 people in line ahead of you, you leave in frustration.

The next day you return to the hardware store's paint counter with a good book to read to pass the time. To your surprise, Mr. Blocking Thread has been fired and replaced with Mr. Asynchronous. Mr. Asynchronous takes an order, starts the paint mixer, and immediately returns to help the next customer. When a customer's paint has finished mixing, he retrieves it and completes the transaction.

A full discussion on asynchronous programming is beyond the scope of this book, but there are many excellent articles available online that lay out the details.

Using HTTP Cache

Many sites use the same static content on each page. Examples include logos, site-wide JavaScript, and style sheets. Because these assets do not change, it makes no sense to repeatedly download them for each page request. Instead, you can specify that browsers should cache static assets for a given period of time and serve all subsequent requests from the cache.

Setting cache control is done by setting the Cache-Control and Expires response headers. You can accomplish this by adding the code shown in Listing 10-5 to the web. config file.

Listing 10-5. Web.config Code That Sets the Cache-Control Response Header to public and the Expires Header to Tue, 19 Jan 2038 03:14:07 GMT

```
<system.webServer>
    <staticContent>
        <clientCache cacheControlMode="UseExpires"
            cacheControlCustom="public" httpExpires="Tue, 19 Jan 2038 03:14:07 GMT" />
    </staticContent>
</system.webServer>
```

Setting cacheControlMode to UseExpires allows us to ask browsers to cache static assets until a date that is far in the future. Setting cacheControlCustom to public also allows web proxies to cache static content.

If we republish the Turtles web application to Azure, reload the site, and examine the results in Chrome DevTools' Network tab, we see that for the Turtle.jpg image, the Cache-Control response header has been set to public, and the Expires has been set to Tue, 19 Jan 2038 03:14:07 GMT (Figure 10-6). This is just as expected. If we look at our JavaScript or CSS bundle, we'll see that the Expires response header has been set exactly one year in the future. This is a "feature" of using bundles, and there is currently no way to change the Expires response header.

▼ **Response Headers**   view source
    Accept-Ranges: bytes
    Cache-Control: public
    Content-Length: 10715940
    Content-Type: image/jpeg
    Date: Thu, 30 Mar 2017 19:25:23 GMT
    ETag: "89cb3ef0d7a7d21:0"
    Expires: Tue, 19 Jan 2038 03:14:07 GMT
    Last-Modified: Tue, 28 Mar 2017 15:28:23 GMT
    Server: Microsoft-IIS/8.0
    X-Powered-By: ASP.NET

Figure 10-6. *The response headers for* `Turtle.jpg` *after enabling HTTP client caching*

Just to prove that subsequent requests will be served from disk, please `clear` the Disable Cache check box on the Chrome DevTools Network tab, then reload the Turtles web app main page. You'll see the value (from disk cache) or (from memory cache) in the Size column of the Network tab for our bundles and `Turtle.jpg` image. Notice that the total load time for the page has dropped from 2.13 seconds to 368 `milliseconds`.

Using Appropriately Sized and Optimized Images

You might've noticed that our `Turtle.jpg` file is a 10.1 MB behemoth of an image. It's 4,000 pixels wide at a 400 dpi resolution. Because I was a lazy developer, I included the image in the project without bothering to see what could be done to optimize it.

Right off the bat, there are a few things that we can do to decrease the image's file size. At the largest screen size, Bootstrap limits the Turtle image to 1,020 pixels wide. In addition, most images on the Web are set at a 72 dpi resolution. Let's fire up your favorite photo editor and resize this image to a width of 1,020 pixels while preserving the aspect ratio. We'll also drop the dpi from 400 to 72. I'll skip detailed instructions for doing so because they will depend on the photo editor you choose. If you're working at a large company that has an art department, make them do it for you.

Resizing the image dropped the file size from 10.1 MB to 139 KB. This will definitely decrease our page load time, but we can do better still.

Several companies have created tools to shrink the size of images without a noticeable loss of quality that's detectable by the human eye. My personal favorite is a company called JpegMini (`http://www.jpegmini.com`). They are kind enough to allow you to minify test images through their web site, and their desktop tool is a paltry $29 at the time of this writing. Depending on the image, I've seen size savings from 0% to 80%.

In summary:

- Don't use an image that is larger than what you will display at maximum resolution. This wastes bandwidth and increases page load time.

- Set images to 72 dpi unless you have a compelling reason for a higher resolution.

- Consider an image optimization tool such as JpegMini to further reduce file size.

Using External CSS and JavaScript Files

When defining CSS and JavaScript, you have two options: You can store script and styles directly within a page, or you can move them into external `.css` and `.js` files. You should elect to store JavaScript and CSS in external files. The reason is that external files can be cached by the browser, meaning that you do not have to incur the penalty to transfer those bytes with each request. If you put CSS and script into a dynamic page, you'll incur the cost in time to transmit those bytes every time the page is requested.

Notice that in our `_layout.cshtml` markup, we have inline styles defined within the `<head>` tag. Remove these styles and place them at the bottom of the `Site.css` file. These styles will now be moved into our CSS bundle that is cached in the browser.

Moving External JavaScript Files to the Bottom of the Page

Earlier in the chapter, we learned that external JavaScript files are parser blocking resources, and CSS is a render blocking resource. Whereas a page will not start rendering until all CSS has been downloaded and parsed, the page will render even if not all

JavaScript has been downloaded and executed. We can exploit this fact by moving our external JavaScript files to the bottom of our page and placing them just above the closing body tag.

Using Async for Certain External JavaScript Files

We've already touched briefly on what happens when a page is requested. All JavaScript and CSS files must be downloaded and parsed before a page can be completely rendered. There's an exception to this rule, though. Marking an external `<script>` tag with the async attribute instructs the browser to continue processing the page, and to parse and run the script when it becomes available. Essentially, the async attribute designates an external JavaScript file as nonblocking for the page loading process. Here's an example of using the async attribute:

```
<script src="/scripts/soMuchScript.js" async></script>
```

So when should you use the async attribute? If you have script that doesn't interact with the DOM, you should use the async attribute. This typically applies to third-party vendor scripts such as user tracking pixels or analytics packages.

If you mark an external JavaScript file that interacts with the DOM with async, you're going to have a bad time. In this scenario, it's possible that the async script fill finish downloading and will be executed before the DOM has been fully constructed. If your script attempts to reference a DOM element that hasn't yet been created, JavaScript errors will occur. And you will likely hear about it in your Monday morning staff meeting. Don't be that guy.

Using a Content Distribution Network

A content distribution network (CDN) is a global network of servers that cache content from your web application. Typically, cached content is static such as CSS, JavaScript, or image assets. CDN servers are usually located on Internet backbones and therefore have high bandwidth. When a user requests content that is cached by a CDN, that request is fulfilled from the server within the CDN that is closest to the user making the request.

Using a CDN has several benefits for scalability and performance.

- Because requests for content are served by the CDN server closest to the requestor, network latency is reduced. For example, if a user in Tokyo requests content from your web application that is hosted in the Azure East US region it is much faster if static content is delivered from a Tokyo-based CDN server than making a trip that is literally halfway around the globe. Reduced network latency leads to increased performance.

- Each request that is served from a CDN server is one less request that your servers have to handle. This allows your servers to spend more time doing important things like updating your data store and generating dynamic responses. Fewer requests for static content allow your servers to do more before having to scale up or out.

How Azure CDN Works

Let's make this a little more concrete by walking through how a request is served from a CDN. We'll use our Turtles web application for this high-level illustration. I'm going to gloss over the details of how to set up a CDN, which is covered in the next section. For now, assume that our Turtles app is hosted at `https://eltortuga.azurewebsites.net`, and our CDN can be reached at `https://eltortuga.azureedge.net`.

When setting up our web application and CDN, we have to decide which content will be cached and served from Azure's CDN servers. For our Turtles app, we'll use the CDN to serve our CSS and JavaScript bundles along with our images.

Previously, our main `Turtle.jpg` image was linked in our `index.cshtml` file as `"<img src='/content/images/turtle.jpg'>"`. Because we want to serve this file from our CDN, we're going to change this link to our `index.cshtml` file to `"<img src='https://eltortuga.azureedge.net/content/images/turtle.jpg'>"`.

When a browser makes a request to download `https://eltortuga.azureedge.net/content/images/turtle.jpg`, the Azure CDN will check its cache. If it doesn't find the file, it will make a request to the origin. You guessed it: The origin is our Web App located at `https://eltortuga.azurewebsites.net`. It will fetch the asset, cache it, then serve it back to the browser.

The next time the `Turtle.jpg` image is requested, the CDN has the image in the cache and will return it to the caller. Our Web App never even sees the second through Nth request for `Turtle.jpg`; these requests are handled by the CDN.

Creating a CDN for the Turtles Web Application

To make this concept much more concrete, let's add a CDN for our Turtles web application.

Our first step is to provision a CDN within the Azure Portal. The steps to do so are as follows:

1. Create the CDN service. Click the plus sign to provision a new service. The CDN service is located under the Web + Mobile menu option (Figure 10-7).

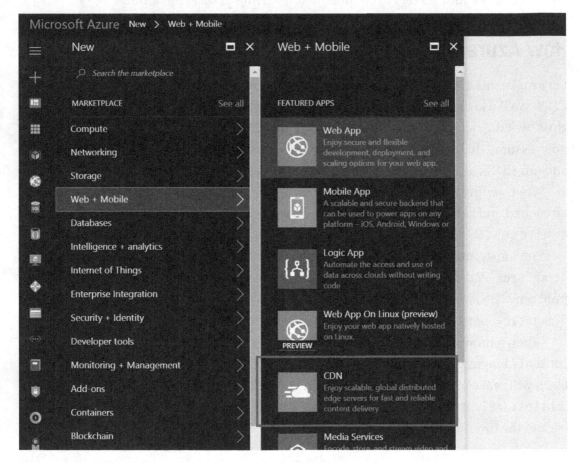

Figure 10-7. *Select the CDN service*

We then need to fill out our CDN profile (Figure 10-8).

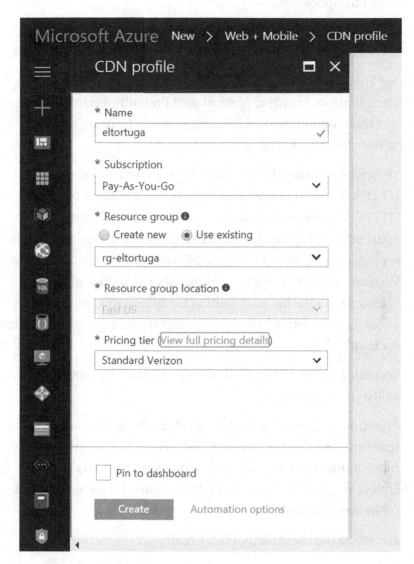

Figure 10-8. *The CDN profile*

Enter values for the following fields:

- *Name*: This is the name of your CDN resource. Name it something meaningful, and perhaps even endearing.

- *Subscription*: This is the subscription that will be billed for your CDN usage charges.

- *Resource Group*: I placed the CDN in the same resource group as my Turtles web application.

- *Resource Group Location*: You cannot actually choose a resource group location. It is set by the resource group that you choose.

- *Pricing Tier*: There are three separate pricing tiers that you can use: Standard Verizon, Standard Akamai, and Premium Verizon. All three of these options will cache static content. Here are the main differences between the options.

  - *Standard Akamai*: This tier does not support custom domain HTTPS. It does, however, allow you to serve content over HTTPS. The endpoint URL will be `https://<cdn name>.azureedge.net`. Also, the Standard Akamai tier is ready to begin serving content within a minute of being provisioned. Standard Verizon can take up to 90 minutes. For this demo, we're using Standard Akamai because waiting for 90 minutes just sounds awful. In the words of a famous American, "Ain't nobody got time for that!"

  - *Standard Verizon*: This tier does offer custom domain HTTPS as well as asset preloading.

  - *Premium Verizon*: This tier has handy features such as reporting, real-time stats, real-time alerts, URL redirects and rewrites, and token authentication. This is also the most expensive option. Unless you need these features, I'd recommend using one of the other standard tiers.

  After filling out these fields, click Create.

2. Define a CDN endpoint. An endpoint is a cache for content that is pulled from a particular origin. An origin can be a Web App, Azure Storage, a cloud service, or a completely custom source. To define an endpoint, navigate to the Overview blade for the CDN profile, then click + Endpoint to define a new endpoint (Figure 10-9).

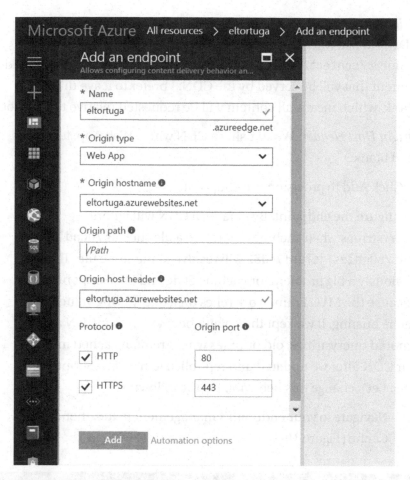

Figure 10-9. *The CDN endpoint fields*

The fields are described here.

- *Name*: This is the name for your endpoint.

- *Origin Type*: An Azure CDN isn't just limited to caching assets from Web Apps. It can also cache assets from Azure Storage, Cloud Storage, or custom sources. The origin type that you choose will determine the options in the Origin Hostname field. Select Web App for the origin type.

- *Origin Hostname*: The options for this field are based on what's been selected in the Origin Type field. If you selected Web App for the Origin Type, all Web Apps that are provisioned in this subscription will appear in this drop-down list. Select your Turtles Web App.

- *Origin Path*: You can specify a path within your Web App that the CDN will use when requesting content. For example, you could define a `/content/cdn` directory in your Web App and use it to hold content that will be served by the CDN. I prefer to leave this field blank, which means all content will be requested relative to the root.

- *Origin Host Header*: When using a CDN with a Web App, leave this field blank.

     Click Add to provision the endpoint.

3. Configure the endpoint. By default, a CDN will ignore querystrings when caching. Therefore a file such as `/bundles/js` and `/bundles/js?aef7cd82` will resolve to the same file. This is obviously a big problem for caching Style and JavaScript bundles because the MVC Framework relies on a querystring value for cache busting. If we kept the default behavior in our CDN and ignored querystrings, old bundles would remain cached in our CDN after we updated and republished new JavaScript or CSS. Let's change this behavior. Do the following:

   a. Navigate to your endpoint's management blade, then select Cache (Figure 10-10).

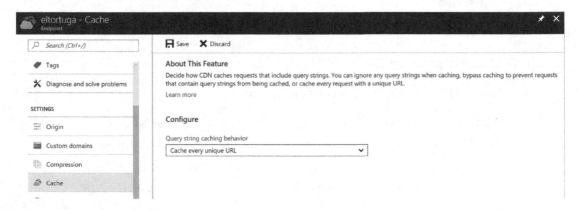

Figure 10-10. *The CDN Cache configuration blade*

   b. Change the Query String Caching Behavior value in the drop-down list to Cache Every Unique URL, then click Save.

4.   Test. Let's make sure that our CDN is working as expected. If you chose the Standard Akamai tier, your CDN should be ready to service requests within 60 seconds. If you chose the Standard Verizon tier, your endpoint won't be ready for another 90 minutes. I recommend either reprovisioning with Standard Akamai or taking a break and having a few cups of coffee.

To test, fire up your favorite browser and navigate to our static image. Because the `Turtle.jpg` image is located within our Web App at `/content/images/turtle.jpg`, you can append that path to your CDN's hostname, and you should see the `Turtle.jpg` image in all its glory. Because I named my endpoint eltortuga, my Azure CDN endpoint can be addressed at `https://eltortuga.azureedge.net`. The full URL to request the cached `Turtles.jpg` image is therefore `https://eltortuga.azureedge.net/content/images/turtle.jpg`.

Integrating a CDN with an ASP.NET MVC App

We now have our CDN set up, an endpoint defined, and have proven that we can serve content from the CDN. The last step is to integrate our CDN with the Turtles web application.

Integrating Bundles

We'll start with serving our CSS and JavaScript bundles from the CDN. There's a bit of complexity in doing so.

First, we'll revisit our `BundleConfig.cs` file. First, we have to set the `BundleCollection`'s `UseCdn` property to true. In our application, this is simply:

```
bundles.UseCdn = true;
```

The `ScriptBundle` and `StyleBundle` classes have overloaded constructors that will take a `cdnPath` argument, which is the path to the bundle when using the CDN. For example, if our CDN was at `https://fastcdn.azureedge.net`, our overloaded constructor for a new `ScriptBundle` would be:

```
bundles.Add(new ScriptBundle("~/scripts/js", "https://fastcdn.azureedge.
net/scripts/js")   .Include("~/scripts/bootstrap.js"));
```

Unfortunately, this isn't going to work very well for us. When the MVC Framework renders this to our HTML output when a page is requested, it will render:

```
<script src="//eltortuga.azureedge.net/scripts/js"></script>
```

You have probably already spotted the problem: Our hash that is appended to the end of the bundle for cache-busting has been omitted. This is, in my opinion, a glaring oversight by Microsoft. Because by default `StyleBundles` and `ScriptBundles` have their cache expiration date set a year in the future, the CDN will continue to cache your old bundles for an entire year. It'll lead to loads of support problems when you introduce breaking changes in future updates and your users are still using old styles and scripts that are cached in the CDN.

You'll find several articles online (even one from Microsoft) that recommend appending a version number to your script and style bundles. Although this will solve your CDN caching problem when new updates are released, it will cause much more mayhem with the bundles' `cache-control` and `expires` response headers. Recall that these headers are what instructs the browser to store content in the browser's HTTP cache. Unfortunately, deep in the bowels of the `System.Web.Optimization` library, the `cache-control` and `expires` headers are not set correctly unless the bundle hash that is calculated by the MVC Framework is properly appended to each bundle's query string.

The last few paragraphs have been somewhat mind-bending. If understanding the intricacies of this issue make your head hurt, skip it and follow the steps given next to properly cache bundles in the CDN and ensure that the `cache-control` and `expires` headers are properly set.

First, we'll need to make updates to our `BundleConfig.cs` file. The complete text of the file is shown in Listing 10-6.

Listing 10-6. The BundleConfig.cs File

```
using System.Web;
using System.Web.Optimization;
using System.Configuration;

namespace Turtle.Web
{
    public class BundleConfig
    {
        public static void RegisterBundles(BundleCollection bundles)
        {
            //we have to go ahead create and add our Bundles as if there is no
            //CDN involved.
            //this is because the bundle has to already exist in the
            //BundleCollection
            //in order to get the hash that the MVC Framework will generate
            //for the
            //querystring.
            Bundle jsBundle = new ScriptBundle("~/scripts/js").Include(
                "~/Scripts/jquery-{version}.js",
                "~/Scripts/modernizr-*",
                "~/Scripts/bootstrap.js",
                "~/Scripts/respond.js");

            Bundle cssBundle = new StyleBundle("~/content/css").Include(
                "~/Content/bootstrap.css",
                "~/Content/site.css");

            bundles.Add(jsBundle);
            bundles.Add(cssBundle);

            bool useCDN = bool.Parse(ConfigurationManager.AppSettings["UseCDN"]);
            if (useCDN)
            {
                //only execute this code if we are NOT in debug configuration.
                bundles.UseCdn = true;
                //grab our base CDN hostname from web.config...
```

```
        string cdnHost = ConfigurationManager.AppSettings["CDNHostName"];

        //get the hashes that the MVC Framework will use per bundle for
        //the querystring.
        string jsHash = GetBundleHash(bundles, "~/scripts/js");
        string cssHash = GetBundleHash(bundles, "~/content/css");

        //set up our querystring per bundle for the CDN path.
        jsBundle.CdnPath = cdnHost + "/scripts/js?v=" + jsHash;
        cssBundle.CdnPath = cdnHost + "/content/css?v=" + cssHash;
    }
    else
    {
        bundles.UseCdn = false;
    }
}

/// <summary>
/// This method calculates the bundle hash. The hash is what the MVC
/// Framework
/// appends to the bundle querystring for cache busting.
/// Based on the code by Frison B Alexander as shared on
/// Stackoverflow.com.
/// (http://stackoverflow.com/questions/31540121/get-mvc-bundle-
/// querystring)
/// Licensed under the Creative Commons license.
/// </summary>
private static string GetBundleHash(BundleCollection bundles, string
bundlePath)
{
    //Need the context to generate response
    var bundleContext = new BundleContext(new
        HttpContextWrapper(HttpContext.Current), BundleTable.Bundles,
        bundlePath);

    //Bundle class has the method we need to get a BundleResponse
```

```
Bundle bundle = BundleTable.Bundles.GetBundleFor(bundlePath);
var bundleResponse = bundle.GenerateBundleResponse(bundleContext);

//BundleResponse has the method we need to call, but its marked as
//internal and therefore is not available for public consumption.
//To bypass this, reflect on it and manually invoke the method
var bundleReflection = bundleResponse.GetType();

var method = bundleReflection.GetMethod("GetContentHashCode",
    System.Reflection.BindingFlags.NonPublic |
    System.Reflection.BindingFlags.Instance);

//contentHash is what's appended to your url (url?###-###...)
var contentHash = method.Invoke(bundleResponse, null);
return contentHash.ToString();
        }
    }
}
```

There are a few things to note here:

- We start by defining our ScriptBundle and StyleBundle just as we had before. We then check a web.config property called UseCDN to see if the CDN is enabled.

- If the CDN is enabled, we'll get our CDN hostname from the web.config property called CDNHostName. We'll then call our GetBundleHash for our style and script bundles. This method will calculate the same hash that the MVC Framework appends for cache-busting when a CDN is not in use. If you look in the GetBundleHash method, you'll see that we have to use Reflection to call the BundleResponse's GetContentHashCode method, which is internal.

- Finally, we set the CdnPath for each of our bundles. This is composed of our CDN hostname, our bundle name with the hash appended as a query string value.

We now need to add the CDNHostName and UseCDN variables to our web.config file. The code to do so is shown in Listing 10-7.

Listing 10-7. Adding the Necessary Values to Our web.config File

```
<appSettings>
    [... other settings omitted...]
    <add key="UseCDN" value="true" />
    <add key="CDNHostName" value="//<your endpoint name>.azureedge.net"/>
</appSettings>
```

If you set the UseCDN property to true, deploy to Azure, and then request the main page, you'll see the following output in the Chrome DevTools Network tab for our JavaScript bundle (Figure 10-11). Note that this is for the first request. You'll see it's served from the CDN (https://eltortuga.azureedge.net) and has an expires date set exactly one year in the future.

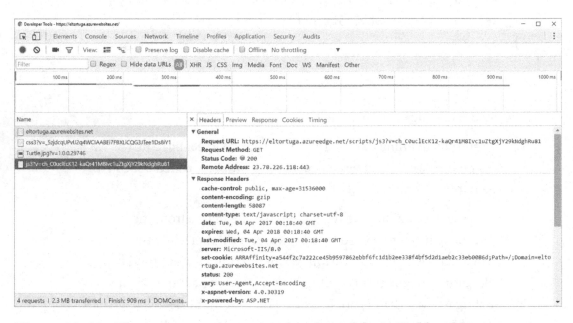

Figure 10-11. *The request and response headers of the initial load for our ScriptBundle*

On the subsequent load, you'll see that the bundle is served from the disk cache. Finally, if you modify any script or stylesheet in a bundle and redeploy, a new hash will be appended to the query string, and the new file will be cached fresh in the CDN.

Integrating Image Files

Unfortunately, there are no framework classes or helpers that will allow you to easily switch between loading an image from the origin while developing, and loading an image from a CDN for production. Fortunately, though, creating the code to do so is pretty straightforward.

We'll build our own custom `HtmlHelper` extension method to make the magic happen. First, let's add a new class to the project called `CDNHelper`. The full text of the `CDNHelper.cs` file is shown in Listing 10-8.

Listing 10-8. The Full Text of the CDNHelper.cs File

```
using System.Configuration;
using System.Web.Mvc;

namespace Turtle.Web
{
    public static class CDNHelper
    {
        public static string CDN(this HtmlHelper helper, string imageNameAndPath)
        {
            bool useCDN = bool.Parse(ConfigurationManager.AppSettings["UseCDN"]);
            useCDN = true;
            if (useCDN)
            {
                //we ARE using the CDN.
                var cdnHostName = ConfigurationManager.AppSettings["CDNHostName"];
                string cdnHostAndPath = cdnHostName + imageNameAndPath;

                //cache bustin'. To generate a unique query string, we'll append the
                //assembly version number to the image URL.
                var version = System.Reflection.Assembly.
                GetExecutingAssembly().GetName()
                    .Version.ToString();
                cdnHostAndPath += "?v=" + version;
                return cdnHostAndPath;
            }
```

413

```
        else
        {
            //Use the relative path. We're not using the CDN.
            return imageNameAndPath;
        }
    }
  }
}
```

Using this class is very simple. Jump to the project's Views\Home\Index.cshtml file and replace the previous <img> tag that linked to the Turtle.jpg image with the following line:

```
<img src="@Html.CDN("/Content/Images/Turtle.jpg")" class="main-image"/>
```

If we've enabled the CDN in our web.config, our CDNHelper class will emit a fully qualified file name for the image that's served from our CDN. If not, it will emit the relative path, which will be served from the origin.

Summary

In this chapter, we've discussed various techniques to decrease page load time and scale your web applications. Most of these techniques are simple to implement. In certain circumstances, the effects on performance can be dramatic.

In the next chapter, we'll look at various tools and techniques for troubleshooting Web Applications.

CHAPTER 11

Troubleshooting Web Applications

Try as we might, it's impossible to always catch every potential problem during testing. Sooner or later, you'll receive The Call. The Call can come at any time, but often it happens when you're doing something fun away from the office. It's usually along the lines of this: "Something is broken in production and users are being affected. Help!"

The bad news is that you can't simply attach a debugger to a release build in a production environment and step through the code until you find the problem. The good news is that Microsoft has provided several extremely useful tools that can help you figure out why things have gone sideways. Some of these tools are proactive and will alert you to problems and attempt to diagnose the issues. Others help you analyze what went wrong after the fact.

This chapter introduces you to the troubleshooting tools available and offers guidance on how they can be used to discover what's going wrong in your web applications. Let's dive in.

An Overview of Available Tools

Most of the troubleshooting tools we discuss are made available by Kudu or Application Insights.

Kudu

Kudu is an application that runs as a separate process within an App Service. Kudu is responsible for managing Git deployments, managing WebJobs, and providing instrumentation that you can use for debugging and optimizing your Web Apps and

© Rob Reagan 2018
R. Reagan, *Web Applications on Azure*, https://doi.org/10.1007/978-1-4842-2976-7_11

WebJobs. Kudu is included in the cost of your App Service Plan, so there's nothing that you must install to make use of its functionality.

Note   Kudu is open source. In fact, the Microsoft team responsible for building and maintaning Kudu commits their code directly to their public GitHub repo. If you're ever curious about the finer details of how Kudu works, you can clone or browse the latest code at `https://github.com/projectkudu/kudu`

Kudu provides several services that we're particularly interested in, including these.

- *A process explorer*: You can quickly tell which processes are consuming memory and CPU time.

- *Diagnostics-as-a-Service (DaaS)*: This little gem of a tool will collect a memory dump and review web server and application logs. It will then apply rules and generate a report informing you of any issues that it sees.

- *Log stream*: You can see logs echoed to the screen in near real time.

- *Debug console*: This is an online Explorer window that lets you browse your Web App's file system. This is useful for verifying that what you think is currently deployed is actually deployed, and for checking to make sure that you did actually deploy the correct values in your `web.config` file.

- *Auto-heal*: Auto-heal allows you to create triggers such as max requests within a given interval, memory utilization, or HTTP response codes within a certain interval. When a trigger fires, you can elect to recycle the process, create a log message, or take a custom action.

We discuss each of these features in further detail in upcoming sections.

There are a couple of ways to access Kudu functionality. Each App Service has a companion Kudu site that can be reached via the URL `https://[yoursitename].scm.azurewebsites.net`. Authentication for each Kudu site is single sign-on, so you can use the same credentials that you use to log into the Azure Portal.

You'll notice that the Kudu console is a bit unrefined (Figure 11-1). Over time, Microsoft has been exposing various Kudu features within the Azure Portal as menu options on the Web App management blade.

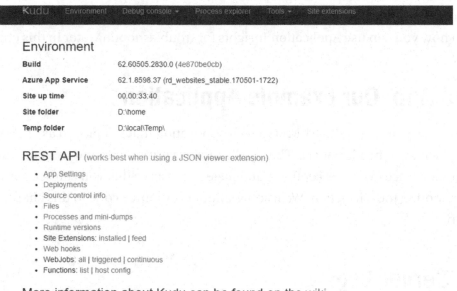

Figure 11-1. *The Kudu site landing page*

Application Insights

Application Insights is a tool that ingests performance data, custom traces, and exceptions. This information is collected from browsers, your application code, and the underlying Azure hosting platform. Application Insights processes the collected telemetry and presents it to you in an easy-to-use format within the Azure Portal. You can then use Application Insights to find out how users are using your application, troubleshoot performance problems, and track down the root cause of exceptions.

Application Insights was designed to be simple to integrate with your application. Because data is batched and sent to the server on a separate thread, you won't see much of a performance impact on your application.

Like most Azure services, Application Insights has a Basic tier that is free to use. The Basic tier includes 1 GB of free data per month. Additional data is available in the Basic tier and is priced per GB. The Enterprise tier includes 200 MB of data per application node per day, and as of this writing is priced at $15 per node per month.

I highly recommend making use of Application Insights in your Web Apps. We'll walk through how you can use Application Insights for troubleshooting later in this chapter.

Awful App: Our Example Application

We'll use a very simple ASP.NET MVC 5 web application that's deployed as an Azure Web App scaled to two instances. This application is very simple, and its main purpose it to generate trace events, exceptions, and page requests so that you can see various troubleshooting tools in action. We'll show snippets of source code in this chapter when appropriate.

Web Server Logs

Web Server Logs show each HTTP request to your Web App. Logged information includes the request timestamp, URL, requester's IP address, browser, resulting HTTP status code, ARR Affinity token (if ARRA is enabled), and the time taken to service the request. All Web Server Logs are in W3C Logging format.

If you have scaled out to more than one Web App instance, all logs for all instances are combined.

Web Server Logs are not enabled by default. To enable Web Server Logs, navigate to your Web App's management blade. Select Diagnostics Logs under the Monitoring heading. Toggle the setting for Web server logging from Off to either Storage or File System. Selecting File System will write your logs to your Web App's file system. If you select Storage, you'll be prompted to select an Azure Storage account and Blob container where your logs will be written.

To access Web Server Logs, you have several options. If you elected to write logs to Azure Storage, you'll need to use a tool such as Azure Storage Explorer to view logs. If you chose to write logs to the file system, you can browse logs within Visual Studio, browse them within the Kudu site, or download log files via FTP.

Browsing Web Server Logs Written to the File System
Using Visual Studio

The easiest way to view Web Server Logs written to the file system is to use Visual Studio. To browse logs using Visual Studio, do the following:

1. In Visual Studio, select View ➤ Server Explorer.

2. In Server Explorer, right-click within the pane and select Connect to Microsoft Azure Subscription. You'll be prompted for your Azure credentials.

3. After logging in, expand App Service ➤ [Resource Group] ➤ [Web App Name] ➤ Log Files ➤ http ➤ RawLogs (Figure 11-2). Click any log file to download and view it in Visual Studio.

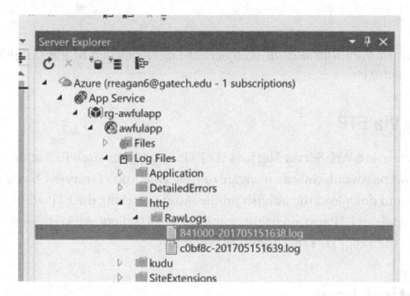

Figure 11-2. *Viewing Web Server Logs through Visual Studio's Server Explorer*

Using the Kudu Debug Console

We've mentioned that every Web App has a companion Kudu site located at `https://[yoursitename].scm.azurewebsites.net`. For example, if your Web App name was awfulApp, the Kudu site would be located at `https://awfulapp.scm.azurewebsites.net`.

If you visit your Kudu site and sign in with the same credentials that you use to access the Azure Portal, you can view logs by doing the following:

1. On the menu bar, select Debug Console. In the drop-down menu, select CMD. This will open a File Explorer along with what looks like a command prompt.

2. You can then navigate to the LogFiles ➤ http ➤ RawLogs directory. All of your Web Server Logs will be listed (Figure 11-3). Click the Edit icon next to the log you'd like to see to view it in the browser.

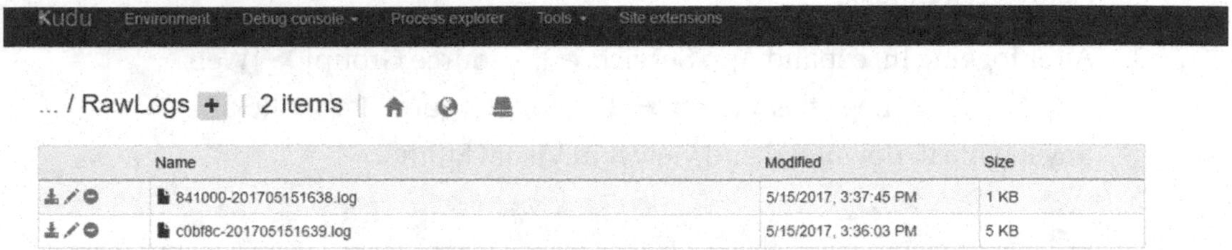

Figure 11-3. *In the Kudu site, all Web Server Logs are listed in the \LogFiles\http\ RawLogs directory*

Browsing Via FTP

You can also retrieve Web Server Log files via FTP. To get your site's FTP address, username, and password, you can navigate to your Web App's Overview blade in the Azure Portal and download the publish profile. After retrieving the FTP address and credentials, open an FTP session using your favorite FTP client. All Web Server Log files are located in the /LogFiles/http/RawLogs directory.

Application Logs

Application logs capture trace and exception information.

Using the System.Diagnostics.Trace class, you can emit messages to any registered trace listeners. The Trace class allows you to choose the log level: Verbose, Information, Warning, or Error.

If you've used tracing before, you know that normally you have to register one or more trace listeners to capture emitted tracing information. By default, Azure Web Apps already have a Trace Listener defined that will write output to the Application logs.

Setting Up Tracing

To make use of tracing in your web application, do the following:

1. First, you must enable tracing. Navigate to your Web App's management blade, then click Diagnostics Logs under the Monitoring heading.

2. Set Application Logging to On. You'll also need to specify the logging level using the drop-down list. Your choices are Verbose, Information, Warning, and Error. Note that Application Logging will disable itself 12 hours after it is initially set.

3. Finally, we need to emit tracing information in our code. In the AwfulApp's `HomeController`, I've added a WebAPI method called `TraceLogInfo` (Listing 11-1). When called, this method emits a trace using the Information logging level. The TraceLogInfo Was Called message will then appear in the Application log (Figure 11-4).

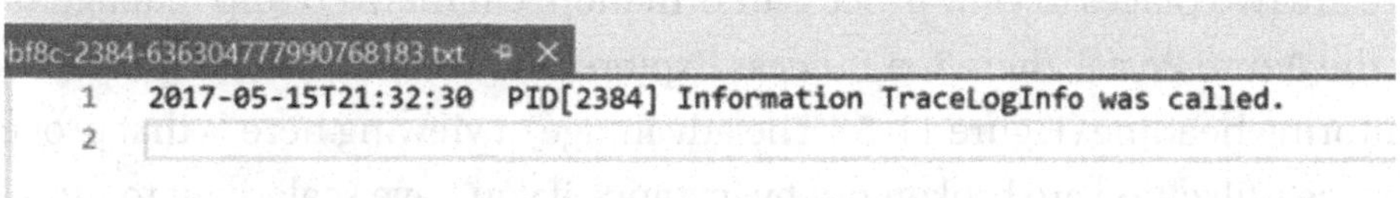

```
bf8c-2384-636304777990768183.txt    ⊕ ✕
  1    2017-05-15T21:32:30  PID[2384] Information TraceLogInfo was called.
  2
```

Figure 11-4. *The Application log will include a timestamp, process ID (PID), logging level, and message for each trace*

Listing 11-1. The TraceLogInfo Method, Which Will Emit a Trace of TraceLogInfo Was Called at the Information Level

```
public void TraceLogInfo()
{
    System.Diagnostics.Trace.TraceInformation("TraceLogInfo was called.");
}
```

Viewing Application Logs

Just like Web Server Logs, Application logs are stored on either your Web App's file system or in an Azure Storage Blob container. They can be accessed via Visual Studio, the Kudu console, or FTP.

When viewing Application logs using Visual Studio, expand App Service ➤ [Resource Group] ➤ [Web App Name] ➤ Log Files ➤ Application. All Application log files will be listed in the Application folder. Similarly, when viewing files via FTP or the Kudu console, Application log files will be located in the /LogFiles/Application directory.

Kudu Process Explorer

The Process Explorer shows all processes running in a Web App. For each process, you can see the process ID (PID), process name, thread count, memory utilization, and total CPU time. This is useful as a quick gauge to see if memory, threads, or CPU utilization are running amok. Note that the displayed metrics are a snapshot in time and do not offer a historical graph.

There are two places to view process information. On the Web App management blade in the Azure Portal, there is a Process Explorer menu option that's located under the Monitoring heading (Figure 11-5). The advantage of viewing here is that processes and resource utilization are broken out by instance if you have scaled out to more than one instance.

	PID	PROCESS	THREAD COUNT	WORKING SET	PRIVATE MEMORY	TOTAL CPU TIME
INSTANCE ID : 841000						
⊞	7060	w3wp	18	2.09 MB	6.92 MB	
K	6252	w3wp	30	27.74 MB	60.43 MB	2s
INSTANCE ID : C0BF8C						
⊞	2384	w3wp	30	5.50 MB	60.62 MB	4s
K	11876	w3wp	29	59.46 MB	53.99 MB	2s

Figure 11-5. The Azure Portal's Process Explorer for a two-instance Web App

The second place to view process information is in the Kudu companion site. Unlike the Azure Portal's Process Explorer blade, the Kudu site shows combined metrics across all instances of your Web App (Figure 11-6). However, within Kudu you can click a process's Properties button to view extended details such as what modules are loaded, individual thread states, and environment variables. To view the Process Explorer within Kudu, navigate to your Web App's Kudu companion site located at https://[yourSiteName].scm.azurewebsites.net. After authenticating with the same credentials you use to log into the Azure Portal, click Process Explorer in the top navigation bar.

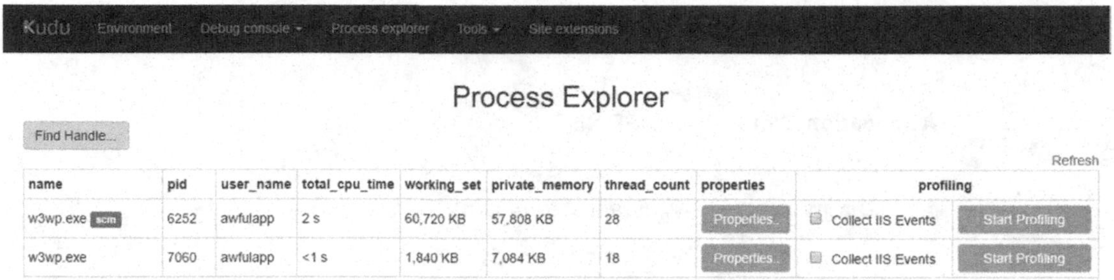

Figure 11-6. *The Process Explorer within the Kudu companion site*

Diagnostics-as-a-Service

When your web application is experiencing poor performance or availability issues, DaaS is an excellent tool to help identify the problem.

DaaS is a WebJob that will execute as a separate process within your Web App. When launching DaaS, you can choose if you'd like it to take and analyze a memory dump, your event logs, your HTTP logs, or some combination of these. Based on the input given, DaaS will then apply a set of rules to attempt to determine exactly what's wrong with your Web App.

Because DaaS examines the current state of your Web App, it should only be run when you are experiencing problems. Note that because DaaS consumes computing resources, it can have performance implications when run. Also, in extremely dire circumstances where your Web App's memory or CPU utilization is maxed out, DaaS might fail to run due to resource starvation.

Running DaaS

To launch DaaS, do the following:

1. In the Azure Portal, navigate to your Web App's management blade.

2. In your Web App's menu, click Diagnose and Solve Problems.

3. On the Diagnose and Solve Problems blade, click the Diagnostics as a Service link in the lower right corner of the page.

4. On the Diagnostics as a Service page (Figure 11-7), you'll need to provide some parameters before launching.

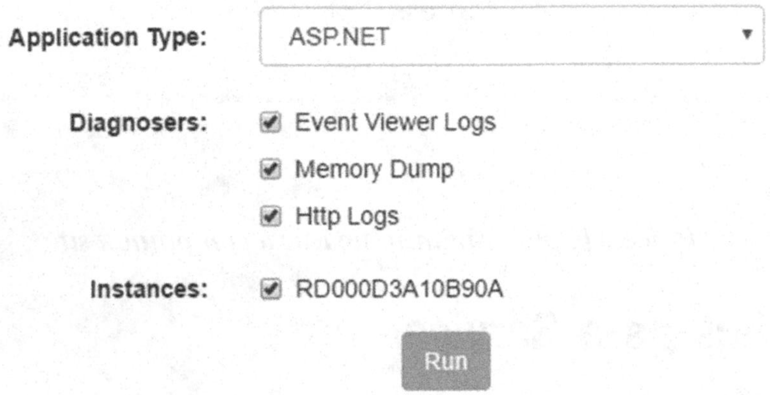

Figure 11-7. *Starting the DaaS*

a. From the drop-down list, select the application type you'd like to analyze. Your options are ASP.NET, Node.js, or PHP.

b. Choose the diagnosers you'd like to use. You can choose to analyze the Event Viewer Logs, Memory Dumps, and/or HTTP logs. I recommend running them all.

c. Finally, choose the instances you'd like to include in the analysis. Click Run.

Once launched, DaaS will run for several minutes. Once data has been collected, it will take some time to complete the analysis. When complete, you'll have the option to download and view each report.

Application Events

Application events show all traces and exceptions in a slightly more readable format than the Application logs. To access Application events, navigate to the Diagnose and Solve Problems menu item located on your Web App's management blade. Once there, click the Application Events link in the page's lower right corner. You'll then be taken to the Application Events blade (Figure 11-8).

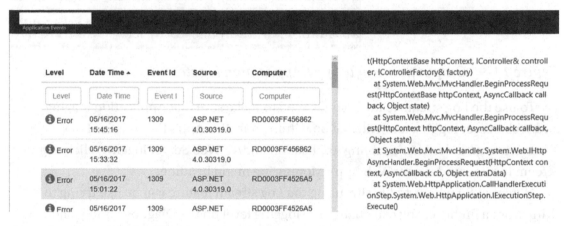

Figure 11-8. *The Application Events blade*

Note that you can filter the event log by severity level, date, event ID, source, and instance.

Clicking a row in the Application Events table will display the event details in the right pane.

Log Stream

Log stream allows you to see Application and Web Server Logs echoed to the Azure Portal Log Stream blade in near real time (Figure 11-9). This is useful if you want to see what's happening within your application at the current moment.

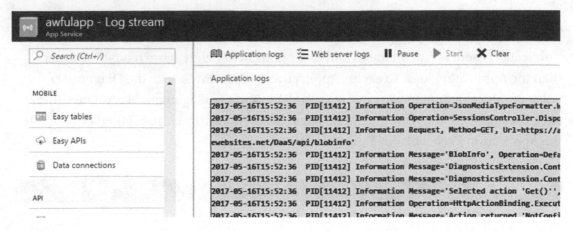

Figure 11-9. *Output from AwfulApp's Application log stream*

To use the Log stream feature, you'll need to make sure that Application logging and Web Server logging are switched on within your Web App's Diagnostics Logs management blade. After enabling Application and/or Web Server logging, click Log Stream located under your Web App's Monitoring menu heading.

Note that for a high-traffic site, using the Log stream feature can be like trying to drink from a firehose. You can change the logging level on the Diagnostics log blade to cut down on logs that are echoed. You can also use the Pause button on the Log Stream page to stop logs from being echoed, thus giving you time to examine logs in more detail.

Failed Request Tracing Logs

Failed Request Tracing logs (FREB logs) show detailed information for your application's failed requests. By default, any request that generates an HTTP response of 400 or greater will be logged.

For each failed request, Azure creates an XML file containing information such as:

- The requested URL that generated the failure.

- The App Pool.

- The Site ID.

- Whether the user was logged in or anonymous.

- The HTTP response code.

- Total time taken to process the request.

- All request headers.

- The complete response, including response headers.

This gives you an excellent toehold when trying to figure out exactly what went wrong.

Before you can access FREB logs, you first must enable the Failed request tracing setting on your Web App's Diagnostics Logs blade. After enabling Failed request tracing, you can click on your Web App's Diagnose and Solve Problems menu item. On the Diagnose and Solve Problems blade, click the Failed Request Tracing Logs link in the lower right corner of the screen. The FREB Logs screen lists all traces in tabular format (Figure 11-10). Click the .xml file to view trace details.

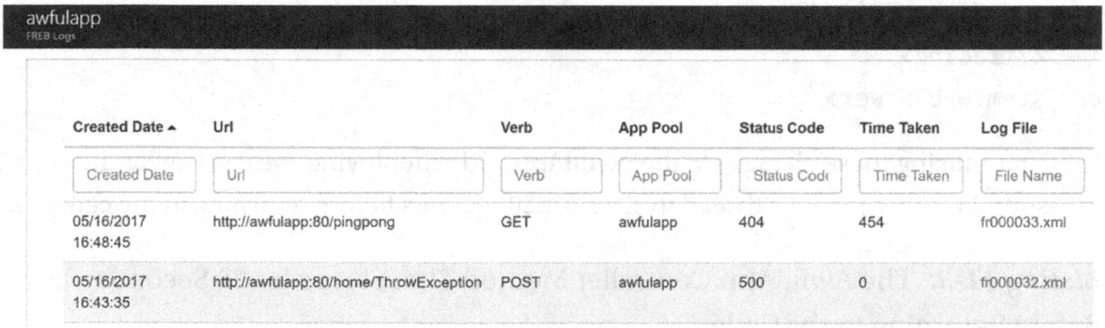

Created Date ▲	Url	Verb	App Pool	Status Code	Time Taken	Log File
Created Date	Url	Verb	App Pool	Status Cod	Time Taken	File Name
05/16/2017 16:48:45	http://awfulapp:80/pingpong	GET	awfulapp	404	454	fr000033.xml
05/16/2017 16:43:35	http://awfulapp:80/home/ThrowException	POST	awfulapp	500	0	fr000032.xml

Figure 11-10.   *The Failed Request Tracing blade*

You're not just limited to tracing calls that resulted in an HTTP 400 or greater status code. Azure also allows you to define your own criteria for what constitutes a failed request, and you can do so in your web.config file via the <tracing> section. The web.config settings shown in Listing 11-2 trace all requests that issue a 400 or greater response code, or take more than five seconds to complete.

Listing 11-2.   Defining Custom Failed Request Tracing in the web.config File

```
<system.webServer>
  <tracing>
    <traceFailedRequests>
        <remove path="*" />
        <add path="*">
          <traceAreas>
```

```
                     <add provider="ASP" verbosity="Verbose" />
                     <add provider="ASPNET"
                     areas="Infrastructure,Module,Page,AppServices"
                        verbosity="Verbose" />
                     <add provider="ISAPI Extension" verbosity="Verbose" />
                   <add provider="WWW Server" areas="Authentication,Security,Filter,
                        StaticFile,CGI,Compression,Cache,RequestNotifications,
                        Module,FastCGI"
                        verbosity="Verbose" />
                 </traceAreas>
                   <failureDefinitions timeTaken="00:00:05" statusCodes="400-599"/>"
               </add>
           </traceFailedRequests>
        </tracing>
</system.webServer>
```

After making these changes to the AwfulApp and redeploying, we can trigger the code in Listing 11-3 that puts the thread to sleep for 20 seconds before returning to the caller.

Listing 11-3. The AwfulApp Controller Method That Sleeps for 20 Seconds Before Returning to the Caller

```
[HttpGet]
public void SlowRequest()
{
    System.Threading.Thread.Sleep(20000);
}
```

After specifying that requests taking longer than five seconds should be included in our FREB logs, and invoking the SlowRequest method, we can see that the SlowRequest was traced (Figure 11-11).

Request Diagnostics for GET http://awfulapp:80/home/SlowRequest			
– Request Summary			
Url	http://awfulapp:80/home/SlowRequest	Site	1546638444
App Pool	awfulapp	Process	8592
Authentication	anonymous	Failure Reason	TIME_TAKEN
User from token	IIS APPPOOL\awfulapp	Trigger Status	0
Activity ID	{00000000-0000-0000-CA04-0080000000DD}	Final Status	200
		Time Taken	5844 msec

Figure 11-11. *A request taking more than five seconds in our FREB logs. Note that the Final Status returned is HTTP 200, and the time taken to trigger is just over five seconds*

Auto Heal

I once spent a couple of months chasing a very subtle bug in an MVC application that was hosted within an Azure Web App. During bursts of traffic, memory would spike, requests would slow, and then the Websocket component of the application would quit working. Then I would get The Call, and I'd remedy the situation by restarting the Web App.

For the first couple of weeks during this bug hunt, this seriously disrupted my life. I took my laptop everywhere just in case. Then I learned about Auto Heal, which is one of Azure's more useful debugging and mitigation features.

Auto Heal lets you define triggers for your application. When a trigger fires, you can specify an action that Azure should automatically take. The following triggers are available in Auto Heal.

- *Requests in a time period*: If your Web App receives more than X requests within a specified time period, take an action. This is useful if you know that your app becomes unstable under a certain load.

- *Status codes within a time period*: If you see X number of requests that return a specified status code in a given time period, take an action. For example, if your application begins raining down 200 HTTP 500 errors in a five-minute period, something is wrong and an action should be taken.

- *Slow requests*: If X number of requests occur within a time period, take an action. You get to specify the number of seconds that constitutes a slow request.

- *Memory threshold*: If memory exceeds a threshold that you specify, take an action.

Once a rule is triggered, the actions that you can execute are as follows:

- *Recycle the Process*: Since the earliest days of Windows on the desktop, turning it off and turning it back on has solved 90% or more of issues. Why should things be any different on the server? The Recycle action will recycle the W3WP process along with any of its child processes.

- *Log Event*: This action writes an entry to the Application Event log informing you that a rule has fired.

- *Custom Action*: By specifying a custom action, you can call any executable that you've loaded onto your Web App. By default, the selected executable is `DaaSConsole.exe`, which is already included in your Web App's `D:\home\data\DaaS\bin` folder. By specifying the `'-CollectKillAnalyze "Memory Dump" 60'` argument to `DaaSConsole.exe`, Auto Heal will capture a memory dump from your W3WP process, recycle the W3WP process, and kick off a DaaS analysis of the memory dump, which will be waiting for your review.

Setting Up Auto Heal

Auto Heal is available to all Web Apps that are on an App Service Plan of Basic or higher.

To set up Auto Heal, navigate to your Web App's management blade, then click Diagnose and Solve Problems. On the Diagnose and Solve Problems blade, click the Mitigate link under the Tools heading in the lower right corner of the screen to open the Auto Heal screen in a separate browser tab (Figure 11-12).

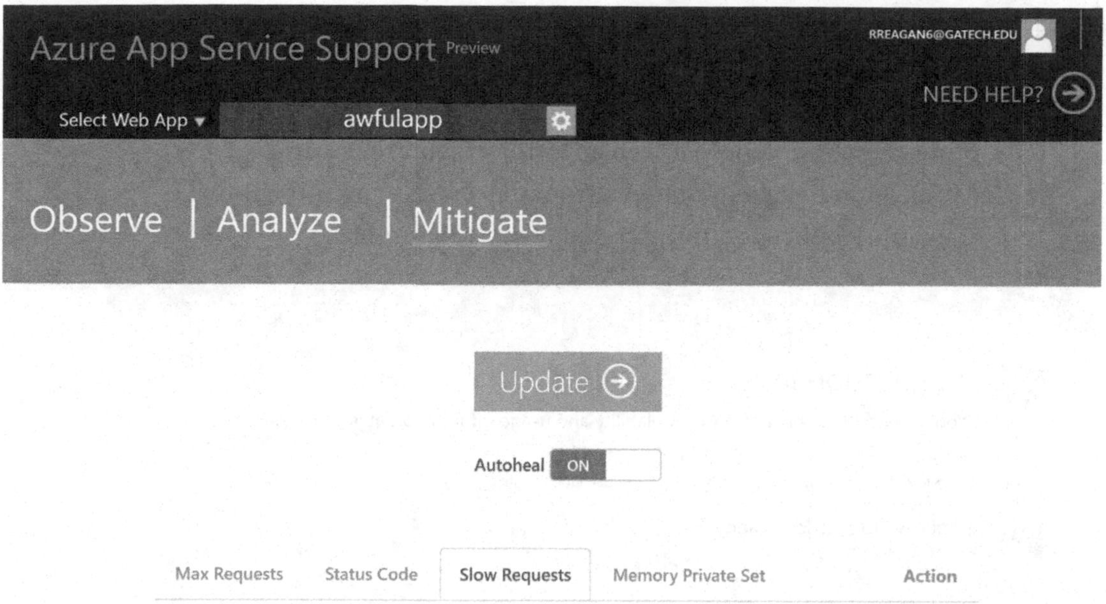

Figure 11-12. *The Auto Heal management console*

The first step is to enable Auto Heal by toggling the Auto Heal button to On. This will enable the trigger and action definitions.

To define triggers, simply click Max Requests, Status Code, Slow Requests, or Memory Private Set tabs. Note that you can only define one trigger of each type.

After setting up triggers, click the Action tab. At the time of this writing, you can only set up one action that will be invoked when any of your defined triggers fire. Therefore, you cannot choose to log an event when a Slow Request trigger fires, and also Recycle when a Max Requests trigger fires.

When you're done defining your triggers and action, don't forget to click Update to save your changes.

Application Insights

Application Insights is an excellent tool for tracking down application errors, performance problems, and availability issues. Let's walk through an example by troubleshooting our AwfulApp application.

Installing Application Insights

To add Application Insights to an existing ASP.NET web application, do the following:

1. Right-click your ASP.NET web app project, and select Add
   Application Insights Telemetry from the shortcut menu. This will
   open the Application Insights dialog box (Figure 11-13).

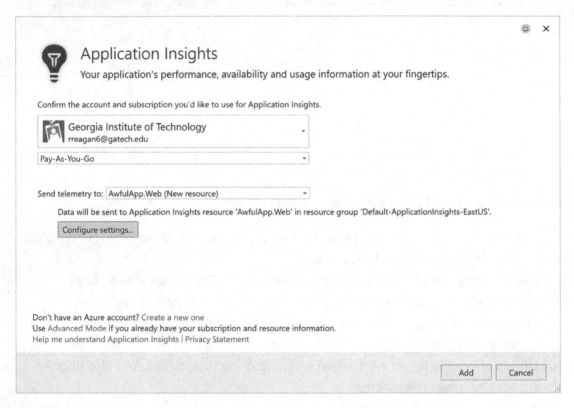

Figure 11-13. *Adding Application Insights to an existing ASP.NET web application*

2. Specify the Microsoft account you'd like to associate with your
   new Azure Application Insights resource. You'll then be able to
   choose a subscription, and whether you want to use an existing
   Application Insights resource, or have Azure create a new one for
   you. You can click Configure Settings if you'd like to change the
   resource group, Application Insights resource name, or region.
   Unless you have a compelling reason to do so, choose the same
   region that will host your Web App.

3.   Click Add. Visual Studio will install several Application Insights
     NuGet packages and update your web.config file.

After adding Application Insights, publish your web application to Azure and make
a few requests to generate metrics. Log into your Azure account, and you'll see your
new Application Insights resource listed in your list of all resources. If you browse to
the Application Insights overview blade, you'll see telemetry for the recent requests you
made after publishing (Figure 11-14).

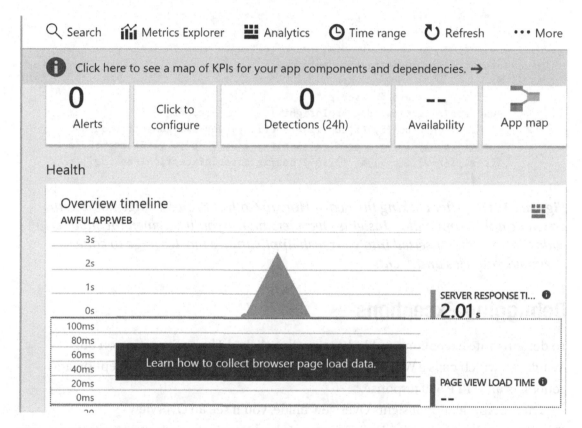

Figure 11-14.   *The Application Insights Overview blade shows server response time,*
page load time, the number of server requests, and the number of failed requests

Notice that in Figure 11-14, the Page View Load Time value is blank. Click the Learn
How To Collect Browser Page Load Data banner, and you'll be taken to a screen that
provides Application Insights telemetry JavaScript for client side metrics and events
(Figure 11-15). Paste this code into your master page, which will be _Layout.cshtml if

you're using ASP.NET MVC. After saving changes to your master page, republishing, and making a few requests, you'll see page view load time metrics in Application Insights.

Guidance

 Easy to get started. Simply paste the following into your master page

```
<!--
To collect end-user usage analytics about your application,
insert the following script into each page you want to track.
Place this code immediately before the closing </head> tag,
and before any other scripts. Your first data will appear
automatically in just a few seconds.
-->
<script type="text/javascript">
  var appInsights=window.appInsights||function(config){
    function i(config){t[config]=function(){var i=arguments;t.queue.
"https://az416426.vo.msecnd.net/scripts/a/ai.0.js";u.getElementsByTa
,i(c+a),i(h+v),i(c+v),i("flush"),config.disableExceptionTracking||(r
    }({
```

Figure 11-15.   After clicking the Learn How to Collect Browser Page Load Data banner on the Application Insights Overview blade, you'll be given the JavaScript code that must be inserted into your web application's master page to collect client-side metrics and events.

Debugging Exceptions

To demonstrate exception troubleshooting, I've clicked Throw Exception on our AwfulApp, which calls a WebAPI method on the server that throws an exception and generates an HTTP 500 response.

On the Application Insights Overview blade, you'll see an Overview Timeline heading, beneath which are several charts stacked on top of one another (Figure 11-16). These include Server Response Time, Page View Load Time, Server Requests, and Failed Requests. Each of these charts displays aligned time series data. In the Failed Requests graph, we can see all requests that generated a 400 or greater HTTP response code (excluding HTTP 401 Unauthorized). Clicking the pink Failed Requests bar opens the Failed Requests blade, which will provide us with more details on exactly why the request was unsuccessful.

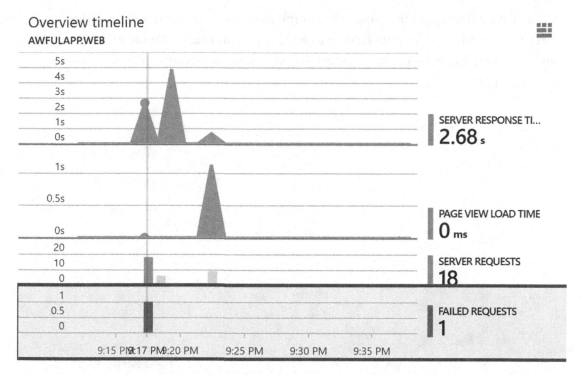

Figure 11-16. *The Application Insights Overview blade includes aligned time series charts that show Server Response Time, Page View Load Time, Server Requests, and Failed Requests.*

The Failed Requests blade has a similar interface showing aligned time series charts. On a minute-by-minute basis, we can see the Total Failed Requests, Dependency Failures, Server Exceptions, the number of server requests, and the number of users affected (Figure 11-17).

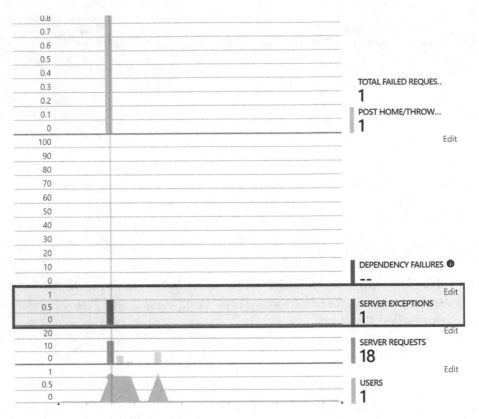

Figure 11-17.   *The Failed Requests time series charts give details on how many requests failed, whether the failure was due to a dependency (like a database) or a server exception, and how many users were affected*

To get details on the server exception, click the pink Server Exceptions bar. This opens a new blade showing the exception details (Figure 11-18).

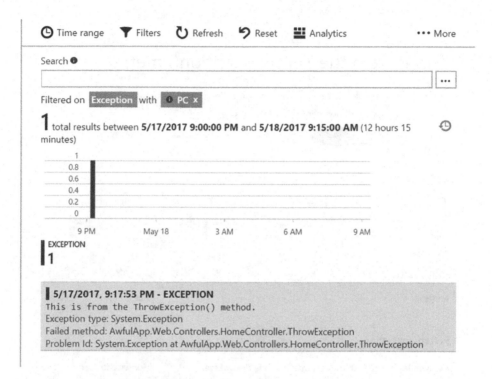

Figure 11-18. *Clicking the server exception drills down into the exception details*

Application Insights still has more data to give us. Click the exception (highlighted with a blue background in Figure 11-18), and you'll see the exception details (Figure 11-19). These include the URL for the request that generated the exception, the method that failed, the requester's device type, and a stack trace. You can also click links to view full telemetry for the session, for a five-minute window before and after the exception, or examples of requests that experienced the same problem.

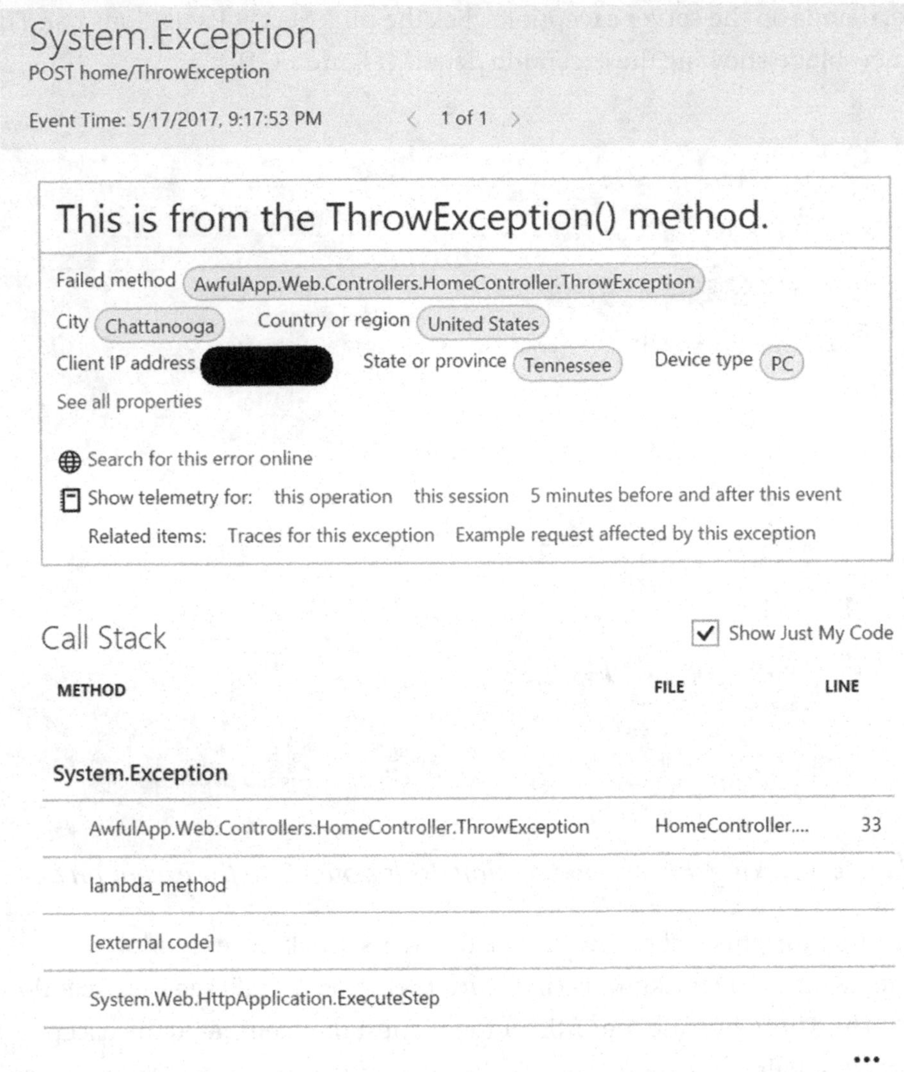

System.Exception
POST home/ThrowException

Event Time: 5/17/2017, 9:17:53 PM   ‹   1 of 1   ›

This is from the ThrowException() method.

Failed method (AwfulApp.Web.Controllers.HomeController.ThrowException)

City (Chattanooga)   Country or region (United States)

Client IP address ████████   State or province (Tennessee)   Device type (PC)

See all properties

🌐 Search for this error online

🖥 Show telemetry for: this operation   this session   5 minutes before and after this event

   Related items: Traces for this exception   Example request affected by this exception

---

Call Stack   ☑ Show Just My Code

METHOD	FILE	LINE

System.Exception

| AwfulApp.Web.Controllers.HomeController.ThrowException | HomeController.... | 33 |

| lambda_method | | |

| [external code] | | |

| System.Web.HttpApplication.ExecuteStep | | |

• • •

Figure 11-19. *Application Insights provides a great deal of information on exceptions*

Alerts

Application Insights Alerts notify you when various metrics have exceeded a defined threshold. This is useful for information purposes, or to give you advance notice that something bad is about to happen to your Web App. You can receive alerts via e-mail, webhook, or both.

To set up one or more alerts, do the following:

1. Open your Application Insights Overview blade, then click the Alerts box (Figure 11-20). This will open the Alert Rules blade.

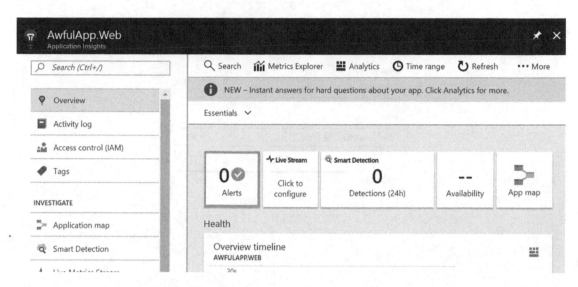

Figure 11-20. *The Alerts box in the Application Insights Overview blade*

2. The Alert Rules blade will list all active alerts. Click on Add Alert to create a new alert. This will navigate you to the Add an Alert Rule blade (Figure 11-21).

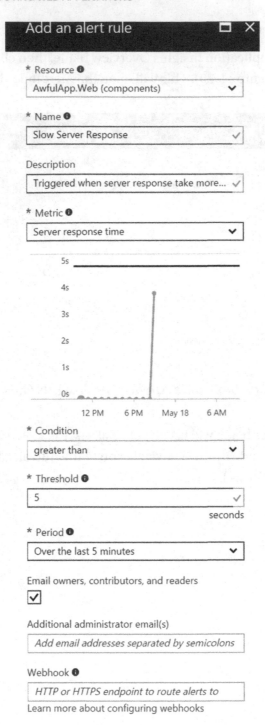

Figure 11-21. *The Add an Alert Rule blade, which allows us to create a new Application Insights Alert rule*

3. The Add an Alert Rule blade allows you to choose a metric,
    condition, threshold, and time period when defining a new rule.
    You'll also be able to choose who receives an e-mail when the
    alert is triggered, and to optionally specify a webhook to be called.

Summary

Troubleshooting an application can be a difficult task, especially if done in a high-
pressure situation such as a period of degraded performance or unavailability. In this
chapter, we examined tools that can help you quickly pinpoint and mitigate issues, or
even detect issues before they become a problem. I recommend reviewing these tools
carefully and becoming comfortable with their feature sets *before* you have to use them
in a production environment in a critical situation.

In the upcoming final chapter, we'll cover tools that can automate your app's
infrastructure provisioning and deployment process, thus eliminating checklists and
manual steps that are often the source of deployment errors.

CHAPTER 12

Deployment

Let's start this chapter with a horror story. Many moons ago, I was involved with building a web application for a new startup. We provisioned the necessary Azure resources manually using the portal, downloaded our publish profile, and published our app to Azure through Visual Studio. When we first launched, I think we had three daily active users, with two of those being our mothers. Over time, though, the site's popularity grew, and so did the site's features and complexity.

Even when we were then dealing with multiple Azure services, we were still performing manual deployments. To deal with this complexity, we made sure to first test our code in a staging environment (which we also provisioned manually in the Portal), then used a checklist to perform the multiple steps necessary to push our deployments to production. We deployed late at night to make sure that site interruptions were minimized and to give ourselves a buffer for any potential "oops" scenarios.

The battle-hardened veterans reading about our deployment process are probably thinking, "Boy, I'll bet they paid for that." We did. Eventually a deployment went bad, and we had several hours of late-night downtime while we scrambled to diagnose the problem and fix the site. Everyone was sleep-deprived and grumpy the following day.

What exactly was so terrible with our deployment approach? Our sins were as follows:

- We manually set up our production and staging environments. Did the environments match from day one? Possibly. Did the environments match six months later after a steady stream of new features and deployments? Probably not. This environment drift meant that we were not testing our code in an environment that mirrored production. Eventually, this led to errors slipping through to production that could've been identified in staging.

© Rob Reagan 2018

R. Reagan, *Web Applications on Azure*, https://doi.org/10.1007/978-1-4842-2976-7_12

- We were manually performing multistep deployments. Developers who perform a multistep deployment from memory are begging for punishment, and eventually they'll get it. Checklists can cut down on errors but might miss new or updated steps in a rapidly evolving code base. With more complicated deployments, Murphy's Law oftent rears its ugly head.

Proper Deployment Practices

Deployments don't have to be stress-inducing; you can deploy with confidence and ease. When deploying, developers should do follow the practices outlined here.

Follow a Proper Code Promotion Strategy

Code promotion simply means that code is deployed and tested in a series of (hopefully) identical environments before being deployed to production. A simple code promotion strategy begins with each developer working on his or her own machines. Each developer's machine is referred to as a development environment. Once developers check in code to a revision control system such as Git, the code can be built and deployed to an environment that mirrors production. This environment is called staging or integration. After thorough testing in staging, the build can then be deployed to production.

It's not often possible for each developer's environment to exactly mirror the production environment, but it is vital that staging environments match production. If your web application runs in production on an Azure S1 Standard Web App with two instances in the East US datacenter with certain settings, your staging environment should consist of an identical Azure S1 Standard Web App with two instances in the East US datacenter with the same settings. Failure to test your code in a staging environment identical to production can allow defects to slip through the cracks and show up in production.

Prevent Environment Drift by Treating Infrastructure as Code

Manually provisioning staging and production environments is an invitation for environment drift over time. If staging and production environments don't quite match up, defects that should be caught in staging can slip through to production. Your Azure resources in staging and production should always be in sync.

To help accomplish this, Azure offers Azure Resource Management (ARM) templates. ARM templates are just JSON files that specify all of the Azure resources and their respective settings that make up an environment. You can describe the desired environment within an ARM template and deploy the template to Azure using one of several methods. Azure will then ensure that your environment matches the template by updating settings or provisioning new resources. You can precede your code deployment with an ARM deployment to ensure that your environment is provisioned as expected. We discuss the details of building and deploying ARM templates in this chapter.

Automating Deployments

Pushing code to production should be scripted. You should use the same script to publish code to your staging environment that you use for publishing to production. Scripting deployments ensures that steps aren't left out or performed incorrectly.

If your staging and production environments are identical, you can use the same script to target different environments to publish your application to staging and production. You can then test your code thoroughly within the staging environment, and deployment to production can be drama-free.

In this chapter, we start by talking about ARM templates and how to create them. Next, we put together a demo web application, add an Azure Resource Group project to the solution, and deploy. We finish the chapter with a look at how to automate your deployments to both staging and production.

ARM Templates Overview

Azure ARM Templates are JSON files that describe resources within an Azure Resource Group. These template files can specify both resources and resource settings. You can create almost any type of Azure resource using an ARM template.

When published, Azure will ensure that the specified resource group contains the resources defined in the ARM template. If a resource within the template doesn't exist, it will be created. If a resource does exist but has settings that differ from those defined in the template, the existing resource's settings will be updated to match the template.

This is an excellent tool to provision resources and protect against environment drift. Because ARM templates are just JSON, they can be checked into source control along with your code.

Take a look at Listing 12-1 for an example of an ARM template that defines an App Service and a single Web App.

Listing 12-1. An Azure ARM Template That Provisions an App Service Plan and a Web App

```
{
  "$schema": "https://schema.management.azure.com/schemas/2015-01-01/
  deploymentTemplate.json#",
  "contentVersion": "1.0.0.0",
  "parameters": {
    "DemoAppServicePlanName": {
      "type": "string",
      "minLength": 1
    },
    "DemoAppServicePlanSkuName": {
      "type": "string",
      "defaultValue": "F1",
      "allowedValues": [
        "F1",
        "D1",
        "B1",
        "B2",
        "B3",
        "S1",
        "S2",
        "S3",
        "P1",
        "P2",
```

```
      "P3",
      "P4"
    ],
    "metadata": {
      "description": "Describes plan's pricing tier and capacity. Check details
      at https://azure.microsoft.com/en-us/pricing/details/app-service/"
    }
  }},
"variables": {
  "DemoWebAppName": "[concat('DemoWebApp', uniqueString(resourceGroup().
  id))]"},
"resources": [
  {
    "name": "[parameters('DemoAppServicePlanName')]",
    "type": "Microsoft.Web/serverfarms",
    "location": "[resourceGroup().location]",
    "apiVersion": "2015-08-01",
    "sku": {
      "name": "[parameters('DemoAppServicePlanSkuName')]"
    },
    "dependsOn": [ ],
    "tags": {
      "displayName": "DemoAppServicePlan"
    },
    "properties": {
      "name": "[parameters('DemoAppServicePlanName')]",
      "numberOfWorkers": 1
    }
  },
  {
    "name": "[variables('DemoWebAppName')]",
    "type": "Microsoft.Web/sites",
    "location": "[resourceGroup().location]",
    "apiVersion": "2015-08-01",
```

```
        "dependsOn": [
          "[resourceId('Microsoft.Web/serverfarms', parameters('DemoAppService
          PlanName'))]"
        ],
        "tags": {
          "[concat('hidden-related:', resourceId('Microsoft.Web/serverfarms',
          parameters('DemoAppServicePlanName')))]": "Resource",
          "displayName": "DemoWebApp"
        },
        "properties": {
          "name": "[variables('DemoWebAppName')]",
          "serverFarmId": "[resourceId('Microsoft.Web/serverfarms', parameters
          ('DemoAppServicePlanName'))]"
        }
      }],
    "outputs": {}
}
```

ARM Template Components

Let's break this template down and look at its constituent parts.

ARM templates can have up to four major sections: parameters, variables, resources, and outputs.

Parameters

Parameters are values that are passed into a template that allow you to modify its behavior. Examples include resource names, resource properties, or whether the template is being deployed to a staging or production environment.

Parameters are provided in one of two ways: either on the command line if the template is deployed via Powershell or in a separate JSON parameters file.

In Listing 12-1, take a look at the parameters node. You'll see that the template defines two parameters named DemoAppServicePlanName and DemoAppServicePlanSkuName. Each parameter must specify a data type. You can optionally provide a default value to use if none is specified. Also, you can specify an array of allowed values that restrict what can be specified for a parameter's value.

A parameters section is optional and can be omitted.

Variables

Variables allow you to store the output of one or more ARM template expressions or functions for use later within the template. Expressions and functions are contained in a string literal and are denoted by opening and closing brackets. For example, `"[concat (variables('ServiceBusNamespace'), '-staging')]"` will concatenate the value of the `ServiceBusNamespace` variable with the string literal `"-staging"`. There are quite a few functions that are built-in and available for your use. You can find a complete list at `https://docs.microsoft.com/en-us/azure/azure-resource-manager/resource-group-template-functions`.

In Listing 12-1, you'll see a single variable named `DemoWebAppName` that is defined as follows:

```
"DemoWebAppName": "[concat('DemoWebApp', uniqueString(resourceGroup().id))]"
```

This concatenates the string literal `"DemoWebApp"` with the hashed value of the Resource Group ID to create a unique name for our Web App. By storing the output from these functions in the `DemoWebAppName` variable, we can reuse the value without having to muddy our template by reevaluating these functions each time. Variables are primarily for convenience within a template. A variables section is not required within an ARM template.

Also, note that variable names are not case sensitive.

Expressions and functions aren't restricted to the variables section; they can be used anywhere in a template.

Resources

The Resources section contains an array of Azure resources that will be created or updated when the template is deployed. Each type of resource has its own properties. For example, the valid and required properties for defining a Web App will differ from the properties for defining a Cosmos DB resource.

In our example in Listing 12-1, the template's resources array defines two separate resources: an App Service Plan (whose type is `Microsoft.Web/serverfarms`) and a Web App (whose type is `Microsoft.Web/sites`). Here's a short description of the various properties in each.

- *Name*: This is the name of the resource. Several types of resources require that resource names must be unique. Examples include Web Apps and Service Bus. This is always required.

- *Type*: This is the type of resource that's being provisioned. This is always required.

- *ApiVersion*: This is the version of the REST API that's being used to create resources. This will vary by resource type. `ApiVersion` is always required.

- *Location*: This specifies the region where you want to provision the resource. Note that not all services are available at all region. The list of valid options will change by resource type.

- *Comments*: This covers any comments that you'd like to include in the template. These have no bearing on deployment. Please note that whereas Visual Studio will happily color-code C#-style comments within a template, the deployment process will not and will error out if you try to use them. This field is both recommended and optional.

- *DependsOn*: If a resource requires that another resource is already provisioned, you can specify the dependency here. When an ARM template is deployed, resources are provisioned in parallel. Defining a dependency ensures that the required resource is deployed before the dependent resource. You can only specify a dependency on another resource that is within the template. Note that in our example, the Web App depends on the App Service. If there are no dependencies, this is not required.

- *Properties*: These are resource-type-specific properties. Notice that the properties for our Web App differ from the properties in the App Service.

- *Resources*: This section is used for the definition of child resources. There are no child resources in the example in Listing 12-1, but we'll see them in the upcoming demo project. For example, Azure SQL Databases are defined as child resources of Azure SQL Servers.

How do you know exactly which properties are available for each resource type? Microsoft has a handy reference for each under the expandable Reference menu at `https://docs.microsoft.com/en-us/azure/templates/`.

Outputs

ARM templates can be nested, where one template calls another to do some work. This decomposition is useful as your templates become more and more complex. Breaking templates apart also allows template reuse. This decomposition is similar to how procedural programs are broken into multiple functions; doing so helps manage complexity and allows for code reuse.

The fourth and final major section within ARM templates are outputs. Outputs allow a template to pass an object to its calling template. This is useful for providing calling templates with constructed values like new resource names.

Creating ARM Templates

When I viewed an ARM template for the first time and looked over the few hundred lines of JSON that it contained, my shoulders slumped and I thought to myself, "Great. Here's another tedious technology that I'll have to spend a few hours learning." The good news is that you'll rarely, if ever, start with a blank template and type JSON by hand. Microsoft has made it very easy to start with an existing template and modify it to fit your needs.

There are several ways to get started authoring ARM templates.

- Provision resources within the Azure portal to create your environment, then download the ARM template for your resources from the portal.

- Microsoft has a large gallery of example templates in GitHub. Find one that is most similar to your architecture, then modify it to meet your needs.

- Visual Studio has an Azure Resource Group project that includes various templates that you can choose from. You can choose resources from a list to add to the template, and the JSON for each new resource will be added for you.

Let's look at each of these methods in turn.

Downloading ARM Templates for Preexisting Resources in the Azure Portal

From previous chapters, you're already familiar with provisioning Azure resources using the Azure Portal. Within the Portal, every existing resource within Azure has an Automation Script menu item on its management blade. Clicking Automation Script takes you to an Automation Script blade that will allow you to download code to provision the resource. On the Automation Script blade, you can choose between downloading an ARM template, a Powershell script, a CLI script, or .NET code. Let's run through a quick example to demonstrate.

1. First, log into the Azure Portal and provision a new Storage Account. If you need a refresher on how to provision a Storage Account, review Chapter 6 for a walkthrough. Because scripting an ARM template will script all objects in a resource group, create a new resource group for this Storage Account.

2. After your new Storage Account is created, navigate to its management blade. You'll see an Automation Script menu item located under the Settings heading. Click Automation Script to bring open the Automation Script blade (Figure 12-1). Note that each resource, regardless of type, will have an Automation Script menu item. We're just using a Storage Account as our example.

3. The Automation Script blade has several tabs, which include Template, CLI, PowerShell, .NET, and Ruby. Clicking a tab will show you the tool-specific deployment script. Because we're interested in ARM templates, click the Template tab to see the ARM script.

4. Click Download (Figure 12-1) to download the all scripts. This will initiate a zip file download that contains the JSON template, a JSON parameters file, and a Powershell script that will perform the deployment. The .NET, Ruby, and CLI scripts will be included in the zip file at no extra charge.

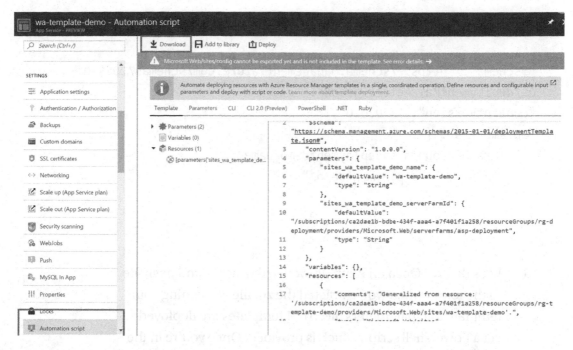

Figure 12-1. *The Automation Script management blade*

5. Unzip the zip file and open `template.json` in your favorite editor. You'll notice that there is a single parameter for the Storage Account's name.

Next, open `parameters.json`. This is the parameters file that feeds `template.json`. You'll see a single parameter for the Storage Account's name that corresponds to the parameter defined in `template.json`. The parameter name will depend on what you named your Storage Account in the Azure Portal, so the parameter names in your template will differ from mine.

To demonstrate deployment, we're going to use the template and parameters file to provision another Storage Account with the same settings as the one we just provisioned in the Portal. Jump back to the `parameters.json` file and change the value of your Storage Account name parameter. Finally, save your `parameters.json` file. My `parameters.json` file is shown in Listing 12-2.

Listing 12-2. My parameters.json File After Step 5

```
{
    "$schema": "https://schema.management.azure.com/schemas/2015-01-
    01/deploymentParameters.json#",
    "contentVersion": "1.0.0.0",
    "parameters": {
      "storageAccounts_sadeploymentdemo_name": {
        "value": "sadeploymentdemo2"
      }
    }
}
```

6. Let's deploy! Open an Azure Powershell window and navigate
    to the folder where you extracted the zip file containing your
    template and parameters file. ARM templates are deployed
    via a Powershell script, which is provided. Once you're in the
    same directory as your scripts, run the following command in
    Powershell:

    ```
    .\deploy.ps1
    ```

    You'll be prompted for a few pieces of information (Figure 12-2).

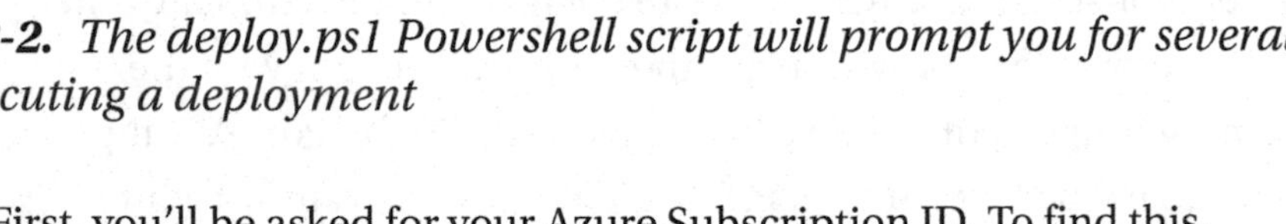

Figure 12-2. *The deploy.ps1 Powershell script will prompt you for several inputs before executing a deployment*

First, you'll be asked for your Azure Subscription ID. To find this,
go to the Azure Portal and search for Subscription. All of your
subscriptions will be displayed, and you can copy the appropriate
subscription ID.

Next, you'll be asked for the name of the resource group you'd like to deploy the template to. Enter the name of a resource group that already exists. You'll then be asked for a deployment name, and you can name the deployment anything you like. The entered deployment name will show up in the resource group's deployment logs. Finally, you'll be prompted to log in to your account. Enter your credentials, and the deployment will begin.

After the deployment finishes, you can log in to the Portal to see the new Storage Account that was provisioned.

That exercise demonstrates how you can start with an existing template and use it to create a completely new resource. The other major use for an ARM template is to tune up existing resources to ensure that their settings match what's defined in the template. To demonstrate this, follow these steps.

1. Open the `template.json` file that you deployed in the previous exercise. Scan down until you find the `sku` property in the resources section. The SKU defines the Storage Account's pricing tier and data replication. Set the SKU's name to `Standard_GRS` and save the file.

2. Redeploy the template just as we did in Step 6 in the previous exercise. After the template is successfully published, log back into the Portal and check the Performance and Replication settings on the Storage Account's Overview tab. You'll see that they've been set to Standard and Geo-redundant storage (GRS), just as specified in the template.

I'd like to point out that there's nothing magic about the `deploy.ps1` Powershell script that we downloaded with our Automation Script. If you open it in your favorite editor and have a look, you'll notice that several commands prompt you for information before running the cmdlet `New-AzureRmResourceGroupDeployment`. Instead of using the predefined `deploy.ps1` script, you can run this command yourself with the appropriate arguments to perform your deployment.

Choosing a Gallery Template

Before starting just about any new project, I first look to see if I can find a codebase to build from rather than starting from scratch. Microsoft has created an ARM template gallery that accepts community submissions that conform to a set of guidelines. This is a great place to start when building out a new ARM template.

You can browse the gallery here at `https://azure.microsoft.com/en-us/resources/templates/`. Note that each template listed in this URL will link you to the template's folder located on GitHub at `https://github.com/Azure/azure-quickstart-templates/`.

Each template lists all parameters required and includes a Powershell script for deployment.

Even if you don't start with one of the gallery templates, they're a great resource for learning how to accomplish certain tasks using ARM.

Creating Templates with a Visual Studio Azure Resource Group Project

The Azure Resource Group Project can be added to any solution. The project template will create an ARM template, an ARM parameters file, and a Powershell script to use for deployment.

The real magic of using an ARM Project is that when editing an ARM template, Visual Studio will display a JSON Outline (Figure 12-3).

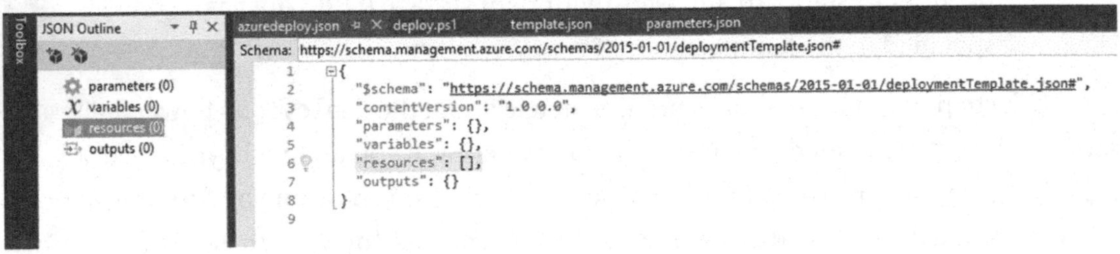

Figure 12-3. *Editing an ARM template in Visual Studio*

By right-clicking the Resources node and selecting Add New Resource, you'll be taken to the Add Resource dialog box, where you'll have the opportunity to choose from a list of resource types (Figure 12-4). Once chosen, Visual Studio will automatically insert the necessary JSON and associated parameters into your ARM template. You can then edit the new resource's JSON as needed.

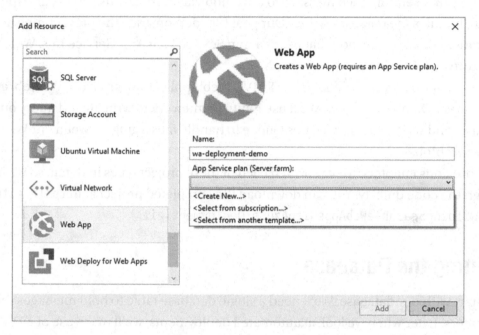

Figure 12-4. *The Add Resource dialog box lets you choose from a list of resource types to add to your ARM template*

As an added bonus, the Add Resource dialog box will handle the provisioning of any additional required resources. For example, if you add a Web App but don't already have an App Service Plan defined within the template, Visual Studio will add the necessary App Service Plan for you.

We'll make use of an Azure Resource Group Project in our upcoming demo app.

The Deployment Web Application

Before we can dive into ARM templates and automated deployment, we first need an example application to deploy. The Deployment Web Application is a Rube Goldberg contraption that writes messages entered by a user to an Azure SQL database. It does so by first sending each message to a WebJob via a Service Bus Queue, and the WebJob handles the database writes. Our goal is to demonstrate the provisioning and deployment of an application that uses an App Service Web App, Service Bus, WebJob, and Azure SQL Database.

The solution consists of an ASP.NET MVC Web Application, an Azure WebJob, and a SQL Server Database Project. We'll use Entity Framework to write to and query our database, and we'll use a Service Bus Queue to handle messaging between our Web App and the WebJob.

In previous chapters, we've covered each of these project types in detail, so we'll run through the code quickly. You can download the completed project at `https://github. com/BuildingScalableWebAppsWithAzure/Deployment.git`.

Creating the Database

Let's start with our database. We'll need a single database table to hold messages that the user enters. Later when we look at automated deployments, we'll make use of a DACPAC to create and execute TSQL statements to create our database, and later to upgrade our existing database during subsequent deployments. The easiest way to create a DACPAC and allow us to version our database scripts is to use a SQL Server Database Project.

1. Open Visual Studio and create a new project. In the Add New Project dialog box, select Templates ➤ SQL Server ➤ SQL Server Database Project. Let's name the project `Deployment.Database`, and the solution `Deployment`. Click OK to create the project and solution.

2. Let's add our single database table. Right-click the Deployment. Database project and select Add ➤ Table. Name the new table `ReceivedMessages`. In the resulting `ReceivedMessages.sql` file, add the code in Listing 12-3.

Listing 12-3. The TSQL for Creating Our ReceivedMessages Table

```
CREATE TABLE [dbo].[ReceivedMessages]
(
    [Id] INT NOT NULL PRIMARY KEY IDENTITY,
    [Message] NVARCHAR(256) NOT NULL
)
```

We're now done with our database project. Let's move on to our database access code.

Accessing the Database

Both our web application and WeJob will need to talk to the database, so let's place all data access code in a common Class Library project.

1. Right-click the solution, and select Add ➤ New Project. In the Add New Project dialog box, select the Class Library template located under the Windows menu item. Name the new project Deployment.Persistence and click OK.

2. Now we'll add our Entity Framework package via NuGet. Right-click the Deployment.Persistence project and select Manage NuGetPackages. On the Browse tab in the NuGet Package Manager, search for EntityFramework and add the latest stable version to the project.

3. Rather than walk through the wizards to create our Entity Framework model and Context, we'll just copy and paste in the necessary class files. Add a new class to the Deployment. Persistence project and call the file ReceivedMessage.cs. The complete code listing for ReceivedMessage is shown in Listing 12-4.

Listing 12-4. The ReceivedMessage Class

```
namespace Deployment.Persistence
{
    using System.ComponentModel.DataAnnotations;

    public partial class ReceivedMessage
    {
        public int Id { get; set; }

        [Required]
        [StringLength(256)]
        public string Message { get; set; }
    }
}
```

4. Now we'll add our DbContext subclass. Right-click the Deployment.Persistence project and select Add ➤ New Item. Under the Code menu item, select the Class template, then name the new class file DeploymentContext.cs. The code for DeploymentContext is shown in Listing 12-5.

Listing 12-5. The DeploymentContext Class

```
namespace Deployment.Persistence
{
    using System.Data.Entity;
    public partial class DeploymentContext : DbContext
    {
        public DeploymentContext() : base("name=DeploymentContext")
        { }
        public virtual DbSet<ReceivedMessage> ReceivedMessages { get; set; }
        protected override void OnModelCreating(DbModelBuilder modelBuilder)
        { }
    }
}
```

That wraps up our Deployment.Persistence project. Next, we'll create our web application.

The Deployment Web Application

Our web application will allow users to submit messages that will eventually be written to the ReceivedMessages table in the database. We'll also create a page that reads the ReceivedMessages table in the database and displays all messages. You can see the rendered page for inputting messages in Figure 12-5. The message history page is shown in Figure 12-6.

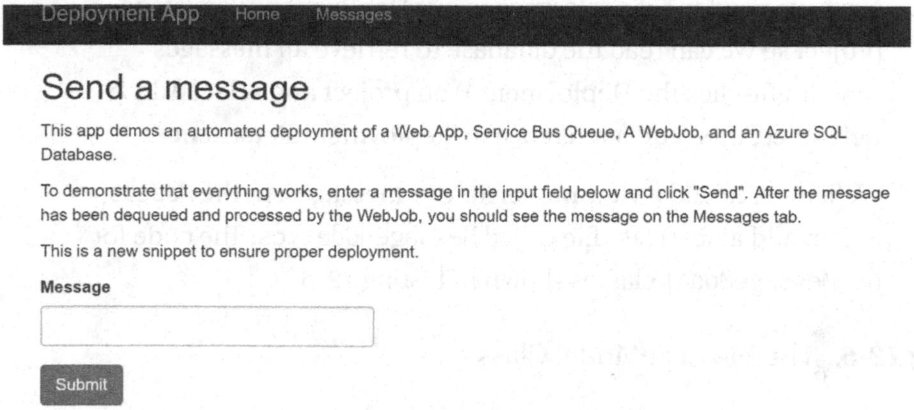

Figure 12-5. *Our main page allows users to enter messages*

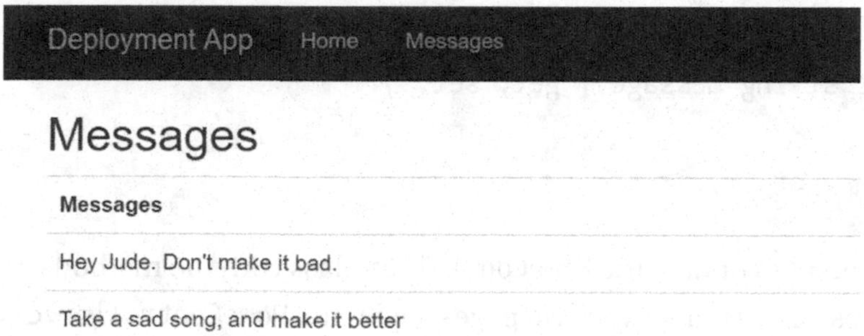

Figure 12-6. *Listing all messages that have been entered*

1. Let's start by creating our ASP.NET MVC project. Right-click the Deployment solution and select Add ➤ New Project. Under the Web menu item, select the ASP.NET Web Application (.NET Framework) template, name the project Deployment.Web, then click OK. You'll be prompted to select a template. Choose the MVC template, then click OK to create the project.

2.   We'll use a Service Bus Queue to send the messages entered to our WebJob, and the WebJob will handle writing the messages to the database. Therefore, we'll need to add a reference to the WindowsAzure.ServiceBus library via NuGet. To do so, right-click the Deployment.Web project and select Manage NuGet Packages. On the Browse tab in the NuGet Package Manager, search for WindowsAzure.ServiceBus and install the latest version.

3.   Next, we need to set a reference to our Deployment.Persistence project so we can read the database to retrieve all messages sent. Right-click the Deployment.Web project and select Add ➤ Reference, then add a reference to Deployment.Persistence.

4.   We'll need to add a view model for our messages. In the Models folder, add a new class file called MessageModel.cs. The code for the MessageModel class is shown in Listing 12-6.

Listing 12-6. The MessageModel Class

```
namespace Deployment.Web.Models
{
    public class MessageModel
    {
        public string Message { get; set; }
    }
}
```

5.   We need to update the HomeController class with the methods necessary to render our two pages. Open the HomeController.cs file located in the Controllers directory, then add the code from Listing 12-7.

Listing 12-7. The HomeController Class

```
using System.Web.Mvc;
using Deployment.Web.Models;
using System.Configuration;
using Microsoft.ServiceBus.Messaging;
```

```csharp
using Deployment.Persistence;
using System.Collections.Generic;
using System.Linq;

namespace Deployment.Web.Controllers
{
    public class HomeController : Controller
    {
        [HttpGet]
        public ActionResult Index()
        {
            return View(new MessageModel());
        }

        /// <summary>
        /// Takes a message submitted from our main form and enqueues
        /// it in a Service Bus Queue.
        /// </summary>
        [HttpPost]
        public ActionResult Index(MessageModel model)
        {
            //enqueue our message.
            string serviceBusConnectionString = System.Configuration.
            ConfigurationManager.AppSettings["ServiceBusConnectionString"];
            string queueName = ConfigurationManager.AppSettings["ServiceBus
            QueueName"];
            var client = QueueClient.CreateFromConnectionString(serviceBus
            ConnectionString);
            BrokeredMessage msg = new BrokeredMessage(model.Message);
            client.Send(msg);
            return View(model);
        }

        /// <summary>
        /// Shows a list of all messages that have been written to the database.
        /// </summary>
        /// <returns></returns>
```

```
    [HttpGet]
    public ActionResult Messages()
    {
        using (var deploymentCtx = new DeploymentContext())
        {
            List<ReceivedMessage> allMessages = deploymentCtx.
            ReceivedMessages.ToList();
            return View(allMessages);
        }
    }
}
}
```

6. Entity Framework and the QueueClient need to read database
   and Service Bus connection strings from the web.config file.
   After opening the web.config file, add the following entry in the
   <appSettings> section:

```
<add key="ServiceBusConnectionString" value="[Your Service Bus Connection
String]"/>
```

Next, add the following entry in the <connectionStrings>
section. You might need to add thetags below the closing </appSettings>
tags if Visual Studio did not include it in the default template.

```
<add name="DeploymentContext" connectionString="[Your SQL Server Connection
String]" providerName="System.Data.SqlClient"/>
```

For now, you can even leave the value and connectionString
attributes blank for both entries. In the real world, this would
be where you would specify settings for your development
environment. We'll return to these settings after provisioning our
Azure resources with the ARM template.

7. Finally, let's update the markup. For brevity, the markup is available in this project's Git repo. You'll need to update the markup for the _Layout.cshtml in the Views\Shared folder, and the Index.cshtml file in the Views\Home folder. You'll need to add Messages.cshtml to the Views\Home folder as well.

Finally, let's create our WebJob.

The Deployment WebJob

Our Deployment WebJob will monitor the Service Bus Queue for any messages sent from our web application, and will write the contents of any messages received to the database.

1. Right-click the solution file, and select Add ➤ New Project. In the Add New Project dialog box, select the Cloud menu item, then select the Azure WebJob project template. Name this project Deployment.WebJob, then click OK.

2. Because we're monitoring a Service Bus Queue, we need to add a reference to the WindowsAzure.ServiceBus library. Right-click the Deployment.WebJob project, select Manage NuGet Packages, and seach for WindowsAzure.ServiceBus on the Browse tab. Add a reference to the latest version. While you're on the Manage NuGetPackages screen, also add a reference to Microsoft.Azure.WebJobs.ServiceBus. This package is needed for our Service Bus Trigger.

3. We'll also need a reference to our Deployment.Persistence project so that we can write received messages to the database. Right-click the Deployment.WebJob project, select Add, and then select Reference. Add a reference to the Deployment.Persistence class in the Reference Manager dialog box, then click OK.

4. The Program class is the entry point for our WebJob, and we need to make a few changes so that the WebJob API knows that we're making use of a Service Bus Queue. The completed code for the Program class is shown in Listing 12-8.

Listing 12-8. The Program Class

```
using Microsoft.Azure.WebJobs;

namespace Deployment.WebJob
{
    class Program
    {
        static void Main()
        {
            var config = new JobHostConfiguration();
            config.UseServiceBus();
            var host = new JobHost(config);
            // The following code ensures that the WebJob will be running
            // continuously
            host.RunAndBlock();
        }
    }
}
```

5. The `Functions` class holds our `ProcessQueueMessages` method, which gets called when new messages are placed in the Service Bus Message Queue called `messages`. The source is shown in Listing 12-9.

Listing 12-9. The Functions Class

```
using Microsoft.Azure.WebJobs;
using System.IO;
using System;
using Deployment.Persistence;

namespace Deployment.WebJob
{
    public class Functions
    {
        // This function will get triggered/executed when a new message is written
```

```
// on an Azure Service Bus Message Queue called "messages"
public static void ProcessQueueMessage([ServiceBusTrigger("messages")]
    string message, TextWriter log)
{
    Console.WriteLine(message);
    ReceivedMessage msgModel = new ReceivedMessage();
    msgModel.Message = message;
    using (var deploymentCtx = new DeploymentContext())
    {
        deploymentCtx.ReceivedMessages.Add(msgModel);
        deploymentCtx.SaveChanges();
    }
}
}
```

6. This WebJob will read the database and Service Bus connection strings from the app.config file. Although we don't have to specify values for either at the moment, we do need to make sure that there's a placeholder for each. Open the app.config file and add the following entries in the <connectionStrings> section:

```
<add name="AzureWebJobsServiceBus" connectionString="[Service Bus
Connection String]"/>
<add name="DeploymentContext" connectionString="[Database Connection
String]" providerName="System.Data.SqlClient"/>
```

Our solution is now complete and would run if we'd specified a SQL Server database, an Azure Storage Account (which is required to run a WebJob), and a Service Bus. We'll handle the creation of each of these resources via an ARM template, and we'll create the ARM template by adding an Azure Resource Group Project to our solution.

Deploying Azure Resources Using an Azure Resource Group Project

The Azure Resource Group Project simplifies the creation of an ARM template that will script the deployment of Azure resources. After creating an Azure Resource Group Project, you can deploy the ARM template directly from Visual Studio or integrate it into a separate deployment process using tools such as the Visual Studio Team Services Build system.

Creating the Azure Resource Group Project

To add an Azure Resource Group Project to the solution, right-click the solution and select Add ➤ New Project. In the Add New Project dialog box, you'll find the Azure Resource Group Project template located under the Visual C# ➤ Windows ➤ Cloud menu item (Figure 12-7). Name the new project Deployment.ARM and click OK.

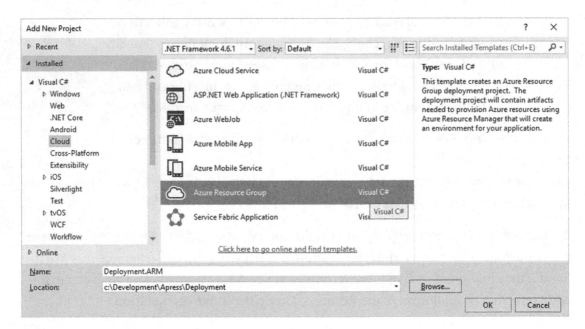

Figure 12-7. *Adding an Azure Resource Group Project to the solution*

Before the project is added to the solution, you'll be asked what template you'd like to use (Figure 12-8). For this exercise, select Blank Template.

Figure 12-8. *Choosing a template before the Azure Resource Group Project is added to the solution*

Note that in the upper left corner of the dialog box, there is a drop-down list labeled Show Templates from This Location. The Azure QuickStart option will display all templates from Microsoft's template gallery, which are also listed on GitHub.

After the project is created, you'll notice that we're given the following three files to begin with:

- *Azuredeploy.json*: This is the ARM template that will contain our parameters, variables, resources, and outputs.

- *Azuredeploy.parameters.json*: This file contains values for all parameters that do not have default values declared within azuredeploy.json.

- *Deploy-AzureResourceGroup.ps1*: This is our Powershell script that will be used to publish the template to Azure.

To provision resources for our Deploy web application, we'll need to define a SQL Server, SQL Database, Service Bus, Service Bus Authorization Rule, Service Bus Queue, App Service Plan, and a Web App. Some of these resources, such as the Service Bus Queue and SQL Database, depend on other resources. Let's start with defining our SQL Server.

Adding a SQL Server

To add a SQL Server definition to our ARM template, click the `azuredeploy.json` file. You'll see that we have the JSON for a bare-bones ARM template along with a JSON document outline on the far left (Figure 12-9).

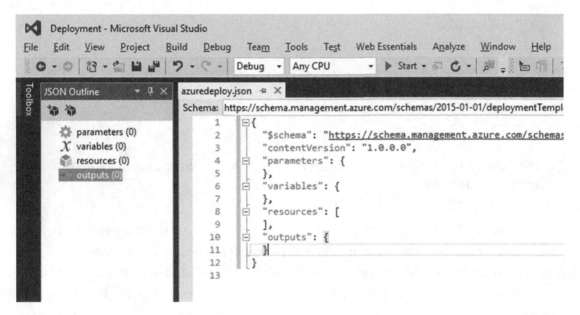

Figure 12-9. *The bare-bones azuredeploy.json ARM template and the accompanying JSON outline*

To add a new resource to the template, you have the option of typing code directly into the template, copying and pasting JSON for a new resource, or letting Visual Studio do the work. For our SQL Server definition, let's let Visual Studio do the work. Right-click the Resources node in the JSON Outline window and select Add New Resource from the shortcut menu.

When you select Add New Resource, the Add Resource dialog box opens (Figure 12-10). You can scroll through available templates on the left, and enter relevant properties for the selected resource type on the right. Note that not all Azure resource types are listed; as we'll see when we create our Service Bus, we won't be able to rely on Visual Studio to provide us with a starting point.

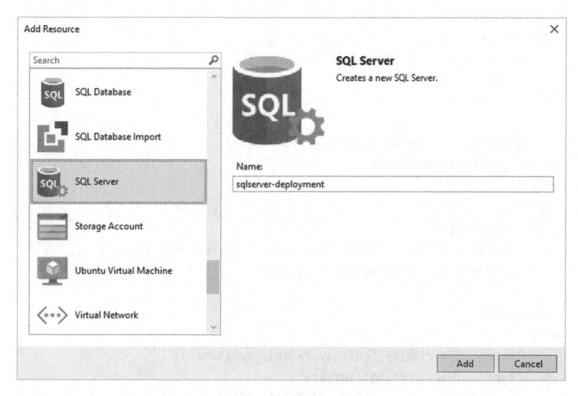

Figure 12-10. *The Add Resource dialog box lets you choose from the most common resource types to add to your ARM template*

Scroll down until you find the SQL Server resource type. Select it, and enter `sqlserver-deployment` in the Name field. Click Add to add the SQL Server definition to the template. The resulting code inserted into our `azuredeploy.json` file is shown in Listing 12-10.

Listing 12-10. Our azuredeploy.json File After Adding a SQL Server Resource
Definition

```
{
  "$schema": "https://schema.management.azure.com/schemas/2015-01-01/
  deploymentTemplate.json#",
  "contentVersion": "1.0.0.0",
  "parameters": {
    "sqlserver-deploymentAdminLogin": {
      "type": "string",
      "minLength": 1
    },
    "sqlserver-deploymentAdminLoginPassword": {
      "type": "securestring"
    }
  },
  "variables": {
    "sqlserver-deploymentName": "[concat('sqlserver-deployment',
      uniqueString(resourceGroup().id))]"
  },
  "resources": [
    {
      "name": "[variables('sqlserver-deploymentName')]",
      "type": "Microsoft.Sql/servers",
      "location": "[resourceGroup().location]",
      "apiVersion": "2014-04-01-preview",
      "dependsOn": [ ],
      "tags": {
        "displayName": "sqlserver-deployment"
      },
      "properties": {
        "administratorLogin": "[parameters('sqlserver-deploymentAdminLogin')]",
        "administratorLoginPassword": "[parameters(
          'sqlserver-deploymentAdminLoginPassword')]"
      },
```

```
    "resources": [
      {
        "name": "AllowAllWindowsAzureIps",
        "type": "firewallrules",
        "location": "[resourceGroup().location]",
        "apiVersion": "2014-04-01-preview",
        "dependsOn": [
          "[resourceId('Microsoft.Sql/servers',
              variables('sqlserver-deploymentName'))]"
        ],
        "properties": {
          "startIpAddress": "0.0.0.0",
          "endIpAddress": "0.0.0.0"
        }
      }
    ]
  }
],
"outputs": {
}
}
```

Let's take a closer look at what's been done.

First, you'll notice that two parameters have been added to the `parameters` section: `sqlserver-deploymentAdminLogin` and `sqlserver-deploymentAdminLoginPassword`. There are no default values specified. This means that parameters will have to be specified in a separate parameters JSON file, or that we'll need to provide values via our chosen deployment tool when the deployment takes place.

Second, you'll see that a single variable called `sqlserver-deploymentName` has been defined. This is a concatenation of our chosen SQL Server name and the ID of the resource group that we ultimately deploy to. Because a SQL Server name must be unique across Azure, appending the resource ID is an attempt to ensure uniqueness. Storing the name in a variable makes it much easier to refer to throughout the rest of the template.

The last point I'd like to bring to your attention is the use of a child resource. Note that within the SQL Server object contained in the template's resources section, there is a nested `firewallrules` resource that specifies what IP addresses can connect to this server.

473

To finish up, let's specify a value for the `sqlserver-deploymentAdminLogin` parameter in our `azuredeploy.parameters.json` file. We won't be specifying a value for `sqlserver-deploymentAdminLoginPassword` because it's declared as a `securestring` type. We'll enter a value for this password parameter at the time of deployment.

Open the `azuredeploy.parameters.json` file and input the script in Listing 12-11.

Listing 12-11. A Parameter Value Specified in azuredeploy.parameters.json

```
{
  "$schema": "https://schema.management.azure.com/schemas/2015-01-01/
    deploymentParameters.json#",
  "contentVersion": "1.0.0.0",
  "parameters": {
    "sqlserver-deploymentAdminLogin": {
      "value": "serveradmin"
    }
  }
}
```

We're now ready to deploy our template.

Deploying from Visual Studio

Because we have a SQL Server resource defined, we can deploy this template to Azure to ensure that it works as expected. To deploy with Visual Studio, do the following:

1. Right-click the Deployment.ARM project, then select Deploy ➤ New to open the Deploy to Resource Group dialog box (Figure 12-11). Within this dialog box, you'll need to log in to Azure, then specify the following:

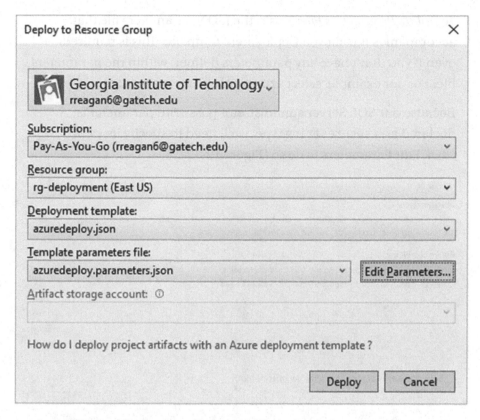

Figure 12-11. *The Deploy to Resource Group dialog box*

- *Subscription*: Choose the subscription that contains the resource group you'd like to use for deployment. You'll also have the option of creating a new resource group in the subscription that you choose.

- *Resource Group*: This is the resource group to which all resources will be deployed. You can choose an existing resource group within your selected subscription, or you can select Create New in the drop-down list to create a new resource group.

  For this demo, select Create New. Name your new group `rg-deployment-staging`.

- *Deployment Template*: This drop-down list lets you choose the ARM template to deploy. This is necessary because you could have multiple templates within an Azure Resource Group Project. Choose the `azuredeploy.json` file for this example.

- *Template Parameters File:* This is the JSON parameters file that accompanies the chosen Deployment template. This is required, even if you don't have any parameters defined within the parameters file. For our example, select `azuredeploy.parameters.json`.

  Because our SQL Server administrator password parameter is declared as a `securestring` type, we'll need to specify its value. Click Edit Parameters to do so (Figure 12-12).

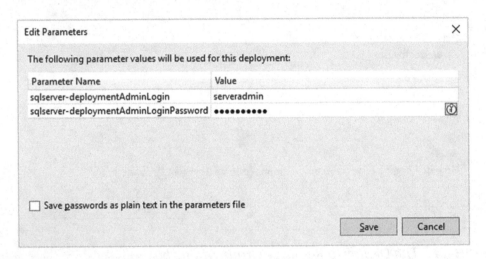

Figure 12-12. *The Edit Parameters dialog box lets you override parameters defined in the ARM parameters file*

2. When the fields in the previous step are specified, click Deploy to initiate a deployment. You'll see output echoed to the console. You'll also notice that a Powershell window is launched. Within the Powershell window, you'll be prompted again for the value of any parameter of type `securestring`.

   When the deployment completes successfully, you can log in to the Azure Portal, browse to your specified resource group, and see that the SQL Server has been successfully deployed.

Improving Our ARM Template

The JSON that Visual Studio provided for our SQL Server definition is very flexible: It allows us to parameterize the admin username and password. It also concatenates the SQL Server name that we provided with the Resource Group's ID to create a unique name.

Remember, though, that our goals are to make sure that we have identical staging and production environments that we can use to test and deploy our code. We don't need to parameterize every possible value because this means that we have to specify each parameter when we deploy.

We'll apply the following rules of thumb to the JSON generated by Visual Studio:

- Keep parameters to a minimum. If a value can be calculated, store it in a variable instead of passing it in to the template as a parameter.

- If a value isn't needed more than once, hard-code it.

- For each parameter that we use, define a default value if at all possible.

- When creating variables, it's possible to have nested properties. I prefer to define one variable per resource, then define as many nested properties as needed. This makes the template easier to read and use.

The modified version of our JSON template is given in Listing 12-12.

Listing 12-12. The Modified azuredeploy.json Template

```
{
  "$schema": "https://schema.management.azure.com/schemas/2015-01-01/
  deploymentTemplate.json#",
  "contentVersion": "1.0.0.0",
  "parameters": {
    "environmentName": {
      "type": "string",
      "minLength": 1,
      "defaultValue": "staging",
      "metadata": {
```

```
          "description": "The environment type. This will typically be
          'staging' or 'production'"
        }
      },
      "sqlServerAdminPassword": {
        "type": "securestring",
        "metadata": {
          "description": "The administrative password for the SQL Server"
        }
      }
    },
    "variables": {
      "sqlserver": {
        "adminLogin": "adminuser",
        "deploymentName": "[concat('sqlserver-deployment-',
        parameters('environmentName'),
            '-', uniqueString(resourceGroup().id))]"
      }
    },
    "resources": [
      {
        "name": "[variables('sqlserver').deploymentName]",
        "type": "Microsoft.Sql/servers",
        "location": "[resourceGroup().location]",
        "apiVersion": "2014-04-01-preview",
        "dependsOn": [],
        "tags": {
          "displayName": "sqlserver-deployment"
        },
        "properties": {
          "administratorLogin": "[variables('sqlServer').adminLogin]",
          "administratorLoginPassword": "[parameters('sqlServerAdminPassword')]"
        },
```

```
  "resources": [
    {
      "name": "AllowAllWindowsAzureIps",
      "type": "firewallrules",
      "location": "[resourceGroup().location]",
      "apiVersion": "2014-04-01-preview",
      "dependsOn": [
        "[resourceId('Microsoft.Sql/servers', variables('sqlserver').
        deploymentName)]"
      ],
      "properties": {
        "startIpAddress": "0.0.0.0",
        "endIpAddress": "0.0.0.0"
      }
    }
  ]
  }
],
"outputs": {}
}
```

We've also updated our `azuredeploy.parameters.json` file to account for our new `environmentName` parameter. It's shown in Listing 12-13.

Listing 12-13. The Updated azuredeploy.parameters.json File

```
{
  "$schema": "https://schema.management.azure.com/schemas/2015-01-01/
  deploymentParameters.json#",
  "contentVersion": "1.0.0.0",
  "parameters": {
    "environmentName": {
      "value": "staging"
    }
  }
}
```

You'll notice that we've done the following:

- All SQL Server settings are either hard-coded or changed to properties in our `sqlServer` variable.

- Because we want a duplicate environment between staging and production, we've introduced an `environmentName` parameter. This is appended to our SQL Server's name. Therefore, if our `environmentName` parameter is set to `production`, our SQL Server's name will be `sqlserver-deployment-production`.

Adding Service Bus Resources

Visual Studio doesn't offer a template for declaring a Service Bus Namespace, Service Bus Queue, or Service Bus Authorization Rules. To get the necessary JSON, the easiest solution is to provision these Service Bus resources in the Azure Portal, then download an ARM template containing their definitions. You can then copy and paste the Service Bus resources into our `azuredeploy.json` file.

If you need to review how to export a template for existing resources, refer back to the "Downloading ARM Templates for Preexisting Resources in the Azure Portal" section earlier in this chapter.

Adding Other Resources

The remaining resources that we need to add to our template are a SQL Database, App Service Plan, and a Web App. You've already seen the mechanics for doing so. You can choose between provisioning resources in the Portal, downloading the ARM template from the Automation Scripts tab, and then copying the necessary JSON into your own template. Alternatively, you can use Visual Studio to insert JSON for the necessary resources into your template. Regardless of the approach, you can then edit generated JSON to fit your needs.

Let's look at the completed template.

The Completed Template

The completed template containing all resources needed for our web app is shown in
Listing 12-14.

Listing 12-14. The Complete azuredeploy.json File

```
{
  "$schema": "https://schema.management.azure.com/schemas/2015-01-01/
  deploymentTemplate.json#",
  "contentVersion": "1.0.0.0",
  "parameters": {
    "environmentName": {
      "type": "string",
      "minLength": 1,
      "defaultValue": "staging",
      "metadata": {
        "description": "The environment type. This will typically be 'staging'
            or 'production'"
      }
    },
    "sqlServerAdminPassword": {
      "type": "securestring",
      "metadata": {
        "description": "The administrative password for the SQL Server"
      }
    }
  },
  "variables": {
    "sqlserver": {
      "adminLogin": "adminuser",
      "deploymentName": "[concat('sqlserver-deployment-',
      parameters('environmentName'),
          '-', uniqueString(resourceGroup().id))]"
    },
```

```
    "sqldb": {
      "deploymentName": "[concat('sqldb-deployment-', parameters('environment
      Name'))]",
      "edition": "Basic",
      "serviceObjective": "Basic",
      "collation": "SQL_Latin1_General_CP1_CI_AS"
    },
    "storageAccount": {
      "deploymentName": "[concat('sadeployment', parameters('environment
      Name'))]",
      "deploymentType": "Standard_LRS"
    },
    "serviceBus": {
      "namespace": "[concat('sb-deployment-', parameters('environmentName'),
      '-', uniqueString(resourceGroup().id))]"
    },
    "serviceBusQueue": {
      "name": "[concat(variables('serviceBus').namespace, '/messages')]"
    },
    "serviceBusAuthRule": {
      "listenSendAccessKeyName": "[concat(variables('serviceBus').
      namespace, '/ListenSend')]"
    },
    "appServicePlan": {
      "deploymentName": "[concat('asp-deployment-', parameters('environment
      Name'))]",
      "sku": "F1"
    },
    "webApp": {
      "deploymentName": "[concat('wa-deployment-', parameters
      ('environmentName'), '-', uniqueString(resourceGroup().id))]"
    }
  },
```

```
"resources": [
  {
    "type": "Microsoft.ServiceBus/namespaces",
    "sku": {
      "name": "Basic",
      "tier": "Basic"
    },
    "kind": "Messaging",
    "name": "[variables('serviceBus').nameSpace]",
    "apiVersion": "2015-08-01",
    "location": "[resourceGroup().location]",
    "tags": {
      "displayName": "sb-deployment"
    },
    "properties": {
      "serviceBusEndpoint": "[concat('https://', variables('serviceBus').
      nameSpace,'.servicebus.windows.net:443/')]"
    },
    "dependsOn": []
  },
  {
    "type": "Microsoft.ServiceBus/namespaces/AuthorizationRules",
    "name": "[variables('serviceBusAuthRule').listenSendAccessKeyName]",
    "apiVersion": "2015-08-01",
    "properties": {
      "rights": [
        "Listen",
        "Send",
        "Manage"
      ]
    },
    "tags": {
      "displayName": "sb-deployment: sendListen"
    },
```

```
    "dependsOn": [
      "[resourceId('Microsoft.ServiceBus/namespaces', variables('serviceBus').
      namespace)]"
    ]
  },
  {
    "type": "Microsoft.ServiceBus/namespaces/queues",
    "name": "[variables('serviceBusQueue').name]",
    "apiVersion": "2015-08-01",
    "location": "[resourceGroup().location]",
    "properties": {
      "defaultMessageTimeToLive": "14.00:00:00"
    },
    "tags": {
      "displayName": "sb-deployment: queue"
    },
    "dependsOn": [
      "[resourceId('Microsoft.ServiceBus/namespaces',
      variables('serviceBus').namespace)]"
    ]
  },
  {
    "name": "[variables('sqlserver').deploymentName]",
    "type": "Microsoft.Sql/servers",
    "location": "[resourceGroup().location]",
    "apiVersion": "2014-04-01-preview",
    "dependsOn": [],
    "tags": {
      "displayName": "sqlserver-deployment"
    },
    "properties": {
      "administratorLogin": "[variables('sqlServer').adminLogin]",
      "administratorLoginPassword": "[parameters('sqlServerAdminPassword')]"
    },
```

```
"resources": [
  {
    "name": "AllowAllWindowsAzureIps",
    "type": "firewallrules",
    "location": "[resourceGroup().location]",
    "apiVersion": "2014-04-01-preview",
    "dependsOn": [
      "[resourceId('Microsoft.Sql/servers',
          variables('sqlserver').deploymentName)]"
    ],
    "properties": {
      "startIpAddress": "0.0.0.0",
      "endIpAddress": "0.0.0.0"
    }
  },
  {
    "name": "[variables('sqldb').deploymentName]",
    "type": "databases",
    "location": "[resourceGroup().location]",
    "apiVersion": "2014-04-01-preview",
    "dependsOn": [
      "[resourceId('Microsoft.Sql/servers',
          variables('sqlserver').deploymentName)]"
    ],
    "tags": {
      "displayName": "sqldb-deployment"
    },
    "properties": {
      "collation": "[variables('sqldb').collation]",
      "edition": "[variables('sqldb').edition]",
      "maxSizeBytes": "1073741824",
      "requestedServiceObjectiveName": "[variables('sqldb').
      serviceObjective]"
    }
  }
]
```

```
    },
    {
      "name": "[variables('storageAccount').deploymentName]",
      "type": "Microsoft.Storage/storageAccounts",
      "location": "[resourceGroup().location]",
      "apiVersion": "2016-01-01",
      "sku": {
        "name": "[variables('storageAccount').deploymentType]"
      },
      "dependsOn": [],
      "tags": {
        "displayName": "sadeployment"
      },
      "kind": "Storage"
    },
    {
      "name": "[variables('appServicePlan').deploymentName]",
      "type": "Microsoft.Web/serverfarms",
      "location": "[resourceGroup().location]",
      "apiVersion": "2015-08-01",
      "sku": {
        "name": "[variables('appServicePlan').sku]"
      },
      "dependsOn": [],
      "tags": {
        "displayName": "asp-deployment"
      },
      "properties": {
        "name": "[variables('appServicePlan').deploymentName]",
        "numberOfWorkers": 1
      }
    },
```

```
    {
        "name": "[variables('webApp').deploymentName]",
        "type": "Microsoft.Web/sites",
        "location": "[resourceGroup().location]",
        "apiVersion": "2015-08-01",
        "dependsOn": [
          "[resourceId('Microsoft.Web/serverfarms', variables
          ('appServicePlan').deploymentName)]"
        ],
        "tags": {
          "[concat('hidden-related:', resourceId('Microsoft.Web/serverfarms',
          variables('appServicePlan').deploymentName))]": "Resource",
          "displayName": "wa-deployment"
        },
        "properties": {
          "name": "[variables('webApp').deploymentName]",
          "serverFarmId": "[resourceId('Microsoft.Web/serverfarms',
          variables('appServicePlan').deploymentName)]",
          "siteConfig": {
            "connectionStrings": [
              {
                "name": "DeploymentContext",
                "connectionString": "[concat('Server=tcp:',
variables('sqlServer').deploymentName, '.database.windows.net,1433;Initial
Catalog=', variables('sqldb').deploymentName, ';Persist Security
Info=False;User ID=', variables('sqlServer').adminLogin, ';Password=', para
meters('sqlServerAdminPassword'), ';MultipleActiveResultSets=False;Encrypt=
True;TrustServerCertificate=False;Connection Timeout=30;')]",
                "type": 2
              }
            ]
          }
        },
```

```
"resources": [
  {
    "name": "appsettings",
    "type": "config",
    "apiVersion": "2015-08-01",
    "dependsOn": [
      "[resourceId('Microsoft.Web/sites', variables('webApp').
      deploymentName)]",
      "[resourceId('Microsoft.Storage/storageAccounts',
      variables('storageAccount').deploymentName)]"
    ],
    "tags": {
      "displayName": "appSettings"
    },
    "properties": {
      "ServiceBusConnectionString": "[listKeys('ListenSend',
      '2015-08-01').primaryConnectionString]",
      "AzureWebJobsDashboard": "[Concat('DefaultEndpointsProtocol
      =https;AccountName=',variables('storageAccount').deployment
      Name,';AccountKey=',listKeys(resourceId('Microsoft.Storage/
      storageAccounts', variables('storageAccount').deploymentName),
      providers('Microsoft.Storage', 'storageAccounts').
      apiVersions[0]).keys[0].value)]",
      "AzureWebJobsStorage": "[Concat('DefaultEndpointsProtocol=
      https;AccountName=',variables('storageAccount').deployment
      Name,';AccountKey=',listKeys(resourceId('Microsoft.Storage/
      storageAccounts', variables('storageAccount').deploymentName),
      providers('Microsoft.Storage', 'storageAccounts').
      apiVersions[0]).keys[0].value)]"
    }
  }
]
}
],
```

```
"outputs": {
  "appServiceName": {
    "type": "string",
    "value": "[variables('webApp').deploymentName]"
  },
  "sqlServerName": {
    "type": "string",
    "value": "[concat(variables('sqlserver').deploymentName, '.database.
    windows.net')]"
  },
  "sqlDatabaseName": {
    "type": "string",
    "value": "[variables('sqldb').deploymentName]"
  }
}
}
```

If you deploy this template with the environmentName parameter set to "staging" and then navigate to the resource group that you deployed to, you should see all resources listed (Figure 12-13). This confirms that our template works as expected.

NAME ∨	TYPE ∨	LOCATION ∨
asp-deployment-staging	App Service plan	East US
sadeploymentstaging	Storage account	East US
sb-deployment-staging	Service Bus	East US
sqlserver-deployment-staging	SQL server	East US
sqldb-deployment-staging	SQL database	East US
wa-deployment-staging	App Service	East US

Figure 12-13. *After navigating to the rg-deployment-staging resource group in the Azure Portal, we can see all resources that were deployed using our ARM template*

Creating a Production Environment

Now that we've deployed our staging environment using an ARM template, let's create a duplicate production environment.

1. Open the `azuredeploy.parameters.json` file and change the `environmentName` parameter value from `"staging"` to `"production"`.

2. Next, right-click the Deployment.ARM project in the Visual Studio Solution Explorer and select Deploy ➤ New. In the Deploy to Resource Group dialog box, we want to create a new resource group called `rg-deployment-production`. Click Deploy to initiate the deployment. Don't forget to open the spawned Powershell window to reenter the SQL Server admin password.

After the deployment, log in to the Azure Portal and click through to the rg-deployment-production management blade, then take a look at the resources that it contains. You'll see all of the resources defined in our template, each with an appended `-production` (Figure 12-14).

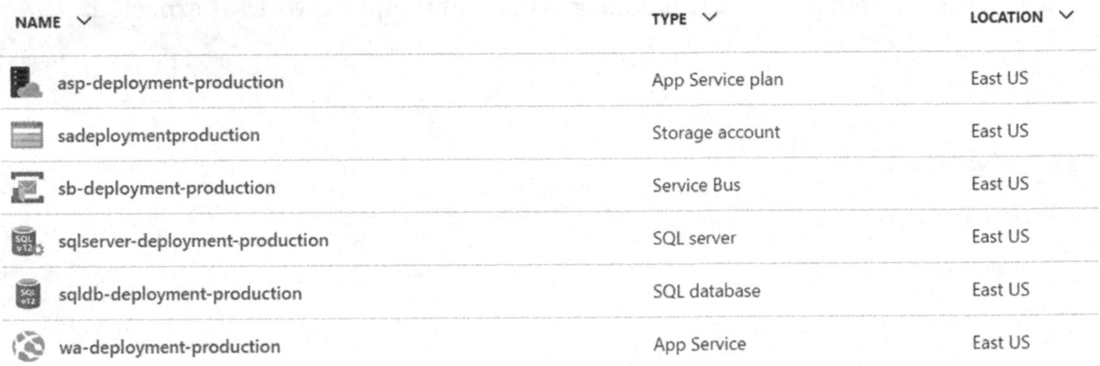

NAME ⌄	TYPE ⌄	LOCATION ⌄
asp-deployment-production	App Service plan	East US
sadeploymentproduction	Storage account	East US
sb-deployment-production	Service Bus	East US
sqlserver-deployment-production	SQL server	East US
sqldb-deployment-production	SQL database	East US
wa-deployment-production	App Service	East US

Figure 12-14. *All resources in the rg-deployment-production resource group*

Deploying the Application

Now that we've got the provisioning of our Azure environments under control, it's time to turn our attention to deploying our actual application. In this section, we cover three topics.

First, we talk about how we can set up configuration transforms so that our web.config and app.config files automatically incorporate the correct settings based on the build configuration. We close the chapter by automating the entire deployment process.

Setting Up Build Configurations and Configuration Transforms

We want to be able to promote our code from development to staging, and from staging to production. However, settings like database connection strings and Azure Storage accounts will vary from environment to environment. Manually updating these settings in configuration files before each deployment is almost guaranteed to lead to errors over time and is best avoided. Fortunately, we can let our build tools do the job of updating settings in our configuration files based on our selected build configuration.

Defining Build Configurations

Build configurations allow you to change how a solution and its projects are compiled. You're likely familiar with the two default solution configurations: Debug and Release. We're not limited to these two configurations; Visual Studio will let us define as many as we need. With each build configuration, we have the option to create a configuration-specific transform file for our web.config and app.config files. We'll demonstrate creating these transforms in the next section.

Our development environment will use the Debug build configuration. Our production environment will use the Release build configuration. Therefore, we need to define a new build fonfiguration called Staging, which will be used in our staging environment. To create a new Staging build configuration, do the following:

1. In Visual Studio, click Build in the top-level menu. Click the Configuration Manager submenu option to launch the Configuration Manager dialog box.

2. The Configuration Manager dialog box allows you to select an active solution configuration, and to create new configurations. To create a new configuration, expand the Active Solution Configuration drop-down list and select New (Figure 12-15).

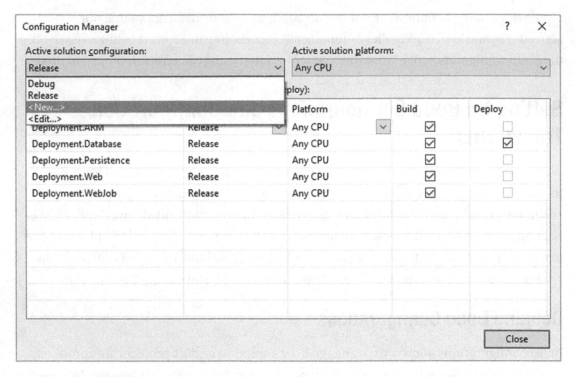

Figure 12-15. *The Configuration Manager dialog box. Click New to define a new build configuration. This opens the New Solution Configuration dialog box*

3. In the New Solution Configuration dialog box, enter `Staging` for the new configuration's name, then choose to copy settings from the existing Release configuration. Because we want the code that we're testing in our staging environment to mirror production as closely as possible, we're going to build with the same Release settings.

We now have a Staging build configuration. Let's create our configuration file transforms for our `web.config` and `app.config` files.

Adding a Staging Transform for Web.config

Navigate to the Deployment.Web project and locate the `web.config` file. You'll notice an arrow next to the `web.config` file that indicates that the menu item can be expanded. When you click the expansion arrow, you'll see the transform files for the Debug and Release configurations. These are named `web.Debug.config` and `web.Release.config`, respectively (Figure 12-16).

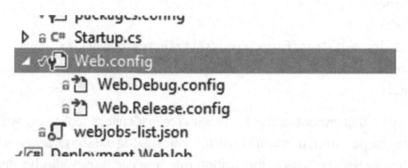

Figure 12-16. *Expanding the Web.config node shows the build-specific configuration transform files*

These transform files are applied at compile time. The transform used is based on the active build configuration. To define a new transform file for a build configuration, right-click the `Web.config` file and select Add Config Transform. This will add transformation files for any build configuration that doesn't already have one listed. You should now see a `Web.Staging.config` transform file listed beneath the `Web.config` file.

Next, we need to populate the `Web.Staging.config` and `Web.Release.config` files with the appropriate transforms. The syntax is simple: We'll specify the entries that we want transformed, then apply special transform attributes that let our compiler know how these entries should be applied to the original `web.config` file. Note that we only have to specify the entries that we want to transform. The complete `Web.Staging.config` file is shown in Listing 12-15.

Listing 12-15. The Web.Staging.config File

```
<?xml version="1.0"?>
<configuration xmlns:xdt="http://schemas.microsoft.com/XML-Document-
Transform">
  <connectionStrings>
    <add name="DeploymentContext" connectionString="[Your Staging database
```

```
    connection string]"providerName="System.Data.SqlClient"
    xdt:Transform="SetAttributes" xdt:Locator="Match(name)"/>
  </connectionStrings>
  <appSettings>
    <add key="ServiceBusConnectionString" value="[Your Staging Service Bus
      Connection String]" xdt:Transform="SetAttributes"
xdt:Locator="Match(name)"/>
  </appSettings>
  <system.web>
    <compilation xdt:Transform="RemoveAttributes(debug)"/>
  </system.web>
</configuration>
```

The values for `DeploymentContext` and `ServiceBusConnectionString` will vary depending on the password that you chose for your staging database, and the SAS key generated for your Service Bus's authorization rule. You can retrieve both values from the Portal.

The `Web.Release.config` file looks exactly the same as the `Web.Stagin.config` file, with the exception that you must swap the `DeploymentContext` and `ServiceBusConnectionString` values with those used in your release environment.

Transforming the Deployment.WebJob's App.config

Visual Studio 2015 doesn't yet have support for adding configuration transforms to `app.config` files, so we'll need to install additional tooling. I recommend adding the SlowCheetah XML Transforms package to do so. It can be downloaded and installed from the Visual Studio Marketplace at `https://marketplace.visualstudio.com/items?itemName=VisualStudioProductTeam.SlowCheetah-XMLTransforms`.

Once it is installed, simply right-click the `app.config` file in the Deployment. WebJobs project, then select Add Transform. Transform files will be added for each build configuration.

You'll then need to update settings within the `app.staging.config` and `app.release.config` files based on each environment. The transform file for `app.staging.config` is shown in Listing 12-16.

Listing 12-16. The app.staging.config File

```xml
<?xml version="1.0" encoding="utf-8" ?>
<configuration xmlns:xdt="http://schemas.microsoft.com/XML-Document-
Transform">
  <connectionStrings>
    <add name="AzureWebJobsDashboard" connectionString="[Staging storage
      account connection string]" xdt:Transform="SetAttributes"
      xdt:Locator="Match(name)"/>
    <add name="AzureWebJobsStorage" connectionString="[Staging storage account
      connection string]" xdt:Transform="SetAttributes"
      xdt:Locator="Match(name)"/>
    <add name="AzureWebJobsServiceBus" connectionString="[Staging Service Bus
      connection string]" xdt:Transform="SetAttributes"
      xdt:Locator="Match(name)"/>
    <add name="DeploymentContext" connectionString="[Staging database
    connection string]"
      providerName="System.Data.SqlClient" xdt:Transform="SetAttributes"
      xdt:Locator="Match(name)"/>
  </connectionStrings>
</configuration>
```

Building and Deploying with Visual Studio Team Services

Visual Studio Team Services (VSTS) is an online platform for source control, project
management, load testing, build, and release. VSTS is free for small teams of up to five
developers. You might recall that we used VSTS for load testing our Web Apps in
Chapter 2. If you haven't already signed up for an account, you can do so at
https://www.visualstudio.com/team-services/.

Setting Up VSTS

After signing up and logging in for the first time, you'll be prompted to name your
VSTS account, your first project name, and the type of repository you'd like to use
(Figure 12-17). Enter a name of your choice, enter your desired project name, select Git,
and then click Continue.

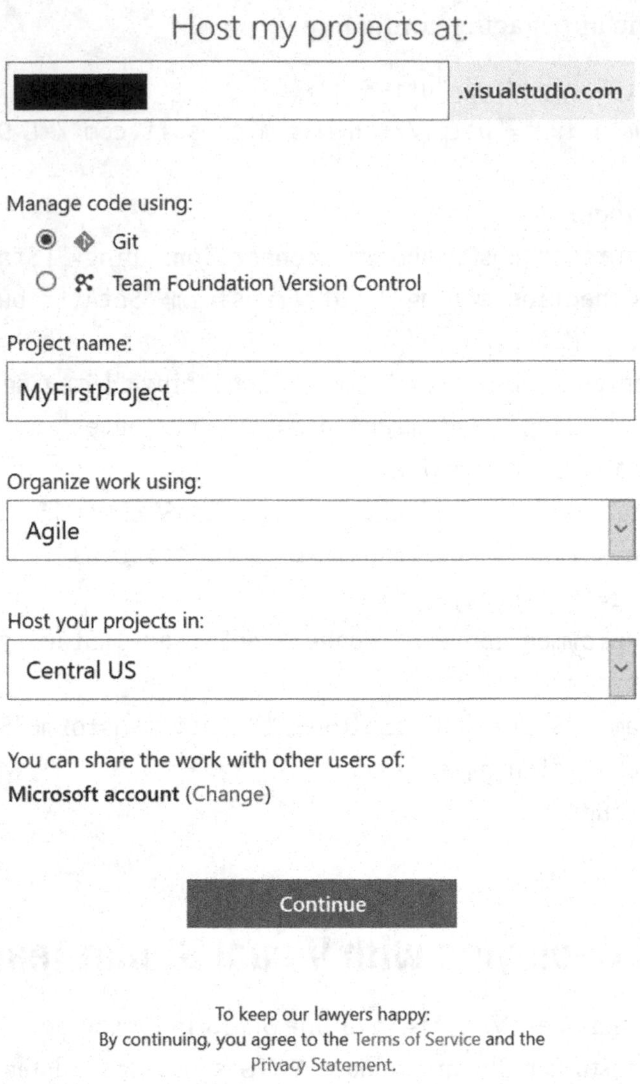

Host my projects at:

[   ]   .visualstudio.com

Manage code using:

- ⦿ ◈ Git
- ○ ⚒ Team Foundation Version Control

Project name:

MyFirstProject

Organize work using:

Agile ⌄

Host your projects in:

Central US ⌄

You can share the work with other users of:

Microsoft account (Change)

Continue

To keep our lawyers happy:
By continuing, you agree to the Terms of Service and the
Privacy Statement.

Figure 12-17. *The initial setup screen in VSTS*

Next, we'll need to push code to our project's Git repository. When we set up our automated build process, the initial step will be to check out all source from our Git repo.

Click Code in the top toolbar. You'll see the project's Git repo details and can import code using your favorite method. After importing code into the repo, we're ready to move on to defining our automated build.

How VSTS Build Works

The build process begins when you define a build. A build definition is a chain of build tasks that are executed sequentially to create and deploy an application. There are many different tasks available in VSTS's build tool. If there's not a task that meets your needs, there are provisions for writing your own.

Builds can be triggered manually, or they can be launched in response to a code check-in on a specific branch in a repository. Launching in response to a code check-in allows you to set up continuous integration to automatically deploy to a staging environment.

The VSTS build tool has other incredibly useful features, such as automating the execution of unit tests and e-mailing interested parties when any part of a build fails.

Now that we've hit the highlights, let's dive into the specifics using our example application.

Defining a Build in VSTS

We start by creating our build definition.

1. In VSTS, click Build & Release on the top menu bar. This will take you to a listing of all of your build definitions for the current project. Click New to create a new definition.

2. You'll now be taken to a template selection page (Figure 12-18). There are several templates to choose from, each with a different arrangement of build tasks. If you choose a template, you'll be able to edit, add, and delete tasks as needed. For this example, click the link to start with an empty process.

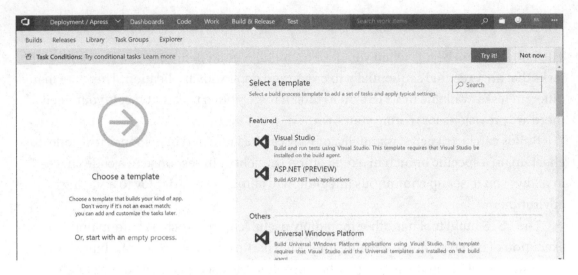

Figure 12-18. *The build template selection page*

Build Task: Pulling Source from the Repository

After choosing a template or electing to start with an empty process, you'll be navigated
to the Edit Build page (Figure 12-19). Let's start by renaming our build definition from
the default name of Deployment-CI to something more meaningful, like Deployment-
Staging. After renaming, let's configure our first task, which is to pull in source from
the correct branch in our Git repository. We'll then initiate a build to see how the build
process works.

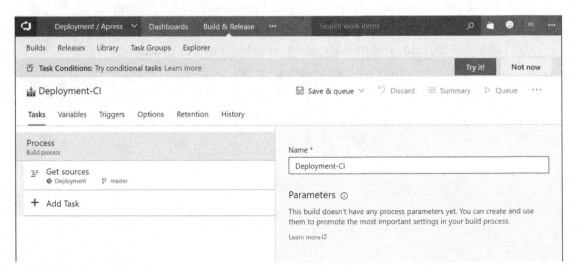

Figure 12-19. *The Edit Build page*

1. You'll see that the first and only task in our build is the Get Sources task. This allows us to specify the repo and branch where VSTS should pull from. Click it and verify that we're pulling from This Project, the correct repository, and the branch of your choice. Note that if you prefer to host your Git repository elsewhere, you are still able to do so.

2. At this point, we have a build defined, even though it only has one step. Click Save & Queue to save the definition. This will also queue a build. Queueing a build places the build in a task queue, where it will be picked up by a hosted agent to execute. As the build executes, you'll see status echoed to the console within the browser. After the build completes, you'll see a message showing that the build was successful or that the build failed (Figure 12-20).

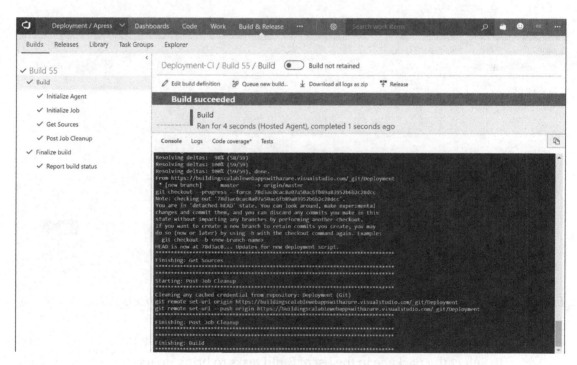

Figure 12-20. *The console echoes the output from build tasks as they execute. When the build is complete, a message will indicate if the build was successful or failed.*

If the build failed, then it's time to click the Logs link next to the console and start the debugging process based on the output.

Now that we've proven that we can execute the build, click Edit Build Definition to return to our Edit Build page.

Build Tasks: Restoring NuGet Packages

We've successfully pulled the latest source on the desired branch to our build server. Before we can actually compile, we need to make sure that all of the necessary NuGet packages are present. This involves adding a NuGet Restore task to our build definition.

1. Click Add Task at the bottom of our tasks lists. This opens a list of all tasks in VSTS in the right pane. On the All tab, scroll down until you find the NuGet Restore task, then click Add (Figure 12-21).

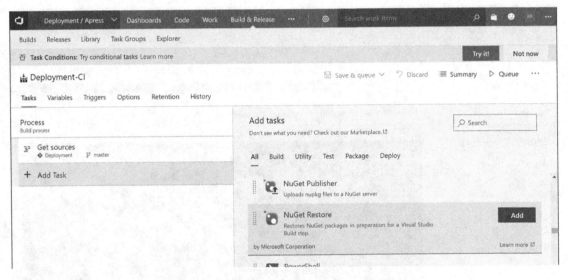

Figure 12-21. *Adding a NuGet Restore task to the build definition.*

2. After adding the NuGet Restore task, we still need to configure it. Select the package in the list of Build tasks to bring up its properties.

In our case, all of the default properties are fine. The default values instruct the task to restore NuGet packages for all projects in the solution.

3. Click Save & Queue to launch a new build to ensure that we haven't broken anything. During the build, you should see NuGet restore statements echoed to the console.

Build Tasks: Building the Solution

We have source pulled to the build server and all NuGet packages are restored. Now it's time to actually build the application.

To build, we'll use the Visual Studio Build Solution Task. To add and configure it, do the following:

1. Click Add Task to open a list of all available tasks. You'll find the Visual Studio Build task on the Build tab. Click Add to add it to the solution.

2. Select the new Build Solution task in the left pane to bring up its configuration options. We'll need to change the MSBuild Arguments setting to the following:

    ```
    /p:DeployOnBuild=true
    /p:WebPublishMethod=Package  /p:SkipInvalidConfigurations=true
    /p:PackageLocation="$(build.artifactstagingdirectory)\\"
    ```

    This instructs the build task that we want to create a web deploy package and place it in the artifacts staging directory. A task that we'll add later in the build process will pick up the package and deploy it to Azure.

3. Click Save & Queue to launch a new build. You should see MSBuild output in the console window when the Build Solution task executes.

Build Tasks: Deploy ARM Template

We have our build successfully defined that packages code for deployment. Now we just need a place to deploy. We'll provision our Azure resources using the ARM template that we created in the Deployment.ARM project. We'll use an Azure Resource Group Deployment build task to do so.

501

Here's where the magic happens: We can deploy our ARM template with every single build. If all resources already exist and have the appropriate settings, nothing in our target Azure environment will change. If resources defined in the ARM template are missing, however, they'll be provisioned. If settings differ from what's defined in the ARM template, they'll be updated. This ensures that every time, we're deploying to the environment that we expect.

To set up the Azure Resource Group Deployment task, do the following:

1. Click Add Task. The Azure Resource Group Deployment task is located on the Deploy tab. Add the task to the build definition.

2. Click the newly added task to configure it. We'll need to update the following settings:

   - *Display Name*: Let's set this to `Deploy ARM Template` because the default name is both wordy and uninspiring.

   - *Azure Subscription*: Using the drop-down list, choose the Azure subscription you'd like to use when deploying resources.

   - *Action*: Leave the default setting, which is Create or Update Resource Group.

   - *Resource Group*: Type the name of the resource group you'd like to deploy to. For this exercise, please enter `rg-deployment-staging`. If this resource group doesn't exist, it will be created.

   - *Location*: Choose the region you'd like to deploy to. I recommend choosing the one closest to you to reduce network latency.

   - *Template Location*: Select Linked Artifact. This will allow you to browse for the template within your code base. The other option is to specify a URL where the template can be found. This is useful if you're making use of a gallery template that can be reached via a URL.

   - *Template*: Because you selected Linked Artifact for the template location, you can click Browse to the right of this text field to browse to the `azuredeploy.json` file located in the Deployment. ARM project.

- *Template Parameters*: Click Browse and navigate to the `azuredeploy.parameters.json` file located in the `Deployment.ARM` folder.

- *Override Template Parameters*: This gives us the option to supersede any default parameter values or values defined in the parameters file. Enter the following in this text field:

```
sqlServerAdminPassword [Your SQL Server Password]
-environmentName staging
```

When done, click Save & Queue to save and initiate a deployment. After the deployment completes successfully, you can log into the Azure Portal and see all resources that were provisioned to the rg-deployment-staging resource group.

When creating a build definition, it's sometimes useful to disable long-running tasks such as this. You can right-click any task and select Disable Selected Task(s) from the shortcut menu to prevent this task from executing each time. Don't forget to enable it when you've finished defining the build.

Build Tasks: Copy Files Between Directories

When VSTS builds our application, output is written to the `$(System.DefaultWorkingDirectory)` directory. Because we are using a DACPAC to deploy our database to SQL Azure, we will need to use an Azure SQL Database Deployment task to do so. The problem is that the Azure SQL Database Deployment task doesn't have access to read the `$(System.DefaultWorkingDirectory)`. We're going to need to move our DACPAC file to a directory that our Azure SQL Database Deployment task can read.

To add a new Copy Files task, do the following:

1. Click Add Task, and select the Copy Files task. The Copy Files task is located under the Utility heading.

2. Click your new Copy Files task to configure it. The necessary fields are as follows:

   - *Display Name*: The display name should be something descriptive, such as Copy DACPAC to Staging Directory.

- *Source Folder*: Our source folder is
  `$(System.DefaultWorkingDirectory)`. This is where the
  DACPAC build files will be placed.

- *Contents*: Enter `**\Deployment.Database.dacpac`. The double
  asterisk instructs the task to copy all files in the source folder, as
  well as the files in all subfolders. This will ensure that we grab the
  DACPAC file needed.

- *Target Folder*: The target folder should be `$(build.`
  `artifactstagingdirectory)`. The upcoming Azure SQL
  Database Deployment will be able to read this folder.

Build Tasks: Azure SQL Database Deployment

The Azure SQL Database Deployment task will deploy the DACPAC contents to the
specified Azure SQL Database instance. The DACPAC file must be in a directory that is
accessible to the task.

To add an Azure SQL Database Deployment task, do the following:

1. Click Add Task, then select the Azure SQL Database Deployment
   task located under the Deploy heading.

2. Configure the Azure SQL Database Deployment task as follows:

   - *Display Name*: Name the task something descriptive, such as
     Deploy DACPAC.

   - *Azure Connection Type*: Set to Azure Resource Manager.

   - *Azure Subscription*: Select the subscription that will contain the
     Azure SQL Database.

   - *Azure SQL Server Name*: Enter the full name of the Azure SQL
     Server that hosts your Azure SQL database. You can find this after
     deploying the ARM template for the first time.

   - *Database Name*: This is the name of the database that the
     DACPAC should be deployed to.

- *Server Admin Login*: The administrative username for your Azure SQL Server instance.

- *Password*: The password for the aforementioned Server Admin Login.

Build Tasks: Deploy Web App to Azure

Our Visual Studio Build task compiled and packaged our source code, then copied it to an artifact staging directory. The package is ready to be picked up and deployed to an Azure Web App. To handle the deployment, we'll use the Azure App Service Deploy task.

1. Click Add Task to open the list of available tasks. On the Deploy tab, select the Azure App Service Deploy task and add it to the build definition.

2. Please update the properties for this task as follows:

   - *Display Name*: Enter something meaningful, such as Deploy Web Application.

   - *Azure Subscription*: Using the drop-down list, select the subscription that contains the App Service where the web app will be deployed.

   - *App Service Name*: Select the App Service where our web application will be deployed. For this example, please choose wa-deployment-staging.

   - *Package or Folder*: This tells the task where it can find the package to be deployed. If you'll recall, in the Visual Studio Build task we specified the web package output directory as `$(build.artifactstagingdirectory)`. Therefore, set the value of this field to `$(build.artifactstagingdirectory)/Deployment.Web.zip`.

   All other fields can be left blank or use the default values.

3. Click Save & Queue to save this new task and launch a build. After the build successfully completes, you will be able to browse to your web app's staging directory to see the published application.

Putting It All Together

Last but not least, we need to update our web.config file in the Deployment.Web project with the appropriate database connection string and Service Bus connection string. We also must update our Deployment.WebJob's app.config file to point to the appropriate storage account for the AzureWebJobsDashboard and AzureWebJobsStorage settings. Make sure you also set the database connection string and Service Bus connection string as well. Commit these changes to your Git repository to trigger a new build.

If all goes as expected, your entire VSTS build process should run successfully. If you navigate to your Web App's address, you should see the index page for our application (Figure 12-22).

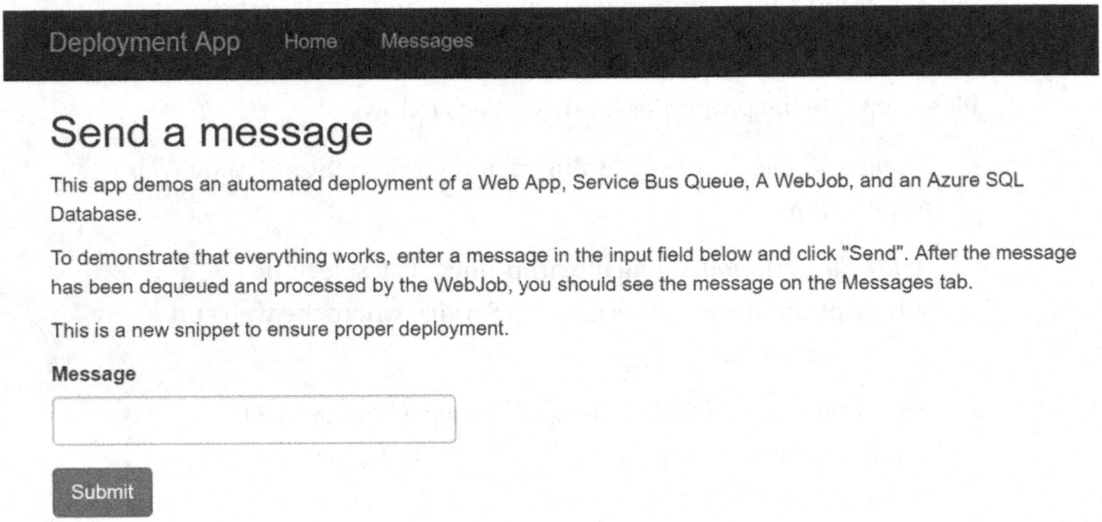

Figure 12-22. *Our Deployment application was successfully deployed to our provisioned Web App*

Summary

In this chapter, we've covered deployment best practices, MS Build configurations, ARM templates, deploying infrastructure using an ARM template from Visual Studio, and how to set up an automated deployment with Visual Studio Team Services build tools.

Index

A

C

D

E

Get the eBook for only $5!

Why limit yourself?

With most of our titles available in both PDF and ePUB format, you can access your content wherever and however you wish—on your PC, phone, tablet, or reader.

Since you've purchased this print book, we are happy to offer you the eBook for just $5.

To learn more, go to http://www.apress.com/companion or contact support@apress.com.

Apress®